PENGUIN BOOKS

BOLLYBOOK

Diptakirti Chaudhuri is a salesman by day and writer by night.

This is his third book, and the second on Hindi cinema. He is currently working on a biography of India's most explosive screenwriters, Salim–Javed.

He lives in Gurgaon with his wife, a son and a daughter. They don't share his obsessive love for the movies. Yet.

BOLLYBOOK

The Big Book of Hindi Movie Trivia

DIPTAKIRTI CHAUDHURI

PENGUIN BOOKS

An imprint of Penguin Random House

PENGUIN BOOKS

USA | Canada | UK | Ireland | Australia
New Zealand | India | South Africa | China

Penguin Books is part of the Penguin Random House group of companies
whose addresses can be found at global.penguinrandomhouse.com

Published by Penguin Random House India Pvt. Ltd
7th Floor, Infinity Tower C, DLF Cyber City,
Gurgaon 122 002, Haryana, India

Penguin
Random House
India

First published by Penguin Books India 2014

10 9 8 7 6 5 4 3 2

ISBN 9780143422174

Typeset in Minion by R. Ajith Kumar, New Delhi

Printed at Repro India Limited

www.penguin.co.in

MIX
Paper from
responsible sources
FSC® C047271

Contents

'Iss ilaake mein naye aaye ho, sahab?'

I am only like a boy playing on the seashore, and diverting myself in now and then finding a smoother pebble or a prettier shell than ordinary, whilst the great ocean of Bollywood lay all undiscovered before me.

—With apologies to Isaac Newton

Inspired by Sir Isaac's cosmic pronouncement and my desire to waste time watching Hindi movies, I present here the definitive (*Terms and conditions apply) book of Bollywood trivia.

There are—hold your breath—100 lists in this book that cover everything from history ('Which father–son duo killed Curzon and Dyer?') to geography ('How many Ramgarhs are there in India?') to arithmetic ('How much did Kamal Kishore Khosla buy the plot for his ghosla for?') to physics ('How is Boyle's law related to the *Ooh la la* song of **The Dirty Picture**?') to chemistry ('Who was the first actress to wear a swimsuit on screen?').

It is the book-on-your-bedside-table to flip through before you start dreaming about Katrina or Ranbir. It is the book that is supposed to referee your vodka-fuelled debates with friends. It is the book that is supposed to remind you of the time you bunked college to see **DDLJ**. And if it inspires you to go back to Maratha Mandir once again, my job here is done.

Before you dig in, let me confess that you are likely to come across some missed notables, some overlooked trivia and maybe even (gasp!) an error or two. If you encounter any such thing (or just want to say hi), drop me a mail (diptakirti@gmail.com) or a tweet (@diptakirti) or a comment on my blog (diptakirti.blogspot.com) and I will correct them in the next editions.

But do remember that for the next editions to happen, this edition has to sell out.

QUIZ: AND ABOVE ALL . . .

A quiz on some of our quirkier credits from some of our biggest hits and most favourite films. Let's see how many you can get.

1. This actor starred in **Jaani Dushman** (1979) and **The Burning Train** and in both cases, he was credited as 'And above all . . .' Who is this stratospheric dude?

2. 'And . . . with his Wonder Bird . . .' Name the actor and his pet from this film, which incorporated the bird's image in the logo of the film's title.

3. Amitabh Bachchan and Rishi Kapoor acted together in five movies (not counting guest appearances). In only one of them, Rishi's name appeared before Amitabh in the titles. Which one and why?

4. Which Hindi film had the following as part of its cast: '. . . and Lord Bertrand Russell in . . .'?

5. Who is credited with the story of **Shahenshah**?

6. Complete the following credits from **Queen**: 'Dialogue: Anvita Dutt, Additional dialogue . . .'

7. In films written by Salim–Javed, what distinction do the following four people hold: Gulzar, Inder Raj Anand, Nasir Husain and Manoj Kumar?

8. Which film had the following as part of its credits: Anupam Kher (Principal), Rani Mukherji (Tina), Kajol (Angie), Shah Rukh Khan (Rocky)?

9. Which film had the following stars: Waheeda Rehman, Mala Sinha, Sharmila Tagore, Simi, Indrani Mukherji, Bindu, Komila Wirk, Prema Narayan, Simple Kapadia?

10. Kundan Shah and Saeed Mirza were Script Associates. Sudhir Mishra was Dialogue Assistant. Naseeruddin Shah was credited with the still photography. Which is this film?

ANSWERS

1. Jeetendra
2. Pran and Sheroo in **Dharam Veer**.
3. **Amar Akbar Anthony** because Rishi Kapoor played Akbar whose name was announced before Anthony in the hospital where the credits played out.
4. **Aman** (starring Rajendra Kumar) had an anti-war message and convinced Bertrand Russell Peace Foundation to get the British philosopher to appear in a cameo.
5. Jaya Bachchan
6. Kangana Ranaut, who wrote most of the lines for her character.
7. They are the only four people who were credited with the dialogues in Salim–Javed films, which the writer duo usually preferred to write themselves. For **Andaz**, **Seeta Aur Geeta**, **Yaadon Ki Baaraat** and **Kranti** respectively.
8. **Koochie Koochie Hota Hai**, an animation film around the love stories of a pack of dogs, borrowed the character names from **Kuch Kuch Hota Hai**.
9. **Naseeb**. These were the female stars who participated as guests in the John Jaani Janardhan song.
10. **Khamosh**, Vidhu Vinod Chopra's second feature film had this stellar cast partly because the budget dictated a lot of gratis work.

x

1

Title Track

Hum jahan khade hote hain, line wahin se shuru hoti hai.
—*Bob Christo in* **Kaalia**[1]

People meet. Ideas pop up. Mahurats happen. Trailers launch. Movies start. Stars debut. This section—cleverly placed at the beginning of the book—is about, well, beginnings.

---

[1] If you are thinking this is a mistake, then that was exactly the intention. You see, Amitabh Bachchan did not say this iconic line in **Kaalia**. Michael (Bob Christo) said it first and then Kaalia (Amitabh) said, '*Hum bhi woh hain jo kabhi kisi ke peechhe nahin khade hote hain.*' Happy? Impressed? Yes, that was also the intention.

Lights, Popcorn, Action: 12 Opening Credits

The moving finger writes ...
—Opening line from Yash Chopra's **Waqt**

As you struggle to open the slightly oily packet of chips, the lights go off, making the already difficult job of locating the seat impossible. You also stop tugging at the polythene and concentrate on the list of people who are going to fill your next three hours—and maybe the rest of your life—with meaning.

No amount of pre-release hype or music-channel song promos can bring about a surge of adrenaline the way a rocking opening credits sequence does. And while some do it with mirrors, Bollywood does it with a mix of cool devices.

Pre-credit Backstory Compression[1]

Pre-credit backstory compression—very popular till the 1980s—was an attempt to knock off the socio-historical context of the film, the motivation of the hero and the emergence of the key characters before the titles so that the 'real' story could begin. It took economy of expression to a completely new level, saying more in the first 22 minutes than in the next 222!

There were many film-makers who employed this device but nobody did it better than Manmohan Desai.

In his biggest hit, he separated a family of five in a matter of eight minutes. The father got into a gun-battle with a smuggler and escaped with a crate of gold biscuits. The mother was rendered blind by the falling branch of a tree. Their three sons were picked up by a Hindu police

---

[1] Acknowledgements are due to Rajorshi Chakrabarti, who defined this concept in his essay 'Perchance to Dream' published in the anthology *The Popcorn Essayists* (edited by Jai Arjun Singh). The book cannot be recommended enough.

officer, a Muslim tailor and a Christian priest each, but not before all of them had left behind tons of identifiers to pick up years later. Years passed, and we are brought to an accident site where a blind flower-lady was hit badly and needed blood urgently. A Christian do-gooder took her to the hospital. A Hindu police inspector was at the hospital to lodge the case. A Muslim qawwali singer was also there, flirting with a lady doctor. All of them were found to be of the same blood group as the blind lady, and were all roped in to donate some blood.

As the transfusion started, a doctor asked them their names. And as the titles came on, they told us—*Amar Akbar Anthony*.

Hit Song

One of the most popular 'previews' of a Hindi film is always the music. And no better way to promote it than to put it right up front when the audience is settling down and the stars of the film are being announced.

An Evening in Paris had a great title track, in which Shammi Kapoor wooed Parisian blondes in the glittering streets of the city while Mohammed Rafi belted out the hit number. Well-known landmarks zoomed past the audience as Shammi jumped up and down on the Champs-Élysées while wide-eyed Frenchmen tried to grasp the exotic notion of an Indian dancing in their midst.

Another great title track was from *Maine Pyar Kiya*—though it did not feature the lead pair. It showed instead two figures in silhouette doing a sexy (as sexy as Rajshri allowed them) dance routine to the tune of the title track, swearing that incredibly beautiful things happened to them only because they fell in love. The superhit song also had impeccable pedigree because it was lifted from Stevie Wonder's '*I just called to say I love you*'.

Musical Titles

Apart from the hit music from the film, titles often have customized music—played usually to a set of mood-setting visuals. R.D. Burman had perfected the art of creating rocking title music by putting together a medley of the film's tunes.

The Greatest Film Ever Made opened with a jailor getting off a train and climbing on to a horse, accompanied by the trusted manservant of a thakur. We did not know this when the movie started but the entire title sequence staked out the rocky, rugged terrain that was going to be the setting of the movie. As the two riders moved from the outskirts to the villages, the tune—which started on a grand scale—slowly incorporated a melody more suited to a regular village scene. We soaked in the atmosphere that was so germane to the film, and the music that was going to be the beat to which *Sholay* would unfold.

Ramesh Sippy and R.D. Burman collaborated again five years later with **Shaan**—one of the grandest Hollywood-style thrillers from India. Its titles paid homage to the biggest series of thrillers that exists: James Bond. A slithering female figure shimmied and sashayed on a scarlet screen as Usha Uthup's husky voice sang '*Doston se pyar kiya*' and R.D. Burman deftly mixed the strains of that song with refrains of all the other songs of the film.

The Innovations

And sometimes, nothing works better than a quirky new thing. Film-makers down the ages have come up with some nifty moves for those elements that would bring a smile and kick off some roller-coaster (and some not-so-rollicking) rides.

The two cons in **Do Aur Do Paanch** devoted their lives to trumping each other. And the title sequence of the film was exactly about that. Shot as a cartoon, it had animated versions of Amitabh Bachchan and Shashi Kapoor in the best Spy vs Spy traditions of *MAD* comics. The animation was done in the visual style of *The Pink Panther* and was all about the duo tiptoeing through alleyways, cutting each other's climbing ropes, planting bombs or bomb-shaped diamond cases on each other. As the cast and crew appeared in starbursts, the sequence ended with the duo being marched away to jail.

A completely obscure movie from the mid-'80s—**Jaal**—had an amazingly neat revelation of the credits. The entire title sequence was about Vinod Mehra getting released from jail and going around, sick and unwanted. The lead actors' names were painted in red on the walls of Central Jail. The next set of names was painted on the road Vinod Mehra walked on. A co-passenger on a bus was reading a newspaper that had the names of the writers, while a door (banged on his face) and a roadside signboard had the other crew members' names. And as a finale, Vinod Mehra stumbled into a *kotha* bearing the director's name on its walls!

Rohan Sippy's directorial debut was **Kuch Naa Kaho**, an intelligent take on the usual love story, although the Aishwarya–Abhishek starrer didn't do too well commercially. Apart from the cool dialogues, the film had a super opening sequence with the names of the cast and crew of the film appearing on various parts of Abhishek's room and bathroom as he took a bath. The editor appeared on the edge of a pair of scissors, the lyricist on a CD cover, the composers on a music system, while the financiers appeared on a credit card. The story–screenplay–dialogue guys were on spines of books while the publicity people were on a boldly coloured toothpaste tube! And Aishwarya was on the shower curtain while Abhishek was on a bar of soap. And the names of the two most important people—the director and the producer—were written with a finger on steamed glass. Ironic—check. Creative—double check!

The titles of **Taare Zameen Par** were suffused with the magic of a child's hyperactive imagination. Created in the style of a child's drawing book, the titles floated between underwater scenes, octopus and fish blew blue ink which became outer space, planets jostled for space with spaceships, aquaria became playgrounds and delightfully creative things happened. The titles roll during a bus ride from school to home—the former was all about dictatorial teachers reading out poor marks and the latter was where the fears and insecurities of the parents took over. And the imagination of Ishaan Awasthi was such a beautiful refuge from both.

Sometimes, stars turn up in person for opening credits. And no, I don't mean the ones in the film that is to follow.

Yash Chopra's paean to romantic, Valentine love—**Dil To Pagal Hai**—had visuals of couples publicly displaying affection as Lata Mangeshkar sang 'Ek duje ke vaaste' in the background. At least three of the couples in that sequence were very well known. The director himself appeared right at the end with his wife Pamela, embarrassing her with an impromptu hug. Before him came Yash and Hiroo Johar, squabbling like a regular couple as she snatched away his cordless phone. Also featuring in the opening sequence were Sanjeev Kohli (son of composer Madan Mohan, and erstwhile CEO of Yash Raj Films) with his wife.[2]

Sometimes, it is not the face but the voice of a star that makes an impact.

In **Paa**, Jaya Bachchan read out the names of the cast and crew in her inimitable style—pausing sometimes to remember a few names and giggling like a schoolgirl when saying 'Introducing Amitabh Bachchan'.

This device of her reading out the titles was probably a belated return of favour that Amitabh Bachchan had done for her film **Bawarchi**, some four decades earlier.

Before the camera focused on Chamanganj in Kanpur for the opening scenes of **Tanu Weds Manu**, we heard a radio announcement. Starting with the static and the interference of changing radio channels, it segued into an advertisement for Vicco Turmeric Ayurvedic Cream and went on to list the people who had sent in song-requests to a radio programme anchored by the inimitable Ameen Sayani. The twist was that Ameen bhai read out the names of the characters in the movie. So, *Dilli se Manoj Sharma urf Manu, Kanpur, Uttar Pradesh, se Tanuja*

---

[2] Trivia hunters have often mistaken him for Aditya Chopra, the reclusive YRF scion, but when **Dil To Pagal Hai** released, Aditya was neither married nor convinced about making a screen appearance. He is now married but still unconvinced about making appearances anywhere.

Trivedi urf Tanu; and all their friends (including *Lucknow se Raja Awasthi* and *Azamganj se Pappi Tiwari*) requested for the song that played on the radio of a household getting ready to receive a would-be groom for their daughter.

The song was from **Bawarchi**—'*Bhor aayi gaya andhiyara*'.

Achha, ab picture chalu karo re . . .

OPENING MESSAGES

Several Bollywood films start with the strangest—or the most obvious—messages.

- **Bluff Master**: The con caper starring Shammi Kapoor invoked Abraham Lincoln's famous dictum before it started: '*Kabhi kabhi aap saari duniya ko thodi der ke liye bewakoof bana sakte hain. Kabhi kabhi aap kuch logon ko hamesha ke liye bewakoof bana sakte hain. Lekin aap sabko hamesha ke liye bewakoof nahin bana sakte.*'
- **Upkar**: Based on the iconic slogan *Jai jawaan, jai kisaan*, 'This film is humbly dedicated to the sacred memory of one of the greatest sons of India: Shri Lal Bahadur Shastriji.'
- **Anand**: Hrishikesh Mukherjee dedicated the film to 'the city of Bombay & Raj Kapoor', the latter being the inspiration for the character of Anand.
- **Jaani Dushman**: We had a taste of what was to come when the film opened with '*preton ke upar aadhaarit kalpnik kahani hai. Jo bhoot preton mein maante hain, unke liye is film mein koi sandesh nahin hain. Jo nahin maante hain, unko manane ka koi prayatna nahin hain.*'
- **Masoom**: Shekhar Kapur's directorial debut was 'in the memory of Shri Guru Dutt [and] Smt. Geeta Dutt'.
- **Waisa Bhi Hota Hai Part II**: Shashanka Ghosh's laugh riot declared, 'This film is a mindless work of fiction. The characters happen to be fictional, despite our sincerest efforts. The locations, however, are real. The story has been plagiarized from several films.'

Pehli Mulaqat: 5 Famous First Meetings

Hindi films would be nothing if not for the legends surrounding most of them. All the stars, all the movies, all the hits would have come to naught if you did not have that hanger-on who claimed to be there when it all happened.

I think one of the greatest heroes of Bollywood is the guy who stopped Amitabh from boarding the train to Allahabad after his twelfth flop. That man also introduced him to Prakash Mehra who was looking for an actor for a film called *Zanjeer*. There is no such guy? What rubbish! In fact, that guy was featured in a scene in *Rangeela*, where he recounted this story. That guy was Neeraj Vohra? That guy was *played* by Neeraj Vohra. He actually exists. No, really.

Of all the legends around stars, the most interesting ones are about the first meetings between them. There is an element of suspense and drama around these. Thanks to our predisposition to astrology, there is something inherently attractive about a chance meeting between two Masters of the Universe.

STATUTORY WARNING: Some of the stories have been embellished by the author's imagination.

Guru Dutt and Dev Anand

Dev Anand was an employee of the Indian Postal Service. During the Second World War, he worked as a censor and read hundreds of letters daily to edit out passages unwanted by the government. While doing this boring job, he was completely taken aback by the passionate fan letters addressed to film stars and dreamt of getting some letters like that himself.

One day, when the dhobi returned his laundry he found in it a shirt which was not his. It was of the same size but definitely not the same sartorial elegance Dev was used to. On inquiring, the dhobi speculated that the shirt could belong to this other fellow—who lived in the same chawl—who was working on odd jobs at Prabhat Talkies. To get a little dope on the film industry, Dev decided to take the shirt back to the owner himself. And became so thick with Gurudutt Shivshankar Padukone that, very soon, the most famous pact of Hindi cinema was made: if Dev produced a film, Guru would direct it. If Guru produced one, Dev would star in it.[1]

Balraj Sahni and Johnny Walker

Badruddin Jamaluddin Qazi was a conductor with the Dadar depot of BEST. His standard routine consisted of entertaining passengers while handing out their tickets. A stammering lover proposing to his girlfriend for Mr Braganza. An out-of-tune singer doing a ghazal for Mrs Apte. A drunkard getting harangued by his wife for Mr Sahni. Balraj Sahni, that is.

Balraj Sahni was working on a script for a film called *Baazi*, most parts of which were filled except for one: that of a comedian. He was impressed enough by Badru's antics to fix up an appointment for him with the director, Guru Dutt.

On the day of the meeting, Badru staggered into the room completely drunk, proceeded to fall over furniture and almost kissed the studio receptionist, Miss Lobo. Only when the director was about to call the police did he confess that he was acting. Thanks to his drunken turn, when the time came to decide a screen name (B.J. Qazi is not what screen legends are called), Guru Dutt unilaterally decided to infringe on the copyright of the world's most famous brand of Scotch whisky. And for generations after that, Indians thought that Johnny Walker did drunken roles so well that they had named a whisky after him.

Raj Kapoor and Nargis

Baby Nargis had acted in a few films as a child artiste. She grew up to be a raving beauty and acted in a few forgettable films as well.

During that time, Prithviraj Kapoor's eldest son was getting on everyone's nerves on the sets of a film where he was the clapper boy. (It is a common filmi family tradition to send the new-generation kiddos as assistants to directors who cannot refuse them.) There were rumours that the clapper boy took more time to get ready than the hero.

Anyway, Raj decided that there were better films to be made, cocked a snook at his bosses, used his father's clout to get financing and even got a script written. To save some money, he decided to act in the lead role himself. By this time, he had screen-tested many girls for the lead role and did not like any. Just when he was getting really impatient, he happened to see some footage of Nargis and decided that the girl had some magic. An appointment was fixed and the young Mr Kapoor went off to meet the girl.

Either Ms Nargis did not know the time of the director's arrival or she could not care less;

---

[1] For the record, Dev kept his part of the bargain with *Baazi*. Guru did not.

she was busy in the kitchen when the door was knocked on. Actually, she was deep-frying some stuff in *besan*—with her hands wrist-deep in the batter. With no servants around, she ran and opened the door herself. Tousled hair, hands in a mess . . . but she was very impressed by the light-eyed, fair-skinned good looks of Mr Kapoor. And in a dazed manner, when she used the back of her hand to push back a few strands of hair from her forehead, she smeared some besan on to her hair.

Mr Kapoor remembered this scene for the rest of his life and immortalized it in his teen-romance *Bobby*.

Satyajit Ray and Sharmila Tagore

Ray developed a reputation for giving chances to newcomers right from his first film. He did not really have a choice during his first film, *Pather Panchali*, as none of the actors of Bengali cinema then fitted the bill for most of the roles—and more importantly, he did not have the money to pay any of them.

When he was testing actresses for the lead role in *Apur Sansar* (the third film of the Apu Trilogy), it turned out to be one long haul because none of the hopefuls had the innocence, beauty and sensitivity needed for the role. A common friend told Ray of a fourteen-year-old who was distantly related to Rabindranath Tagore. He wanted to refuse but could not do so because of his 'bhadralok' upbringing. His worst fears were confirmed when the girl in question landed up in a short yellow frock and a fringe cut. But something must have come through in her English diction, because Ray asked his wife to take the girl inside, tie her hair in a bun using a wig and dress her in a traditional saree.

And that's how Sharmila Tagore became a Ray heroine. Along the way in her journey, she went on to become the biggest female star in Bollywood of her time.

Ramesh Sippy and Amjad Khan

The offices of Sippy Films had a room which was ostensibly for their story department. In 1972, the story department was all but disbanded as the scion of the company—Ramesh—was always closeted with two Muslim boys of the same age (which was very young, by filmi standards). Salim Khan and Javed Akhtar were given full use of the story room as they were working on a two-line story idea commissioned by G.P. Sippy: 'A police officer's family is massacred by a dacoit. To take revenge, the officer takes the help of two small-time crooks.'

Of the four characters mentioned in the two lines, three had already been cast—Sanjeev Kumar, Dharmendra and Amitabh Bachchan. And as the screenwriter duo worked towards the climax of the screenplay, they realized that the dacoit was turning out to be the most charismatic of the lot. And with two major stars of the day slated to play the police officer and one of the crooks, the actor playing the dacoit had to match up to them. All major villains of the day were evaluated and rejected for lack of menace. Danny Denzongpa was almost signed on but he withdrew because he had committed to doing Feroz Khan's *Dharmatma*.

At this point, Satyen Kappu recommended to Salim Khan a young actor who was acting in an IPTA production with him. Salim saw the actor and asked him to come and meet Ramesh Sippy for the finest role of the film.

When the actor walked into the dimly lit story room, Ramesh Sippy was lying on a mattress on the ground with his back to the door. Hearing a voice, he turned around and looked up to see a guy who was medium in build but, because of Ramesh's perspective from the floor, looked like a menacing figure who loomed across the entire frame of the door. Ramesh Sippy turned around and met Amjad Khan for the first time.

After that first meeting, Amjad left and later returned for the screen test in army fatigues, with blackened teeth and a grubby, bearded look. Now, Ramesh Sippy met Gabbar Singh for the first time.[2]

WHEN RAJ 'MET' ZEENAT

When Raj Kapoor was hunting for an actress to star in **Satyam Shivam Sundaram**, sex siren Zeenat Aman was the last person on his mind. The role was that of a village girl with a badly scarred face. Zeenat—who wanted the role badly—arrived at Raj Kapoor's residence dressed as a village girl, and in make-up to look scarred. Raj Kapoor was mighty impressed and signed her on the spot with a gold coin as the signing amount.

What was on full display was Zeenat's body and not so much her acting talent though Raj Kapoor felt that this was required to draw in the public to his film and its message. 'Let people come to see Zeenat's tits, they will go out remembering the film,' he had famously said.

---

[2] Acknowledgements are due to Anupama Chopra, who recounted the story of this meeting in her bestselling book, *Sholay: The Making of a Classic*.

Starting Small: 13 Low-profile Debuts

A lot of actors from film families have either stood in for others or have been pushed into small scenes. This was obviously before their 'launches', which are a little better planned and publicized, not to mention more anticipated.

Raj Kapoor's three children—Randhir, Reema and Rishi—appeared in the immortal love song '*Pyar hua ikrar hua*' of **Shree 420**, looking tremendously cute in their raincoats and umbrellas as the lyrics prophetically declared that the RK lineage will ensure the show goes on—'*Hum na rahenge, tum na rahoge / Phir bhi rahengi yeh nishaniyaan*'.
　　Rishi, who was the youngest of the three, was bribed with chocolates by Nargis in order to shoot in the rain.

Sanjay Dutt had a brief screen appearance before he made his 'formal' debut in *Rocky*. He appeared in **Reshma Aur Shera** (produced by Sunil Dutt) as a sidekick to the main singer in a qawwali. He was there (with his trademark goofy smile) clapping in the standard qawwali style (open-palms-wide-rotate-palms-in-opposite-directions-clap-delicately).

Aamir Khan's first movie role was that of the child version of his youngest uncle (Tariq) in their home production, **Yaadon Ki Baaraat**. He appeared in the title song, during which he excused himself to take a leak. Apparently, the entire family teased him about that for a long time.
　　Aamir's nephew, Imran Khan, carried on this family legacy by appearing as the kid version of his uncle in two home production blockbusters—**Qayamat Se Qayamat Tak** (in a virtually invisible role) and **Jo Jeeta Wohi Sikandar** (a substantial role, including a beautiful song).

Hrithik Roshan's dancing skills were evident from a very early age as he danced alongside Sridevi and Rajinikanth (wow!) in **Bhagwaan Dada**. He also acted in a film called **Aap Ke Deewane**.

11

Both the films were produced by his father and the former was directed by his grandfather.

Even when it is not a home production, if a star-child is present on the location and looks cute enough, the temptation is great for the producer to (a) save money by shoving the kid in and (b) thereby earn brownie points with daddy. This is probably what happened when Bobby Deol was requisitioned to play the junior Dharmendra in Manmohan Desai's **Dharam Veer**.

If it is not the star's son, it could be the producer's—saving a packet by using home-grown artistes. For *Sangharsh*—a remake of *The Silence of the Lambs*—the cost-conscious Bhatt brothers put Mahesh's daughter Alia to play the child Preity Zinta, contrasting the horrors of Punjab terrorism with her pigtailed charm.

In the early scenes of **Kabhi Khushi Kabhie Gham,** Jaya Bachchan was seen playing with her kid son, who grew up to become Shah Rukh Khan in the film. Then a toddler, Aryan Khan was recruited to play his real daddy's kiddie version there.

While **Dilwale Dulhania Le Jayenge** was strictly not his home production, Karan Johar still played an important part in it—as assistant to Aditya Chopra, and even in the cast. He played Rocky, SRK's chubby friend. But this was not his acting debut.

Karan Johar's first acting assignment was in a TV serial of the 1980s called **Indradhanush**—in which a gang of schoolboys inadvertently built a time machine. He played a bumbling friend of the hero. In one scene, when the hero was wondering how to make a computer chip, he good-naturedly offered him his packet of potato wafers.[1]

The **Mr India** gang of kids comprised at least two later stars—Aftab Shivdasani (who had earlier been seen as the Farex baby) and Ahmed Khan (who is a choreographer and has directed *Fool 'n' Final* in recent times). Ahmed showed promise right at the beginning, when he breakdanced through his role in **Mr India**.

Before he achieved fame as the yodelling gypsy of 'Mehbooba mehbooba' (in **Sholay**), Jalal Agha made a regal debut in one of the greatest epics in Indian cinema as one of the most famous characters in Indian history. He was the young Shahzada Salim in **Mughal-e-Azam**.

Just as surprising is the kid who played the role of the young Ashok Kumar in the landmark

---

[1] SRK's other friend in **DDLJ** (Robby) was played by Arjun Sablok, who went on to direct **Na Tum Jaano Na Hum** and **Neal 'n' Nikki**. In hindsight, he should have stuck to acting.

hit of the 1940s—*Kismet*. Mehmood debuted and later came back to become one of the most famous comedians of Hindi cinema.

And as a sort of ending, it would be interesting to showcase the lowest-profile debut of a member of the highest-profile family of Bollywood. Shweta Bachchan Nanda made an appearance in the Greatest Film Ever Made while she was still unborn. Jaya Bachchan was pregnant with her while shooting for *Sholay* and the make-up crew had a tough time making the glowing Jaya look like a lifeless widow in the film.

THE NAWAB OF LOW-PROFILE DEBUTS

When Nawazuddin Siddiqui got noticed for his amazing performances in *Kahaani* and *Gangs of Wasseypur Part 2*, he was actually being rewarded after more than a decade of struggle. When people started digging into his past, they found a long list of bit parts in several well-known and not-so-well-known films. And since Nawazuddin doesn't remember himself, there may be more—waiting to be discovered.

Some of the better known films are:

- *Sarfarosh*: He was one of the labourers interrogated by Mukesh Rishi and Aamir Khan in the police lock-up who confessed after being threatened with an 'encounter'. He enacted another police lock-up scene with Aamir Khan in *Talaash*.
- *Munna Bhai MBBS*: He was the pickpocket who tried to steal Sunil Dutt's wallet, and was beaten up before being brought to Sanjay Dutt's false clinic for treatment.
- *Black Friday*: In his first role with Anurag Kashyap, he played Asgar Muqadam who was (yet again) beaten up in a police lock-up for information about the bomb-blasts.
- *Dev.D*: In this cult classic, he was one of the '*Patna ke Presley*' who performed the '*Emotional Atyachar*' song with uninhibited glee!
- *Peepli Live*: He played Rakesh, the local reporter in Peepli who first reported the story of a farmer committing suicide to waive off his loans, and then became the point person for the reporter from the English channel.

Apart from the above, his credits include *Shool*, *Manorama Six Feet Under*, *Ek Chaalis Ki Last Local*, *Aaja Nachle*, *New York* and *Firaaq*. According to film blog Moi Fight Club (and its contributor @silverlightgal), *Kahaani* was Nawazuddin's thirtieth role. Talk about low-profile careers!

QUIZ: WHAT ARE STAR PARENTS INSPIRED BY?

Before we enter the world of families and fraternities, here is a quick quiz to see if you can figure out how and where our stars got their names from.

1	Parineeti Chopra	A	From a poem written by his father for his mother
2	Kareena Kapoor	B	Suggested by poet Sumitra Nandan Pant
3	Karisma Kapoor	C	A film by Prakash Jha
4	Javed Akhtar	D	Exact match with grandfather
5	Raveena Tandon	E	Heroine of a David Lean movie
6	Ranbir Kapoor	F	An Italian actress and sex symbol
7	Amitabh Bachchan	G	An epic novel by Leo Tolstoy
8	Lara Dutta	H	A mashup of both parents' names

ANSWERS

1C Parineeti's parents liked Prakash Jha's socially conscious *Parinati* enough to name their daughter after the film. 2G Babita was reading *Anna Karenina* when she was pregnant with Bebo. 3F Gina Lollobrigida impressed Randhir and Babita enough that they named their first born Lolo. 4A Jaan Nisar Akhtar wrote to his wife Safia, 'Lambha lamba kisi jadoo ka jasana hoga . . .' when they got married and for a long time, their son was called Jadoo—inspired by this line—before a formal name was given. 5H What else will you call Ravi and Veena Tandon's daughter? 6D Ranbir Raj's son Rishi named his son Ranbir Raj too. 7B Harivansh Rai wanted to name his son Inquilaab but his good friend suggested a less revolutionary but more illuminating option. 8E Boris Pasternak's *Doctor Zhivago* was filmed by David Lean with the haunting Lara's Theme music and the Duttas were hooked.

14

2

Rishtey Naatey

It's all about loving your parents.
—Publicity line from **Kabhi Khushi Kabhie Gham**

AbRam is my best production.
—Shah Rukh Khan

Bollywood is nothing without relationships. From parents to dogs, from children to chaddi buddies.

This section looks at how people are related in movies—from make-believe relationships to real ones.

Cine-Maa: 15 Mothers

If one character distinguishes Hindi cinema from that of the rest of the world, it is the Mother. No other country in the world has so many different variations on the mother–son relationship (almost never mother–daughter though) as in Bollywood. And thanks to the predominance of the 'formula' in Bollywood, one can even categorize the mothers of Bollywood and list the 'top moms'.

Mother India

Starting with Nargis in the role of the heroic mom, Mother India is the self-righteous mother who puts nation, honour and duty before her son. So, the son may have killed a guy double his size for her and may have bought her an apartment block in south Mumbai but she would still give him up for the greater good of society. Or better, shoot him. Nargis showed the way as she gunned down her dacoit son to save the honour of her village in *Mother India*.

A mother's dilemma between love and duty was brilliantly articulated in *Deewaar* when Nirupa Roy handed over the gun to her police officer–son and 'prayed' for his weapon to remain steady—'*Bhagwaan kare goli chalate waqt tere haath na kaanpe.*' Having done her duty as a woman, she left to wait for her errant son immediately afterwards. '*Aurat apna farz nibha chuki. Ab maa apne bete ka intezaar karne jaa rahi hai.*'

Agneepath's mother (Rohini Hattangadi) was a watered-down version of the above character, for she berated her son for his gangster ways but promptly forgave him when he promised 'to return to the village'. Eventually, the son died on the mother's lap—having cleansed himself of all sin by passing through the path of fire.

16

A recent avatar of this mother was seen in **Vaastav**, where an obviously doting mother (Reema Lagoo) shot her gangster-son (Sanjay Dutt), partly for his wrongdoings and partly to end his suffering as a fugitive and drug addict.

This character received a 180-degree makeover in **Aatish**, where the mother (Tanuja) defended her smuggler-son's (Sanjay Dutt) actions to her police officer–son (a wimpy Atul Agnihotri) by pointing out that the elder brother's criminal takings had funded the latter's education and career.

Hip Mom

Reema Lagoo broke off her B-grade shackles and emerged as the nation's coolest mother when **Maine Pyar Kiya** became the first movie to have a 'Mom' instead of a 'mother'. Here was a really cool lady who threw darts, was okay with a bob cut (though not for her own daughter-in-law), actually mouthed the word 'miniskirt', and even dyed her hair. She was such a relief from the grey-haired, saintly souls that she had millions of similar roles to do after that one.

Farida Jalal of **DDLJ** was the other iconic representation of the Hip Mom—especially when she talked to her daughter about her dream man and even egged her on to elope. Her son-in-law was, of course, a chauvinistic wet blanket and refused to run away without the dad's permission—somebody slap him!

After these two, almost each movie of the Yash Chopra genre has had a variation on this kind of mom.

An extreme variation on this kind of Hip Mom is the smoking and promiscuous kind—made famous by Mita Vasisht in **Oops**. The lady thought nothing of having an affair with her son's friend and went about in slinky clothes, with a sultry look and a lighted cigarette for most of the film.

Monster-in-Law/Stepmom

Now, these are the moms who are after blood. It is usually the blood of the rebellious daughters-in-law that they are after, although property, villainous uncles and children from the husband's earlier marriages bring about similar levels of dementia. Of course, in all such 'social' films, the mother never dies. She just reforms.

Bindu and Lalita Pawar are the most famous practitioners of this genre.

Bindu's role in **Biwi Ho To Aisi** was one of the greatest examples of unintended hilarity in Hindi cinema. Her refrain, 'Secretary, follow me,' and her constant harangue against her bahu

Rekha were the stuff legends are made of. All this while her wimpy son (Farooque Shaikh) looked on balefully.

Aruna Irani in **Beta** had one such epic battle with her daughter-in-law (Madhuri Dixit) as the stepson (Anil Kapoor in the most undeserved title role of all time) looked on, smiled foolishly, was torn between the two super-heroines and finally got poisoned before rising from the dead to save his mother.

Tragedy Queens

These are the Single Moms—women who are punished for having sex before getting married. Actually, they did get married in the eyes of God but that does not count in the real world. So, the object of their affection either dies on them or deserts them after impregnating them during a night of passion. They are left to lead a life of sacrifice and determination in order to bring up their sons (always sons) so that they can make *roshan* family names or take *badla*.

It was the former in the case of **Aradhana** as Sharmila's son grew up to be yet another dashing air force pilot with the same drop-dead good looks as his father. The mother survived unwed motherhood, a jail sentence and very bad make-up to bring up a son as her would-have-been husband would have wanted.

Badla was the objective in **Trishul** as Waheeda Rehman's son grew up to take on top industrialist and his 'illegitimate father', R.K. Gupta, for his mother's humiliation. He did not fear death or destruction because he was used to his mother's slow descent into death, and he articulated that with the explosive line: '*Jisne pachchees baras apni maa ko har roz thoda thoda marte dekha ho, usey maut se kya dar lagega?*'

Mandakini in **Ram Teri Ganga Maili** probably falls in this category too but nobody remembers anything from that film except the waterfall song.

Heartless Moms

These are the terrible mothers who abandon their families either on the provocation of evil relatives or—even worse—to pursue a career. But the Bollywood mom *never* leaves her children. So each one of them comes right back, sacrificing wealth and career to be with their brats.

The desi version of **Kramer vs Kramer**—**Akele Hum Akele Tum**—had Manisha Koirala leaving super-chauvinistically-atrocious hubby (Aamir Khan) to put up a fight for a career in films.

Then, horror of horrors—she got into an ugly custody battle for which the now-martyred Aamir had to sell off his precious musical compositions.

Karisma Kapoor, the rich kid, had a whirlwind romance, a quick marriage and a quicker son with taxi-driver **Raja Hindustani** before she left him at the behest of her 'evil' mamaji. She came back just in time for the climax in which her *laadla* son was tossed around like a football in the Super Bowl, by the aforementioned mamaji.

HONOURABLE MENTIONS

Aruna Irani had a classic 'mom'-ent in **Doodh Ka Karz**, when she breastfed a snake (yes, a 100-per-cent authentic, ISO-certified serpent and not an *ichhadhari* one) along with her son (who grew up to be Jackie Shroff). Of course, her milky ways earned her the eternal gratitude of the snake, who returned time and again to help her (human) son.

Saawan Kumar Tak (of **Souten** fame) made a film that was initially called 'Mother 98' (because it was supposed to release in that year) but was eventually released as **Mother** three years later with a storyline quite similar to *Mamma Mia*. It had Rekha in the title role, and the object of the game in the film was to find out which of her three lovers was the father of her daughter. The contestants were Rakesh Roshan, Jeetendra and Randhir Kapoor.

TIMELESS MOTHERS, AGELESS CHILDREN

Actresses always bear the brunt of having to play mothers to older heroes. A selection:

- *Sharmila Tagore and Rajesh Khanna*: Sharmila played Rajesh Khanna's lover and mother in **Aradhana**, despite being two years younger.
- *Rakhee and Amitabh Bachchan*: Rakhee played Amitabh's lover in 1981 (**Barsaat Ki Ek Raat**) and mother in 1982 (**Shakti**), despite being five years younger.
- *Preity Zinta and Hrithik Roshan*: Preity played Hrithik's lover in **Koi Mil Gaya** and his mother in the sequel (**Krrish**) though she did not share screen time with him as his mother. She is a year younger than Hrithik.
- *Dimple Kapadia and Salman Khan*: While Dimple belongs to the 1970s generation and Sallu-bhai is still strutting around, their age difference was only nine years but that did not stop Dimple playing mother to Salman in **Dabangg**.

The Baap of All Lists: 11 Fathers

The father figure recurs in our movies in different ways. Sometimes he creates an impact with his presence and sometimes with his absence. A taskmaster, a darling, a hero, a villain—he's been all of those characters and more.

The Photographic Father
An alarmingly large number of fathers in Hindi movies have been two-dimensional. They have existed only in photographs for their widows to stand in front of them and declare tearfully to the son, '*Kaash tere Babuji aaj zinda hote...*'

The most striking example of this was in **Jaane Tu Ya Jaane Na**, in which Naseeruddin Shah showed just how good great actors can be, even when they are confined within a frame. As a Ranjhaur ka Rathore, he was quite sick of the pacifist bull his wife was feeding his son, and from his perch, he made his displeasure clear. And in the end, he had a victory of his own.

The Missing Father
In **Deewaar**, the father—for the most part—was missing. He was only invoked through the tattoo of his elder son which was a mark not just on his left forearm but on his soul, his existence, his entire being. The son didn't understand why his father had run away. He didn't know that his father had made a huge sacrifice for him and the family. He was just plain angry with him.

When his turn came, he decided not to run away because he was not about to let his unborn son face the same accusation he had faced—'*Mera baap chor hai.*'

In **Masoom**, the son was thrust upon the father suddenly—when he wasn't even aware of his existence. The illegitimate son entered the happy family of his father, without knowing why, and yet enjoying the experience. The son's affection for the father and the father's restrained emotions were gut-wrenchingly real.

20

In a poignant scene, Jugal Hansraj drew a bespectacled figure and introduced it to Naseer as his father. Naseer asked, 'Aap ke papa chashma pehnte hain?' When the boy said yes, he paused and slowly took off his glasses.[1]

The Hitler

With more films on the education system that go beyond 'Maa, main pass ho gaya', it is only natural that the overambitious (but well-meaning) parent would be depicted in some form or the other. The name of this category is taken from *3 Idiots*, where Farhan's father was referred to as Hitler Qureishi. Here was a man who thought 91 per cent was a disastrous performance but, at the same time, installed an AC in his son's room so that he could sleep comfortably. He thought photography was a dumb career choice but gave in when he realized that it made his son really happy.[2]

One hideous character—falling under the same heading—whose writ ran farther than academics was Bhairav Singh of Vikramaditya Motwane's *Udaan*. Imperious in nature, impervious to others' wishes and often violent, here was a man who made one want to wring his neck. Ronit Roy put in the performance of a lifetime to portray a man whom everyone hated from the bottom of their hearts.

The Romance Killer

For decades, this gentleman of regal countenance has stormed down the ornate stairs of his haveli to stop his daughter (or son) from marrying a person unworthy of his *khandaan*. And obviously, the suitor never did anything to help his cause.

Look at the best example. In *Dilwale Dulhania Le Jayenge*, Shah Rukh vandalized Amrish Puri's store, ran away with a crate of beer and then tried to run away with his daughter as well. Amrish Puri—on his part—wagged his never-ending finger, upped the volume of his baritone, and made his eyes so big, you could play ice hockey on them.

But then, for all their fury, these dads are dads after all. When he realized how much the upstart from London loved his daughter (and maybe, what his net worth was), he let her go and garnered the maximum applause for that.

(Repeat after me in Amrish Puri style, '*Jaa Simran jaa . . .*')

---

[1] Naseeruddin Shah seems to have made a career out of playing illegitimate fathers. His illegitimate offspring include Farhan Akhtar (*Zindagi Na Milegi Dobara*), Kalki Koechlin (*The Girl in Yellow Boots*), Ajay Devgn (*Raajneeti* and *Naajayaz*), Shah Rukh Khan (*Main Hoon Na*) and Urmila Matondkar (*Chamatkar*).

[2] To understand the genesis of the Hitler dad, a perusal of the chapter on spiritual ancestors on page 45 is recommended.

The Friend

DDLJ had a counterpoint too. Shah Rukh was brought up by a father who spoilt his son silly. He raised a toast to his son's great achievement of flunking in England ('*Hum toh sab Hindustan mein fail huye, tu ne London mein fail hoke dikha diya . . .*') and urged him to live life to the fullest.

First of all, he was not Dad. He was Pops. He was a friend who shared a beer. He was a confidant who conspired to get his son the girl he loved. And under the friendly banter, there was the doubled love of a single parent ('*Main sirf tera baap nahin, teri maa bhi hoon*').

The Fighter

After the father dies, the son grows up and takes revenge for his death. But sometimes, it is the son who dies, and the father who takes up arms.

In the most famous example of this, the father did not take up arms in a literal sense. But in a metaphorical way, ex-headmaster B.V. Pradhan found a new meaning in life after his son passed away. In *Saaransh*, Anupam Kher played the role of a lifetime as he took on the recalcitrant state, first in a bid to get his son's ashes home and then to seek justice for a helpless young woman.

The Priest

All fathers are not biological. Some of them are theological too.

The familiar, benevolent figure in the white gown uttering words of solace is someone we have grown used to. After all, he's the go-to man for confessing our sins and getting sane advice that we eventually ignore.

Naseeruddin Shah in **Kabhi Haan Kabhi Naa** is one such lovable father—who was constantly ticking off his wayward parishioners and commandeering vehicles to hitch rides in opposite directions. When met with protests, he inevitably said that all roads led to God. So there.

The Odd Ones

And finally, we have two oddball fathers who were way out of the ordinary and were both, quite coincidentally, played on screen by two actors related to each other.

In *Paa*, Abhishek Bachchan was the father of Amitabh Bachchan, a patient of progeria (an advanced ageing disease)—a very unusual casting choice. Writer–director R. Balki said that he got the idea in a meeting in which Amitabh was fooling around while Abhishek was all serious. So, he researched and dug out a disease that could make this happen. Simple. Amitabh's make-up and acting, however, were not that simple.

And finally, the last word must belong to the 'father of them all'—***Shahenshah***. You know, the guy who said '*Rishtey mein toh hum tumhare baap hote hain . . .*'

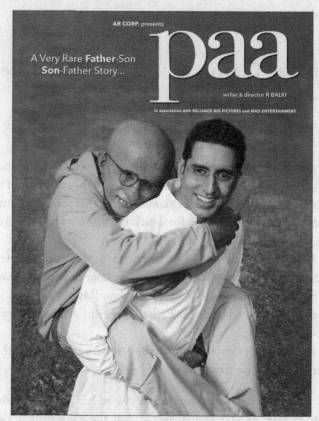

The son who became the father. Abhishek Bachchan in and as Paa.

Phoolon Ka, Taaron Ka: 12 Brother–Sister Pairs

Brothers and sisters in Hindi cinema should be the easiest to write about since they appear in every second film, and a sister's rape and brutal murder is always the chief reason for docile village bumpkins to become AK-47–toting vigilantes. Either that scenario, or maudlin weddings in which the sisters tearfully sit in the *doli* for which the brothers have worked night and day to accumulate the necessary dowry.[1]

Interestingly, *3 Idiots* injected a vial of wicked humour into the usual despondent theme of unmarried sisters. All the clichés of '*bimaar baap*', '*lachaar maa*' and '*kunwaari behen*' were brought together in a Triveni Sangam of spoofs as Raju Rastogi's unwed sister popped up every now and then as a potential bride for Farhan Qureishi. And a potentially insignificant track in the film became a laugh riot.

However, this section is not merely about all the brothers and sisters in the world; it is also about star pairs in the sibling domain.

The most high-powered brother–sister duo in Bollywood has to be the Aishwarya Rai–Shah Rukh Khan pairing in *Josh.* As Max and Shelley leading the Eagle gang in Goa, Ash and SRK were twins in the film. Despite putting up a decent show as siblings with the typical traits of overprotectiveness, rivalry and affection in equal measure, they could not save the film from sinking, and thus, nearly putting an end to the casting of top stars as siblings.

Aishwarya has played sister to two of Bollywood's biggest stars—SRK and Big B. She was the sister of her real-life father-in-law in *Hum Kisi Se Kum Nahin* (where he played a shrink) and was wooed simultaneously by Ajay Devgn and Sanjay Dutt (who was also a mafia don and AB's patient). Shades of the Robert De Niro and Billy Crystal–starrer *Analyze This* crept into this intended-to-be comic caper by David Dhawan but nothing seemed to click.

---

[1] Incidentally, it is always '*bhai ki padhaai*' and '*behen ki shaadi*' for which a man works. It is never the other way round.

Talking of top stars as siblings, **Andhaa Kaanoon** paired Hema Malini as Rajinikanth's elder sister—putting a distaff twist to the usual Bollywood formula of a righteous outlaw and his dutiful blood relative. Hema Malini did everything to stop her brother from killing their father's killer (including wearing a *havaldar*'s cap at a jaunty angle) but the now-red-eyed-now-white-eyed Rajini escaped to the accompaniment of tossed cigarettes and flaring nostrils.

No sibling discussion can be complete without a mention of Sooraj Barjatya and his films. The poster-child of Great Indian Family Values gave half of India and their *bhabhi*s diabetes with his saccharine-sweet brothers and sisters living under one huge roof.

In **Hum Saath-Saath Hain**, we had two reigning stars (Salman Khan and Saif Ali Khan), and one major character artiste (Mohnish Behl) playing brother to Neelam—one of the top heroines of her time. They all ate together, prayed together, pulled legs together, smiled together, simpered together and even whimpered together before getting one big group hug . . . *Bhaiyya*!

All people remember of **Trishul** is the Three Faces of Man—Sanjeev Kumar, Amitabh Bachchan and Shashi Kapoor—and all they speculate about is whether the rivalry between two construction tycoons is inspired by real life. What they forget is that Poonam Dhillon—fresh from the success of **Noorie**—was Shashi Kapoor's sister (and Amitabh's stepsister). She was the archetypal spoilt kid sister—who sang inane songs ('*Gapoochi gapoochi gum gum*'), drove Merc convertibles recklessly, and fell in love with short men in yellow pullovers. Her wedding—or whatever was left of it—ultimately formed the climax of the film.

Smita Patil was the reigning deity of art cinema. Mithun Chakraborty was the god of pelvic thrusts. Nobody really expected them to come together but they did. In **Dance Dance**, Smita was the elder sister who brought up her snotty kid brother to make him the country's biggest all-singing-all-dancing star. And she was not merely the backroom manager but the lead vocalist in the band as well. She eventually married the drummer, Shakti Kapoor (inexplicably called Resham), and settled down to happy domesticity. And if you know good ol' Shakti, you wouldn't dare think that was the end of it.

In **Fiza**, we had two huge stars as siblings. Hrithik Roshan was on his way up and Karisma Kapoor was on her way out. Written and directed by noted film critic Khalid Mohamed, the film was about a sister's quest for her missing brother, an unusual enough storyline. Add to that the complexities of a Muslim youth's alienation post the Bombay riots of 1992–93, his allegiance to terror networks, and Sushmita Sen's item song while his sister was looking for him—and you have **Fiza**. The film did not do too well—as movies featuring top stars in sibling roles never seem to do.

There is a general custom in India of tying a rakhi on the wrists of neighbourhood goons, to ward off their clumsy (and potentially dangerous) romantic advances. Conversely, brothers of bombshells have thankless jobs, for they are entrusted with the aforementioned task: of protecting the sisters. Leading the list are Anil Kapoor and Nana Patekar, who had the unenviable task of shepherding Katrina Kaif in *Welcome*. On the one hand, they had a bespectacled sissy like Akshay Kumar with whom their sister was hopelessly in love. On the other, they had international dons called RDX (Feroz Khan, quite naturally) to ward off.

In recent times, one of the funniest—and most natural—sibling relationships has been portrayed by Genelia D'Souza and Prateik Babbar in *Jaane Tu Ya Jaane Na*. There were no maudlin moments, no promises to protect honour and no rakhis either. Instead, there was the beautiful wistfulness of a brother who saw his sister make other friends, and a sister's quiet pride at her brother's talent. And several kick-ass sibling banter moments. One of which stands out for its deadpan humour:

> Genelia: *Do minute baith jaoon?*
> Prateik: *Tera ghar, tera bum—baith.*

My Brother Nikhil had Juhi Chawla and Sanjay Suri playing siblings in a tragic tale. Built around the theme of homosexuality, AIDS and our intolerance of both, debutant director Onir put together a fantastic depiction of sisterly love and helplessness. Sanjay Suri—not quite an A-list star—created a niche for himself as an actor of sensitivity and a producer of distinction, who then went on to do several offbeat films of value.

Many real-life brothers and sisters have been depicted in Bollywood too, all wildly successful and at least one big enough to become a spoof.

In *Golmaal Returns*, Tusshar Kapoor's character had a sister called Ekta—who watched soaps, got totally immersed in them and made important life decisions based on what she learnt from the serials. Played by Kareena Kapoor, Ekta was not beyond using the names of popular soaps in her daily conversation and the rest of the gang was not beyond thrashing Tusshar just for being his sister's brother.

And the last word has to be that film. The one with the Brother–Sister Song, in which the filmi brother was old enough to be the sister's father in real life. The story was the mirror image of *Fiza*—the brother went looking for his sister, Jasbir, in the dope dens of hippie-infested Kathmandu. In between, there were at least four hit songs (including the grown-up version of '*Phoolon ka taaron ka*'), estranged parents, a stolen deity, Mumtaz, and a girl called Janice who urged us to take a puff. *Hare Rama Hare Krishna*.

Salaamat Rahe: 16 Friends

Ever since one blind boy latched on to the elbow of a disabled boy, singing plaintive songs on the empty streets of 1950s Mumbai, Bollywood latched on to the formula that would not be given up *ever*! Friends have gone on bikes with sidecars, on horseback, in Mercedes convertibles and even on hearses—basically, from here to eternity. Though some pretence of variety is made, there are essentially three genres of 'friendship' in Hindi cinema.

The Sidekick: *Oye pappe!*

This label is applicable when the solo hero is either too intense (or wooden) to carry off comic scenes or too big a star for the producer to afford a second hero. The sidekick anchors the comic subplot without getting involved in any philosophical discussions and restricts himself to buffoonery and providing assistance during elopement.

To start off, we have to rewind to the 1960s and get Rajendra Nath into view as Shammi Kapoor's ubiquitous 'friend'. The most abiding memory of this comic genius is probably *An Evening in Paris*, where he played Sardar Makkhan Singh and romanced the heroine's sidekick with a brilliant invitation to a secluded spot—'*Aaja honey / Mausam hai funny / Charon taraf sannata / Itthe koi na marega mainu chaanta*'. Slapstick was never this poetic.

Coming to the 1990s, we had Deepak Tijori as the leading 'friend' of the industry, playing second fiddle to most of the leading stars of his time. Films with him as the solo hero bombed spectacularly. He started with a not-so-big star in *Aashiqui*. As Rahul Roy's resourceful friend in the film, he had a funny hand gesture that became quite the rage in college campuses at that time.

The most famous female exponent of this character is Guddi Maruti. Despite the predominance of male friendships in Bollywood, this is one glass ceiling that was completely shattered. In her many—almost identical—roles, she overshadowed pretty much everybody else with her girth and glee.

27

Friends who pee together, stay together

And finally, we have the Ultimate Sidekick whose character has got completely welded to the name of the hero, helped in creating a multi-film franchise, and been responsible for a large part of the series' popularity—Munna bhai's Circuit. In Arshad Warsi, we had the Don's henchman who was the right mix of menace and *masti*, reality and fantasy, humour and emotion. Without exaggeration, we can happily borrow a line from their second film and say, '*Jab tak sooraj chand rahega, Munna–Circuit ka naam rahega.*'

The Sacrificer: *Dost dost na raha...*[1]

And then there is the most popular geometrical figure in Bollywood—the triangle.

Employed by producers without the budget for two leading pairs (and thereby calling the film a multi-starrer), this is how you have three stars, get the 'extra' one to sacrifice so that the 'pair' can live happily ever after.

And since it is always about the friend and never about the girl, the reason for sacrifice isn't always the girl.

One of the biggest hits of the genre with three major stars—Raj Kapoor, Rajendra Kumar and Vyjayanthimala—was *Sangam.* Poor-boy fell in love with rich-girl who fell in love with

---

[1] In an attempt to steer clear of the obvious, two films about great sacrifices by friends—*Dostana* and *Yaarana*—are not listed.

rich-boy after poor-boy supposedly died but married poor-boy when he came back from the dead. Don't even bother to keep track of this three-line plot since it took the director the better part of four hours to narrate it on screen.

Shot extensively in Europe, the strangest bit of the triangle was the fact that Raj Kapoor got the girl in the end but still sang the Anthem of the Betrayed—'*Dost dost na raha*'. He apparently apologized to Rajendra Kumar later, saying it was too good a song to give up.

Feroz Khan's crime caper was named after the philosophy of sacrifice and had an energetic title song on the many therapeutic effects of **Qurbani** (among other things, '*Allah ko pyari hai qurbani*'). Feroz Khan and Vinod Khanna were both head over heels in love with Zeenat Aman. With Zeenie Baby slinking around in green bikinis and sheer thigh-slit gowns, you could hardly blame them. She divided her screen time and songs equally between the two heroes and remained blissfully unaware of their feelings—till the last scene. And after the usual drama of misunderstandings and accusations, Feroz Khan exercised the Director's Prerogative (see above) and got Vinod Khanna to take a bullet.

Not all films have to end with a death, though.

In **Saajan**, the heroine fell in love with a poet, whose identity was assumed by a handsome rake and she had, therefore, a perfect boyfriend—uniting a poet's mind with a hunk's body. Of course, the poet and the hunk were the best of friends and they both relinquished their love for the other's sake without asking the lady in question whom she would prefer. Eventually, she did express her choice. This was the 1990s, after all. And soon, one of the two gentlemen handed over the lady to the other and walked off with a smile.

Shah Rukh Khan made his name as a tragic hero—who never got the girl but died trying. In **Deewana**, he was a spoilt brat in love with a widow, but before he could move from singing-in-the-valleys to consummating-a-marriage, the lady's husband returned from the dead. **Deewana** deserves a mention in this list not because one of the two male leads died, but because the usual Rule of Bollywood Triangles was violated and the first person in love with the girl did not get her. If you think about it, all films till then had the second lead as an interloper who always died/left. This film broke that rule.

The Greatest Film Ever Made with The Greatest Star Cast Ever Assembled also had The Greatest Friendship Anthem Ever Composed. '*Yeh dosti hum nahin todenge*' was—and remains—one of the most hummed songs as two fast friends did unbelievable things with a motorcycle, a sidecar and a two-sided coin. Their friendship remained tongue-in-cheek as Jai tried to marry off his friend in a manner you reserve for your worst enemies, while Veeru had no stated use of his friend except to babysit his children. Except in the final showdown, when Jai pitched in with a non-romantic sacrifice.

When initial box-office reports of *Sholay* came in as lukewarm, the team debated whether to reshoot the end to make Jai live on. Thank God they didn't because Bollywood's most perfect film is so much the better for the slight heartbreak at the end.

The Eventual Lover: *Ladka ladki kabhi dost nahin ban sakte...*

This type encompasses the To-Become-Sexual Friendship. Bollywood has never been able to keep heroes and heroines from pawing each other—eventually. The progression from friends to lovers happens only when the heroine (initially a tomboy) starts to develop her femininity. Basically, a guy finds a girl (sexually) unattractive when she is playing basketball or getting into fisticuffs. The moment she puts on false eyelashes, Tarun Tahiliani lehengas and Saroj Khan–induced coquettishness, he gets a hard-on from here to Ludhiana and rides off into the sunset with her.

Maine Pyar Kiya was the first time the lead players of a romantic film did not get into mock quarrels or battles of one-upmanship. They became friends. And they did not say 'sorry' or 'thank you' either—by some strange code of their friendship. Prem and Suman remained the best of friends (for all of one song and three scenes) till someone pointed out '*ladka ladki kabhi dost nahin ban sakte*'—and nobody explained the concept better.

Incidentally, **MPK** managed to incorporate two kinds of Bollywood friendship—Sidekick (Salman and Laxmikant Berde) and Sexual (Salman and Bhagyashree)—in the same film.

Rahul thought love started with friendship ('*Pyar dosti hai*') and that lovers should be friends first. In **Kuch Kuch Hota Hai**, he happily made friends—and then tied the knot— with college belle Tina while his best friend Anjali was left bouncing a basketball. Of course, his pronouncement came back to him via his dead wife's letters and a precocious daughter. And he had to meet Anjali once again. Except this time, she had a hunk by her side, to whom she was engaged. Again, two kinds of friendship: Sacrifice (Salman and Shah Rukh) and Sexual (Shah Rukh and Kajol). Again, a record-breaking hit. Is there a formula here?

Jaane Tu Ya Jaane Na had all the ingredients of this genre of buddy films. Tomboy heroine— check. Friendship mistaken as love—check. Promises to find mates for each other—check. Boorish boyfriend of heroine—check. Incompatible girlfriend of hero—check. Late realization of love—check. Déjà vu—check. In fact, the director very cleverly channelized the déjà vu into a plot device by turning the story around and narrating it in flashback. You always knew the boy and girl would marry, right? You only wanted to know how.

Khubsoorat is a slightly sly entry into the ladka–ladki friendship list because the two friends were Ashok Kumar and his would-be daughter-in-law, Rekha. Rekha started a game to point out to her sister's conservative in-laws that a girlfriend–boyfriend thing can't be all that bad. She deduced that since Ashok Kumar was neither a female nor her enemy, he could only be her boyfriend—thus embarrassing him ceaselessly. And in the end, Ashok Kumar returned the compliment by calling Rekha his girlfriend. Keeping the family audience in mind, Rekha turned suitably coy and insisted on being called bahu. As I said, '*Ladka ladki kabhi . . .*'

Three of Three

Three buddy films with three friends each—***Dil Chahta Hai***, *3 Idiots* and ***Zindagi Na Milegi Dobara***—are the most difficult to slot into any of the above types. Despite one of the friends in each of the films being played by a much bigger star (Aamir Khan and Hrithik Roshan), the other two friends got equal importance and had well-developed characters and backstories. There was an air of sacrifice though no sexual tension among the friends. They were as real as friendship got in real life, and friendship sometimes means nothing more than having cake, getting drunk and pulling legs. And, of course, being suitably sympathetic when crushes on teachers happened.

SONGS OF FRIENDSHIP

Five not-so-obvious friendship songs, which talk not about friendship but about doing stuff with friends:
- *Diye jalte hain*: Amitabh Bachchan and Rajesh Khanna in ***Namak Haram***
- *Ek ek ho jaye, phir ghar chale jaana*: Amitabh and Mithun in ***Gangaa Jamunaa Saraswathi***
- *Imli ka boota, beri ka ped*: Dilip and Raaj Kumar in ***Saudagar***
- *Dil chahta hai*: Aamir Khan, Saif Ali Khan and Akshaye Khanna in ***Dil Chahta Hai***
- *Tum hi ho bandhu*: Saif Ali Khan, Deepika Padukone and Diana Penty in ***Cocktail***

The Truth about Cats and Dogs: 10 Filmi Pets

In Bollywood, friends turn into foes and foes turn into friends at the drop of a hat. However, it would be apt to introduce a different kind of friend who won't turn foe for anything.

These friends are the four-legged stars of Bollywood, the valiant and honourable pets who have fought villains, shed tears (crocodiles not included), taken bullets for their masters, danced to Bappi Lahiri's tunes and even umpired cricket matches.

The logic was impeccable. If Dhanno—a mare—could pull a tonga, why couldn't a woman drive one? And thus was born probably the most famous human–beast friend combo in the history of Bollywood—Basanti and Dhanno. Thanks to **Sholay**'s iconic status, Dhanno has become a full-fledged character that has stayed on and on

But for all her loyalty, she was treated rather cavalierly by her *malkin*. We didn't get to see her at the end of the film. Veeru and Basanti left in a train and not on her tonga . . .

Bonus Joke: Why did Dhanno run so fast to save Basanti? Well, there were four horses after her as well!

Try jumping off the roof of a train. With a gun in one hand, and a falcon perched on the other. Whenever you are unconvinced of the divinity of Amitabh Bachchan, visualize any scene from **Coolie** and your atheism will vanish faster than the falcon flutters its wings.

The falcon—named Allah Rakha—featured in the supercharged 'entry dialogue' by Amitabh in which he pegged his identity to the protection of Allah and the assistance of his faithful feathered friend—'*Bachpan se hai sar pe Allah ka haath, aur Allah Rakha hai apne saath . . .*'

The falcon appeared in key sequences—snatching guns off villains, dropping garlands during courting songs—and his presence reached a climax when Amitabh ascended an election podium with a huge falcon on the backdrop and the real one perched on his forearm. What did I say about '*Allah Rakha hai apne saath*'?

Bonus Falcon: Manmohan Desai's penchant for the bird led to a falcon, Sheroo, becoming a star attraction in **Dharam Veer** as well. Pran played an outlaw who had the supercool bird to assist him in his guerilla wars against the tyrant raja. And yes, Sheroo got a star billing at par with leading character actors.

How many films can you remember that were named after an animal? Well, **Haathi Mere Saathi** was one for sure. Rajesh Khanna shared equal screen time and less-than-equal screen space with the four tusk-eteers—whom he called his 'brothers'. And their roles in the film were no different from that of the standard-issue 'good brother' in Hindi cinema. They helped Rajesh Khanna grow up, earn money, woo Tanuja and scare away villains. The only thing they did not assist the hero in was—presumably—fathering the child.

Most dog-lovers have asked—how much can a dog do? The question the maker of **Teri Meherbaniyan** (the legendary K.C. Bokadia) asked was different—what do you want a dog to do? Moti, the ubiquitous black Labrador of Bollywood (who always got separate billing as 'Wonder Dog') was literally the hero of the film as he did matchmaking, shed copious tears, performed the last rites of his master (Jackie Shroff) and took revenge.

Rub your eyes and read those last ten words again. Yes, Moti carried the water-filled *kalash* ahead of the funeral procession, went around the pyre with a burning log and finally lit the fire.

When he went on to kill Amrish Puri after that, it seemed like an anticlimax.

Only one question: How much was Jackie paid for this film? And Moti?

A dynamic horse–dog duo was the main supporting cast behind **Mard** *tangewala*'s crusade against the British Raj. Moti returned (as Moti) as did Badal, the white steed that has been the preferred mode of transport for a million characters in historical—or even not-so-historical—films.

Badal got his separate comic subplot where he fell in love with Lord Curzon's mare (which was part of a statue) and even eloped with his lady-love at the very end. Moti got his action subplot where he stormed a Britishers Only club—assisted by one Mr Amitabh Bachchan—

and managed to uproot that insulting notice once seen at the entrances of British-owned establishments: 'Dogs and Indians Not Allowed'.

Imagine two animals getting star-billing and separate subplots in an Amitabh Bachchan movie. That probably makes them bigger stars than Deepak Parashar.[1]

Bollywood's favourite black Labrador returned in **Bol Radha Bol,** a David Dhawan thriller in which an industrialist (Rishi Kapoor) was being swindled out of his inheritance. As the industrialist returned from a romantic sojourn in a village, he came face-to-face with a lookalike who had taken his place. The industrialist called for his trusted dog to prove his identity but the dog turned out to be an impostor, thus making it a very rare animal double role. Of course, the heroic duo overcame the evil machinations of the villainous clique to chase the impostors—human and canine—out.

Salman Khan and Sooraj Barjatya's debut—**Maine Pyar Kiya**—was a history-altering hit and also had the biggest pet hit song in '*Kabootar ja ja ja*'. The pigeon in the song delivered love letters—ping-ponging between Bhagyashree and Salman. The pigeon was no ordinary bird—as it got star-billing in the credits as 'Handsome'.

But if we delve into the history of the pigeon (in the film, not real life!), we realize that he actually belonged to Seema (the vamp, played by Pervin Dastur) whose cruel brother (Mohnish Behl) planned to use the bird for target practice. On being saved by the simpering Bhagyashree, Handsome pledged undying allegiance to her and even returned in the climax to take revenge on Mohnish Behl, thus rendering PETA largely redundant.

Whenever Indian cricketers get out to dubious umpiring decisions, we miss cute little Tuffy (the cuteness quotient debatable, though) who wore an umpire's hat, sat on a high chair and put up notices with umpiring decisions in **Hum Aapke Hain Koun.** And that was just the first scene. Sooraj Barjatya maintained his tradition of a 'complete' happy family by showcasing the only Pomeranian in the world which didn't snap at strangers. During the film, Tuffy assisted wedding rituals by couriering shoes, did matchmaking (a basic minimum requirement of Bolly pets), acted cute, and finally brokered a happy ending by delivering a letter to the wrong person. Overall, Tuffy upstaged Handsome, the pigeon of **Maine Pyar Kiya** and—some dog-lovers claim—even Laxmikant Berde.

---

[1] Moti has got separate subplots in several films. For example, he single-handedly cared for an infant in **Maa** when the baby's mother passed away.

Bonus Pet: In a bid to upstage the pigeon and the dog, Sooraj Barjatya introduced an animated parrot in **Main Prem Ki Diwani Hoon**, which spoke only in film titles. It was unarguably the most irritating cartoon character in Bollywood history.

A monkey—called Bajrangi—formed a seamless trio with Govinda and Chunky Pandey in **Aankhen,** and all of them did a lot of monkeying around, with the real one being the most serious of the lot. The monkey's place in the sun was assured when the trio had to perform in front of the Gateway of India to earn their daily bread (after Kader Khan kicked them out of their house). The monkey was the top dog in the song as he was compared to fighting–dancing stars ('*Nache to Jeetender, maare to Dharmender . . .*')—which may have melted Maneka Gandhi's heart but the reactions of the aforementioned stars remain unavailable.

Mandatory Chunky Bashing: When asked why he didn't have a double role in a film where everyone else seemed to have one, Chunky Pandey said, 'Haven't you seen the monkey?'

The crocodile in **Shaan** was a pet with a difference. You couldn't have possibly petted it. Neither did it have a name. But the efficiency with which it discharged its carnivorous duties was very commendable. Swimming in an enclosed pool under rotating chairs (which had traitors shackled to them) was a dirty job but Mr Croc did that too. The moment the traitor was upturned into the pool by his master—bald-headed villain Shaakaal—he came charging in and promptly dug in. Except when he met his match in Amitabh Bachchan at the climax who drove a stake through his jaws and—to quote Arnold Schwarzenegger—'he was luggage'.

You could say that the cat called Radha had a guest appearance in **Jaane Tu Ya Jaane Na**. Actually, not even a guest appearance—since the film opened with the announcement of her death by a solemn doctor, and Ms Aditi (Genelia D'Souza) grieving at her funeral. But the cat's contribution has to be seen in a greater context because both the heroine's depression and a first-class A.R. Rahman song ('*Kabhi kabhi Aditi*') were the clear by-products of her untimely death.

HONOURABLE MENTIONS

The length of a role is never its measure of importance to a movie. Remember, even Naseeruddin Shah never came out of the photo frame in the same movie.

STATUTORY DECLARATION: No animals were harmed during the making of this chapter.

Heartbreak Hotel: 13 Unlucky Star Children

Kapoor. Bachchan. Deol. Roshan. Khan. The Bollywood firmament is crowded with stars of the same surname, that perpetuate fan following across generations, wonderfully symmetrical photos ops and casting possibilities. But there have been so many who didn't make it. So many whose debuts were bankrolled by their fathers who were great judges of audience taste, and yet collapsed.

What happened to them?

Kumar Gaurav

The son of Rajendra Kumar aka Jubilee Hero tops the list. A decent actor with chocolate-boy looks, he was supposed to pose a challenge to Bachchan's throne. Sadly (and inexplicably), *Love Story* remained his only hit.

He did several promising movies after that, all of which flopped. When he did act in (and produce) a hit—*Naam*—his brother-in-law[1] garnered all the praise. More than a decade after his debut, Rajendra Kumar made a last-ditch attempt with a film called *Phool*, with Madhuri Dixit opposite his son, but that sank as well. Later on, he acted in *Kaante*—a pretty decent performance—but that was not enough to resurrect his career. When last heard, he had acted in an English film (*Guiana 1838*) and garnered some praise for it. But right now, he seems to be too old to be the hero's friend and too young to be the hero's father.

Rajiv and Kunal Goswami

Manoj Kumar's brother Rajiv Goswami was paired opposite Meenakshi Seshadri in *Painter Babu*, a film—needless to say—produced and directed by Manoj Kumar.[2] It would be fair to

---

[1] Kumar Gaurav is married to Namrata, Sanjay Dutt's sister.

[2] See 'Canvas on Celluloid: 10 Artists' for plot details, if you are into masochism. I won't direct you there. Go, if you dare.

add here that the only thing more tragic than the plot was the direction. While not in the league of the Worst Films of All Time (which was achieved in a later film by Manoj Kumar—*Clerk*), his brother's direction was probably why poor Rajiv sank without a trace.

Manoj's son Kunal was the hero of *Kalakaar*. But the music of the film (especially the fantastic '*Neele neele ambar par*') overshadowed everything else in the film, including Kunal. Later on, he was the lead in *Vishkanya* where Pooja Bedi's venomous vibes administered a lethal shot to his career.

Suneil Anand

Dev Anand launched his son, Suneil, in a film called *Anand Aur Anand*. It is one of the best examples of unintended hilarity in Hindi cinema—where Suneil was chased by drunken elephants in the climax. The film could also have been called '*Sharaabi Meets Haathi Mere Saathi*'. Later, Suneil wrote, directed, produced and acted in a film called *Master* on a martial arts theme, where the hero was framed and imprisoned in Hong Kong. He learnt kung fu from a fellow inmate and took revenge when he was released. There was, however, no mention of the trademark dialogue of kung fu films—'Kiyaah Choo Mash-tah Sinchuang Kung Pao Mash-tah Honourable Mash-tah'.

Probably that's why it failed.

Sanjana, Karan and Kunal Kapoor

Sanjana Kapoor was the first Kapoor woman to act in movies, much before her nieces Lolo and Bebo joined the party. In *Hero Hiralal*, she played a film star falling in love with a Hyderabadi auto-driver. But an extremely crappy climax and Sanjana's obvious inability to look like a plump, made-up matinee idol spelled doom for this movie. She also acted in *Junoon* and *36 Chowringhee Lane*—both her father's productions—as a child artiste. She continues to be a leading theatre actress and producer, who brought back the buzz to Prithvi Theatre almost single-handedly.

Karan Kapoor found stardom as the male face of Bombay Dyeing. As a blonde hunk, he was a very successful model when he made his Bollywood debut in *Sultanat*. He was cast opposite Juhi Chawla (in her debut role as well) and got completely overshadowed in the fisticuffs between Dharmendra and Sunny Deol in the middle of a desert sultanate.

He also starred in *Loha* and *Zalzala*, both of which starred Dharmendra, making them co-stars in 100 per cent of Karan's Hindi films, which weren't too many (read: three) due to his foreign-accented Hindi and very furniture-like acting.

Kunal Kapoor was launched in *Vijeta*, set during the 1971 Indo-Pak War about a complex father–son relationship (played by Shashi and Kunal respectively). He was a young air force cadet with a budding romance to nurture and an impending war to fight. Directed by Govind

Nihalani, the film garnered a lot of critical acclaim and Kunal did a few small roles thereafter, before vanishing.

Faisal Khan

Aamir Khan and his brother Faisal Khan 'debuted' in the same film. In **QSQT**, Faisal appeared as a sidekick of a side-villain (played by Makarand Deshpande) who tried to molest Juhi Chawla. He helped reduce the family's junior artiste budget again in *Jo Jeeta Wohi Sikandar*, where he was a St Xavier's student.

Faisal got a proper launch in *Madhosh*—produced by dad Tahir Hussain—opposite another newcomer, Anjali Jathar. Despite heavy promotion and pretty good music, the film tanked.

His perfectionist brother got him a second lead in *Mela*, a very meaty role for someone with one flop. Despite very good action and competent acting, *Mela* did nothing for Faisal. Come to think of it, neither did it do anything for Aamir.

In recent times, Faisal was diagnosed with schizophrenia and fell out with Aamir, but we hear rumours about his returning to acting.

Puru Raaj Kumar

Raaj Kumar's son, Puru, made his debut in a film called *Bal Bramhachari* directed by Prakash Mehra, opposite the super-successful Karisma Kapoor, and with no apparent help from his dad. This means Raaj Kumar cannot be blamed for the devastation of distributors brought about by the film.

He followed it up with a villainous act in the film called *Hamara Dil Aapke Paas Hai*, where he raped Aishwarya Rai only to be beaten to a pulp by Anil Kapoor—not for the rape, but for offering to marry Ash to atone for the rape. Yes, that was the plot. And Happy Women's Day.

He did yet another villainous turn in *Mission Kashmir* as a smiling Kashmiri terrorist, a chilling character out to wreak havoc. He has also acted in *Umrao Jaan*, *LOC Kargil*, and in a few films in small roles but is nowhere near reaching the eccentric stardom of his father.[3]

Armaan Kohli

Rajkumar Kohli is one of the moderately successful producer–directors of Hindi cinema—with several decent hits to his credit. His son—Armaan Kohli—is a contender for the world record for the maximum number of launches (relaunches?) of an actor by a relative. He debuted in a film called *Virodhi* way back in the 1990s and has been seen in several of his dad's productions.

---

[3] Raaj Kumar's daughter is Vastavikata, who has recently appeared in a film called *Ei8ht: The Power of Shani*. With a name like that, we cannot pretend that it will be easy for fans to scream out her name.

This trend ended with a film called *Jaani Dushman—Ek Anokhi Kahani,*[4] where he played a snake (*ichchhadhari naag*) and proceeded to kill almost the entire star cast, which included but was not restricted to Sunny Deol, Akshay Kumar, Sonu Nigam, Aditya Pancholi, Sunil Shetty and Aftab Shivdasani. A filmful of heroes polished off by a relative newcomer—only an indulgent dad would agree to make this script.

Sanjay Kapoor

The youngest brother of Boney and Anil debuted in a film in production for an inordinately long time, *Prem.* He starred opposite Tabu (also in her debut) and lip-synced to what went on to become the National Anthem of Constipation—'*Aati nahin, aati nahin*'.[5] Sanjay's brother Boney bankrolled his forays in several big-budget movies opposite really big-ticket heroines—including Madhuri Dixit in *Raja.*[6] Sanjay acted in several films outside the Kapoor banner as well—most notable among them being *Chhupa Rustam* (opposite Manisha Koirala and Mamta Kulkarni), *Qayamat* (as a villain in a copy of *The Rock*), *Sirf Tum* (opposite Sushmita Sen) and his crowning glory *Kal Ho Naa Ho* (as the gorgeous Sonali Bendre's husband). He threatens to (and does) surface once in a while in reasonably visible movies (*Luck By Chance*, for example) so there is still some time before we can give him a Lifetime Achievement Award.

Uday Chopra

The world record for the maximum relaunches by the family is a difficult one to decide when Uday Chopra also enters the fray. He was launched by his family in *Mohabbatein*—as a happy-go-lucky student out to woo a girl. Of the ten-odd films he has done, only two (*Charas* and *Supari*) have not been made by family or friends. The scathing reviews he has got and the terrible box-office fate of his solo ventures have done nothing to cramp his style. His doting daddy and brother have continued to express faith in him, with top actresses opposite him and lavish budgets backing each one of his films—most notably the *Dhoom* franchise. As the Twitter

---

[4] *Trivia Alert*: Rajkumar Kohli directed another film called *Jaani Dushman* in the mid-'80s—again a multi-starrer which was about a psychotic King Kong kind of monster, which went about killing brides amidst a firmament of top stars (like Sunil Dutt, Jeetendra, Shatrughan Sinha, Sanjeev Kumar, Vinod Mehra, Neetu Singh, Reena Roy and who-not).

[5] There is another school of thought which feels that '*Dum maro dum*' is the Constipation Anthem, and '*Aati nahin*' is merely the National Song.

[6] Both the Kapoor brothers have the dubious distinction of acting in films named after them but remembered more for Madhuri. Anil's effort is *Beta*.

joke went, Aamir Khan had to audition for *Dhoom 3*, Uday Chopra simply had to turn up![7]

He is now busy in Hollywood, leading Yash Raj Films' foray in international markets.

Mahakshay Chakraborty

The industry waited with bated breath for the launch of Mahakshay Chakraborty aka Mimoh[8] in a film named after one of his father's biggest hit songs—*Jimmy*. The multiplexes were unmoved, and reports from the smaller centres—which have worshipped his father—were lost in transit.

He made another attempt with **Haunted**, India's first 3D horror movie, but people were horrified in an unintended sort of way. The box-office collections have ensured that horror films, 3D films and Mahakshay are not coming back in a hurry.

But the industry waits . . .

――――――――――――――――

HONOURABLE NEW ENTRANTS

Two bold young sons of veteran producers have rocked the debut scene like no other – Harman Baweja and Jackky Bhagnani.

Harry Baweja's son, Harman, attempted a dream debut opposite Priyanka Chopra in *Love Story 2050* that tanked pretty quickly but rumours of a liaison with the heroine generated a lot of curiosity. He acted in a few other films like *Victory*, *What's Your Raashee* and *Dishkiyaoon* but is yet to make an impact.

Vashu Bhagnani's son, Jackky did not get anywhere with his debut (*Kal Kissne Dekha*) though his next film (*F.A.L.T.U.*) had one hit song and got noticed. He took audience incredulity to a new high when he played India's Prime Minister in *Youngistaan* and a tweeter (@akshaykanitkar) commented, 'Jackky Bhagnani is playing Rahul Gandhi in *Youngistaan* while Rahul Gandhi is playing Jackky Bhagnani in real life.' Enuff said!

――――――――――――――――

―――――――――

[7] His love interest in **Mohabbatein**—Shamita Shetty—has retired from films and taken on interior decoration. A few days after her announcement to this effect, Uday too 'retired' (though he appeared in **Dhoom 3** after that)—thus making both their entries and exits coincide perfectly.

[8] Mimoh is named after his father's two idols—Michael Jackson and Mohammad Ali.

Naya Daur: 9 Fathers and Sons Playing Fathers and Sons

With decades of practice, the Bollywood press is great at sniffing out connections that would make super photo ops. Old flames, children of co-stars, stars at historical locations and old stars in new remakes make for great (if not great then space-filling) copy. Dad and Junior of real life playing Dad and Junior in reel life is one such draw.

Prithviraj Kapoor played the father of his son Raj in *Awara*. He was the judge who threw his wife out suspecting infidelity and his estranged son grew up to be a criminal. As is ordained in Bollywood, the son was produced in his father's court, accused of murder. Cue clashing cymbals and ominous drums for the final showdown between father and son.

They repeated their father–son pairing in *Kal Aaj Aur Kal*, representing the *kal* (past) and *aaj* (present) while Raj's son Randhir was brought in to play the future (*kal*). In this social comedy, the present lubricated the friction between the past and the future.[1]

When Kishore Kumar took a break from his manic comedies, he directed a film of rare sensitivity. ***Door Gagan Ki Chhaon Mein*** was a father's quest to cure his son (who had lost his speech in an accident) and their tribulations in doing so. Kishore Kumar played the father to his real son, who performed brilliantly and got credit as Amit Gangoly. After this opening pathos, they were father and son in the zanily named, crazily plotted ***Shabash Daddy***—where Kishore Kumar was about to get married before his son. Amit Kumar made occasional sorties into acting—most often with his father—in some very quirky films like ***Badhti Ka Naam***

---

[1] In a prescient move, Mehmood—playing a triple role—spoofed the three Kapoors hilariously in ***Humjoli***, a film which released about a year before *Kal Aaj Aur Kal*.

Dadhi and *Chalti Ka Naam Zindagi*,[2] in both of which he played his father's nephew.

Kunal Kapoor played the son of *Siddhartha* in Conrad Rooks's eponymous film. He had a small part as the son of the prince seeking enlightenment, though all we remember of this film was his father Shashi Kapoor's famous pose before a topless Simi Garewal. His first full-fledged role as air force cadet Angad Singh came in *Vijeta*. Shashi and Kunal Kapoor played a very real father–son pair, who were going through the same tensions all parents and children go through at the cusp of college and adulthood.

The 'launch' of the star-son is usually a grand affair, traditionally orchestrated by the father. Jubilee Star Rajendra Kumar pulled out all stops for the launch of his son, Kumar Gaurav, in *Love Story* and even joined the cast as the hero's indulgent, pseudo-strict father. The rosy-lipped hero turned up late at official functions, ran away from home and wanted to marry the arch-enemy's daughter. The father got a backstory when it was shown that the arch-enemy had married the father's lady-love in his youth, causing him to become the arch-enemy.

Though it was released after *Betaab*, *Sunny* was the first film Sunny Deol worked on.

Daddy Dharmendra bankrolled the former and acted as Sunny's father in the latter. He 'guest-appeared' as a tycoon caught in an unhappy marriage, had an affair with a virginal prostitute (standard-issue Bollywood character played by Sharmila Tagore) and died promptly after getting her pregnant. Their son Sunny (not to be confused with the sensational TV programme *Sansani*) took over the movie from this point.

The triple-combo knockout punch was delivered when Dharmendra and his two sons Sunny and Bobby appeared as an ageing boxer and his two sons in *Apne*. The boxer's dream of having a champion son was shattered when the younger son was terribly wounded in the ring. But not for long since the older son donned the gloves and started training. You know the rest, don't you?

Again in *Yamla Pagla Deewana*,[3] Dharmendra and Bobby Deol played a father–son con, visited by a Canadian millionaire (Sunny Deol) who turned out to be the estranged elder son. They repeated their triple-combo casting in a sequel (and we, Indian audiences, have nerves of steel).

---

[2] While the former film (*BKND*) was a sequel only in name, the latter (*CKNZ*) was a proper sequel to the classic *Chalti Ka Naam Zindagi* with the three brothers running a hotel instead of a garage.

[3] The movie title is taken from a song in the Dharam-starrer *Pratiggya*.

Sanjay Dutt's child debut (**Reshma Aur Shera**) and adult debut (**Rocky**) were both directed by his father. However, it was some time before Sunil Dutt played on-screen father to his real-life son. That happened in **Kshatriya**. He was Maharaja Bhavani Singh, father of Vikram Singh (Sanju baba) who was killed while his son was still a child and did not share any screen time with the elder Dutt. Sunil Dutt then became involved in full-time politics and did not act in films. Ten years later, he returned as the principled father of the lovable goon in **Munna Bhai MBBS**. His short role was a mix of the trademark emotions that had made him a star—a softy who could be tough when required. As Hari Prasad Sharma, he was the proud village sarpanch exasperated by his son's wayward behaviour. While it was Sanjay Dutt's film all the way, his father too made a solid impact in his last screen role.

Dutt-saab and Sanju-baba sharing screen space in Munna Bhai MBBS

Many fathers have directed their sons in movies. Directing a son as well as acting alongside him is relatively uncommon, playing on-screen father to the son while directing him even more so.

Rakesh Roshan directed **Koi Mil Gaya**, in which he also played a scientist searching for extraterrestrial life. His obsession led to his death in a car crash, leaving behind a pregnant wife. His son grew up to be Hrithik Roshan. While they shared no screen time (and Rakesh had a very small role), it is nevertheless an important piece in the father–son saga of Bollywood.

Rakesh and Hrithik Roshan appeared together in two films—**Aap Ke Deewane** and **Bhagwaan Dada**—when Hrithik was still a child. The former was just a song appearance for Hrithik but in the latter, he had a reasonably large role as a street-smart kid.

Akshaye Khanna made his debut in **Himalay Putra**, which was produced by father Vinod. It was a standard-issue estranged-parents story in which Vinod Khanna and Hema Malini were in love but could not marry due to parental opposition. She was pregnant when they separated due to misunderstandings emanating from a wedding card (don't ask!). Hema Malini brought up Akshaye who started hunting for his father when he grew up. All was well in the end (what did you expect?) and as a bonus, Akshaye even destroyed a drug-trafficking racket.

Trivia Alert: Farhan Akhtar was an assistant director for **Himalay Putra**. Did he narrate the **Dil Chahta Hai** role to Akshaye Khanna during the shooting?

Amitabh and Abhishek Bachchan first played father and son in **Sarkar**—an apt story since it was about an inheritor taking over the father's mantle. Amitabh Bachchan as the 'Godfather' brought an amazing intensity to his role while Jr AB held his own against his illustrious father.

Their next dad–son act came in **Kabhi Alvida Naa Kehna**, where Junior Bachchan looked on in horror as Senior Bachchan played Sexy Sam, living it up in flashy clothes, flashier women and leopard-printed handcuffs.

They reprised their **Sarkar** pairing in the sequel **Sarkar Raj**, before turning the tables and becoming yet another father–son duo in **Paa**, but with a twist: Abhishek played the father of Amitabh Bachchan, whose body aged six times faster than his brain. This was probably the strangest father–son casting in Bollywood and the duo obviously had a ball doing it.

FATHERS AND DAUGHTERS

While there have been many star daughters in the movies, most of them haven't appeared on screen with their dads yet.

- *I.S. and Ambika Johar*: Bollywood comedian and director I.S. Johar acted in a few films—like **5 Rifles**, **Nasbandi** and **Jai Bangladesh**—with his daughter Ambika.
- *Mehmood and Ginny Ali*: Mehmood and his kid daughter Ginny Ali acted in **Ginny Aur Johnny**, where she played a smoking-wisecracking kid to Mehmood's conman. (The film was a remake of Hollywood hit *Paper Moon*, also starring real-life dad and daughter, Ryan and Tatum O'Neal.)
- *Ashok Kumar and Preeti Ganguli*: The father–daughter duo acted in short roles in several films, the most notable of which was **Khatta Meetha** (where they played stepfather and daughter).
- *Kabir and Pooja Bedi*: In his daughter's debut film **Vishkanya**, Kabir Bedi played her reel dad—a righteous forest officer who was bumped off so that the daughter could take revenge.
- *Dharmendra and Esha Deol*: In **Tell Me O Kkhuda** (directed by Hema Malini), Esha Deol played a girl out to find her real father, and Dharmendra did a short role as one of the people likely to be the elusive dad.

Spiritual Ancestors: 5 Sets of Characters
Who Grew into Each Other

Bollywood is a great place for stereotypes and formulas. The moment a character becomes a hit, a million clones appear. Angry Young Man. Romantic Young NRI. Ghost Seeking Revenge. Megalomaniac Villain in Outrageous Costume. We have seen each one of these characters a million times. Sometimes, just sometimes, we get to see characters that seem different, yet familiar. They have a freshness but we have this niggling feeling that we have seen them somewhere before. And when we think about it, we realize that sometimes characters in different movies are related. One grows up to become the other.

Zanjeer/Khakee

Inspector Vijay Khanna of *Zanjeer* battled with his inner demons and a gang of smugglers. Towards the end of the film, the two merged as smuggler Teja turned out to be his father's killer. Having killed both, he was expected to have a stellar career in the police force. But hot-headed and sincere officers have strange fates in India. In fact, his superior had mentioned '*paanch saal mein gyarah transfers*' in the initial scenes. And there was nothing to suggest that it would have changed.

If we projected Inspector Khanna's career, it would be littered with frequent run-ins with powerful, well-connected criminals and subsequent transfers, leading to his increasing cynicism. Eventually, he would probably be shunted as Head of the Police Training College, the protagonist of Rajkumar Santoshi's *Khakee.*

DCP Anant Kumar Srivastava, an upright and capable officer, counted the days until his resignation, and that became a sad commentary on the fate of strong officers in our police force. *Zanjeer*'s Vijay became *Khakee*'s Anant because nobody wanted him to work to his full potential.

D/Company

Company came first and when Ram Gopal Varma produced *D*, he called it 'a prequel in spirit' and made it quite obvious by naming the films to denote the most dreaded gangster outfit in India.

In *Company*, we had an upcoming ganglord of Mumbai, Malik, building a scary army through coercion, reward and alliance. Soon, he came under the police's radar and shifted his operational base out of India to continue running his 'company'. The story was built around his international career and, eventually, the schisms that broke his gang apart.

In *D*, we had the short-tempered son of a police constable, Deshu, deliberately and logically deciding to embark on a 'career' of crime after a rational cost–benefit analysis when he got into trouble with the police. He grew under a bigger don, consolidated his empire outside Mumbai and then slowly rooted his tentacles in the Mumbai underworld.

Strictly speaking, there was an overlap between the two movies—of the period of consolidation of the gangs in Mumbai—but in character (from Angry Young Man to Cold Calculating Leader) and tenor (from 'violent aggression' to 'deliberate infection'), Deshu 'grew up' to become Malik.

Taare Zameen Par/3 Idiots

In *Taare Zameen Par*, Aamir Khan rejected the concept of rote-learning and urged us to look at non-academic talents. The worst censure in the film was reserved for the well-meaning but blinkered parents of Ishaan Awasthi, who refused to accept his disability and forced him to emulate his more conventional elder brother. As a maverick art teacher, Aamir Khan coached the child, discovered his artistic talents and made the parents see reason.

If Mr Awasthi hadn't met the art teacher, he would have turned into Mr 'Hitler' Qureishi of *3 Idiots*, a father whose only benchmark of success was an engineering degree and who refused to accept that this son would be much happier if he became a photographer. Mr Qureishi also ran into a different avatar of Aamir Khan. This time, it was Rancho—his son's maverick classmate.

Essentially, Aamir Khan delivered a message of unearthing talent and following dreams in both the films. And in the process of doing so, he counselled the same character in them—but about fifteen years apart.

Do Dooni Chaar/Band Baaja Baaraat

Habib Faisal wrote and directed *Do Dooni Chaar*. He also wrote the blockbuster *Band Baaja Baaraat*. Both were heart-warming tales of middle-class success set in Delhi, though the latter was a bit more filmi.

According to Habib Faisal, Payal Duggal (Rishi Kapoor's daughter, played by Aditi Vasudev) of *Do Dooni Chaar* grew up to be Shruti Kakkar (Anushka Sharma) of *Band Baaja Baaraat*. And when we put the two characters together, they match perfectly. An ambitious girl from Delhi University decides on an entrepreneurial career path (probably after seeing the hardships of her 'service class' father). She puts together a plan, gains experience, gets hold of a partner and takes the plunge. The ambition, the level-headedness, the intelligence, the mental make-up and their affection for their respective families—those of Payal and Shruti—were just identical. In *Do Dooni Chaar*, she had just started college and the seeds of ambition were sown. In *Band Baaja Baaraat*, she had just graduated and they had borne fruit.

Jalwa/The Blueberry Hunt

The last entry on the list is a slightly obscure one because *The Blueberry Hunt* is an offbeat film starring Naseeruddin Shah, whose character (called Colonel) owned a marijuana plantation. Naseer sported a Bob Marleyish look, with matted hair, in the film. On the other hand, *Jalwa*— Naseer's first solo commercial success—was about a narcotics cop in Goa, who managed to clean up the scene by killing off the head honcho of the drugs ring.

In an interview to acclaimed film writer Jai Arjun Singh,[1] Naseer noted that he prepared for the character of *The Blueberry Hunt* by imagining that 'Colonel' was an extension of his character in *Jalwa*. He said that any cop who killed off a top gang boss would be 'f***ed for life' and probably dismissed from service. So, he would want to screw the system back and decide to make a living out of growing marijuana! By applying this twisted logic, Naseer decided that these two characters of his were actually one and the same—maybe thirty years apart.

---

[1] The full text of the interview is available at Jai Arjun Singh's blog, Jabberwock (http://jaiarjun.blogspot.com/2010/03/conversation-with-naseeruddin-shah.html).

EK SE BHALE DO, DO SE BHALE . . .

As we go from familial identities to national ones, we take a look at some films which took not one, not two but three people with diverse identities and fused them into an integrated title. They don't call Bollywood the epitome of national integration for nothing.

- *Amar Akbar Anthony*: Undoubtedly, this is the biggest triple decker combo in Hindi film history—Manmohan Desai's lost-and-found comic–action–romantic melodrama that packed three of Bollywood's biggest stars of the times along with three top-notch leading ladies, not to mention all the character actors registered with the Actors' Association at that time.

- *Gangaa Jamunaa Saraswathi*: Towards the end of his career, Manmohan Desai returned to triple-named films but not all three titular roles were female. Amitabh Bachchan played Gangaa Prasad, a displaced scion of a royal family who ended up becoming a truck driver and the object of two women's affections. The two women were Jamunaa (Meenakshi Seshadri) and Saraswathi (Jaya Prada). Mythology repeated itself when the mythical Saraswathi vanished (read: died) at the sangam of Gangaa and Jamunaa. Oops, did I give away a spoiler?

- *Seeta Salma Suzy*: This time, the titular trio consisted of heroines. This film could have been momentous had it not got lost in the mire of 1990s Bollywood. Archana Puran Singh, Sudha Chandran and Moonmoon Sen played the title roles with great effort and enthusiasm but they could not salvage the movie. If not for the audience, the movie is at least memorable for Sudha Chandran who met her future husband Ravi Dang on the sets as he was an Assistant Director.

- *John Jaani Janardhan*: Triple role of Rajinikanth, playing a father and two sons – one Hindu and one Muslim. Rascals, you still want read about it instead of watching it?

- *Eena Meena Deeka*: Kishore Kumar's hit song from the 1950s got resurrected in the form of a David Dhawan comedy as three title characters – Rishi Kapoor, Juhi Chawla and Vinod Khanna respectively – went on the run from the police in a major mishmash of desi emotions (ailing mother) and videshi inspirations (Hollywood film *Three Fugitives*).

- *Om Jai Jagdish*: India's most popular prayer song was personified in the form of Anil Kapoor, Fardeen Khan and Abhishek Bachchan – three brothers out to prove that the universe's most valuable things are love, honesty and a sea-facing bungalow in Juhu. Anupam Kher's directorial debut tied together three diverse occupations – music industry executive, automobile engineer and software geek – in the story.

3

Indian Idols

Tu hindu banega na mussalman banega, insaan ki aulaad hai insaan banega
—Manmohan Krishna (in Mohammed Rafi's voice) in **Dhool Ka Phool**

Some say Bollywood is like a sea in which rivers from different parts of India come and merge. You could also say Bollywood is like an airport where people from different parts pass through and go places.

This section is about diverse groups of people, about how Bollywood portrayed them and how they portrayed themselves in Bollywood.

Christian Brothers: 12 Depictions of Christianity

Christians in Bollywood drink a lot (sometimes run bars), swear in English, pepper their dialogues with 'man', have bombastic names and are by and large Good Samaritans. There have been a large number of priests as well. Usually a solemn person hovering in the background presiding over marriages and the occasional confessional, his dialogues have a profusion of 'my son' and '*Lord tumko shanti de*'.

Of course, there have been a lot of Foreign Devils (made famous by Bob Christo and Tom Alter, with their exaggerated accents) but they were mostly British Oppressors (or The Foreign Hand) and had nothing to do with religion.

The most important signpost of the Bollywood Christian is a suitably polysyllabic name.

Anthony Gonsalves is undoubtedly the best known Christian name in India and even overshadows Vijay Verma occasionally. Actually, it is probably Amitabh's only screen name that came close to overwhelming his actual name. Post the stupendous success of ***Amar Akbar Anthony***, people started calling him Anthony bhai on the streets.[1] Of course, the added allure of the name came from the fact that it was the name of Pyarelal's (of Laxmikant–Pyarelal fame) violin teacher.

The second most popular Christian name in Bollywood is probably Bobby Braganza in Raj Kapoor's film named after her. She spoke like an Indian teenager, performed a mean dance in a part-Koli–part-tribal outfit although her father (Prem Nath) managed to live up to every single stereotype of the filmi Christian—as he played a heavy-drinking fisherman.

It would be apposite to take up the story of Shiney Ahuja's second film since we have already

---

[1] This fandom was immortalized in ***Gol Maal*** where a schoolgirl asked Amitabh Bachchan for an autograph but wanted him to sign 'Anthony bhai'.

talked about the stereotype of the benevolent Catholic Father. In **Sins**, Shiney played the role of a priest (William, if you must know the name) who fell in love with a young woman, impregnated her, got her to abort, married her off to somebody else to hush up the affair and then killed pretty much half the town in a love-crazed spree. He smashed the stereotype of the Catholic priest as well as most tenets of Christianity so violently that there was an avalanche of protests against this Vinod Pande film.

The drunkard is the other Christian cliché in Bollywood, generally seen in a street corner, slurring over dialogues and slobbering over life.

Pran's part in **Majboor** was probably the first time this character had a major role and even got to sing a song about the ill effects of mixing water in bottles of alcohol— '*Daaru ki botal mein kaahe pani bharta hai / Phir na kehna Michael daaru peeke danga karta hai*'. And it was not only the song, but he even had a massive say in the climax due to a big clue he held to solving the murder mystery.

The stereotype of the Christian drunkard is so strong that even in a realistic film like **Ardh Satya**, there was a bit part called Lobo (played by Naseeruddin Shah)—a former police officer who turned alcoholic due to the frustrations of the job.

In **Julie**, the social divide shown between a 'cultured' Hindu family and a 'crass' Christian family was rather exaggerated. An engine-driver's daughter fell in love with a Hindu classmate, got pregnant and was promptly accused of 'loose morals'. And of course, because it was a Christian family, they sang songs in English. But thank God for that cliché because we got Preeti Sagar's wonderful '*My heart is beating*'.

If we get into art-house territory, we have **Albert Pinto Ko Gussa Kyoon Aata Hai**—in which Naseeruddin Shah played the title role of the angry son of a retrenched millworker. The economic crisis slowly descending on Bombay's thousands of millworkers was sensitively depicted in the film, and Naseer did a stellar job in the part of a motor mechanic.

It is rumoured that Albert Pinto was the name of one of the vendors (caterer/costume/something) from one of the producer's earlier projects, who hadn't been paid. In order to placate him, the lead character was named after him. This story remains tantalizingly unproven, like many of Bollywood's urban legends.

Prahaar is one of the few films to have depicted Indian Christians realistically—with their language, milieu, fears and motivations clearly etched out. Madhuri Dixit gave a stellar performance as Shirley Pinto, the stoic fiancée of an Indian commando, as did the ensemble cast, borrowed from the world of theatre, and all of them directed very well by Nana Patekar.

Baton Baton Mein was set in an authentic Christian milieu and that was part of the novelty of the film, but there was nothing in the story that was exclusive to the community. A love story set in Bombay peppered with a genial uncle, a crazy brother and a pestering mother is as cute and relevant today as it was thirty years back. And it painted a loving portrait of India's Maximum City by setting the romantic scenes in local trains, on seasides and amidst cute Christian grannies (Leela Mishra in a floral dress) in drawing rooms.

Bada Din was a Hindi movie that Bengali film director Anjan Dutta made on the Anglo-Indian community of Calcutta. In the former, Marc Robinson played a young man wanting to make a mark on the music scene as murderous goons, an angry girlfriend (Tara Deshpande) and an irate landlady (Shabana Azmi) descended on him like a ton of bricks. The film was set around Christmas, its name being the Hindi version of 'big day'.

> *English Classic Alert*: Aparna Sen's directorial debut, **36 Chowringhee Lane**, was in English but worth a mention for being probably the finest depiction of the Anglo-Indian community through the eyes of Miss Violet Stoneham (played by the amazing Jennifer Kendal).

Moral dilemmas have never been the forte of Bollywood, and Christian moral dilemmas, even less so. In fact, probably the only one presented was in **Aakhree Raasta**, where David (played by Amitabh Bachchan) went into a church and confessed to crimes he was about to commit. His rationale was that at the end of the three murders he was about to start on, he might not be around for a confessional. The priest broke the sacred oath of secrecy and reported it to the police. He declared that while it was a sin to divulge details of a confession, he was doing so because he considered saving three lives more important. The police officer (David's lost son—AB in a double role) logically concluded that if the guy was indeed a devout Christian, he would get really upset at the priest's betrayal and would try to kill the priest in retribution. So he arranged a ring of security around the priest. He probably forgot that it was a Bollywood movie because, later, David did the most illogical thing in the world: he walked into the police headquarters and murdered his first victim—the police commissioner himself.

Ajit's villainy (which grew exaggerated in the subsequent series of jokes) was always centred on a group of henchmen and molls with 'Christian' names, though no allusion was ever made to their religion and Ajit was quite happy with Punjabizing the pronunciations. Raabert, Tawny and Mona have been flogged to death, actually.

And finally, we have Commissioner De Mello of *Jaane Bhi Do Yaaro*, who has to be one of the funniest corpses in cinematic history. Though I am not sure if he can be counted as a Christian character, because he was hardly alive.

HONOURABLE MENTIONS

ALBERT PINTO BAAR BAAR KYON AATA HAIN?

While not as popular as Anthony and Bobby, Albert Pinto nevertheless has appeared in several films as a quirky character name.

- *Jaane Bhi Do Yaaro*: Both *Albert Pinto Ko Gussa Kyoon Aata Hai* and *JBDY* shared crew members. Kundan Shah wrote both the scripts, for example. And he sneaked in the name as a code word for an elaborate operation around spying on shady builder Tarneja.
- *Jalwa*: Naseeruddin Shah traded his name with (real-life brother-in-law) Pankaj Kapur, who played a Goan police officer out to bust a gang of drug-runners.
- *Jolly LLB*: Harsh Chhaya was Albert Pinto, who came to lawyer Arshad Warsi offering crucial witness in a hit-and-run case. And like most characters with borrowed names, he was not what he seemed like.
- *Chaalis Chauraasi*: In this film about four criminals pretending to be cops, Kay Kay Menon's name was Albert Pinto. In fact, all four of them had names borrowed from classic films. Naseeruddin Shah was called Sir, Ravi Kissen was Shakti, and Atul Kulkarni, Bobby.

Jo Bole So Nihaal: 12 Depictions of Sikhs

Probably the only community in India with a sense of humour, Sikhs have had to take a lot of rubbish. Putting up with an unending stream of sardar jokes cannot be funny. Bollywood's portrayal of Sikhs in character roles is—as usual—one-dimensional. The sardar is always the jovial guy breaking into bhangra at the drop of a turban and running into a fight equally rapidly. Though, it has to be said, there have been many sardar lead characters in recent times and nearly every A-list star has played one.[1]

One of the earliest Sikh characters in Bollywood was played by Dharmendra in *Jeevan Mrityu*. He was an honest bank employee who was framed for embezzlement and sentenced to prison. When he was released, he was a broken man. Due to a freak incident, he was pronounced dead, giving him the chance to take revenge on his enemies by taking on a different identity. Dharmendra came back as Bikram Singh, a shrewd and calculating Sikh businessman whose agenda was not only to destroy the villains but also win back the love of his fiancée (Raakhee) who had also given him up for dead.

Govind Nihalani made *Vijeta*, a film on the confusion and eventual resolution of a teenager's dilemmas. His career choices, the disagreements with his father, the beginnings of romance, were all dealt with sensitively and realistically. Kunal Kapoor played the troubled youngster and his real-life father (Shashi Kapoor) carried out his duties on screen as well. In an interesting piece of detail, the father was clean-shaven while the son maintained the traditional beard and turban. The son did the traditional thing to rebel against his father—ironic.

---

[1] We are avoiding the real-life Sikh of *Bhaag Milkha Bhaag*, whose exploits are covered in the chapter on sports on page 211.

Easily the most popular actor playing a sardar on screen is Sunny Deol. In *Border*, he played a real-life war hero, Major Kuldeep Singh Chandpuri. During the 1971 Battle of Longewala, a small squad of 150 men had resisted a full company of 2,000 Pakistani soldiers, fortified with tanks, from taking over the strategic post. Sunny Deol represented this on screen by hollering at the Pakistani commander, demanding the best out of his own men even more loudly, and glaring so hard at the Pakistani tanks that they almost melted. Wonder if the real major did it the same way.[2]

If people had any doubts about the strength, sense of humour and tolerance of Sikhs after *Border*, Sunny Deol returned to dispel all of them—and more—in *Gadar: Ek Prem Katha*. As truck-driver Tara Singh, he sang songs to charm convent-educated girls (mercifully he did not dance). Then he saved a Muslim girl caught in the Partition riots, wooed and eventually married her. After she was forcibly taken to Lahore by her father, he went there and brought her back. Oh—there was the small matter of the Pakistani army in his path so he vanquished them using a good ol' hand pump.

> *Bonus Movie*: Sunny Deol did one more much-publicized turn as a Sikh in *Jo Bole So Nihaal* but the profusion of scantily clad women on the posters caused too much offence in religious circles and the film had a very limited release due to protest-induced boycotts in cinemas.

A British film-maker came to India to make a film on the freedom struggle and found a gang of frivolous friends to play the parts of revolutionaries. Karan, Sukhi, Aslam and DJ were part of the devil-may-care generation that *Rang De Basanti* sought to portray. DJ was actually Daljeet, whose mother ran a highway dhaba and whose grandfather was a gurdwara priest. He was a Delhi Universiy student who hung around the university because he didn't have the courage to face the outer world. His language was the Punjabi-infused Hindi that is so common in Delhi. His religion was almost incidental to the plot. You only realized later on that the group consisted of Hindu, Muslim and Sikh boys, but it was done subtly and without any hint of tokenism.

It was as if the film was made for the return of the UPA to power in 2009. Every paper in the land went completely gaga over Manmohan Singh's second term in office and dubbed him *Singh Is Kinng*. Akshay Kumar rocked the box office with a film that was fabulously inane,

---

[2] Sikhs have done stellar duty in the Indian Army and there have been many depictions of the same in Bollywood as well. In a relatively unknown film—*Heroes*—Salman Khan appeared in a cameo as a Kargil war hero.

a negative that Akshay and his favourite directors have not only converted to a positive but raised to an art form. A Punjabi village bumpkin's trip to Australia (via Egypt to sing a song) and transformation into becoming the 'Kinng' of the underworld was as fantastic as they got. But if you wanted realism, you would do well to avoid Anees Bazmee movies. The story was just an excuse to wrap around the gags, hit songs and Katrina Kaif around Akshay. So that's what happened and even Snoop Dogg appeared to pay homage to the Singhs—Happy, Lucky, Mika, Guruji et al.

Love Aaj Kal traced the changing face of love, yesterday and today.

In the modern day, Jai (Saif Ali Khan) and Meera (Deepika Padukone) broke up a near-perfect relationship to pursue their dream careers. This was completely incomprehensible to middle-aged Sikh restaurateur Veer Singh (Rishi Kapoor), who had travelled the breadth of the nation for one glimpse of his beloved. Their stories intercut each other and Saif also played the younger Veer Singh, the rowdy who transformed himself to win his love. Could Veer Singh have been something else instead of a Sikh? Probably, but the turban helped because the moment you show a Sikh on screen, the stereotype of a large heart takes over. And love stories are all about large hearts. Yesterday, today and tomorrow.

Enterprising Sikhs have travelled halfway across the globe to set up thriving businesses. One of the first such outposts was London, where Southall can easily be mistaken for a town in Punjab. This is the area where *Patiala House* was located. Apparently based on the life of Monty Panesar, this was the story of a Sikh boy (Akshay Kumar) who passed up the chance to play for England because his autocratic father (Rishi Kapoor) refused to allow him to represent the 'enemy'. His father, having borne the brunt of extreme xenophobia when he had first come to the country, had developed bitterness towards his adopted country; his son had to overcome this.

Harpreet Singh Bedi did not want to waste his time doing an MBA. His ambition was to become *Rocket Singh: Salesman of the Year.* True to the industrious nature of his race, he plunged headlong into a job—that too, in action-packed sales. As a salesman for computer firm AYS Corporation, he was exactly what we know Sikhs to be—

You can't be a Sikh unless you have a nickname. Harpreet Singh Bedi aka Rocket with his grandpa.

honest and hard-working, jovial and *jugaadu*. Starting from the Guru Nanak wallpaper on his computer to the turbans to the slightly Punjabi accent, Ranbir Kapoor got the nuances of a young sardar just perfect.

And no, the stereotypes of sardarji jokes weren't true either since he wasn't short of brains. '*Mere number kum hain, dimaag nahin . . .*'

At least one entry in the list has to be a girl: a Sikhni from Bhatinda—Geet Kaur Dhillon, played by Kareena Kapoor in *Jab We Met*. As the hyper-talkative, super-gregarious Punjaban, Kareena made the role her own and gave the character depth. Her mannerisms, her slight accent, her clothes were straight out of small-town Punjab.

Her entire family—including Dara Singh as her strict grandfather—was credible and the ensemble gave the film its warmth.

Bachchan has played a Sikh character in just a couple of not-so-great movies. In Mehul Kumar's *Kohram*, he played Colonel Balbir Singh Sodhi who went underground after an assassination attempt on a corrupt home minister and reappeared in a clean-shaven avatar.

He played another Sikh soldier—Major General Amarjeet Singh—in *Ab Tumhare Hawale Watan Sathiyon*.

> *Bonus Sikh Disguise*: In *Suhaag*, the Big B played the boisterous Sikh in the traditional costume singing and dancing '*Teri rab ne bana di jodi*' with gusto, all for the good cause of uniting lovers.

Baby sardars could have been certified by the *Guinness Book of World Records* as the cutest species on earth. No one epitomized this cuteness better than the silent sardar kid in *Kuch Kuch Hota Hai*, who went about counting stars and kissing girls without speaking a word. Parzan Dastur, who played the kid, became an overnight sensation and his last-scene entreaty for Kajol to stay back ('*Tussi na jao*') became a catchphrase. Karan Johar—the king of emotions—just knew that nobody but a cute sardar kid could pull this off.

Bawas in Bollywood: 9 Depictions of Parsis

It's true that Parsis are not very visible people. But Bollywood does worse than make them invisible. Every time a member of this particular minority community appears on screen, more often than not, he or she is a caricature. Of all stereotyped communities, the Parsis are probably the worst hit.

The men are always shown wearing the traditional black hat and a white *bandhgala* coat, driving a vintage car loaded with a large family. The women wear sarees in the traditional style and carry Japanese hand fans. They speak in an accent with all their 'T's pronounced hard, and use a whole lot of *dikra*s in their conversation. Has anyone met a Parsi like that in real life?

Khatta Meetha was the movie which probably had the highest number of Parsi characters ever. A loose remake of *Yours, Mine and Ours*, it had two single parents, Homi Mistry (Ashok Kumar) and Nargis Sethna (Pearl Padamsee), marrying each other and uniting their gigantic families to make a family of oh-my-God proportions. Firoze, Freni, Fardeen, Peelu, Russi, Jaal and Fali went about doing the usual sibling rivalry stuff before The Great Family Bonding happened.

None of the on-screen Parsis spoke in any kind of exaggerated accent and even their clothes were quite regular. In fact, probably the only reason the lead characters were made Parsi was to take recourse to the liberalism of a community that allows a second marriage between two elderly people.

Pestonjee was the story of two good friends—Naseeruddin Shah and Anupam Kher—who fell in love with the same woman (Shabana Azmi). One sacrificed his love for the other. Sounds likes standard-issue Bollywood love triangle, doesn't it? Except that there was a twist in the tale when the sacrificer returned to meet the couple after some years and found out that his friend was having an extramarital affair. Directed by Vijaya Mehta, this was what was called an 'art film' in the 1980s and had a different mood and tempo from Bollywood. The three lead actors' acting credentials were never in any question; they got under the skin of their characters effortlessly, and returned one of the most authentic depictions of Parsis on screen.[1]

Many films have had cameos of slightly batty Parsi characters, but I would choose only one— *Muqaddar Ka Sikandar*—where the character was not a real Parsi but a fake one, making the imitation way more outrageous. In a zany subplot, budding lawyer Vinod Khanna decided he had to help a young girl elope (which would help his case in a convoluted way). He infiltrated the girl's house as a gatecrashing Parsi guest, in complete (aforementioned) costume. And as if that wasn't enough, he chose to bring along Ram Sethi (veteran character actor, playing a character called Pyarelal Aware) as his daughter (dressed in Parsi drag). Wait—it got better! Oranges were used to create certain parts of the female anatomy; eventually the girl eloped and Vinod Khanna abandoned his Parsi accent, clothes and mannerisms.

Deepa Mehta depicted the tensions of Partition in *1947 Earth* through the eyes of a little girl from a rich Parsi family. The retinue around her mansion—the maid, the masseur and the ice-candy man—were from the two sides of the divide and their relationships in the context of romantic and political developments were seen from a 'neutral' point of view.

The original novel (*Ice-Candy Man*) was written by Bapsi Sidhwa, a Parsi[2] who co-wrote the screenplay as well, and the film had the Parsi community as an interesting backdrop to Hindu–Muslim relationships. Rahul Khanna and Aamir Khan turned in great performances as the suitors of Nandita Das.

Parzania too had a Parsi family caught in the crossfire of Hindu–Muslim riots, this time the post-Godhra riots of 2002 Gujarat. A poignant tale of a Parsi boy lost in the riots and his parents' attempts to find him did not find too much of a commercial audience due to its bleakness. It did not help matters when the Gujarat government decided to ban the film for what they felt was an unfair depiction of the communal situation. Naseeruddin Shah was his customary excellent self as the father, while Sarika—making a Hindi film comeback after her separation from Kamal Haasan—gave a surprisingly touching performance as the mother who had lost her son.

Munna Bhai MBBS chugged along to become a pan-Indian success with its formula of love, fresh air and hugs; it also brought on two of the most noticed Parsi characters in Bollywood—

---

[1] *Trivia Alert*: The cast includes one Kiran Thakursingh-Kher in one of her earliest film roles—then newly married to Anupam and not yet transformed to Kirron.

[2] *Trivia Alert*: In the last scene of the film, the author appears in a brief cameo as the grown-up version of the little girl.

Dr Rustom and his dad. Dr Rustom (played by a real-life Parsi, Kurush Deboo) looked exactly the part of a brilliant doctor prone to the occasional bout of madness. His accent was authentic without going overboard, and he stayed in a house with large balconies—something only Parsis have access to in Mumbai. His juice-swigging, carom-flicking father only talked about carom, juice and *majjani* life, exuding Parsiness through his vest and cap.

As a vehicle for star Saif Ali Khan trying his hand at acting, *Being Cyrus* succeeded admirably at telling a tight story well and not letting the star overpower the rest of the cast. Saif reciprocated by doing a great job of playing Cyrus Mistry, a mysterious guest in the extended Sethna family. Naseeruddin Shah as the doped artist Dinshaw, Dimple Kapadia as his high-strung wife Katy, Boman Irani as the brother with the persecution complex and Simone Singh as Boman's wide-eyed child wife were all spectacular in bringing alive an eccentric Parsi family. That the director (Homi Adjania) and co-screenwriter (Kersi Khambatta) were both Parsis probably helped the milieu to be bang-on.

In Mani Ratnam's *Guru*, the aristocratic anglicized Parsi was the villain. The Contractors represented the old money of Bombay, blocking the entry of new entrepreneurs into the textile-trading community. They had swanky cars, swish suits and clipped accents, along with the confidence of old money. With those, the Contractors (junior played by Arjun Bajwa, senior played by Dhritiman Chatterjee) tried to block Gurukant Desai's meteoric rise to industrial superstardom. (But the author-backed Bollywood hero is like an idea whose time has come. Nobody can stop it.)

And finally, we have to talk about the Greatest Film Ever Made—*Sholay*—and there was a Parsi in it as well!

Remember the engine driver in the train that got attacked by dacoits in Jai and Veeru's introduction sequence? Well, that was Mushtaq Merchant looking suitably harassed by the attack of the northies in his domain, but doing a decent job of cranking up the speed and providing Veeru with liquor.

Of course, the twist is that he was also the only person to have a double role in *Sholay*. Remember a thin figure who screamed and jumped up and down as Jai–Veeru drove off in the double-carrier bike of '*Yeh dosti*'? That was Mr Merchant again—he played the guy whose bike got stolen by the heroes. (There was a full sequence devoted to the theft but that got chopped at the editing table.)

Just what I said . . . they are always on the sidelines!

It would be appropriate to mention a Parsi actor—Boman Irani—whose amazing versatility is revealed by the fact that he has played a Hindu (in several films), a Muslim (*Veer Zaara*), a Sikh (*Lage Raho Munna Bhai*), a Christian (*Honeymoon Travels Pvt Ltd*) and a Parsi (*Shirin Farhad Ki Toh Nikal Padi*).

MULTICULTURAL MEGASTARS

Leading Indian superstars have played characters of different religions on extremely few occasions. If we take eight stars down the ages—Ashok Kumar, Dilip Kumar, Dev Anand, Raj Kapoor, Shammi Kapoor, Rajesh Khanna, Amitabh Bachchan and Shah Rukh Khan—their non-Hindu roles range in low single digits.

- Dilip Kumar has played a Muslim character only once, as Shahzada Salim in *Mughal-e-Azam* and never a Christian character. He has played (Caesar's heir) Marcus in *Yahudi*, which could count as an ancient Roman religion.
- None—except Ashok Kumar in *Khatta Meetha*—has played a Parsi character except in disguises and guest appearances. In fact, Amitabh Bachchan appeared in Preeti Ganguli's dreams as her Parsi husband in *Khatta Meetha*.
- The first multicultural star is actually Amitabh Bachchan who has played several Muslim and Christian characters, many of which have become iconic—Iqbal of *Coolie* and Anthony of *Amar Akbar Anthony*. He has also played Sikh characters (*Kohram*, *Ab Tumhare Hawale Watan Sathiyon*) though they have not been as iconic. He has tried his hand at Parsi roles as well, disguising himself as a *bawa* in *Shahenshah*, and in his maiden Hollywood appearance, played a Jew in *The Great Gatsby*.
- SRK's multicultural score is also decent, with one Christian (*Josh*) and several very well-known Muslim characters (*Chak De India*, *My Name Is Khan*). We are waiting for a kickass Sikh character, although he has already notched up a Buddhist score with *Asoka*.

Crossing the Vindhyas: 14 Depictions of South Indians

South Indians are dark. They wear white *mundu*s or checked lungis. They have an accent thicker than coconut chutney. And they are either part of the intelligentsia or the mafia. All of the above, more often than not, contributes to the character becoming a comic sidekick. But sometimes, the character becomes memorable—the accent notwithstanding—and is not a sidekick. (Some of them are still funny, though.)

Mehmood was the worst offender in this category. With his exaggerated accent and dark make-up, he imprinted the stereotype on the Bollywood audience's mind. But the film that is most famous for a stereotypical south Indian character is such a comic masterpiece that you can't stop laughing long enough to feel offended.

As the music maestro Master Pillai in **Padosan**, Mehmood was the perfect foil to Kishore Kumar's histrionics. Add to that Manna Dey's classically trained voice belting out a Carnatic version of '*Ek chatur naar*' and you had mayhem. The character was the villain of the piece, made fun of, given a ridiculous 'get-up' and vanquished in the battle for Saira Banu's attentions.

No wonder they don't like to speak Hindi south of the Vindhyas.

While the north Indian tendency is to lump all south Indians together as Madrasis, there's life beyond Chennai—as hot and spicy Hyderabadis would tell you. Theirs is the only south Indian city where people speak a decent smattering of Hindi—though with a distinctive *Dakhni* accent. Many characters have imitated that but none better than the ever-helpful, film-crazy auto-driver who called himself **Hero Hiralal**.[1]

---

[1] *Hyderabadi Poti Alert*: While on the topic Hyderabadi heroes, we might as well doff our cap to a heroine from the city of Charminar. Dilkas Ahmed became **Bobby Jasoos** and put on several disguises and accents during her crime-solving missions. But when she was being herself, there was an authentic Hyderabadi accent that came through.

A Mumbai film crew landed up in Hyderabad and our hero fell in love with the heroine. Thanks to a completely predictable plot, rather shoddy production values and zilch star power (despite major acting talents), the film sank without a trace. Pity nobody heard Naseeruddin Shah getting the Dakhni accent right . . .

Exaggerated Accent Alert: Mehmood played a Hyderabadi *bawarchi* in **Gumnaam**, complete with a super-exaggerated accent, check lungi and extra-dark make-up! He even made a virtue of his dark skin and large heart with the '*Hum kaale hain to kya hua dilwale hain*' song!

Exaggerated Skin Colour Alert: The dark skin colour stereotype of south Indians came to us in a crazy version in **Immaan Dharam** where the normally dusky Rekha put on cakes of dark brown make-up to 'look Tamil'. Even Shashi Kapoor—he of the dazzling white skin—appeared in Rekha's dreams with his entire face painted black!

What a tragedy it is that the holder of a master's degree from Kerala University would be selling coconuts on the streets of Bombay. That is exactly what Krishnan Iyer, MA (pronounced 'Yem Yeh'), did in (the older) **Agneepath.** When he wasn't saving mafia dons from assassinations, that is. Hard-working and honest, he was also a proud member of his community, evident by his invoking the names of (then) President R. Venkataraman as well as C.V. Raman and S. Radhakrishnan to prove his community's intellectual superiority.

Mithun Chakraborty won a Filmfare Best Supporting Actor award for this film—for which he apparently took the help of a Tamil spot boy for specific words. The accent in which he spoke Hindi was entirely his own, though.

Sambar Mafia Alert: In the hullabaloo over Krishnan, we tend to forget the other south Indian in the film—villain Anna Shetty (played by Deepak Shirke), whose accent was also as thick as they get.

More Mafia Alert: The more famous Anna-named don was played by Nana Patekar with chilling perfection in **Parinda**. Anna had no accent, no obvious dressing preferences, and yet the set design of his house screamed out the south Indian–ness of his character. When Feroz Khan remade Mani Ratnam's classic *Nayakan* in Hindi as **Dayavan**, yet another south Indian don made his Bollywood debut—Shakti Velu.

When Kamal Haasan debuted in Hindi, he had a thick Tamil accent. This disadvantage was turned to an advantage in *Ek Duje Ke Liye*—where south Indian Kamal and north Indian Rati Agnihotri were kept apart because of their cultural differences. The culture, the language and even eggs were causes of friction between two warring neighbours from different sides of the Great Indian Divide. Kamal Haasan's knowledge of Hindi seemed to comprise only of Hindi-movie titles and he sang an ode to his beloved with just that, before learning Sanskritized Hindi stumped his north Indian in-laws.

New Age Hero Alert: In *Raanjhanaa*, southern superstar Dhanush debuted as a *Banaras ka launda* and his Tamil accent was explained through the backstory of his father (a south Indian priest) who had settled down in the holy city. He used his Tamil background with aplomb when he approached a fellow Tamil IAS officer in the 'local language' and averted a major crisis.

Talking of Tamil IAS officers, we must remember T.A. Krishnan of *Shanghai*: a Punjabi *munda*—Abhay Deol—turned into a Tamilian with pitch-perfect accent and diction. He was the model bureaucrat destined for greater things when he was called in to conduct an inquiry of an attempt on a political activist's life. Dibakar Banerjee—known for his eye for detail—got the small things perfect as Krishnan spoke like a Tamilian, prayed like a Tamilian and even had a family who spoke like one. In a short conversation where Krishnan spoke to his family on the phone, the voices at the other end were those of a Tamil lady and her real daughter, dubbed in.

The Iyer must marry another Iyer—Old Jungle Proverb.

In the frothy romantic comedy *Hum Hain Rahi Pyar Ke*, this was probably not the intended message but that's what is relevant to the topic at hand. Mr Iyer decreed that his daughter—Vaijayanthi (played by the forever-bubbly Juhi Chawla) would marry a boy from the community (and he even found a classical-dancing 'pansy' to fit the bill). Vaijayanthi had other plans and ran off to become the governess to a handsome bachelor's (Aamir Khan) nephews and nieces. The mayhem that followed was interspersed with Carnatic music, Tamil-accented Hindi and several stretches of Tamil dialogues—spread between the heroine and her father. A part of it was also high-quality Tamil wisdom. When Mr Iyer was asked what was wrong with Aamir for marriage with his daughter, he said with all honesty—'*Buraai kuch nahin. Woh achha chhokra hai. But he's not an Iyer.*' Can't argue with that.

To counter the muscle and guts of the Mumbai underworld, you need a logical, calculating mind. As the foil for Chandru and Malik in Ram Gopal Varma's **Company**, we had Commissioner Sreenivasan—played by Mohanlal. Said to be modelled on real-life Mumbai police commissioner D. Sivanandan, this character was all logic and seemingly slow. Yet, behind the calm demeanour and Malayali accent was a steely resolve. Sreenivasan fought the battle effectively and towards the end of the film, he was eased out and made the head of the Police Training College. The cerebral cop was supposed to be writing a book on the Mumbai underworld—called *Company*.

A south Indian actor playing a south Indian character is rare but that's what Tamil superstar Prithviraj did in his Hindi debut—**Aiyyaa**. His flagrant fragrance triggered off an avalanche of fantasies in Rani Mukherji's fertile imagination, supplemented by 1990s' Bollywood and 'Midnight Masala' on Tamil TV channels. It involved singing a faux Tamil song—'*Dreamum wake-upum critical conditionum*'—amidst props made famous by *The Dirty Picture* and a Maharashtrian Brahmin girl salivating over a dark-skinned Tam-Greek god.

> *South Indian Woman Alert*: Celina Jaitley played a south Indian woman by the name of Meera Nair(!) in **Golmaal Returns**. As Shreyas Talpade's wife in the film, she went around in heavy Kanjeevarams, spewing '*aiyo rama*'s. While the character remained stereotypical, at least the choice of her name raised a chuckle.

The image of the reclusive mathematical genius follows from the figure of Srinivas Ramanujan and that image has been propagated with a clear south Indian feel. But it is not a common image in Bollywood. The Bollywood hero has never been too comfortable with the Binomial Theorem. One exception to this rule is Venkat Subramaniam, played by Amitabh Bachchan in **Teen Patti** (his name inspired probably by the name of one of its scriptwriters, Shivkumar Subramaniam). He played the maths professor out to redefine the laws of probability. And when he tried to prove his theory in real casinos, all hell broke loose.

> *Southie Nerd Alert*: Chatur Ramalingam of **3 Idiots** was your not-so-friendly neighbourhood south Indian engineer. He was studious. He aggressively chased grades. And he found a high-flying job in the USA after graduation (which he was not averse to bragging about), thus merging with the NRI stereotype as well.

If we manage to get past the special effects of **Ra.One** and look at the geek who came up with this video-game supervillain, we find he was Shekhar Subramaniam!

Shah Rukh Khan played a Tamil video-game designer who loved giving deep, meaningful advice to his son and eating noodles with curd. By professing this love for curd-noodles and interspersing his dialogues with Tamil phrases (most notably, '*inge vaa*'), SRK managed to piss off almost everyone in the southern part of the country. When his alter ego was in serious trouble, Rajinikanth (as Chitti from *Robot/Enthiran*) came to the rescue but even that wasn't enough to placate them.[2]

Deepika Padukone has played two hilarious[3] parts both as a south Indian lady with an indeterminate accent and an interminable name. In ***Housefull***, she was Soundarya Bhagyalaxmi Venkateshwari Basappa Rao. In ***Chennai Express***, she was Meenamma Lochini Azhagusundaram, daughter of Big Don (aka Periya Thalai) with a *bakuwaas* accent.

Tamil weddings have come to the forefront in two recent films.

In ***Gori Tere Pyaar Mein***, the groom was not sure about the wedding. In ***2 States***, he was dying to get married.

In the former, Imran played south Indian engineer (is there any other kind?) Sriram Venkat, who escaped from his wedding using the Tamil custom of the groom pretending to leave and then being convinced to stay back. In the latter, Punjabi munda Arjun Kapoor did no such thing and eagerly solemnized his union with Ananya Swaminathan (Alia Bhatt).

> *Smashing Stereotype Alert*: While on the subject of Ananya Swaminathan, she smashed the *paavam Tamil* stereotype to smithereens by drinking beer and eating chicken, even goading her boyfriend to these blasphemous activities.

How do you solve a problem like Murugan? Shashanka Ghosh, erstwhile head of Channel V, directed ***Quick Gun Murugan***—a full-length feature film based on a character he created for the music channel. The vegetarian cowboy ('one whisky, one masala dosa') took on the nefarious Rice Plate Reddy and Gunpowder while muttering sour nothings to belles like Locket Lover and Mango Dolly. People stopped counting the spoofs after the trailer, wonly.

---

[2] Even in ***Om Shanti Om***, SRK did a manic spoof of a south Indian hero by fighting stuffed tigers in fight scenes and, again, peppering dialogue with a faux-southie phrase ('*Yenna rascala!*').

[3] Terms and conditions apply.

The Big Bong Theory: 11 Depictions of Bengalis

As a much-forwarded internet joke goes, one Bengali is a poet; two Bengalis are a film society; three Bengalis are a political party; four Bengalis are—well—two political parties. As far as stereotypes go, this is at least intelligent, which is not what can be said about most Bollywood stereotypes. As far as Bengalis go, they are more fortunate than the south Indians in depiction— but then there are fewer Bengali characters in comparison as well.

One of the earliest Bengali characters in popular Hindi cinema was Miss Chatterjee, who was the subject of Johnny Walker's attention in the song '*Suno suno Miss Chatterjee*'

from the film **Baharen Phir Bhi Aayengi**. Set in Calcutta, the song moved from Victoria Memorial to trams to a nameless garden where 'modern' young men and women were dancing the twist. But that did not stop the inimitable Johnny Walker from wooing his Bengali girlfriend with many words that (apparently) rhymed with Chatter(jee)—for example, 'Matter', 'Better', 'Letter'!

The massive cosmopolitan cauldron that is Mumbai is home to north Indians, east Indians

Durga Puja. Dhoti. Dhunuchi Dance. Mr Dutt brings out his Bongness in Parineeta.

and even some west Indians (apart from Kieron Pollard, that is). And no film brought this fact home better than the one dedicated to the city—**Anand**. The trio of friends consisted of a Maharashtrian, a Punjabi (recently migrated from Delhi) and a Bengali (presumably settled in Mumbai). And the most famous Bong nomenclature was born. Dr Bhaskar Banerjee aka Babumoshai—in Rajesh Khanna's famous lilt—was the archetypal Bengali. Mercifully without a Bong accent, he was the typical intellectual Bengali who wrote long literary diaries while his friend, Dr Prakash Kulkarni, was minting money at his private nursing home. He was also prone to murmuring poetic sweet nothings to his sweetheart that were thoroughly decried by the loud-mouthed Punjabi, Anand Sehgal.

The affectionate and accurate portrayal was brought about by the Bengali director (Hrishikesh Mukherjee) who based the relationship on his own friendship with the iconic garrulous Punjabi, Raj Kapoor.

In **Do Anjaane**, Amit and Rekha Roy (played by the real-life Amit and Rekha) were happily married though Rekha's ambition (and Amit's lack of it) caused some friction. In walked a '*kebab mein haddi*' (Prem Chopra, strangely named Ranjit Mullick[1]). Soon, Amit was thrown off a train (by Prem, who's never up to any good) and the grieving Rekha became a superstar. If that wasn't enough drama for you, Amit Roy came back as a Punjabi producer willing to produce Rekha Roy's next film.

The story was set in Calcutta but no overt Bongness was displayed till we realized that Rekha was a Bengali superstar and her iconic role was an *ek-chutki-sindoor-ki-keemat* kind of part in a film called *Potibrata* ('Pativrataa' to the rest of the country). And then, to counter the Punjabi producer's immaculate Hindi, a Bengali director, Mr Sanyal (played gleefully by Utpal Dutt), emerged and you had more Bengali accent than a Pranab Mukherjee Budget speech.[2]

Kamal Haasan's magnum opus **Hey Ram** opened with his character returning from an archaeological dig in Mohen-jo-daro. He was greeted by his wife, Aparna—the archetype of the sexy Bengali woman in a traditionally worn saree, with a large bindi, larger eyes and a husky voice to die for. Without offering any explanation as to how a south Indian archaeologist married a Bengali schoolteacher, Kamal Haasan dived under the sheets with her. As the languorous lovemaking scene unfolded, Rani Mukherji recited verses from Jibanananda Das—a famous Bengali poet—in her Juhu-accented Bengali, and broke many hearts by dying soon afterwards.

---

[1] Ranjit Mullick is the name of a well-known Bengali actor.
[2] *Trivia Alert*: Yet another iconic Bengali, Mithun Chakraborty, made his debut in a bit part in the film—as a neighbourhood tough in Amit and Rekha's locality.

Note: Contrary to popular belief (emanating from the promos—seen by considerably more people than those who saw the film itself), Rani Mukherji was raped and killed in the 1946 riots and did not die from Kamal biting her on the bum.

What do you call an alcoholic, eccentric, charismatic Bengali? Uff oh, you idiot—not Ritwik Ghatak. I meant in the movies.

Yes, **Devdas** Mukherjee is the man—arguably the most popular Bengali character in Bollywood. In the better-remembered, more opulent Sanjay Leela Bhansali version, Shah Rukh Khan tripped his way through in a dhoti and kurta (which Bengalis, curiously enough, call a 'punjabi') in supposedly rural Bengal first, and Calcutta's red-light district later on. Sanjay Leela Bhansali's knowledge of Bengali culture and language was limited to one word as Aishwarya Rai went '*Issshhhh . . .*' at varying levels of pitch and volume.

One is at a bit of a loss to understand the reason why even the Punjabi audiences liked this sissy drunkard who couldn't choose between two gorgeous women. After all, they don't really get the difference in the northern parts of the country—'*Chandramukhi ho ya Paro, ki farq painda yaaro . . .*'[3]

In **Parineeta**, Saif Ali Khan played the Bengali to the hilt by wearing batik kurtas (aka punjabis—see above), driving around Victoria Memorial, singing romantic songs and taking the Toy Train to Darjeeling. He was Shekhar Roy, the son of the Bengali millionaire Nabin Chandra Roy. And his childhood sweetheart was Lolita—which can only be described as the Second-Most Typical Bengali Name of All Time (losing the top spot to Paromita, probably). Soon, we had Sanjay Dutt walking in as Girish Sharma. If his name wasn't typically Bengali, his costumes, attendance and dance at Durga Puja pandals clearly were. Between the three of them and 1960s' Bengal, you had an encyclopedia of Bongness that would have been a cakewalk for the director, Pradeep Sarkar, to create.[4]

Bonus Movie: The zamindari Bengal of the 1950s shown in Vikramaditya Motwane's **Lootera** was recreated just as lovingly. Pakhi (Sonakshi Sinha) played the role of an insulated Bengali girl who saw – somewhat uncomprehendingly – her father's property

---

[3] *Hat Tip*: To Salim–Javed for coining this line in **Haath Ki Safai** and to Sujoy Ghosh for repeating it in **Jhankaar Beats**.
[4] *Trivia Alert*: Saif's father's role was played by Sabyasachi Chakraborty, who has played Feluda (Satyajit Ray's detective) in several Bengali films.

and her love being taken away. Her clothes, her surroundings, her preoccupations—but thankfully, not her accent—were lusciously accurate.

An idealistic student leader taking on the entrenched political leadership of a state is the stuff legends are made of. Add to that a migrant henchman helping out the politicos and a frivolous youngster who realizes the power of democracy—and you have *Yuva*.

As Michael Mukherjee, Ajay Devgn was the charismatic student leader of Presidency College who was not beyond solving dense mathematical problems on police lock-up walls. While the faux Bengali accent was completely missing in his case, it was there in super-exaggerated form in the voice of Prosenjit Bhattacharya (Om Puri)—the slimy neta.

In *Mumbai Matinee*—one of the low-budget, offbeat efforts—we met Debu (Debasish) Chatterjee, billed as a 'thirty-something virgin' on the lookout for some 'action'. As is the norm in sex comedies, our mild-mannered hero got caught in unwitting adventures including an encounter with a sexologist baba, an inadvertent part in a porn film and, eventually, a run-in with a Bengali police officer. The language of Rahul Bose's character would have remained immaterial to the story if not for the aforementioned police officer. In a completely over-the-top comic scene, the police officer arrested Debu from a brothel and proceeded to lecture him on the collapse of Bengali moral fibre—in theatrical Bengali. Rahul Bose's feeble attempts to explain himself were lost in the high-pitched monologue. *Maa go . . .*[5]

When Gurukant Desai (*Guru*) hit a roadblock in his quest to become India's biggest industrialist, he was helped by an idealistic newspaper editor. When he bent a few rules to get ahead, it was the same editor who took him on. Manik Dasgupta (played by the forever versatile Mithun Chakraborty) was the upright newspaper editor who was always fair—even if it meant going hammer and tongs after his loved ones. While the character was based on real-life media baron Ramnath Goenka (who wasn't Bengali), Mithun gave it some deft touches of eccentricity—like lapsing into Bengali in the middle of a diatribe and the language didn't seem out of place. After all, some of the best-known editors in this country are Bengalis.

Why would two brothers controlling a betting syndicate in Mumbai be Bengali? Why would their third brother be called Mikhail? Why would their idea of fun be firing empty shots at people? There was no reason whatsoever behind what were probably the most eccentric Bengali

---

[5] Bengali invocation (theatrical) of the mother akin to the Marathi '*Ai la*'.

characters in Bollywood. In **Kaminey**, three Bengali actors—Deb Mukherjee, Rajatabha Dutta and Chandan Roy Sanyal—played the three manic brothers with hand-rubbing glee. AK-47s, missing cash, drugs, and the crowning moment of the film—the '*Dhan te nan*' song sequence—all had one of the three Bongs in it. Bongs rule, don't they?

'*Tussi Bong ho?*'—with this opening line, Vicky Arora thought he would have the Bengali teller at the local bank branch wrapped around his little finger. But Ashima Roy (played by newcomer Yami Gautam) turned out to be a tough nut to crack as was her father, who didn't look too kindly at Punjabis. **Vicky Donor** was the love story between Lajpat Nagar and Chittaranjan Park, with healthy doses of Punjabi boisterousness and Bengali intellectualism. All of it eventually culminating into gallons of liquor at the Bong–Panju wedding and the 'light-bulb dance' to signify the intercourse[6] between two great cultures.

Three characters in the list come together.

They were all corporate professionals—grappling with workplace pressures and personal issues in style. Their qualifications varied between having MBA, architecture and literature degrees. They had none of the 'distinctive' traits of Bengalis—except for their names. Ladies and gentlemen, please put your hands together for Nishigandha Dasgupta (**Corporate**), Shonali Mukherjee (**Karthik Calling Karthik**) and Ayesha Banerjee (**Wake Up Sid**).

While on the subject of Bong women, it might be apt to bring up Abhishek Bachchan's character in the **Dhoom** franchise, who was a son-in-law of Bengal. He was shown married to a Bong woman and being colleagues with another (both played by real-life Bongs, Rimi Sen and Bipasha Basu respectively).

HONOURABLE MENTIONS

---

[6] Pun intended.

East, West, North, South: 8 Regional Superstars

The Indian film industry is not just about Bollywood. Every state of India has its own home-grown superstar(s) with massive fan followings. Many of these stars' regional-language releases get national attention and international releases. In terms of remuneration, many of these stars eclipse their Bollywood counterparts and words fail to describe the hysteria they generate. And at different points of time in their careers, they have attempted to reach a pan-Indian audience with varying degrees of success.

Uttam Kumar

Uttam Kumar—the leading star of Bengal—made his Bollywood debut by producing and starring in a romantic drama—*Chhoti Si Mulaqat*—in the late 1960s. It had all the right trappings including Uttam's dashing looks and undeniable charm, Vyjayanthimala, and a very good music score by Shankar–Jaikishan, but did not fare well commercially. Like all inexplicable failures, this too had a corresponding conspiracy theory attached to it: that the big guns of Bombay did not want Uttam Kumar to succeed. Post this failure, he never did a conventional leading-man role in Bombay again and returned to rule his native Bengal.

Much later in his career, he did Shakti Samanta's *Amanush* and *Anand Ashram* (made in both Hindi and Bengali) as well as a strong supporting role in Gulzar's *Kitaab*. By this time, he wasn't the dashing hero but more of a character actor. The last Hindi release before his death was Manmohan Desai's *Desh Premee* where he—as Paran Ghosh—was one of the parochial leaders of the slum Bharat Nagar, all of whom lived in an atmosphere of intermittent animosity, and received advice from Amitabh Bachchan.

Rajinikanth

The word 'superstar' has got intrinsically linked to the adopted name of Shivaji Rao Gaekwad as his legend has spread far beyond the states in which his language is spoken. Becoming the biggest Tamil superstar by the early 1980s, he made his Hindi film debut in *Andhaa Kaanoon*, and in the company of Amitabh Bachchan, proceeded to polish off his father's three killers with black leather jackets, red eyes and large nostrils.

While the film was a big hit, Rajini did not really follow it up with anything big, and some pretty forgettable action films characterized his output in the 1980s. Most of them managed to tell their stories in their titles—*Jeet Hamaari*, *Dushmano Ka Dushman* and *Insaaf Kaun Karega*, for example. His reputation for doing cool things with cigarettes and sunglasses was exploited to the fullest in *Geraftaar*—where he played Inspector Hussein in a guest appearance; people went asthmatic whistling through his entire role—which ended with him lighting a cigarette as he was about to be killed.[1]

He did some more roles—bit parts, compared to his southern output—and the only film worth remembering was his delightfully comic turn as taxi-driver Jaggu in *Chaalbaaz*.

He also did **Hum**—a triple combo knockout punch—with him, the Big B and Govinda playing to the gallery. The scene with Rajini's bat-dance and his '*Beteylal, teen se bhale do, do se bhala yek*' dialogue is still a cult favourite. Interestingly, the film's biggest draw was supposed to be Amitabh, but in Ooty, where the film was being shot, crowds routinely landed up to touch Rajini's feet and get infants blessed by him.

After that, he made a few more forays doing primarily strong character roles in some really weak films, learnt his lesson and returned to breaking records in Tamil.

When one sees Rajini's friendship with the Big B, one hopes that the two will act together in an epic, and we can all die in peace after that.

Kamal Haasan

Kamal Haasan, the other Tamil superstar, is considered more of an actor and has wooed the national audience with a mix of dubbed versions of Tamil films and starring roles in important films. His initial films were big solo-hero successes, starting with *Ek Duje Ke Liye*—which exploited his south Indian background for the story of a north–south romance. All the stereotypes of Tamil language and culture were duly poked fun at and the film went on to become a huge hit on the back of a brilliant score. After that, he had another rocking

---

[1] An article about Rajinikanth in the *Slate* web magazine (dated 27 September 2010) says, 'Putting his sunglasses on is an operation as complex as a Vegas floorshow.'

music score in *Sanam Teri Kasam* that again became a hit. He followed this up with *Sadma* (the remake of a Tamil hit that established both him and Sridevi as hugely talented stars), and *Rajtilak* (a lost-and-found period potboiler). And as if that was not enough, he had an author-backed role in *Saagar* that should have established him as an A-list star in Bollywood. But—quite inexplicably—he never did any leading role after that and only returned with directorial ventures in the last decade or so. Some of them were cute (*Chachi 420*), some convoluted (*Hey Ram*) and some plain bad (*Mumbai Express*). What a pity we didn't get more of Kamal the actor.

Mohanlal

Mohanlal—the leading light of Malayalam cinema—is not the conventionally handsome film hero and his accent is rather distinctive, to put it politely.

He took on the Mumbai underworld as Police Commissioner Srinivasan in *Company*. A cool, calculating cop who hunted with his brain was a role he sunk his teeth into, and the manic energy of the dons found an interesting counterpoint in his slow gait. Buoyed by this success, Mohanlal returned to work with the same director and an even bigger star cast in a remake of the Greatest Film Ever Made. That film was—tragically—*Ram Gopal Varma Ki Aag*. Everything associated with the movie got blasted into small pieces and poor Mohanlal was no exception. Inspector Narasimha (equivalent of the thakur in the original) was seen as a caricature at worst and ignored at best. He has not come back since. And we can only blame Ramu for that.

Chiranjeevi

If Rajini is the Superstar, Chiranjeevi is the Megastar and Supreme Hero.

Blessed with a mouthful of a name (Sivasankara Varaprasad Konidela), he ruled the Telugu filmdom as Chiranjeevi—with a fan-following as large and mad as it got. His Bollywood debut was in *Pratibandh*, as a trigger-happy cop out to protect the chief minister from the evil machinations of Spot Nana (played by Rami Reddy, who's got to be the Most Deadpan Villain of All Times). With kick-ass action and some giggly relief in the form of Juhi Chawla, the film was a reasonable success and it surely paved the way for more of the same.

That 'more' came in the form of *Aaj Ka Goondaraaj*—the standard-issue clanger the '90s were notorious for—which sank without a trace (or maybe with some trace but we don't know for sure). Chiranjeevi came back as *The Gentleman*, which was the remake of a Tamil film called—well—*Gentleman*, and the significance of the additional 'The' was lost on pretty much everybody. Directed by Mahesh Bhatt in the period when he was simultaneously directing some six films at any point of time, it did quite disastrously. And that was the last we heard of

Chiru in this part of town, and with his ministerial ministrations, there is not much to look forward to anyway.

Nagarjuna

Telugu superstar Nagarjuna made an explosive—albeit deadpan—national debut in Ram Gopal Varma's *Shiva*. The story of a regular student becoming a vigilante to resist the forces of a local don was steeped in reality. The choreographed violence and intentionally jagged film-making style made the film achieve some sort of cult status. The director–star duo got together again to remake one of their Telugu films in Hindi. In *Drohi*, Nagarjuna continued his deadpan act as a hitman finding love and escaping his past. This theme did not work but RGV perfected it by the time he made *Satya*.

Soon after this, Nagarjuna made two forays in quick succession. *Khuda Gawah* gave him a glamorous role where he took on a parallel track of romance and bravado. *Zakhm* was a shorter but critically acclaimed role where he played a film director who sired an illegitimate son with his mistress.

His last two Hindi films have been *Agni Varsha* (the adaptation of an ancient play, where he was seen getting into a clinch with the forever-hot Raveena Tandon) and *LOC Kargil* (where he must have been one of the soldiers but nobody—including J.P. Dutta—can confirm this). The former got lost in the theatres and the latter got lost in the interminable cast.

Ravi Kissen

Bhojpuri has become the latest regional film industry to become big and its great white hope is Ravi Kissen—who has become hysterically famous all over India thanks to his appearances on *Bigg Boss*. His cultivated image of a buffoon hasn't, however, helped him to get lead roles. He has worked with critically acclaimed directors like Shyam Benegal (*Well Done Abba*) and Mani Ratnam (*Raavan*). He has appeared in a wide variety of roles too, though most of them seem to have been extended bit parts. In *Luck*, he was a libidinous crook. In *Tanu Weds Manu*, he was the UP goon out for a scrap. In *Chitkabrey*, he played a ragging victim out to settle scores, though his purported nude appearance garnered more comment than this performance.

Which brings us to the most successful crossover of them all. A man started in Tamil cinema, acquired incredible acclaim and commercial success, had his works dubbed and released in Hindi and, after the unprecedented success of this, made a national debut, became wildly popular and is now an international superstar. Ladies and gentlemen—keep listening to A.R. Rahman.

FEMALE STARS

Female superstars from different regions to have made forays in Bollywood are fewer, though many of Bollywood's top heroines are from the south and the east. Three superstars who made short sorties in Bollywood were:

- *Suchitra Sen*—the enigmatic Bengali actress (who had a legendary screen pairing with Uttam Kumar in Bengali) did few but very impactful roles in Hindi. In Bimal Roy's ***Devdas***, she played Paro opposite Dilip Kumar. She was next seen in a short role in Hrishikesh Mukherjee's ***Musafir*** and opposite Dev Anand in ***Bombai Ka Babu***. She was seen as both mother and daughter in ***Mamta***, a remake of a Bengali hit (which also starred her). Her best-known role is, of course, ***Aandhi***—a film still remembered for the controversy it generated, its brilliant music, as well as the performances by her and Sanjeev Kumar.

- *Vijayashanthi*—she was known as 'Lady Amitabh Bachchan' for her 'action hero' role in the Telugu film ***Karthavyam***, where she played a lady police officer supposedly based on Kiran Bedi's life. The film was remade in Hindi, and though it wasn't very successful, a few forgettable films happened due to the sheer inertia of her success in Telugu. Probably her best known role in Hindi was opposite Anil Kapoor in ***Eeshwar***, another remake of a Telugu hit.

- *Jayalalitha*—the Tamil Nadu CM was a Tamil superstar but did only one film in Hindi. As the second lead opposite Dharmendra in ***Izzat***, she had reasonable screen time (read: song and dance) and performed competently. Nevertheless, she chose to remain in her Tamil stardom and never returned.

4

Supermen

Even ordinary people are extraordinary in Bollywood. Now think how extraordinary people would appear to be. People who have shaped countries. People who have shaped destinies. People who have shaped biceps. People who are too big to be called people.

This section is about extraordinary gentlemen and ladies.

Kryptonite: 10 Superheroes

Any hero who romances the heroine, plays badminton with her (including an under-the-leg shot), sings a song, fights off goons and mouths bombastic dialogue all within nine minutes of screen time is actually a superhero.[1] You could, then, argue that all Bollywood movies of the 1960s and 1970s are superhero movies. But here, we are restricting ourselves to people with specific superpowers[2] (or gadgets with superpowers), cool costumes and preferably a secret identity.

In his first lead role, Jackie Shroff was *Hero*. Almost immediately afterwards, he was Superhero in *Shiva Ka Insaaf*, the first 3D film in Hindi (close on the heels of *My Dear Kuttichaathan*, the first Indian 3D offering). Shiva was a super-combo of superheroes from many genres. His training regimen was straight out of Shaolin. His costume (mask and cape) was from Zorro. His mark-leaving ring was from Phantom. His common-man get-up (and profession) were alarmingly similar to Clark Kent's bespectacled, bumbling reporter routine. Trained by a trio of 'uncles' (Ram, Rahim and Robert), Jackie Shroff went from being Bhola to Shiva and back again, romancing Poonam Dhillon by day and fighting crime also by day—in order to catch the people who killed his parents.

Corrupt policeman by day, black-leather-chain-armguard-salt-and-pepper-wig-clad dispenser of justice by night. Jaya Bachchan came up with the 'story idea' for *Shahenshah*, Amitabh's first outing as a bona fide secret identity superhero. After his honest dad was driven to suicide by the evil machinations of JK (Amrish Puri), AB grew up to become a police officer who always flirted with bribery from shady characters (to find out who was, in fact, shady). And once he got to know, he appeared like a messiah in his jazzy leather costume beating up Olympic-

---

[1] The above sequence of events was executed by Jeetendra in *Humjoli*.
[2] The superpowers of Indian superheroes are usually god-gifted (*Shiva* from Shiva, *Toofan* from Hanuman).

sized wrestlers for running vice dens, stopping the unlawful eviction of slum-dwellers and patrolling the empty streets of Mumbai's western suburbs at night ('*Andheri raaton mein, sunsaan rahon par . . .*').

Apart from his enormous strength, a breath that echoed far and wide and a godly voice, he had that one superpower through which he impregnated the mothers of all villains in the world. As he said, '*Rishte mein toh hum tumhare baap hote hain . . .*'

Puneet Issar was **Superman** in the film of the same name—which has been part of many discussions on the worst Indian movie ever. As Shekhar, Puneet breakdanced to Michael Jackson songs and then quickly changed into his red-brief-on-blue-costume get-up (complete with a lock of hair on the forehead). Dharmendra played the father who was forced to leave his son in the care of foster parents on Earth, although he returned in 'spirit' to guide his son. He performed breathtaking feats like rescuing a hijacked plane by plucking it off the sky and lugging it on his shoulders (except the plane was rolling on its wheels and our good ol' superman was tiptoeing in front with his shoulder touching the side of the plane).

Special Effects Alert: The film had arguably the worst-ever special effects in Indian cinema and apparently lifted substantial footage from the Hollywood *Superman* movie of the late 1970s.

Arun Verma's father was a scientist who invented a '*faarmoolaa*' that rendered people invisible—except in red light. He knew evil monsters (with names like Mogambo) would want to misuse his invention and so he hid the gadget (a blingy bracelet with flashing lights) before he got killed. Years later, his son recovered the bracelet, put it on and became **Mr India**. Mr India took on adulterers, black marketers and smugglers in action settings, and horny crime reporters in romantic ones. He eventually took on Mogambo in his den and was doing phenomenally well till somebody switched on all the red lights. Then Arun Verma realized that to take on villains, you didn't need to be Superman but Mango Man.

Another father died. Another villain escaped. Another police officer looked the other way. When the dead man's son prayed to Bajrangbali for justice, a storm blew across the temple area. A hi-tech bow-and-arrow slid across from the Hanuman idol to the little boy and the idol's garland flew over to the boy's neck. Thus, Toofan was born.

Directed by Ketan Desai, **Toofan** was a superhero with a desi-snazzy costume (black Pathan suit with orange cape), explosive lines ('*Jab jab zulm ki aandhi badhti hai, tab tab usse rokne ke liye toofan aata hai*') and a calling card that literally blew you away. Whenever Toofan arrived on the scene, he was accompanied by a real storm. Wow, that beats the Batmobile hollow! Add deadly villains, shady police officers, a bumbling magician (who was Toofan's twin brother), a mother character and you had a full-blown desi superstar/superman.

Retro Alert: Amitabh Bachchan was not the only *toofani* superhero in Bollywood. Vikram (of *Julie* fame) was also Toofan, a masked character on the lines of Zorro. In the action-packed 1970s, he was a sissy, red-coated wimp by day and black masked-caped-capped superhero by night—spoiling the nefarious goals of Jeevan and his villainous cohorts.

Zorro Alert: Bollywood's Zorro bug was rampant in 1975 as Navin Nischol also played the caped crusader, lifting not only the costume from the original but also the name. Punching the lost-and-found formula with the evil raja, Zorro wielded a mean sword and whip to gain justice for the oppressed.

Ajooba = Zorro + Robin Hood + Braveheart + James Bond.

He wore a mask, shot arrows, robbed the rich to donate to the poor, rebelled against the ruler and was a hit with women. He was, literally, a miracle. When the evil wazir (Amrish Puri) of his sultan father tried to kill him, a dolphin carried him to safety, became his foster mother, and left him with an ironsmith. In anonymity, the prince was trained in martial arts and he grew up to rebel against the wazir, who kept intoning '*Shaitaan zindabaad*'. Finally, Ajooba—whose alter ego was mild-mannered serai owner Ali—made an appearance with a booming slogan, '*Muddai lakh bura chahta hai toh kya hota hain / Wohi hota hai jo manzoor-e-khuda hota hai*', which became his calling card. The final showdown happened between him and Fauladi Shaitaan (a metallic giant which looked like a cross between Johnny Sokko's Flying Robot and Chewbacca) amidst demons, flying carpets and magic swords.

When **Honeymoon Travels Pvt Ltd** put a motley group of six newly married couples on a bus to Goa, many skeletons tumbled out of the closet. Abhay Deol and Minissha Lamba formed the super-compatible Parsi couple, Aspi and Zara, who were together since childhood, wore colour-coordinated clothes, danced synchronously and even managed to finish their sudokus at exactly the same time. And they both had a secret to hide. Aspi and Zara were—hold your breath—superheroes. They got their superpowers when they were both caught in an asteroid fall. And that led to both of them vanishing in the dead of the night to fight crime. A cute bit of misunderstanding later (Gasp! Are you cheating on me?), they went on to become a superer-compatible couple.

Krrish inherited his superpowers from his father who was 'blessed' by aliens (in *Koi Mil Gaya*). The child Krishna drew fantastic pictures, did third-standard maths in the first standard, and cracked an 'IQ Test' (which was really a GK test, but still . . .). His paranoid grandmother took him away from the public eye so that he wouldn't get undue attention but what do you do with a hunk like Hrithik? He soon emerged racing ahead of horses, leaping over mountains and displaying his rippling muscles. Krishna landed up in Singapore following a girl and ended up becoming *Krrish*—wearing a masquerade ball mask, and his overcoat inside out. He saved children in a burning circus, fought goons, leapt over cars in downtown Singapore and finally locked horns with a time-travelling evil scientist (who, conveniently, had also 'killed' his father) in his island hideout. Soon enough, Krrish returned in *Krrish 3*[3] to save crashing flights, take flying leaps over buildings, fight more super-villains in their hi-tech lairs and advocate good manners and Bournvita to kids. Now that he has become a video game, we can expect more of him in films also.

Abhishek Bachchan tried his hand at being a superhero in the semi-mythological fantasy *Drona*—one of the biggest box-office disasters of recent times. He started off as mild-mannered Aditya, unaware that he was one of a long line of warrior princes who had been designated to protect the vessel of amrit that emerged from the *samudra manthan*. His super-strength was unlocked by a 'bodyguard' (Priyanka Chopra, who really put the body in the bodyguard). He donned a flowing kurta, a churidar and a sword (not to mention a jewelled headband) to take on his adversary, Riz Raizada (Kay Kay Menon in the most inexplicable role of his career), a magician–asura with massive pointy sideburns and hair gelled to be shaped like a single black antenna on his head. Despite having all the superhero ingredients, *Drona* tanked under the weight of very ordinary special effects, a slow build-up and a super-unfit AB Jr, whose cheeks jiggled when he took flying leaps.

Superhero movies moved from mythology and spiritual mastery into the hi-tech gaming zone with *Ra.One*. The superhero G.One (pronounced Jiwan, stands for Good One) emerged out of a video game to protect the game-designer's son from the villain, Ra.One (Random Access One, huh? Oh, pronounced Ravan). A cool blue-tinged suit, unblinking eyes and a blinking heart formed the persona of G.One. He took on his form-shifting adversary in a London car pound, Chhatrapati Shivaji Terminus (in a mind-blowing SFX-laden scene) and finally inside

---

[3] One second, where is Krrish 2? Well, the makers explained that *Koi Mil Gaya* was the first story of *Krrish* (i.e. Krrish 1), *Krrish* was the second story of Krrish (i.e. Krrish 2), and thereupon, we had *Krrish 3*. We could, of course, argue that there was no Krrish in *Koi Mil Gaya* but after three films of Hrithik Roshan's energetic acrobatics, we are just too tired to do any of that!

a video game. SRK went from the mild-mannered geek Shekhar Subramaniam to the cool, robotic G.One in an effort to woo the family audience. And children would have loved his pelvic thrusts, discussions on condoms and wooing of Kareena Kapoor with '*Chhammak chhallo*'.

It's a bird! It's a plane! It's Govinda! *Dariya Dil* had the most iconic Bollywood superhero–song ever. Govinda dressed up as Superman and Kimi Katkar as Spiderwoman for a song that has gone on to garner nine million views on YouTube. They hovered over the Mumbai skyline before landing in a garden and singing a romantic duet ('*Tu mera Superman, main teri lady / Ho gaya hai apna pyar already*') that scaled unprecedented heights of WTFness.

After imaginary heroes, some real ones can be found in *Supermen of Malegaon.* Faiza Ahmed Khan made this award-winning documentary on the fledgling film industry in Malegaon, a small town in Maharashtra. To take a break from the depressing reality of their lives, a group of people started making movies on shoestring budgets that were remakes of Indian superhits like *Sholay* and *Ghajini*. The documentary caught them when they were making *Superman*. Without ridiculing their obviously shoddy attempts at film-making, the director focused instead on the strength of their conviction to put out a heart-warming tale of human endeavour.

HONOURABLE MENTIONS

Supermen of Malegaon: Ordinary people doing extraordinary things

Independence Day: 10 Freedom Fighters

India's freedom struggle was full of emotions that Bollywood loves in large quantities. Action, emotion, drama, sacrifice and—most importantly—spine-tingling dialogues and soul-stirring music that energized the nation. The freedom struggle lacked only one Bollywood ingredient: romance. Never one to let truth spoil a good story, Bollywood has gone out and invented romantic angles for real-life revolutionaries or, better still, invented the revolutionaries themselves. Actually, this works best. Make it fictional and keep the pesky history-walas at bay!

FICTIONAL

Nothing great is achieved in a day. One has to shed blood, sweat and tears and it often takes decades of perseverance to reach the ultimate goal. But once that goal is reached, generations look up to it as an acme of human endeavour. And that is how Manoj Kumar became Mr Bharat. (What? You thought I was talking of India's freedom struggle?)

After *Shaheed* and *Upkar*, Manoj Kumar gradually upped the patriotic scale to reach *Kranti* in the early '80s. Set in the nineteenth century, it started off with how a trusting raja gave the British permission to use his port, after which they started smuggling in ammunition while smuggling out priceless artefacts. A packed star cast—Dilip Kumar, Shashi Kapoor, Shatrughan Sinha, Hema Malini, Parveen Babi, Sarika, apart from Mr Bharat—came together to fight the British in their forts, on their ships, in the battleground and wherever Tom Alter even thought of going.

Curzon. Dyer. Simon. All the minions of the evil British Empire broke out in a cold sweat when they heard the name of Raja Azad Singh, who could bring an airplane to a grinding halt just by lassoing a rope around its tail. Dara Singh played the raja who was treacherously defeated and imprisoned by the British. Unknown to all, his son grew up to become a worthy inheritor. First things first, his *naamkaran* happened when his father knifed his name on his chest. When he grew up, he gave arrogant Indian women lessons in manners. He attacked 'Europeans Only' clubs with his dog. He stormed British concentration camps. He united with his father in keeping the Britishers on the run.[1] After all, he was something the Britishers could never be—*Mard*.

Raghuvir Pathak was apparently recuperating from TB in Kasauni. But actually, he was waiting for General Douglas with handmade bombs and a plan. He was also waiting for his ally Shubhankar to come and execute this daring plan. What he hadn't planned for was his daughter falling in love with an Anglophile wastrel and his modus operandi leaking out. What followed was a volatile story of British oppression and Indian defiance, with memorable characters on both sides. A romance in the backdrop of an explosive freedom struggle was least expected but brilliantly etched. It was 1942 but there was time for a love story.

The freedom struggle was not only about guns and bloodshed. In fact, the 'first' act of the Indian freedom movement was to beat the British at their own game. Bhuvan led the villagers of Champaner in a cricket match against the players of the British army camp, a most unusual act of defiance. From the initial scepticism among the villagers to their rallying around to the final level of high confidence was something that has united every group of underdogs, most importantly freedom fighters. Eventually, it all boiled down to the very last ball of the match when Bhuvan swung hard to make the first dent in the British armour. He had to do it. After all, it was about standing up against the oppressive tax regime—*Lagaan*.

After Dara Singh and Amitabh Bachchan, the second most potent father–son freedom fighter combo was undoubtedly Mithun Chakraborty and Salman Khan in *Veer*.

Having lost his kingdom thanks to a traitor raja (Jackie Shroff), Pindari warrior Mithun sent his two sons (Salman and Sohail Khan) to Britain so that they could get to know the enemy first-hand. Having given a chance to hero Salman to wear natty clothes, woo a babe and knock off an enemy or two, the director brought him back to India and unleashed some serious bloodbath on the always-suspecting audience and the unsuspecting British.

Salman let his muscles and hair both loose to become a cross between Robin Hood, Gladiator and Braveheart. The British governor and the traitor raja were no match for Salman and his Pindari army, who soaked the desert sands with British blood and hoisted their flag on enemy soil.

Veer did not do too well at the box office but the legend of Salman spread far and wide, only to become so popular that British rock band Queen even composed a rock song as their tribute to it—'*Veer will, Veer will rock you!*'

---

[1] Wonder why they waited till 1947 to leave the country?

REAL

Bhagat Singh

Bhagat Singh, the firebrand from Punjab is, by far, the most popular freedom fighter in Bollywood.

Shammi Kapoor (*Shaheed Bhagat Singh*), Manoj Kumar (*Shaheed*), Ajay Devgn (*The Legend of Bhagat Singh*), Bobby Deol (*23rd March 1931: Shaheed*) and Siddharth (*Rang De Basanti*) have portrayed him. In fact, Manoj Kumar's patriotic reputation was kicked off by his portrayal of the hero. Public interest was piqued when, around 2002, two major films around Bhagat Singh released almost simultaneously.

His bold pronouncements and daredevil actions were pure dynamite and his mustachioed, suited, hatted visage went from roadside poster stalls to movie theatres across the country. Every retelling invented a girlfriend/fiancée for him, Aishwarya Rai being the most glamorous one (in *23rd March 1931: Shaheed*).

> *Bonus Hero*: Chandrasekhar Azad, Bhagat Singh's close ally and confidant, has been played by two of India's biggest stars—Aamir Khan (in *Rang De Basanti*) and Sunny Deol (in *23rd March 1931: Shaheed*).

Mangal Pandey

You may have only one film made on you but when it remains four years in the making with India's most important star growing hair (cranial and facial) for the role and refusing many offers in the process, it deserves an entry in a list of freedom fighters in Bollywood.

Ketan Mehta directed *Mangal Pandey: The Rising* about the man who is called India's first freedom fighter and who fought during the First War of Indian Independence in 1857. The Brahmin sepoy who single-handedly rose against the might of the East India Company was much glamorized (Rani Mukherji as girlfriend) and much hyped (since very little documented history is available on him) in the film's making. The film opened to great excitement but couldn't sustain the momentum it had built, much like the Sepoy Mutiny itself.

Surjya Sen

A simple schoolmaster from Chittagong, who plotted and almost executed a daring raid on the British armoury, has been the subject of two movies. Popularly known as Masterda, the quietly determined schoolmaster got together a band of his students for an elaborate operation to simultaneously disable communication, loot British arms and take Europeans hostage. The first film was *Khelein Hum Jee Jaan Sey*, helmed by Ashutosh Gowariker. Abhishek Bachchan played Surjya Sen and the movie had a romantic angle between him and Kalpana Dutta (played by Deepika Padukone) but could not whip up viewer interest.

Bedabrata Pain—an ex-NASA scientist—directed *Chittagong* with Manoj Bajpai in the lead. The film was generally accepted as a much better offering though it had a very limited release due to lack of star power and marketing muscle.[2]

Subhash Chandra Bose

The only Indian freedom fighter to launch a full-fledged war against the British Empire hasn't had too many films on him. Shyam Benegal tracked the most exciting part of Bose's life in *Netaji Subhash Chandra Bose: The Forgotten Hero*. Bose escaped house arrest in Calcutta, slipped into Afghanistan and reached Germany to build an alliance with Adolf Hitler. When that didn't work out, he travelled to Japan in a submarine and invaded India with the goosebumps-inducing '*Chalo Dilli*' slogan. His campaign wasn't successful because of Japan's defeat in the Second World War, but his assault on northeast India, his initial victories and his eventual death in an air crash are stuff legends are made of.[3]

> *Bonus Movie*: Subhash Chandra Bose's INA (Indian National Army) assault was the backdrop of *Samadhi*, where Ashok Kumar was a soldier in Bose's army and led a daredevil attack against the British.

Mahatma Gandhi

If we don't count the Hindi-dubbed version of Richard Attenborough's *Gandhi* (the staple of Doordarshan on every 2 October afternoon), the Father of the Nation has relatively poorer representation in Bollywood. He appeared as a character in several films that were not always pure Bolly territory. *Gandhi My Father* focused on his son (where Darshan Jariwala played the Mahatma) while *Sardar* was Vallabhbhai Patel's biopic (where Annu Kapoor played Gandhi). The Mahatma had a very small role (played by Naseeruddin Shah) in Kamal Haasan's magnum opus, *Hey Ram*, and it was made memorable by the mahatma being flung a great distance on being shot.

---

[2] Bedabrata Pain won the National Award for the Best Debutant Director (2012).

[3] *Irreverent/Irrelevant Trivia*: Bose's legendary slogan ('*Tum mujhe khoon do, main tumhe azaadi doonga*') was spoofed by Govinda in *Hero No. 1* when he challenged some goons to a fight with the same line.

Of course, all that changed with *Lage Raho Munna Bhai*, when the Mahatma took a *tapori* turn and Gandhigiri became the word of the season.

FOREIGN DEVILS: BOB CHRISTO AND TOM ALTER

Leading the charge against all our illustrious freedom fighters have been two actors of foreign origin, who have become honorary Indians thanks to their stellar service to Bollywood.

- *Bob Christo*: An Australian engineer who strayed into Bollywood almost by mistake, he was the international face of evil in 100+ movies. In *Namak Halal* and *Disco Dancer*, he was an international hitman hired to kill the hero. Apart from Simon in *Mard*, he was the tyrannical British officer all through his career including *Veer Savarkar*, one of his last roles. He was called Bob in a large number of his films though his most famous name is likely to be Mr Walcott in *Mr India*.

- *Tom Alter*: Born and raised in India, he made his Hindi/Urdu speaking prowess clear right at the beginning when he appeared in Satyajit Ray's *Shatranj Ke Khiladi*. His forte has been playing the smooth but cruel representative of a foreign power with names like Jackson (*Parvarish*) and Rexson (*Karma*). All his roles haven't been villainous as he has played the range from Lord Mountbatten (*Sardar*) to even Maulana Abul Kalam Azad (in Shyam Benegal's *Samvidhaan* made for TV).

If *Lagaan* had been made a decade earlier, we would have surely had Tom Alter as the captain of the English cricket team and Bob Christo as the mustachioed fast bowler!

Uniformed Ladies: 10 Women Police Officers

Everybody loves a woman police officer. Women see a role model, a successful person and a source of inspiration in a person occupying a position of authority. Men see the tight uniform and handcuffs.

Villains polish off dad. A revenge saga is spawned. One child grows up to become a police officer and attacks the villains legally. The other ends up on the wrong end of the law and takes on the villain using methods not found in our Constitution. This oft-repeated story got a distaff twist in **Andhaa Kaanoon,** where the cop child was a girl—Hema Malini. Hema and the He-Man went after the three villains who murdered their father and raped their sister. While Rajinikanth nearly chewed off the villains' balls with reddened eyes and flared nostrils, Hema's job was to stop him from murdering the villains. Her efforts yielded precious little as she was kidnapped by villain-in-chief Pran and he had her tied to his bed (those handcuffs, I tell you!)—to be saved just in time by her brother. Her havaldar cap, worn at a jaunty angle, and angry pronouncements were thoroughly upstaged by the two male superstars in the movie—Rajinikanth and Amitabh Bachchan.

Ornamental police officers are common enough, especially if many male stars are around. That's what happened to Madhavi in **Geraftaar.** With three—three? three!—of India's biggest superstars in a tale of lost-and-found brothers that had to allow Rajinikanth to throw a few cigarettes in the air, she had hardly anything to do (as a police officer). Most of her screen time was utilized in being Amitabh Bachchan's love interest—he was also a police officer. Add to that a dead villain who wasn't really dead and a climax involving bulldozers, and the director literally left her hanging from a hook during the climax. The only consolation was that she escaped soon enough to throw a few punches before assembling for the family group picture.

In *Zakhmi Aurat*, Dimple Kapadia was the tough cop (Copadia?) who rode a mean bike and kicked ass. She messed up the criminal careers of Tej Sapru and Puneet Issar (among others) and they attacked her when she was home alone and a standard-issue titillatory rape scene followed. In an action supposed to underline the victim's humiliation, Dimple's trousers were hung from the ceiling fan as the villains went about raping her. And of course, the villains were let off by proving she 'asked for it'.

What followed next was, well, ballsy. Quitting the police force, Dimple formed a group of rape victims and planned revenge. They lured sex offenders into their den (an easy enough task) and castrated them. Chop, chop, chop the team went as all of Dimple's rapists and several other horny bastards woke up without a ball to bounce, much to their considerable dismay.

I suppose there must be some kind of message in this about the impotence of law and/or the Indian male's penis obsession, but I am missing it.

Apart from Dimple, Rekha was the other champion of 'heroine-oriented' roles in the 1980s. In *Phool Bane Angaray*, she was again the victim of the gratuitous Bollywood rape. To avenge her rape and her husband's murder, she—the mother of two—joined the police force. After that, she went hammer and tongs after the villains, even parading a handcuffed Prem Chopra through crowded streets. Unfortunately, she ended up being thwarted by legal loopholes that released most of her arrests. In the climax, Rekha appeared in a *Jhansi ki Rani* avatar—on horseback and wielding a sword—and chopped up the villains with a mix of bombastic *dialoguebaazi* and gruesome swordsmanship.

While on the subject of physically aggressive (don't get ideas now) lady officers, the first name and the last word in action heroines is Vijayashanthi. Dubbed the 'female Amitabh Bachchan', her Telugu film *Karthavyam* was modelled on Kiran Bedi's life, for which she won many awards and which was also a huge hit. The movie was remade in Hindi as *Tejasvini* where the superstar played the title role of Assistant Superintendent of Police Tejasvini Joshi. She was the archetypal supercop who took on pretty much everybody from goons to MPs to her own boss. And in an interesting twist, her love interest was Deepak Malhotra—a model—who had precious little to do in the movie and ended up being the eye candy.

Produced by Subhash Ghai and directed by Mukul Anand, *Trimurti* had a blockbuster star cast of Jackie Shroff, Anil Kapoor and Shah Rukh Khan. This trimurti's mother was Inspector Satyadevi Singh (Priya Tendulkar). She ran into the demonic Kooka[1] (Mohan Agashe) who had killed her husband, in response to which she shot his son dead. She took the fight into

---

[1] *Dreadful Cricket Joke Alert:* Since he was a very bad man, you can say he was a Kooka-burra!

Kooka's den, but ended up being framed by him for murder. And this was while she was pregnant with her third child. After her jail sentence of twenty years, the police officer in her was no more but a badass vendetta seeker had taken shape. Grrr!

Without any examples of ass-kicking ladies in khaki bringing box-office success, policewomen changed a little to become more of undercover agents, detectives or—well—pure eye candy.

In *Khalnayak*, Madhuri Dixit was a cop. Her opening scene was in Nasik Jail (where she was presumably the jailor of the women's cell) and she was the no-nonsense cop in a khaki saree. Her tough-cop routine ended with a slap to two fighting prisoners and she promptly shifted gears thereafter to sing songs with Jackie Shroff.

When her beau was disgraced due to an escaped convict, she went undercover as part of a dancing troupe to catch the *khalnayak*. Anybody who has seen '*Choli ke peechhe kya hai*' would agree this was a brilliant cover for her; meanwhile Inspector Ganga followed her quarry, and taking a leaf out of the Ramayana, left a trail of her jewellery so that her inspector–boyfriend could follow suit. Oh—the things they teach you at Police Training School!

Very soon, her cover was blown and there was a Ramayana-esque debate on whether she was 'pure' or not. A police officer goes undercover to tail a dangerous terrorist and when she is back, the discussion is not on her mission but on her chastity. Obviously, India TV has been around for longer than we think.

From being undercover agents, women officers have made a move towards becoming CSI-style non-uniformed operatives. Leading the pack in sharply cut business suits was Sushmita Sen as ACP Malvika Chauhan, chasing serial killers in *Samay*. Playing a single mom with a demanding law enforcement job, Sushmita Sen looked perfect for the role and the plot built up brilliantly towards a brutal climax. Her natural poise added a dimension to her role as she investigated the murders of a businessman, an actress and a gangster who were murdered at equal intervals (twelve o'clock, three o'clock, six o'clock) and their hands were placed to match the clock hands. Sushmita was shown as an extremely competent police officer with a stellar record at the Police Training Academy as well as during her career. ACP Malvika Chauhan was probably the most competent woman police officer in Bollywood.

Zeher had Shamita Shetty as a senior officer with the Goa police force, who was married to her subordinate (Emraan Hashmi). Frustrated by his wife's success (and bossing), Emraan had an affair with a married woman (Udita Goswami) while his marriage was already on the rocks. With some twists and turns, Shamita was soon investigating the disappearance of a large sum of money recovered from a raid and the death of Udita Goswami—both of which had a lot to do with her husband. In an interesting twist, the woman wasn't the bumbling cop who had to be rescued by the man. It was the man who had his grubby fingers in every shady pie and was seen hastily covering his tracks as the woman went about solving the crime.[2]

BB (Bipasha Basu) is what you could call a CC (Candy Cop) with an athletic figure, super-tight uniform and occasional (half-hearted) attempts at crime-solving. In *Dhoom 2*, she was ACP Sonali Bose—Jai Dixit's (Abhishek Bachchan) batchmate from college, although her utility seemed purely secretarial as she presented the master-thief's future plans while the hero went about exploring the thief's modus operandi. In between all this, she got into hot pants (while on the job) and even clumsily handcuffed herself. (Oh God, someone kill this cliché! On second thoughts, don't.) After a while, she abdicated her role in favour of her twin sister (Monali Bose), who had no police connections and was a bikini-clad surfer in Rio.

Bonus Movies: In *Chor Machaye Shor*, BB was Inspector Ranjita—a bumbling cop and Bobby Deol's love interest. In *Gunaah*, she was Inspector Prabha who went to arrest a criminal (Dino Morea) but got carried away when she saw him bathing and let him escape. (Feminists, cheer for gratuitous male nudity!)

THE TORMENTORS

If we take some supporting actresses, then we have a stellar list of harridans who harried people in jails and outside.
- Kunika in *Gumrah*: Gave Sridevi hell. Slept with fellow police officer Bob Christo.
- Kalpana Iyer in *Anjaam*: Gave Madhuri Dixit hell. Slept with fellow police officer Kiran Kumar.

Wait, how many more of these do you have? Just these two, I promise. The others are different.
- Seema Biswas in *Ek Hasina Thi*: Competent ACP. Chased Urmila Matondkar down after her escape from prison.
- Isha Koppikar in *Kya Kool Hai Hum*: Mentioned only for her name, Urmila Martodkar.
- Neetu Singh in *Besharam*: As Bulbul Chautala, she tormented the hero Ranbir Kapoor along with reel- and real-life husband Chulbul Chautala (Rishi Kapoor).

---

[2] As is often the case with Vishesh Films, *Zeher* was a straight lift from *Out of Time*, a 2003 thriller starring Denzel Washington in the Emraan Hashmi role.

Men of Mystery: 008 Spies

Bollywood has a major handicap in spy movies. The most popular characters are just not made for a martini–bikini caper. Imagine Goldfinger saying, '*Bond, tumhari maa hamare kabze mein hai . . .*' and you have pretty much cooked the International Man of Mystery goose. But despite such formidable problems, whenever the tyranny of a foreign power has threatened the sovereignty of India, we have turned to Shirdi wale Sai Baba. Oh sorry—wrong movie.

Gopal aka Agent 116 in *Farz* (Jeetendra)

Organization: CID, led by David
Task: Finishing off the job started by Agent 303 (bumped off in the opening scenes) of bringing to justice the evil forces of Supremo, a Chinese villain with ghoulish make-up and a Mao Zedong cap.
Gadgets: Jeetendra's white shoes. No, seriously. By singing '*Mast bahaaron ka main aashiq*' and leaping over Babita wearing white shoes, Jeetu donned the Jumping Jack epithet with this movie.
Other Characters: Babita, as Jeetu's love interest, was the daughter of the man who was a pawn in Supremo's hands. While secret agent Jeetu was singing birthday songs for his daughter, Daddy dear was instructing his henchmen to polish Jeetu off. Talk about moral dilemmas!

> *Bonus Movie*: In a tribute to the agent killed in the opening sequence, Jeetendra borrowed his number and played the title role of ***Bond 303***, another spy caper with terrorist missiles.

Sunil in *Ankhen* (Dharmendra)

Organization: A counterterrorism ring, led by Nazir Hussain
Task: To polish off a weapon-smuggling ring wreaking havoc on India. Complications appeared

in the form of Sunil's nephew being taken hostage and a spy planted in his household. And oh—his cover was blown. Par for the course.

Gadgets: Giant radio system (hidden behind a revolving bookcase). Hidden cameras. Transmitters with footlong antennae. Spiked walls closing in. (PS: That last one was the villain's accessory.)

Other Characters: Mala Sinha as an old flame of Dharmendra (whom he had met during a training mission in Japan) who popped up in Beirut as a dancer in a cabaret troupe, which was actually an Indian spy ring.

Inspector Vijay in *The Great Gambler* (Amitabh Bachchan)

Organization: An unnamed law enforcement agency

Task: Getting back blueprints of a top-secret 'atomic power' gun (worth $500,000 in the international market), which were handed over to the villains by a debt-ridden government officer. The debt happened due to major gambling losses, precipitated by Inspector Vijay's lookalike Jay (who was the titular card shark).

Gadgets: A super-duper video-coder where messages were transmitted through a cabaret dancer's dance moves and the lights blinking behind her. I kid you not when I say that a 'stenographer' sat behind a massive panel of switches 'composing' the code, a recorded version of which reached international operatives in the guise of a dance video.[1]

Other Characters: Neetu Singh in tight tops. Zeenat Aman in a gondola. A character called Marconi (Sujit Kumar) speaking in Italian-accented Hindi about pizza being an 'Italian paratha'.

Gunmaster G9 (Mithun Chakraborty)

Long before sequels became popular and the 'franchise' word wasn't bandied about, Ravikant Nagaich[2] made two movies with Gunmaster G9.

Organization: CBI, headed by Iftekhar

Task: *Surakksha* was all about salvaging a map of diamond mines and protecting India from an artificial tsunami brought about by Shiv Shakti Organization's atomic weather controller. *Wardat* was even more fantastic, requiring to protect the world from giant locusts (made of yellow plastic) unleashed by the bad guys who wanted to destroy crops and make a killing by black-marketeering grains.

---

[1] Look through the Veena Malik videos carefully. Is there a message being passed on?

[2] Ravikant Nagaich is something of a Dadasaheb Phalke of spy movies. His directorial debut was *Farz*. He brought Jeetendra back again as Agent 116 in *Raksha*. He seemed to be in love with the number 116 as he made a Telugu movie called *Gudachari 116*. Not to mention that all his heroes were called variations of Gopal and Gopi.

Gadgets: Nothing but the best for '*CBI ka keemti nagina*'. Flying car with parachute. Car with Gunmaster G9 emblazoned on it. Telescopes to spy on card games. Stun guns. Cigarette lighters with sleeping gas.

Other Characters: A bevy of beauties who insisted on throwing themselves at G9 at every possible opportunity. Including one who tied up G9 and gave a cat-and-mouse analogy ('*Choohe ko maarne se pehle billi usse jee bharke khelti hai*'). And two super-villains—a hunchback called Jambola (*Wardat*) and the world's greatest scientist, Dr Shiva (*Surakksha*).

Agent Vinod (Mahendra Sandhu)

Organization: CBI, headed by K.N. Singh

Task: Rescuing scientist (Nazir Hussain), who had developed a formula that could neutralize 'atom bombs' (and make India powerful), from the clutches of the Bichhoo gang, led by Iftekhar. The Bichhoo gang's members had scorpion tattoos on their thumbs and committed suicide when apprehended.

Gadgets: Beeping transmitter in wristwatch. Back-firing pistol. Guns hidden in sleeves to fire when asked to put 'hands up'. GPS trackers in rings and lockets (working within a ten-mile radius). Micro-bomb that looked like a vitamin tablet. But when you have '*lomdi ka dimaag, sher ka jigar*', you hardly need gadgets.

Other Characters: Jagdeep played James Bond, who ended up becoming our hero's comic sidekick. Yes, Agent Vinod is *that* badass!

> *Bonus Movie*: Director Sriram Raghavan doffed a cap at this classic by making a spy caper with the same name. While trying to retrieve a nuclear bomb, Saif Ali Khan's aliases were Anthony Gonsalves, Vinod Khanna, Freddy Cambatta, Kapil Dev and—in an affectionate tribute—Mahendra Sandhu.

Mr Bond (Akshay Kumar)

Organization: Indian Police Service. Wait a minute, how does that make him a spy? *Arre* baba, what else do you call a man whose name is Bond?

Task: Rescue hundreds of children who had been kidnapped by international don Dragon and his twin brother Daaga (Pankaj Dheer in a double role).

Gadgets: Mr Bond's libido.

Other Characters: This movie was the Yellow Pages of starlets in 1990s' Bollywood. To establish the Casanova image of Bond, every starlet who even drove past Filmistan was recruited to participate in bikini-clad song sequences.

Arun Sharma in *The Hero: Love Story of a Spy* (Sunny Deol)

Organization: RAW, led by Pradeep Rawat (of *Ghajini* fame)

Task: Foil Operation Nishan, ISI's attempts to procure a nuclear bomb. Travel from Kashmir to Canada locking horns with the ISI chief (played by Amrish Puri) and assorted jihadis to save India from a nuclear Armageddon.

Gadgets: Disguises, actually. Sunny Deol appeared as multiple characters, such as Ajay Chakrabarti (a fat Bengali undersecretary), Major Batra (a heroic soldier posted in Kashmir) and Wahid Khan (an Indonesian nuclear scientist).

Other Characters: The Hero's love story involved Reshma (Preity Zinta), a Kashmiri girl who was given up for dead in an operation. And Shaheen[3] (played by Priyanka Chopra), whose love for The Hero remained unrequited.

Avinash Singh Rathore aka Tiger in *Ek Tha Tiger* (Salman Khan)

Organization: RAW, led by Girish Karnad

Task: Monitoring a scientist in Dublin who was suspected of selling missile technology to Pakistan. And falling in love with a Pakistani girl.

Gadgets: *Biff* *Pow* *Kaboom* *Dhishoom*. How dare you suggest Bhai needs gadgets to take care of his enemies? Bhai took apart half of Iran with just a pistol. Bhai stopped a tram with a jacket. Bhai broke Katrina's heart with a flick of his eyebrow. Bhairoxx, okay?

Other Characters: Katrina Kaif as the scientist's sexy caretaker who seemed to be a lot more than what met the eye. (And what met the eye was a lot too. Sigh.)

Hamara spy kaisa ho? Sallu bhai jaisa ho!

---

[3] *Topical Trivia*: Shaheen is the name of Pakistan's short-range ballistic missiles capable of carrying nuclear payloads.

RAW-gh and Tough Alert: After Sallu-bhai's glamorous act as the RAW agent, two gritty and—well—raw films put forward faces of real Indian spies. Or did they?

Shoojit Sircar's **Madras Café** had John Abraham battling personal tragedy and professional failure in the backdrop of India's ill-fated Sri Lankan initiative. Behind enemy lines, he battled traitors and terrorists alike in a bid to save his prime minister.

The RAW agents in Nikhil Advani's **D-Day** were also entrusted with saving lives— by ending one. Irrfan was the deep covert agent in Pakistan, out to assist RAW agents Arjun Rampal and Huma Qureshi in bringing a notorious gangster (Rishi Kapoor) to justice in India.

HONOURABLE MENTION

For both retro value as well as having a leading heroine playing a spy, we have to go back to **Samadhi,** one of the biggest hits of the 1950s. Ashok Kumar played a rich industrialist who joined Netaji Subhash Chandra Bose's INA. He also fell in love with Nalini Jaywant—whose sister turned her into a spy for the British citing their father's murder by the Japanese (who were Bose's allies). Plans that were being carried by Ashok Kumar were stolen and the INA met with serious defeats because of that. Of course, the spy had a change of heart and the world was good once again.

Rakshak: 10 Bodyguards

The hazard-laden landscapes of Bollywood movies are full of terrible trolls, unending ups and downs and vicious villains. To navigate this zone—whether you are an heiress or a tycoon—a bodyguard becomes almost a necessity.

In *Hum Kisise Kum Naheen*, Kajal Kiran was the millionaire's daughter who was wooed by two heroes in succession—a childhood love (Tariq) and a millionaire playboy (Rishi Kapoor). During both the romances, she was chaperoned by not one, not two, not three but four bald-headed bodyguards. These nameless, wordless souls were hoodwinked all the time so that the lead pairs could sing songs that would eventually make R.D. Burman a legend. The car the bodyguards were in was diverted. Laxatives were dropped in their tea. They didn't help their cause either by not being the brightest lighthouses in the harbour.

'If you are the daughter of a don, your father's enemies are your enemies.'—Old Bollywood saying.

When Parveen Babi landed in Bombay, the plot of *Amar Akbar Anthony* was already as convoluted as the Saki Naka traffic. Because the enemies of her father (Pran) were trying to kidnap her, protecting her became the duty of Zebesco (played by Yusuf Khan) who could bend iron rods with bare hands. He lived up to this 'iron man' reputation by beating up a completely drunk Anthony Gonsalves at an Easter party. After that, he abandoned his bodyguard duties and tried to kidnap Parveen Babi himself. He did this (albeit with a few complications) and was duly rewarded with marriage to Parveen in the climax. Well, almost.

Bonus Character: Zebesco was obviously Manmohan Desai's Favourite Bodyguard Name since Manek Irani (popular 'opening goon' of the 1980s) in *Mard* also had the same name. He was lodged in the back seat of Amrita Singh's convertible since her propensity to run over people was very high, thus necessitating protection.

In *Namak Halaal*, Amitabh Bachchan was the bodyguard of Raja sahab (Shashi Kapoor). To be dead accurate, he wasn't employed to be a bodyguard but became one when people realized his loyalty was much better than his English.

Of course, the standard complications of estranged mothers, estranged grandfathers and strange villains (Satyen Kappu, of all people) arose. Amitabh's crowning moment of success came when he managed to apprehend a masked assassin, who had sneaked in while public attention was diverted by Parveen Babi singing '*Raat baaki, baat baaki*'. But he didn't get to say his job description. Parveen Babi said it, during a breathless interval in the song: '*Main tumhe nahin marne doongi, Raja . . .*'

Amitabh's bona fide bodyguard role came much later in *Ek Ajnabee*, where he was an ex-army officer enlisted to protect a little girl under the risk of kidnapping. His initial refusal to befriend the girl—due to tragic experiences in the past—eventually dissolved. But the girl got kidnapped and Amitabh Bachchan put on his vigilante avatar to take apart pretty much half of Bangkok to get her back. In this remake of the Hollywood thriller *Man on Fire*, AB brought his usual flair in depicting the emotionally traumatized character who seeks refuge in alcohol and finally redeems himself by becoming the saviour of the young girl.

Major Ramprasad Sharma was instructed by the army to become a bodyguard to the general's daughter since she was likely to be kidnapped in order to stop Operation Milap (an exchange of prisoners between India and Pakistan). Major Ram took on the identity of a student in the girl's school, which also had his estranged brother as a student. Not one to shirk duty, he screamed *Main Hoon Na* and dived right in. He shadowed the girl during the day. He had a security team posted outside her hostel every night. He sent in regular reports. He neutralized the assailants once outside a cinema (using a rickshaw for support) and once after a prom night (using Sushmita Sen for support). All in all, he was a rockstar.

In *Agneepath*, mafia don Vijay Dinanath Chavan realized his enemies might use his sister (Neelam) for leverage. So when he met a conscientious coconutseller, he promptly enlisted him as his sister's bodyguard.

Okay, one second now. Mafia don. Thousands of henchmen. All willing to die for him. Well-armed enemies. So, a sickle-wielding coconutseller was the best option as bodyguard. Right, got it. Let us move on.

Mithun Chakraborty—as Krishnan Iyer MA—turned out to be a perfect bodyguard who danced disco–Bharatanatyam at his ward's college party, hung on to the bumper of a car used to kidnap her and finally, fell in love with her. And falling in love with the ward is pretty much mandatory in the Bollywood bodyguard's job description.

Just as Sunny Deol fell in love with Pooja Bhatt in *Angrakshak*.

Sunny Deol—he of the 2.5-kilo hands—was enlisted to protect Pooja Bhatt, daughter of a politician. In the hustle of shady politics, bustle of shadier business and muscle of shadiest goons, a threat to the politician's family was anticipated.

They fell in love. The villains struck. Pooja got kidnapped. Sunny got injured. He swore vengeance. Pooja's dead body was discovered. Her father got elected in a sympathy wave. Waiddaminit—did you say Pooja Bhatt's dead body? Well yes, that means there is an obvious twist in the tale. If you want to find out what it is, low volume on the TV and a cheap VCD of the movie are recommended.

Bodyguards falling in love with their protectees are common enough though the situations are imaginative and diverse. Or not.

Mahesh Bhatt's *Dastak* was about a girl called Sushmita becoming Miss Universe and then getting an endorsement contract with Emami. Errr—that wasn't the crux of the movie, which was more concerned with a crazed lover (Sharad Kapoor) stalking Miss Universe with letters soaked in blood, crank calls soaked in passion and songs soaked in *jhankaar* beats. Promptly, a police inspector (Mukul Dev) was requisitioned and put on Sushmita's security detail. He ran helter-skelter at many false alarms and some true ones as well. The movie moved from Mumbai to Seychelles to the dark den of the psychotic villain as Sushmita whimpered and simpered while the bodyguard hemmed and hawed. Achha—so who played the role of Sushmita the beauty queen? You had to ask? Sigh.

Bodyguard started off with Salman protecting Katrina Kaif during a song. What that song and the opening fight didn't do for his reputation, Sharat Saxena's opening speech did: '*Dus guard ke jagah ek bodyguard . . . Kaam ki guarantee warranty ke saath . . . Jahan loyalty ki baat hai, wahan yeh royalty ko bhi nahin chhodte . . .*' With a name like Lovely Singh, this explosive introduction was mandatory.

From here, he was entrusted with saving Kareena Kapoor's life and, needless to say, love blossomed in a convoluted anonymous style. Kareena pretended to be someone else while calling Salman and soon both of them had fallen in love: Kareena with the real-life Salman and Salman with the Kareena of the anonymous phone calls. If this is sounding mind-numbingly complex, let me assure you it was even worse on screen. But then, who am I to argue with the 100-crore box-office collection?

Bonus Trivia: In the movie, Salman is seen wearing the logo of Tiger Security, which is his real-life bodyguard Shera's company.

Talking of undying loyalty, Vishal Bhardwaj's *Maqbool* not only had a bodyguard but the silent giant was an important pivot in the plot. Mafia don Jahangir aka Abbaji (Pankaj Kapur) had Usman (Firdaus Irani), to whom he owed his life. In front of his mistresses and cronies, he took great pride in stripping Usman and displaying the bullet wounds Usman had got trying to save him. As he mumbled '*Byculla mein chhe, Kolhapur mein teen*', his mistress (Tabu) dared teetotaller Usman to drink directly from a liquor bottle in a perverse test of loyalty. His refusal was overruled by Abbaji and he gulped down the raw alcohol. This heavy drink meant that night Usman was indisposed and Abbaji was left unprotected. But then, why would he need protection in his own household?

BODYGUARDS WHO FAILED

Here's a smattering of movies where the heroes or the villains managed to thwart the efforts of the bodyguard(s).

- *Aakhree Raasta*: When Amitabh Bachchan decides to cut down his enemies—people who raped and murdered his wife—everything in his path becomes collateral damage. Even if it is another Amitabh. AB Sr killed Dalip Tahil, Bharat Kapoor and Sadashiv Amrapurkar as AB Jr tried his damned best to stop him.
- *Jurm*: You could argue Vinod Khanna did not fail to protect his ward (Sangeeta Bijlani), but after ending up in bed with her, he was certainly no longer the right person to trail her. Add to that a sulking wife and you have the perfect recipe for a thriller–soap opera.
- *Shola Aur Shabnam*: Govinda is out to kill Mohnish Behl. Mohnish Behl is under house arrest amidst tight security. Mohnish Behl is dying to get out of the house. Mohnish Behl gets news that Govinda has been killed. Mohnish Behl jumps out for a party. BEEEP . . . guess who spread the wrong news?
- *Badshah*: In the twist-o-rama that is typical of Abbas–Mustan, the circle of Chief Minister Raakhee's bodyguards had been infiltrated and they asked SRK to come in and kill her while they looked the other way. SRK obviously had other plans but they were different from the bodyguards'. Let's just say the bodyguards failed.
- *Madras Cafe*: John Abraham played a tormented RAW agent who was entrusted with the security detail of the Indian prime minister and failed. The details of the assassination—the south Indian small town, the Sri Lankan suicide squad, the young leader making a political comeback—were gut-wrenchingly close to reality.

Heavenly Bodies: 10 Unusual Gods

Released in 1975, *Jai Santoshi Maa* kicked off a frenzy of worshipping the goddess (that continues till today) and also a stampede to make religious movies. While none attained its level of popularity,[1] movies based on mythological and divine themes gained momentum. But gods in Bollywood didn't always have the mythological trappings of borrowed-from-theatre costumes and highfalutin Sankritized Hindi. They often eschewed one or both and became 'cool'. Or at least they tried to.

The Hindu concept of Yamraj as the Custodian of Death working with his minions (yamdoots[2]) and coming to 'collect' the souls of dead people is a fertile ground for stories and movies.

In *Vaah! Life Ho Toh Aisi*, Sanjay Dutt was Yamraj MA ('*Maut Ka Ayojak*') driving a red jalopy in the skies, who dropped into Lilavati Hospital to collect Shahid Kapoor's soul after his death. He worked with a swanky computer interface to know about his victims' death status that counted down to the exact moment of death. The death was followed by the usual requests for extension of life, Yamraj's acquiescing to give back life (with some riders) and some bumbling around as invisible 'souls'.

In *Lok Parlok*, Jeetendra was killed and he landed up in heaven. While heaven was similar to that of popular belief, the gods were strangely malleable to human machinations. Soon, Jeetu had exhorted the yamdoots to go on a strike and persuaded Yamraj himself to go on a vacation. Yamraj (Prem Nath) and his bookkeeper Chitragupta (Deven Varma) landed up in Martyalok (Bombay, to be specific) causing deaths to stop in their absence. Add to that, references to the Emergency, the interrogation of Yamraj about his role in Yudhishthir's birth, a voluptuous Padma Khanna as Menaka and you had one cracker of a satire. Even though the

---

[1] *Jai Santoshi Maa* was one of the top-grossing movies of the decade.

[2] There is a joke in this somewhere about recklessly driving Yamaha and Rajdoot bikes but I cannot find it.

script was a bit over the top and the overall look garish, **Lok Parlok** nevertheless was quite a clever film on gods and their mortal ways.

Vinay Pathak was the wannabe Dhirubhai Ambani in **Oh My God**. He was the embodiment of 'Be careful of what you wish for you, you may get it,' since his prayers to God were answered everywhere. Saurabh Shukla played the unlikely God and appeared as a businessman, a havaldar, a lotteryseller and a doctor—offering opportunities to Vinay Pathak literally at every street corner. What would you do if a slightly shady lottery ticketseller prodded you to buy a certain ticket while you wanted to buy a different one? Yes, that's exactly what Vinay did. He ignored the bugger.

A low-budget effort with decent performances, **Oh My God** did not get too much attention but did ensure that Akshay Kumar's home production a few years down the line had a more convoluted title.

Paresh Rawal's hit Gujarati play *Kanji Virudh Kanji* was remade into **OMG: Oh My God**—with Akshay playing an avatar of Lord Krishna himself. The premise was hilarious: Paresh Rawal—as a Gujarati businessman—filed a cased against God for losses incurred due to an earthquake. God had to answer the summons and arrived in blazing style atop a shining bike and rotating his keychain as a surrogate for the Sudarshan chakra. Akshay Kumar, who produced the movie, turned vegetarian for the duration of the movie's shooting at his mother's behest. Playing God was no mean task and this preparation was probably his *mannat* for the movie's success.

An acclaimed Girish Karnad play was made into **Agni Varsha**, a movie which opened with an epic yagna to appease Indra, the god of rains. After a lot of confusion about the priest of the yagna, his two sons, their better halves and the better halves' lovers, the movie came to an end. In the end, Amitabh Bachchan appeared—as Lord Indra—with the promise of one boon for Aravasu who had to choose between the love of his life and genuinely helping someone. In a short last-scene cameo, the Big B performed the godly duties of dispensing advice and fulfilling wishes. He had a glowing halo, a flowing mane, a spiky crown and shiny robes to complete his divine countenance. Thankfully, he didn't appear in a white suit.

The 'modern' God—when he appears—cannot avoid the white suit.

In **Thoda Pyaar Thoda Magic**, it was Rishi Kapoor who donned the spotless suit as he pondered the fate of four kids whose parents had been killed in a road accident and who were entrusted to the care of the guy (Saif Ali Khan) who was driving the car. After fingering his cool goatee, Rishi Kapoor decided to enlist the help of his favourite angel, Geeta (Rani

Mukherji). She turned out to be a mix of Mary Poppins and *The Sound of Music*'s Maria, who managed to solve earthly problems in a jiffy. God reappeared later when Saif and the kids were all enamoured by the angel and wanted her to stay. What do you think he did? Well, the same producer—with more than a passing interest in the angel—called his next movie *Rab Ne Bana Di Jodi*.

After Rishi Kapoor, it was the turn of Amitabh Bachchan to don the white suit. He was the eponymous divine in *God Tussi Great Ho*, a pretty faithful copy of *Bruce Almighty*. The Big B—used to the epithet for most of his career anyway—had to contend with Salman Khan's harangues and finally gave him control of the universe for ten days. He moved about in the clouds and on thin air (though not on water), in computer-generated sylvan surroundings of waterfalls and mountains as he counselled Salman on handling his job, his girlfriend and the universe. He managed to do a bit of a PR job for Himself when He delivered the standard internet forwards (God made the world, man made borders, blah blah), and convinced Salman not to shoot blackbucks.[3]

> *Bonus Fact*: In a strange bout of schizophrenia, the movie managed to doff a hat to AB in his human avatar as well when Salman asked Priyanka Chopra, *'Bachchan se tujhe mila doon, aa chalti kya?'*

In *Hello Brother*, Salman Khan was killed but returned as a ghost, only visible to the guy (Arbaaz Khan) who was saved by transplanting the former's heart. At the end, Salman appeared as an angel (complete with white gown and wings) perched on a cloud and spying on Arbaaz's *suhaag raat*. He was called back by God, using the bait of the many nubile angels (not seventy-two virgins, hopefully!) that inhabit heaven. The baritone (called 'Heavenly Voice' in the end titles) belonged to Amitabh Bachchan. Who else?

Salman and God have an ongoing relationship.

Apart from *God Tussi Great Ho* and *Hello Brother*, he met God again in *Hello* (based on Chetan Bhagat's *One Night @ the Call Centre*). In the novel, the author 'met' God and the story was 'given' to him. In the movie, Salman was the superstar waiting in an airport lounge when Katrina Kaif walked in. She offered to tell him a story on the condition that he would make a movie on it if he liked it. The story had a phone-call from God (literally) and several things only the protagonists could have known. When quizzed how she knew the story, she

---

[3] Yeah, right.

just gave one of her heart-melting smiles and melted away into the night. And *Hello* became probably the only Hindi movie which had a female incarnation of God.

As I said, Salman and God have an ongoing relationship.[4]

There is no heaven. There is no hell. There is no God. After you die, you go up an ancient, creaking lift and get sucked into a great bureaucratic mess where your papers are processed before you are passed into a void. This is what your afterlife is going to be, if you believe *Fatso*.

Purab Kohli's character died; after standing for ages in serpentine queues among boards that said 'Suicide' or 'Senior Citizens', he was told that he wasn't supposed to die and it was all a big mistake. The yamdoot (who looked more like a peon) had brought the wrong soul. When Purab sought redressal, he was taken upwards first to Regional Manager Rahul Vora and then to General Manager Jehangir Kakariya. He was told that while his soul was untangling the red tape, his body had already been cremated so he couldn't go back. Aghast at this injustice, he demanded to be taken to God. The 'managers' replied, '*Bhagwaan toh hain nahin . . .*' And thus ended the saga of God in Bollywood.

Purab Kohli stands in a queue to meet God. In Fatso.

---

[4] Nudge nudge wink wink.

Not-so-scary Movies: 10 Ghosts in
Non-horror Movies

A lady in white carrying a candle and singing a song in Lata Mangeshkar's voice in a foggy jungle—as an overcoat-clad hat-wearing hero chased her—was one kind of ghost. The Brothers Ramsay were the purveyors of the other kind of ghosts who had macabre scars, gigantic red eyes and gargantuan claws with which they killed bathing side-heroines. In between these two kinds, we had the ghosts who were comic, romantic, sentimental, friendly and only occasionally scary (that too, unintentionally).[1] They were like just another character in comic, romantic or sentimental movies who could be seen/heard/felt by only a select few and caused bonhomie or hullabaloo by turns.

Villain killed heroine. Hero wanted to prove it and discovered a lookalike. The lookalike was supposed to pretend to be the dead heroine and extract a confession from the villain. Everything went as per plan—the lights went out, lightning flashed and anklets reverberated. The lookalike walked in and—with much drama—got the villain to confess. Except that she knew much more than she should have known. How so? On cue, the lookalike walked in—she had got delayed due to some unforeseen situation. As the hero processed this information, the first lookalike vanished into thin air. She was the ghost of the dead heroine, returning to take revenge.

Madhumati (Vyjayanthimala) was the first to have this ghostly trick and then tribute-factory *Om Shanti Om* recreated the sequence with Deepika Padukone. Both heroines were, well, deadly in their roles.

---

[1] There seems to be a preponderance of this kind of ghost since the 1990s. Probably Demi Moore and Patrick Swayze's runaway hit, *Ghost*, inspired the slew of friendly ghosts.

Probably the first *Ghost* remake was **Pyaar Ka Saaya**—with a hyper-talkative Amrita Singh essaying the Whoopi Goldberg role while Rahul Roy and Sheeba were the lead players with identical hair styles. Mohnish Behl was the baddie. The story—a Xerox copy of the original—managed to sneak in several desi twists including a 'sexy' song in which Rahul Roy's ghost 'occupied' Amrita Singh's body and got into pretty serious clinches with Sheeba, making it a quasi-lesbian sequence. And you thought ghost movies were simple stuff?

There was also a paradoxical climactic fight where Rahul's ghost managed to land thumping punches on Mohnish Behl while Mohnish's fists passed clear through him. At the end of this unequal battle (for which Rahul was coached by another ghost, Avtar Gill), Mohnish too was killed and six Dementor-like yamdoots sucked him away to, presumably, hell.

'If you disturb the dormant spirits in a graveyard, they will come out.'—Old Bollywood Saying.

In **Chamatkar**, a village simpleton (Shah Rukh Khan) took shelter in a cemetery and awakened a ghost (Naseeruddin Shah). He emerged out of his grave wearing a mustard (eww!) overcoat to the accompaniment of laughter, smoke and bad special effects. Man needed ghost for his earthy pursuits (earn money, get girl, etc.). Ghost needed man for his spiritual ones (clear name, help estranged family, etc.). They formed a team that fought goons, played cricket matches, protected college land and swept women off their feet (sometimes literally).

Subtle Mythology Alert: Naseeruddin Shah came back from the dead to atone for his past sins, thanks to the virtues of his wife, named Savitri.

Raj Malhotra came to Gurukul to study and fell in love with the headmaster Narayan Shankar's daughter. The headmaster believed in *anushaasan*, forbade the romance and rusticated Raj for good measure. The daughter committed suicide. The movie didn't end here though. It started hereafter . . .

In **Mohabbatein**, Shah Rukh Khan returned to Gurukul as cool violin teacher Raj Aryan and proceeded to infuse Romance-ov vodka in the martinet. He played matchmaker to three students and was assisted by his dreamy-eyed girlfriend. Waiddaminit, didn't you say the girl committed suicide? Well, yes. The ethereal, ephemeral Aishwarya Rai was a ghost for the greater part of the movie. In her guest appearance, she appeared only during SRK's dreamy-eyed monologues and songs as he went about defying his bête noire. You could argue that she existed only in his imagination and was, therefore, not a ghost in the truest sense of the word. But face it, you are saying that only because you don't want to call such a beautiful woman a *bhootni!*

Aks was a tale of good and evil as an upright police officer (Amitabh Bachchan) chased an evil criminal (Manoj Bajpai). After the criminal was killed, his 'spirit' took over the police officer's body. It became a perverse retelling of the Bhagavad Gita ('*na koi marta hai, na koi maarta hai*') as the imperishable soul of a man just took residence in a different body. An evil soul's partial control of a good man's body led to crimes being committed for which the good man was blamed. The evil man's moll started believing the change. The good man's wife didn't want to believe what her husband was turning into. As the evil soul tried to complete his agenda, it eventually boiled down to a climax in a surreal wasteland during an eclipse (which had its own connotations for this 'spirit change' operation).

In *Hello Brother*, Salman the courier boy (unambiguously named Hero) of A2Z Courier got bumped off by his boss (Shakti Kapoor) when he found out about the narcotics trade his boss was running. When he got killed, a police officer (Arbaaz Khan) also got shot in the heart and Hero's heart was transplanted to save him. In traditional Bollywood style, not only did Hero's emotions (hots for Rani Mukherji, colds for everyone else) get transplanted into the inspector's heart, he also became the only person who could see and hear Hero. Cue drug-busting with spooky help. As all got settled in filmi style, Shakti Kapoor got picked up in a great hellish ball of fire and Hero—as dead heroes have been before him—got teleported to heaven by a white starry, milky way.

Ghosts form formidable teams with kids. In *Bhootnath*, it was Amitabh Bachchan who played the title role aka Kailash Nath. He died an accidental death and did not get a proper funeral as his son had abandoned him.[2] Therefore, he haunted his own mansion—Kailash Villa—and scared everyone till he met his match in Banku, a little boy who came to stay there. The two—after the usual round of tiffs—formed an unlikely team that took on bullies, principals, thieves and unsuspecting passers-by with Bhootnath's magical powers.

Finally, the prodigal son returned to complete his father's last rites and Bhootnath got mukti from his worldly ties. The mukti was short-lived when he returned from heaven in (the imaginatively titled) *Bhootnath Returns* to team up with yet another precocious kid (Parth Bhalerao) and fight larger battles. This time, Bhootnath became Booth-Nath and stood against a villainous politician (Boman Irani) in the elections. No prizes for guessing who won in the end, and with all those speeches, song and dance, Bhootnath's was a party to—well—die for.

If Bhootnath was a rich man, *Bhoot Unkle* was a pirate who stayed in a lighthouse and had a get-up straight out of Captain Jack Sparrow's fashion book. Jackie Shroff's usual unkempt

---

[2] Clearly, the producer was still in love with his earlier hit, *Baghban*.

looks were bolstered with tons of kohl under his eyes. He became friends with a gang of boys, protecting them not only from class bullies but crooked MLAs as well. As is usually the case, Bhoot Unkle helped the gang solve mysteries, reform naughty people, become the favourites of all, and win a cricket series in Australia[3] as the film wound up to a slightly predictable end that was marred by rather tacky special effects.

Ever since Manoj Night Shyamalan made *The Sixth Sense*, a whole new avenue of 'inspiration' opened up for scriptwriters across the globe. In **Hum Tum Aur Ghost**, Arshad Warsi had the same gift, often not realizing that those he encountered were dead. His fiancée attributed his hallucinations to excessive drinking and a generally scattered brain. Boman Irani was a ghost who had an errand for him (bringing in a lost-and-found track), by which a tribute to the original film was paid. He deadpanned to Arshad, 'You see dead people.' Of course, Arshad's girlfriend (Dia Mirza) gave him hell for his eccentric mumblings and threatened to leave him. Till she died herself. And guess who was the one living guy who could see and hear her? Arshad could have become the first man in history who actually listened to what his wife told him . . . but for a silly plot twist. Tchah!

After hanging around with ghosts in *Om Shanti Om*, *Mohabbatein* and *Bhootnath*,[4] SRK decided to become one himself in his home production, **Paheli**. It was the remake of *Duvidha*, made by Mani Kaul during the early years of the parallel cinema movement in India. Amol Palekar directed this ghost movie (not to be confused with 'ghost-directed this movie'), giving it a glamorous avatar that was absent from the older version. SRK played a ghost who could take any form or shape. He took the place of SRK v1.0 (when he left for the city to earn money) and became the husband women dream of. Rani Mukherji was married to v1.0 but she fell in love with v2.0 as did the entire household; v2.0 even managed to impregnate the wife, in an act of spiritual reproduction. When the real SRK returned, he was still the *khadoos* guy nobody liked while the ghost was, well, Casper. It took an old shepherd to solve the identity crisis and separate the ghost from the man.

---

[3] Nope. Not the last one.

[4] Did I mention SRK and Juhi Chawla had guest appearances in **Bhootnath**? Well, I just did. Rather pointless, if I may add.

5

Here, There, Everywhere

Jidhar dekhoon teri tasveer nazar aati hai
—Amitabh Bachchan (in Kishore Kumar's voice) in *Mahaan*

Bollywood doesn't do realism very well. Even real people and real things are breathtakingly unreal in the movies.

This section is about people and things from all around us, who have appeared in Bollywood movies.

Class Acts: 12 Star Teachers

The college is a common setting for—well—college romances. Heroes on the wrong side of forty have often been seen wooing heroines on the right side of forty (but only just) on the corridors and lawns of H.S. College of Arts and Commerce. The dashing leading men and women of Bollywood have almost always been the students, leaving the act of teaching to the supporting cast. Scratching at the blackboard while love notes are being passed around elsewhere is so not fun.

But there have been a few occasions when the stars have gone on to teach as well—sometimes as the strict disciplinarian, sometimes as the friendly guide. Admittedly, the actual act of teaching has been relatively less portrayed in films.

Dharmendra was supposed to be a professor in *Chupke Chupke*. As Parimal Tripathi, he was the star botany professor (aka '*ghaas-phoos ka daktar*'), whose books were read by students far and wide. He played the watchman, the driver, the husband, the friend and occasionally even the fool—but he completely, totally, entirely forgot to play the teacher.

But that's not why this film is in this list. His friend, the professor of English Sukumar Sinha (played brilliantly by Amitabh Bachchan), came in with a twist. He was co-opted to impersonate Parimal Tripathi, as part of an elaborate practical joke. The English professor had to teach botany to a beautiful girl. Despite his heroic attempts to plug *Julius Caesar* as a 'sublime tragedy', he had no option but to memorize the functions of 'corolla' late in the night to conduct tuitions in the morning.

From being a reluctant teacher, Amitabh was pitched into the role of a full-time college professor in the first of his two roles in *Kasme Vaade*. Though, like most Bollywood professors, he was more gainfully engaged in keeping his spoilt brat of a brother (Randhir Kapoor) out of trouble, singing songs on his birthday and wooing his artist girlfriend (Raakhee). Not much

110

screen time was wasted in class, where he was seen teaching Hindi poetry and throwing rogue students out of class for aiming paper planes at him! The lines that he discussed in class were from the poetry of Harivansh Rai Bachchan and these talked about 'the rush of life' ('*jeevan ki aapadhapi mein . . .*').

Bonus Movie: In **Mohabbatein**, though, there was no ambiguity. We knew exactly what AB taught. He taught anushaasan—which he said with as much passion as Baba Ramdev reserves for his breathing exercises. As the headmaster of Gurukul, he seemed to be only the administrative head, for music classes were better left to frivolous people.

Spectacles are props that signify erudition most easily in Bollywood. Anil Kapoor appeared as a schoolteacher in **Andaz** with oversized ones, just in case everyone thought our favourite neighbourhood tapori was not intellectual enough to be associated with academia. But then, studies were strictly avoided as a love triangle between the teacher, his wife (Juhi Chawla) and a student (Karisma Kapoor—in the mandatory minis of a girl student) developed. In any case, Anil Kapoor's erudition would have been terribly misplaced in a school—hilariously named Nalanda—which counted Shakti Kapoor among its students.

Oh—Anil did teach the students how to eliminate terrorists who attack schools: a very useful life lesson.

Playing the title role of **Sir**, Naseeruddin Shah entered the film with a rain song. Err, not the usual kind. He walked into a classroom on a rainy day and immediately escorted his entire class to a glasshouse (presumably, on the college roof) for a session of music. He good-naturedly told his students that they would anyway copy and pass their exams but such a wonderful day was not to be wasted in class.

Where is Naseeruddin Shah and why wasn't he in my college?

He was soon employed by mafia don Velji bhai (Paresh Rawal) to coach his stammering daughter (Pooja Bhatt) into confidence—and that was the end of any classes in college. Dialogue-training Pooja, stopping gang-wars in Mumbai, keeping Paresh Rawal from killing his daughter's suitor *and* going on college picnics constitute a full-time job, you see.

True to his lover-boy image, Shah Rukh Khan has never indulged in any serious teaching. He has once been seen as the games teacher in **Chamatkar**—where his chief contribution to a cricket victory was to negotiate the participation of a ghost (Naseeruddin Shah) to assist his losing team. Before anyone screams blue murder, let me quickly assure her that the opponents were cheating very badly.

On the other occasion, he walked into the Cradle of Educational Discipline, handing out flowers and playing the violin, offering to teach music to students. The headmaster thought it was a waste of time but indulged him anyway. As is normal for Yash Raj heroes with violins and smart pullovers, SRK floored the entire school with his music and held open-air classes with many students till... till he gave the heroes the bright idea of eloping with their lady-loves.

Chandni Chopra: the chemistry teacher with a great physique

From being a reluctant teacher, SRK went on to become an even more reluctant student when he—as Major Ram—went undercover to guard the general's daughter in **Main Hoon Na**. Part of his reluctance vanished as he landed in picturesque Darjeeling to attend school. The remaining parts vanished when the chemistry teacher, Chandni Chopra, walked in through the school gates. Sushmita Sen turned out to be that teacher we all have crushes on—multiplied by Avogadro's number. She was seen in the posters with a blackboard behind her, but in the film, she did no teaching and was only seen in shimmering chiffons giving grooming tips to Amrita Rao.

If teachers are meant to be crushes, Simi Garewal was the perfect teacher and Rishi Kapoor was the perfect bumbling student. In the first third of **Mera Naam Joker**, she was the 'new teacher'. We were not sure what her subject was because she taught both geometry and PT but she was the go-to madam for holiday camps and life lessons ('laugh at yourself, not others'). Her choreographed fall into a stream and her subsequent disrobing were legends as far as adolescent fantasies go, causing Raju to fall head over heels in love with her. It ended in heartbreak, as such things usually do.

> *Bonus Crush*: In Nagesh Kukunoor's **Rockford**, Nandita Das was the crush-mistress Miss Vegas whose entire role in the film consisted of walking down school corridors chanting 'Good morning' as her devoted students cooked up a storm of sighs. Crushes entail cheesy poems that end only when you realize she is in love with the hunky gym teacher. Oh, the injustice!

Taare Zameen Par is one of the few films where the teacher spent substantial screen time actually doing what he was supposed to do. As the stand-in art teacher Ram Shankar Nikumbh, Aamir Khan directed himself and Darsheel Safary to deliver one of the best adult–child combinations in the history of Bollywood. Appearing only after the interval, the teacher's character was the catalyst in the blooming of the talented dyslexic kid. From letting the child express his talent to coaching him to overcome his disability and from convincing headmasters to counselling parents, Aamir was the teacher-from-heaven.

In **Paathshaala**, Shahid Kapoor was an English teacher at Saraswati Vidya Mandir, seen scrawling William Wordsworth's name (if not his poems) on blackboards. But Wordsworth's poetry was no match for Bollywood lyrics and Shahid was soon doubling as the music teacher and wooing the school nutritionist (Ayesha Takia).[1] Needless to say, music teachers (even part-time ones) are cannon fodder for stern headmasters—in this case Nana Patekar—and a confrontation suitably brought about the climax.

> *Bonus Movie*: While on the topic of Shahid Kapoor, we might as well point out his ex-girlfriend's one teaching assignment. After eloping (and being dumped) in **Jab We Met**, Kareena Kapoor was taken under the wing of a nun and started teaching in a convent. For brief bits within a song, Kareena was shown writing desultorily on the blackboard—before she was rescued by Shahid.

After spending many years as a college student romancing Neetu Singh, Rishi Kapoor returned as maths teacher Santosh Duggal in **Do Dooni Chaar**. The film zipped through the mandatory

---

[1] Ayesha Takia was an inspired choice for playing a nutritionist because she started her career—as a child actor—in a TV commercial for Complan. And while she was the 'Complan Girl', Shahid Kapoor was the 'Complan Boy'.

elements of a middle-class teacher's life—confiscating video games in school, rushing to tuition class, disciplining naughty students, soaking in the adulation of loyal ex-students and maintaining idealism amid the heartbreaks—on his trusted scooter, fondly called Duggal Express. With wife Neetu Singh in an anti-glam but marvellous role, Rishi Kapoor brought a heart-warming dignity to the teacher's character as he constantly balanced his books to make 2 + 2 = 4 (and not 5, as his famous uncle did about two decades earlier).

When education gets contaminated by commerce and politics, only the most idealistic and charismatic of teachers can rescue it. In Prakash Jha's **Aarakshan**, Amitabh Bachchan was Dr Prabhakar Anand, the principal of Shakuntala Thukral Mahavidyalay. He was a teacher who could walk out of a job for his principles as well as make Bernoulli's Theorem look really simple to everybody. Partly based on the person who started Super 30 (where meritorious students from disadvantaged backgrounds are still given free tuition for the IIT entrance), Amitabh's character was really the ideal teacher—strict yet kind, serious yet approachable, solid yet fun. As he kept saying in the film—'QED' (Quite Easily Done).

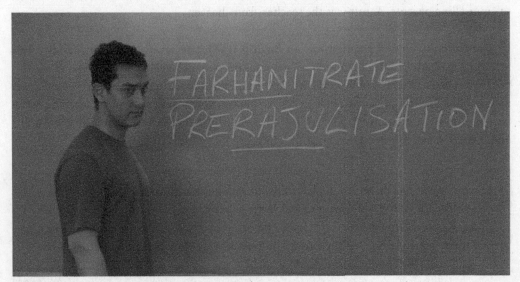

Instead of a teacher, sometimes a student asks tough questions. Aamir Khan in 3 Idiots.

In the Classroom: 10 Blackboards

Stars have been students. Stars have been teachers. But what were their subjects? What was going on in some of these classrooms can easily be gauged from the blackboards and their content. Except that when we have the charisma of a superstar in front of the blackboard, the content on it becomes rather secondary.

One of the earliest blackboards appeared in *Shree 420* when Nargis taught her roadside class some riddles with the '*Ichak dana bichak dana*' song. In response to cute riddles, the children screamed out the answers and Nargis drew them on the board. The four answers—*anaar*, *mirchi*, *bhutta* and *mor*—were drawn with considerable finesse and one can surmise that Nargis was a pretty good artist (and no stunt artists were involved).

In Gulzar's *Kitaab*, Master Raju (a 'veteran' of child roles) put in a wonderful performance as the sensitive yet naughty kid. Obviously, a large part of the film was set in the school and the blackboard provided an apt background to the pranks and lessons. The first time we saw a blackboard was when the English teacher was explaining the 'active–passive' voices. On the blackboard, he had written: 'The cat caught the rat. The rat was caught by the cat.' He was explaining it when a prank disrupted the lesson. Soon entered the inimitable Keshto Mukherjee—a newly married Hindi teacher—and somebody had written on the blackboard, '*Kahiye Panditji, suhaag raat kaisi kati? Mazaa ayaa?*' This rather precocious query led to the principal landing up in the class and a fresh problem erupting at our little hero's doorstep.

Mr India cranked up its Science Quotient with scientist Professor Sinha (Ashok Kumar). He was an assistant to Dr Verma, the inventor of the formula for invisibility. When he wasn't assisting Dr Verma or escaping from Fu Manchu (one of Mogambo's many henchmen), he taught 'science' at the college. If we go by the blackboard behind him in class, what he taught was a fantastic potpourri of all conceivable branches of science. A complicated formula was written as the 'Value of Particle Disturbance'. The 'Theory of Molecular Distance' happily coexisted in close proximity to 'Double Helix' as did an elaborate formula of an organic compound. And if all that failed to stupefy you, there was the subtle ode to the movie's producer—'Boney's Law of Spatial Time–Space Coordinate'!

In *Afsana Pyar Ka*, Aamir Khan and Neelam were both part of Viju Khote's Physics class where he dwelled on the subject of 'light'. He started off with a mistake where he claimed the speed of light to be '1 crore 86 lakh miles per second' (which is exactly hundred times the actual speed). While his monotonous lecture meandered on and the students passed glances and love letters, we could see some diagrams of lenses converging light rays and elaborate formulae worked out on the board. Thankfully, the professor stopped at the factual error and didn't try to explain those concepts to us.

If only we paid attention to the stuff written on blackboards when gorgeous teachers taught us, the world would have been more knowledgeable. In a fleeting sequence in *The Dirty Picture*, Vidya Balan played the role of a voluptuous teacher, whose saree *pallu* never seemed to stay on her shoulder. As she tried to control her clothing, we could see—if we wanted to, that is—$P_1V_1 = P_2V_2$, commonly referred to as Boyle's Law. The law defines the inverse relationship between the absolute pressure (P) and volume (V) of a gas, provided the temperature is constant within a closed system. Vidya's volume and shape were far easier to comprehend than this.

The other shapely teacher—literally one to have great chemistry with her students—was Chandni Chopra of *Main Hoon Na*. Sushmita Sen almost glided into her class and our hearts with a name and wardrobe straight out of Yash Chopra films. As she taught the class in the only one academic session she took in the film, complicated chemical word problems filled the board: 'A sample of pure calcium weighing 1.35 g was qualitatively converted to 1.88 g of CaO. If the atomic weight of oxygen is taken to be 16, what is the atomic weight of calcium?' Whoa.

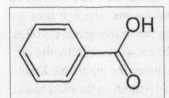

The chemical formula of benzoic acid adorned the remaining part of the board—though no reference was ever made to it. And thank God for that!

Physics was taught by the hilariously disgusting spit-firing teacher (Satish Shah) and then his khadoos replacement (Sunil Shetty). Satish Shah's first class had an unconnected definition ('A phase change or phase transition is an isothermal and isobaric process') on the blackboard while Sunil Shetty's class had the diagram of an electrical circuit including voltmeter, ammeter, external resistance, internal resistance and EMF drawn on the.

In *Taare Zameen Par*, Ishaan Awasthi (Darsheel Safary) went from one tyrannical teacher to another, depicted by a series of blackboards that went from incomprehensible to unbearable to, finally, liberating. It all started in the English class of his Mumbai school, where 'An adjective is a word that describes a noun', examples of 'the red ball, the lazy boy, the bright sun' were inscribed on the board while its left side ominously announced 'Homework'.

The boards came back with a vengeance in the Panchgani school he was then sent to. An arts class had a cube and some pitchers drawn on the board. A comical English teacher appeared on the scene with a plethora of definitions (adjectives, nouns, pronouns, verbs) written on the board behind him. There was some maths (35÷8, 54÷2, 49÷7, 36÷4) and some Hindi before the admonition of the teachers (IDIOT, LAZY, CRAZY, DUFFER) started appearing on the boards. For the dyslexic Ishaan, all the letters on the board merged into a jumble of squiggles causing him to break down and start scratching his nails against it.

Redemption came in the form of a new art teacher who mimicked Da Vinci and wrote on the board, '.ЯƎMUꓘIИ ЯAꓘИAHƧ ƧI MAЯ ƎMAИ YM'. The blackboard then became his playground as he overcame dyslexia by writing words (hate, tape, mate) and numbers, and thus beginning his return to a happy childhood.

In *Desi Boyz*, the hallowed portals of Trinity College (presumably of the University of Cambridge) were further illuminated when Jerry Patel aka Rocco (Akshay Kumar) gave up his lucrative job as a male stripper and rejoined the college to earn his degree in economics.[1] His efforts got a fillip when his college sweetheart (Chitrangada Singh) became his tutor and she did a fine job of posing in low-cut dresses in front of a blackboard with 'Economics 209' written on it. In one song, Akshay Kumar literally swept her off her feet even before she could finish writing 'Elasticity' on the board. The board was a great backdrop for Akshay's verbal duel with a British professor who insisted Indians were of no use. Our hero made ample use of the 'Advanced Principles of Calculus' written on the board to drive home the fact that it was an Indian who invented zero and kicked off mathematics in the first place.

All blackboards don't have lessons written on them. Some of them are also expressions of love.

In *Darr*, 'Jaadu teri nazar' was filmed on Kiran (Juhi Chawla) being serenaded by an unknown lover who insisted that she cannot be anybody else's but his. Kiran ran from one end of the college to another looking for this mysterious singer and eventually landed up in a deserted classroom. Her suitor had left his guitar there and had written a message on the blackboard—'I Love U Kiran'. And in a flamboyant flourish, he had replaced the dot of Kiran's 'i' with a star.

---

[1] For the record, Indian-born Nobel Prize–winning economist Amartya Sen also got his degree from the same university.

Amitabh Bachchan and his cohorts formed an inspirational teaching squad in **Aarakshan** when they rebelled against the 'coaching' mafia and started a free tuition centre for students. Amitabh did a bit of physics and asked tough questions on electric charges ('A charge Q is divided into two parts of q and Q-q. If the Coulomb repulsion between them when they are separated is to be maximum, the ratio of Q/q should be . . .'). Before you could recover from this, he came up with a problem on matrices ('Obtain the universe of the following matrix using elementary proportions . . .'). In another classroom, his daughter Deepika Padukone was throwing biology at us ('Pseudopodia') while his favourite student Saif Ali Khan was holding forth on the Molarity Equation ('$M_1V_1 = M_2V_2$'). And against all this, all Manoj Bajpai could come up with was a pathetic looking '$12N \times V_1$'? Tchah!

This next instance was not a blackboard but a slate. But given its importance to the story, it deserves an entry.

In **Toofan**, Inspector Hanuman Prasad (Pran) was wrongly accused of stealing government gold. He got a tip about the real culprit and left to nab him in a hurry. Just before leaving, he scrawled a message for his sleeping son on the latter's slate—'*Sone ki dacaiti ki saazish mein ACP Sharma aur Daku Shaitaan Singh shaamil hai. Main apni begunahi ka saboot lene ja raha hoon.*' In true Manmohan Desai[2] style, he died trying and a choreographed rain ensured that only the two names in the above declaration were wiped off by some offending droplets! The son grew up to become a bow-wielding superhero, who went all over the world seeking people who could fill in the blanks in his slate. The rain managed to wipe off two names in a matter of minutes. In the ensuing twenty years (or more), however, not even a single word was smudged.

---

[2] The film was directed by Manmohan Desai's son, Ketan.

Author, Author! 7 Men of Letters

Bollywood was never about high literature. Sure, Bimal Roy made the odd Saratchandra novel into a film, but that was that. The overwhelming majority of filmi fodder has come from the made-to-order familiarity provided by Bollywood screenwriters. Till recently, even bound scripts were a rarity in tinsel town—leave aside bound novels.

That hasn't stopped Bollywood from having poets and novelists infesting their films. Dreamy-eyed men of letters have spewed poetic lines and ornate words, enthralling—or pissing off—millions.

In *Pyaasa*, Vijay (Guru Dutt) was the archetypal impoverished poet. He was unemployed, misunderstood and radical. And like the true-blue unsung artiste (think Van Gogh, but with both ears intact), he managed to remain unsold in his lifetime. Only when the false news of his death spread and his girlfriend got his poetry published (as a collection titled *Parchhaiyan*), he became hugely popular though other people duly took credit and the royalties. Vijay, then, made a proper filmi (re-)entry with his trademark poetry renouncing the world, the world of mansions, thrones and crowns (gasp, a communist!). And promptly went back into oblivion. Did he write again? Who knows?

Anand opened with an award ceremony in which Dr Bhaskar Banerjee was the recipient of the Saraswati Puraskar (instituted by the Rustomjee Trust) for his autobiographical book—*Anand*. He was a part-time author, the material for whose book was fed by his day job as a cancer specialist. His story was about having a big life not a long one. It was about realizing that we are all puppets held by strings and it could be curtains any moment now. The subject was a terminally ill patient, Anand Sehgal—who won a million hearts on his way out.

But even after his death, Anand lived on in the pages and on the celluloid of the immortal film. As the author said in the last line of his story—Anand did not die. Anand does not die.

In **Kabhi Kabhie**, Amit Malhotra was not an impoverished poet. We had moved on from *Pyaasa* by then. In fact, Amit was one of the most impeccably turned out poets in history. His poetry (ghost-written by Sahir Ludhianvi) and his voice (provided by Amitabh Bachchan) were magical enough to reduce women to putty though. So when his girlfriend didn't get to marry him, she spent her suhaag raat singing songs from his book of poems as her husband looked on dreamily.

Like so many other things, the Big B is one hell of an award-winning novelist. In **Baghban**, he was Raj Malhotra, a bank manager who used his entire life's savings to prop up his sons' careers and lives—only to be dumped in his old age (along with his beautiful wife, Hema Malini). His philosophy of a man being a gardener who raises his children like flowering plants and his pain at being ill-treated resulted in *Baghban* (meaning The Gardener)—an English novel that was written partly in a youth hangout called Archies Music Café, and partly at night while disturbing his son with the clacking of typewriter keys. All of that got sweet redemption as his novel went on to win the Booker Prize[1] and he hammered his entire family in the acceptance speech.

> *Dramatic Bonus*: The Big B played a poetry-spouting playwright in **Silsila**, even though most of his pursuits were not literary in the film. He did act in an avant-garde play (which, presumably, he wrote himself) and won an award too.

Mess + Muse = Award-winning author. Sanjay Dutt in Shabd.

In **Shabd**, a much-tattooed Sanjay Dutt was Shaukat Vashisht, an author who bagged a Booker Prize (again!) with his very first novel, *Mindscape*. Snippets of various reviews and profiles showed that the novel had a 'deeply human core' while its author was 'a [literary] supernova'. He walked past quick cuts of applauding hands and impressed foreigners, going on to release his second novel,

---

[1] *Fact Check Alert: Baghban* was published by New Wave Publishers of London (offering an advance Rs 10 lakh). Intentionally or otherwise, this covered the condition that a book has to be published in the UK to be eligible for the Booker Prize.

And Time Stood Still. This time, the reviews were as unanimous as the first ones, but in the opposite direction. 'Can we have a real story?' asked one while 'lack of experience leading to unreal characters', proclaimed another. Shaukat's indignation led him to create a real-life experiment where he pushed his wife (Aishwarya Rai) into an affair with a younger colleague (Zayed Khan) to obtain the emotions evoked by marital infidelity realistically. Not short of imagination, surely.

Fans driven to the point of hallucination is not something one usually associates with Bobby Deol. But that did not stop the makers of *Nanhe Jaisalmer* from featuring a camel-riding kid tourist guide in Jaisalmer, who was such a big fan of the youngest Deol that he had imaginary conversations with the star. (Before you scream 'Calvin and Hobbes', let me quickly add that Bobby did indeed land up in Jaisalmer at least once in the film.) The kid's education, his sister's wedding and his experiences as a tourist guide eventually ended up becoming a book that wins the adult Nanhe (Vatsal Seth) the Booker Prize (yet again!). And guess who lands up at the award ceremony? Not Big B but Small B, Bobby Deol!

The stuff that gets read in millions of train rides and during lazy afternoons is not highfalutin literature—but pulp fiction. In *Manorama Six Feet Under*, junior engineer Satyadev wrote exactly that, but he soon found out that writing popular shit was just as difficult as writing critically acclaimed shit. His first—and last—novel, *Manorama*, sold some 200 copies and he was relegated to being a frustrated and corrupt public servant in a desert town. But his reputation as a crime novelist was enough to get him a client who claimed to be the irrigation minister's wife and wanted him to do some snooping on her husband's purported extramarital affairs. Satyadev soon found out that the minister had a nasty bunch of goons on his payroll and a slinky woman on his arm. And his own irate wife wasn't liking his detective-giri. And after all that, his client was not in a position to pay him for his troubles. Surely fodder for another novel . . .

In *Chori Mera Kaam,* Shashi Kapoor broke into a house and found a manuscript called—you guessed it—*Chori Mera Kaam.* He promptly stole it and published it as his own. The book went on to become a runaway bestseller as it was the perfect book to teach one to escape after committing various types of crimes. All was well and royalties kept flowing in . . . till the police started taking interest in how the author managed to acquire such intricate knowledge of thieving. And there was the small matter of the guy whose manuscript it was.

DISHONOURABLE MENTION

Canvas on Celluloid: 10 Artists

Ever since it was revealed that M.F. Husain had painted film posters, poster art gained respectability. Coffee-table books emerged on the subject, shopkeepers in Chor Bazaar increased poster prices and this kitschy art found newer followers. Over time, the hand-drawn Bollywood poster gradually made way for digital art. As poster art changed, so did the artist in the Bollywood film. In the olden days, the artist lived if not in abject penury, at least in tight financial conditions. In fact, the poor artist was always rejected by many a heroine's father in the olden times. The new Bollywood artist is not poor by any stretch of the imagination. His art may not be selling like hot cakes (yet) but he is firmly in Page Three territory, holding a champagne flute and looking handsome.

In *Mr & Mrs 55*, a wealthy dowager wanted somebody poor and malleable enough for a shotgun marriage to her niece. And who fit the bill better than a newspaper cartoonist? All he had to do was to stay married for a few months, collect his money and run. Except the cartoonist was Guru Dutt. He not only had a point of view but dialogues by Abrar Alvi as well. Add to that the drawing skills of R.K. Laxman (who did the cartoons in the film) and you had Preetam Kumar—a struggling cartoonist, an artist with a twist. And a killer introduction. After his speech on the plight of the poor, the aunt taunted him, '*Tum communist ho?*' He smirked and said, '*Jee nahin, cartoonist hoon!*'

An artist and a charmer make for a deadly combination. *Mere Jeevan Saathi* boasted that, as well as Rajesh Khanna's looks. Also add blindness, a cruel princess, a Good Samaritan, a mind-blowing soundtrack and filmi dilemmas . . . Rajesh Khanna did not waste too much time wielding a brush. The paintings on display in his house and studio were—quite inexplicably—of hungry beggars or abstract art. He went around singing songs in shiny velvet waistcoats, and the paintings just paled into insignificance. But really, Rajesh Khanna's artistic style could well have been exhausted by his looks and his gift of the gab. He presented his 'most beautiful work' to his heroine and whipped off the cover with a flourish—only to reveal a mirror. And if that was not enough, he sang '*O mere dil ke chain . . .*'

Women artists are few and far between. Raakhee as Miss Suman in *Kasme Vaade* was one of this rare breed. As an artist, she painted a mother–son piece called *The Heart's Smile* which was adjudged the best painting and immediately went under the hammer. Her own brother-in-law (Randhir Kapoor) tried to buy it but was outbid by his filthy-rich rival (Vijayendra Ghatge). The painting was finally sold for Rs 20,000. If we adjust for inflation, that translates into quite a pretty packet! After her boyfriend's death, she spent the rest of her life painting pictures of him. (Sales reports of these are not available.)

Kasme Vaade: Rakhee captured Amitabh Bachchan on canvas. Amitabh Bachchan captures Rakhee in real life.

Two debuts marked the standard Love in the Times of Choleric Parents film—*Painter Babu*. The hero was Rajiv Goswami, brother of Harikrishna Goswami aka Manoj Kumar. The heroine was Meenakshi Seshadri, whose claim to fame was still one 'heroic' film away. A childhood romance got nipped in the bud when the hero's father fixed an economically motivated match for him, in order to save the family business. The son indignantly walked out, got framed (not for his painting but for murder) and shuttled in and out of jail. When he was finally released, he found out that the heroine was already married . . .

Hello? One second—where is the artist in all this? Why is this film in the list? Arre yaar, the hero was supposed to be interested enough in painting to make it into a profession. On top of that, look at the title. How can it not be included?

Confess, you never realized Aamir Khan was an artist in *Mann*. Confess, you also never realized that *Mann* existed in the first place. Well, it did exist and Aamir was a rocking filmi painter at that. He started off as a gold-digging playboy—with an artistic bent—till he met the first woman he couldn't seduce (Manisha Koirala). Almost immediately, he broke off his engagement to a rich heiress and became a pauper. And just when you thought it couldn't get any more filmi, he decided to make a fortune for himself by painting. And like all famous painters (see the M.F. Husain story earlier), he kicked off his career by painting film posters and, before you could say 'Raja Ravi Varma', people were buying his art in droves and women were throwing themselves at him. If you can withstand the high drama of Inder Kumar films, and Aamir's high art, which was about as artistic as crockery design, you can attempt to watch this movie (and figure out the similarities to *An Affair to Remember*, of which this is supposed to be a copy).

Dil Chahta Hai was about three south Mumbai dudes whose professions were far less interesting than their girlfriends, even though one of them chose a very colourful vocation.

The film opened with a manic dash by Aamir and Saif to reach Akshaye's studio to see his latest painting. Whether the pencil sketch of the Rubenesque nude actually looked like their economics teacher Mrs Kashyap or not was debatable but it set the tone of the film. Akshaye found a muse in Dimple Kapadia, who looked as radiant as ever and was totally deserving of the luscious portraits Akshaye drew of her. And as the portrait session went on, we had probably the most 'artistic' of Bollywood songs in which Akshaye Khanna inhabited a painter's visual landscape of unsaturated dabs of colour. Akshaye Khanna's career as an artist seemed to go through a steady progression from sketching at parties to recommendations from a critic at the exhibition to inclusion in an artist's retreat at a hill station to painting in solitude at an uncle's farmhouse. So did he sell any of those paintings? Your guess is as good as mine.

> *Akhtar Painting Club*: The Akhtar siblings seem to have a soft corner for artists. In *Dil Chahta Hai*'s spiritual sequel *Zindagi Na Milegi Dobara*, Naseeruddin Shah played Salman Habib—a Bohemian painter who abandoned his pregnant girlfriend and went off to Spain in search of his art and muse. He was alternately eccentric and practical, painting flamboyant canvases and then selling them off to pay his bills.

Ishaan Awasthi was the boy with an incorrigible attitude, impossible teeth and incredible talent. Except, everybody was so busy turning him into an engineer that they did not notice. And the poor fellow—already handicapped with dyslexia—moped about for half the film and got sent to a boarding school. Enter Ram Shankar Nikumbh, maverick art teacher by day, and all was well. In Aamir Khan's directorial debut, *Taare Zameen Par*, art was at the centre of it all. A talented boy's journey towards public recognition and self-belief was brought to life by an amazing performance from Darsheel Safary and some evocative art by Sameer

Mondal—who did the kiddie art as well. Starting from Ishaan's hyper-creative images of the solar system to his bright portrait by the art teacher, the paintings added an extra dimension to this film. Even the album and disc covers of this film were full of doodles and scrawls that added wonderfully to the mood.

If the universe conspired to let more sisters into their brothers' rooms, we would have discovered many more talented artists than we have currently. This was a hypothesis put forward by *Jaane Tu Ya Jaane Na*, which had a subplot of sibling rivalry between heroine Genelia D'Souza and her artist brother, Prateik Babbar. That Prateik was an artist was not revealed till quite late in the film when his sister's suitor walked into his room. His room turned out to be a mix of Dali, Munch and maybe even Abbas Tyrewala, with surreal subjects and bold colours. There was art on every wall, window and piece of furniture—so dense that it was difficult to distinguish between painting and sculpture. Eye-catching for sure. But for all his talent, Prateik made no pretence of trying to sell or even exhibit his work in the film. He seemed quite content in his stinking-rich father's bungalow, playing with his pet rat when not spewing pithy epigrams at his sister.

There is something about the brooding, loner image of Aamir Khan that draws artist roles to him like a magnet. His wife, Kiran Rao, cannot but agree. In *Dhobi Ghat*, he was the reclusive, eccentric artist who shifted from house to house in Mumbai and hated the exhibitions where his art got sold. He was obviously affluent (since he lived in big flats in Mumbai) and successful (he had exhibitions in Australia). His art was about the city he lived in and loved. He dedicated his exhibition to Mumbai—'my muse, my whore, my beloved'. His art was as much about the geography of the city as it was about its politics, because the exhibition he introduced was about the migrant labourer population of Mumbai and there was a statement in that. According to the director, some aspects of Aamir's character were modelled on artist Sudhir Patwardhan, and Aamir worked with Ravi Mallick for the art.

While neither the hero nor the heroine was a painter, their learning to paint together was an important element in the premise of *Lootera*. Sonakshi Sinha was the socially insulated, culturally evolved daughter of a zamindar while Ranveer Singh was the stranger who walked into her life and swept her off her feet. He claimed to be an accomplished painter and so she started to learn from him. However, his limited artistic abilities were caught out soon enough. The aborted painting classes involving leaves and trees came handy for both of them—in another life, at another time.

Bonus Salman Connection: Salman Khan often paints as a hobby, and it is said Sonakshi took tips from Salman on how to paint for the camera. Before he became a painter, Salman was a painter's subject in **Hum Aapke Hain Koun** where both Mohnish Behl and Renuka Shahane were hobby-painters. And not one for modesty, Salman revealed his brother's greatest painting to Madhuri—a portrait of himself.

HONOURABLE MENTIONS

M.F. Husain was the ultimate Bollywood fan, not beyond watching favourite films hundreds of times and deriving inspiration from heroines. One of his earlier contributions was in Raj Kapoor's **Henna**—in which he did the paintings for the title cards. Sometime after that, he grew inspired by Madhuri Dixit and promptly knocked off a series of paintings—all of which were sold for figures with countless zeroes in them. He did not stop there and made a full-fledged feature film called **Gaja Gamini** with Madhuri Dixit in the title role and in multiple roles thereafter, including that of Mona Lisa.

THE PICTURES WE SEE IN HINDI MOVIES

- *The Bigass Painting on the Wall*: Aka *Kaash-tere-babuji-aaj* picture, in front of which mothers give sentimental sermons before the children sully the khandaan's name by marrying out of social status.
- *The Crumpled Photo in Wallet*: Aka *Tere-paas-yeh-kaise* picture, which remains with one member of a family separated by a calamity and emerges just before the climax.
- *The Dreamy Romantic Sketch*: Aka *Iska-matlab-tum-mujhse* picture, which is discovered by the heroine just after she has committed undying love to another man. (Doesn't have the erotic charge of Hollywood e.g. Jack painting Rose in *Titanic*.)
- *The Police Mugshot*: Aka *Maine-aapko-pehle-kahin* picture, which populates police stations and walls all around the city, sending the world chasing the (usually wrong) subject.
- *The Psycho Picture*: Aka *Oh-teri-yeh-kaise* picture around which crazy shit happens. Sometimes, there is a dead body behind it (**100 Days**). And sometimes, you can go into the picture (**8x10 Tasveer**).

Alpha Plus: 11 MBAs

Graduates—check. Doctors—check. Engineers—check. All those *honhaar ladkas* who rush to their mothers and announce '*Maa, main pass ho gaya*,' seem to be doing a lot of the conventional courses—except one. Management degrees are rare in Bollywood. But the number has increased in recent times, and you would be surprised to know, some of the MBAs even have a fan following.

In *Trishul*, Shashi Kapoor was the happy-go-lucky son of construction tycoon Sanjeev Kumar. He returned from a foreign education bubbling with the energy and ambition to flirt with everything that hovered around him in skirts. But what foreign education? It was an MBA, sir. On his first day in office, Sanjeev Kumar walked him into his impressive cabin and pointed to the desk from where he would make deals worth millions. That's when we got to know that Sanjeev Kumar had forced him to do a 'course in business administration' from London while Shashi wanted to become a musician. And so, he inherited a massive empire instead of becoming a 'bandmaster'.

London MBAs are worth their weight in gold in Bollywood. Ask Karan Johar.

In *Kabhi Khushi Kabhie Gham*, when Hrithik Roshan decided to unite his estranged brother (SRK) with their father (Amitabh Bachchan), he needed an excuse to go to London. His excuse was higher studies. 'What?' his father asked. 'MBA, Dad!' he answered blithely. There were some murmurs about doing an MBA in India. But Hrithik cited family tradition, of doing it in London. What? You mean Amitabh's father, Amitabh and Shah Rukh were all MBAs in *K3G*? From London? Well, so it seems. And before you could say 'London Business School', Hrithik had zoomed into King's College—hopefully it had a B-school—in a red Lamborghini and the MBA was basically forgotten.

Desi Boyz opened in 2009 with the recession hitting its peak (or rock bottom, if you please) in the United Kingdom (and elsewhere). Akshay Kumar was a college dropout who did odd jobs while John Abraham[1] was a high-flying trader at a seemingly high-flying bank. John Abraham was an MBA from the London School of Economics and that explained his fat bonus (though not his sacking immediately afterwards). His 'London MBA' wasn't of much use during the recession which turned out to be a great leveller, getting both the MBA and the dropout jobs as male strippers.[2]

Fact Alert: The London School of Economics, of course, does not offer an MBA degree. It offers an MSc programme in management that is 'a competitive alternative to an MBA'.

If not a 'London MBA', the next best bet is probably an American one.

In *Kal Ho Naa Ho*, Preity Zinta and Saif Ali Khan were pursuing an evening MBA degree at the University of New York. Saif was working with an advertising agency while Preity was refereeing fights at home. Since they were content with chit-chatting in class, with Saif passing notes for dinner dates in the course of slideshows, academics wasn't high on their priority. However, Preity did carry a thick book—*The Portable MBA Desk Reference*—to highlight her choice of education and stood next to the *Charging Bull* of Wall Street to hint at her choice of specialization.

Hate Story was the story of a slighted woman (Paoli Dam) who used sex to extract revenge. In her quest, she had to seduce Kunwar Rajdev Singh (Joy Sengupta), whose career was outlined in such detail that it had to be a first in Bollywood. He was from the IIM Ahmedabad Class of 1997[3] following which he did a 'leadership' course from Stanford. He had been an AVP at Morgan Stanley and a VP at HSBC before he became the CEO of Cementec Infra. Oh—and he played a mean round of golf too! On meeting him, Paoli breathlessly intoned that she was a big fan of his. Our man modestly commented that he had heard of fans of cricketers and filmstars but a fan of an MBA was a definite first.

If you know the service tax rate is not 12.24 per cent but 12.36 per cent, if you know the 1984 amendment to the Builders' Act, and if you know when to insert a 'rain clause' in a contract,

---

[1] John Abraham actually holds an MBA in real life, from the University of Mumbai.

[2] For a detailed overview of Akshay Kumar's academic adventures, check out the chapter 'In the Classroom: 10 Blackboards' on page 115.

[3] *Batchmate Trivia*: Author Chetan Bhagat is also from the IIMA Class of 1997.

then you are likely to be a legal whizz. Not!

In **Karthik Calling Karthik**, the eponymous hero knew all this and he was not only a college topper and a chartered accountant but an IIM topper as well. Oof! Nobody noticed him in his geeky glasses though, till he walked in to office in a sharp suit, demanding to be made head of Business Development at four times his current salary with the corner office. You see, not all IIM grads get great placement from campus. Some get it with a little bit of on-the-job coaching (from oneself).

While Madhur Bhandarkar littered **Corporate** with management graduates, he named only two of them. Minissha Lamba joined the Sehgal Group of Industries as assistant manager, Operations, and was a giggly fan of Nishigandha Dasgupta, played by Bipasha Basu (MBAs *do* have fans, then). She claimed to be from the same management school as Bipasha and said she had been admiring her ever since *Business Today* called her the '*sabse* best female executive'. Bipasha's designation in her current company was not very clear but she received lucrative offers from rival companies that promised double the salary and perks, stock options and the designation of senior vice president.

> *Job Description Alert*: Almost immediately on Minissha's joining, she was asked to organize the 'region-wise distribution data in a comprehensive table format'. Sigh, the story of MBAs' lives.

In **Sheesha**, Mithun Chakraborty was an MSc from the 'Institute of Science' and an MBA from 'Ahmedabad'. While the three golden letters remained unsaid, there was no doubt about his pedigree. After an excellent academic record in both his master's degrees, he went on to become a general manager at Steel Alloy Company and, eventually, chief executive at PC Drugs Company. You could say he was a 'modern' manager when he asked his subordinates to not call him 'sir', but not when he refused to meet a telephone operator with a grievance citing hierarchy. When he did meet the operator—the smokin' hot Mallika Sarabhai[4]—she accused him of outraging her modesty. And Mr MBA was embroiled in the story Michael Crichton would write two decades later.

From the haloed portals of St Teresa,[5] Alia Bhatt turned up at the country's premier B-school and promptly ran into an engineer (Arjun Kapoor) from IIT Delhi. Their academic credentials

---

[4] Ironically, Mallika Sarabhai holds an MBA from IIM Ahmedabad.

[5] If you haven't seen **Student of the Year**, how can you call yourself cool?

paled into insignificance as their sojourn at IIM Ahmedabad and beyond was defined by the fact that they were from *2 States*. As they tried to get their families into accepting each other, their post-MBA professional lives provided an interesting backdrop to it all. Arjun Kapoor bagged a job at Yes Bank, seemingly on the basis of his assertion at the interview that it was 'the best bank'. Alia joined Sunsilk as a brand manager, and made confident pronouncements about 'modern women'. Of course, when she made her salary public (Rs 50,000), it was likely to have caused a considerable decline in the number of CAT aspirants.

Not all MBAs are from premier institutes. A large number of management graduates are from lesser-known colleges. As was Atul Agnihotri in *Veergati*.

In a movie known for Salman Khan's bare-bodied daredevilry, Atul was his younger brother and star student at the SV (Swami Vivekananda) College of MBA. He was so good that he routinely left exam halls early, having finished well before the allotted time. Needless to say, he topped his MBA and that even made newspaper headlines. Did he get a high-flying corporate job? Well, his girlfriend's father insisted that to marry her, he needed to get Rs 1 crore and finance a project. And how did our management whizz solve this? You see, he got his brother to win that amount of money through *teen patti*. An MBA degree is all about managing resources to deliver optimal results . . .

A very large majority of MBAs in this country are actually engineers, doing nothing to utilize their technical education meaningfully. Rajkumar Hirani found a *gadha* specimen to exemplify this situation in *3 Idiots*. Suhas Tandon was a graduate from Imperial College of Engineering and did an MBA after that and went on to become a banker in the USA. In between, he developed a taste for expensive shoes (for himself) and limited-edition watches (for his fiancée), but he insisted on screaming their prices from the rooftops. He was doing pretty well for himself professionally and personally till . . . till an idiot came by and left him behind. You see, MBAs chase success while the idiot is after excellence.

HONOURABLE MENTIONS

In *Ladies vs Ricky Bahl*, Dipannita Sharma was a 'BTech from IIT and MBA from IIM' although even she got conned while chasing a Husain painting for her boss. So, are all these engineer–MBA types gadhas?

He is an MBA. He wears Rado watches and Gucci perfumes. He plays the guitar and holidays in France. Needless to say, he has tons of money and was born with a silver spoon. What? You don't know him? Arre baba—he's the guy who can't dance, *saala*! How can you forget Pappu of *Jaane Tu Ya Jaane Na*?

Kanoon Ka Haath: 13 Lawyers

The black-caped crusaders who use their intellect and the gift of their gab to fight for justice (or against it) are nothing short of superheroes. Yet, the heroes are always getting on with the business end of the movie (homicide for honour, rowdyism for revenge or stealing for survival) while the elderly lawyers are usually required to fill in the scene just before they are chucked into jail. However, some logically astute and verbally dexterous stars have donned the lawyer's robe to great effect and then taken it off to engage in some good ol' fisticuffs.

One of the earliest high-profile lawyers was Nargis in *Awara.*

In a twist that would be seen in many movies later on, she defended her lover Raj in a courtroom presided over by her foster-father Judge Raghunath (Prithviraj Kapoor), who was also Raj's biological father. To get matters to just the right level of complication that a three-hour Bollywood film needs, the murder victim was the one who was responsible for Raj's estrangement from his father. Nargis appealed to the right brain of all present with a passionate plea about Raj acting in self-defence, but her case was fraught with much interruption as Raj chose to escape and tried to kill his real father as well. But despite these hiccups, the Bollywood lawyer had well and truly arrived with *Awara.*

B.R. Chopra made *Kanoon*, a song-less thriller about an upright lawyer (Rajendra Kumar) who happened to witness a murder and saw a well-known judge, his future father-in-law and mentor Ashok Kumar, committing the crime. Soon, he was appointed public prosecutor in a case against a petty thief arrested—with irrefutable evidence—for the very same murder he had witnessed and which was ironically brought to Ashok Kumar's court. On the one hand, there was the obvious temptation of hushing up the truth and going on with his regular life. On the other, there was the need to answer his conscience. You get no prizes for guessing what our honourable hero chose and soon, the prosecutor had become the defence lawyer, the judge had become the accused, the defence lawyer had also become a suspect and twists happened faster than the court clerk could transcribe.

Middle brother Sunil Dutt was the defence lawyer for big brother Raaj Kumar who was accused of murder, while baby brother Shashi Kapoor was a false witness for the prosecution. And if you are still not short of breath with excitement, then we also had the father (Balraj Sahni) being co-opted as a (truthful) witness. Yash Chopra's *Waqt* was the mother template of long-lost siblings and parents, and it ended with a solid courtroom battle in which all the principals were intricately involved. Sunil Dutt did a stellar job of defending his client, efficiently trashing the prosecution-witness's testimonies, smartly recreating the murder, and inserting enough red herrings to confuse the hell out of both the criminal, and the lawyer for the prosecution.

A senior lawyer is elevated to a judgeship. In the very first case he presides over, his brother is the accused facing the death penalty for murder—except that the judge doesn't know it. But he suspects that something is amiss since he knows the accused to be a good guy. He investigates the case on his own (yes, while the trial is on) and comes back as a lawyer to defend his brother. Sanjeev Kumar played the lawyer-turned-judge-turned-lawyer, defending Amitabh Bachchan in *Khud-daar*. And apart from being an ace lawyer, he was a top-notch investigator as well—adept at sifting through the evidence, following up on leads and tying up shady witnesses in knots. Having done that superbly and having identified the criminal, he left just enough space for the villain to escape so that the Big B could rush after him and complete the climactic fight.

In *Dostana*, Shatrughan Sinha played a flamboyant criminal lawyer though he never silenced the court with his trademark 'KHAMOWSH'. He was Vijay's (Amitabh Bachchan) best friend till they fell out and he swore to destroy Vijay. When Vijay was implicated in a false murder trial, our good lawyer offered to save him for an exorbitant fee. He would do it only if Vijay's girlfriend Sheetal (Zeenat Aman) slept with him. Before you crack the 'Sleepless in Sheetal' joke, let me hasten to add that such dishonourable acts are never done by friends in Hindi films. He realized his folly, they went back to being fast friends and '*Dostana* lived on forever'.

Very few films have managed the raw, visceral impact of Govind Nihalani's *Aakrosh*, where Om Puri played the role of Bhiku Lahanya—a low-caste daily labourer accused of murdering his wife. The brutality of the kill and the blatant manipulation of the system by the actual killers left him speechless, with Om Puri going through the entire prosecution without uttering a single word. This made the task of his well-meaning lawyer, played by Naseeruddin Shah, virtually impossible. Despite his many assurances and sincere attempts, Bhiku did not speak.

The accused and the lawyer turned in brilliant performances (both the actors were given National Awards) and the projected emotions of resignation and idealism against a hostile system were gut-wrenchingly real.

In *Meri Jung*, Anil Kapoor played the boy who saw his father being hanged wrongfully due to the evil machinations of a crooked lawyer (who molested his mother for good measure), and who grew up to be a lawyer himself. The courtroom became the battleground between the young and upcoming Arun Verma (who believed—in true Bollywood style—that innocence doesn't need evidence or witnesses) and G.D. Thakral (Amrish Puri—the same crooked lawyer as above—who was quick to invent *any* evidence should it be required). Director Subhash Ghai orchestrated some kick-ass wars of words—in the courtroom and out of it—as Arun Verma put his life on the line to win cases against Thakral. And then, Thakral's son landed up in court as a defendant in a murder trial.

Amrish Puri has an illustrious record as the evil criminal lawyer. In *Damini*, he was Inderjeet Chadha who played video games in his spare time and had a tuft of hair that needed to be flipped back every now and then. With these tics, XXL-sized eyeballs and supreme confidence, he managed to save his client from a sure-fire murder-and-rape rap by taking apart the testimony of the key witness (Meenakshi Seshadri as Damini) and had her sent to a lunatic asylum (mentally unstable, you see). He hadn't bargained for a heavy-handed[1] lawyer making a comeback. Sunny Deol only used his fists to thump the courtroom table and became the lawyer with the best lines in Bollywood. His 120-decibel scream of frustration—'*Tareekh pe tareekh*'—remains one of the most repeated movie dialogues in Bollywood. When he wasn't screaming like a banshee, he put together a reasonably cogent legal argument. This involved wittily interrogating witnesses and playing cupid between Damini and her husband (Rishi Kapoor). Of course, he didn't stop at that and threatened to beat up Chadha in the courtroom (thankfully, a promise he did not keep).

In *Veer Zaara*, an Indian Air Force pilot (Shah Rukh Khan) entered Pakistan, following his transborder lover (Preity Zinta), and was promptly thrown into jail by her fiancé. He spent decades rotting in a Pakistani jail as no one took a look at his serial number. It took a fresh lawyer, Samiya Siddiqui (Rani Mukherji), to realize Qaidi No. 786 had divine blessings and needed to be released. She took up the case of this convict who hadn't spoken ever since he was thrown in prison, and came up against her mentor (Anupam Kher) in the courtroom. Her courtroom procedure included making emotional paeans

---

[1] Literally. The weight of his hand, 2.5 kilos, is probably the most well-known weight measure in Bollywood.

Advocate Samiya Siddiqui makes a case for the release of Veer Pratap Singh

to romantic love, and the investigation meant visiting her client's hometown in India to prove his identity. Needless to say, no man has ever been able to ignore emotional pleas in Rani Mukherji's sexy voice and the judge was like putty in her hands. Quite grandly, he ordered the release of Veer so that he could cross back to India with his Zaara and a wonderful photo op could be organized.

The Jim Carrey–starrer *Liar Liar* was remade as **Kyo Kii Main Jhuth Nahin Bolta**, where Govinda was the motormouthed fibber, lying his way through his marriage, family, office and courtrooms. From a small-time lawyer crusading for justice, he went on to become a much-sought-after legal star with shady clients (and an even shadier courtroom style) while his wife and son completely turned away from him. After his son made a wish making him incapable of lying, he turned over a new leaf, but had to fight a just cause without lying.

Govinda's courtroom style included taking unscheduled breaks to decide his next course of action, aggressively haranguing judges and witnesses, winking at his mafia clients and attacking witnesses with burning arms (yes, you read that correctly—burning arms!).

When Michael Crichton wrote *Disclosure*, did he imagine that the legal defence of the man accused of sexual harassment could be conducted by his wife?

In **Aitraaz**, Priyanka Chopra (an ageing telecom czar's trophy wife) accused her ex-lover of sexual assault after he refused her advances. The matter ended up in court but the original lawyer (Annu Kapoor) was conveniently murdered (by Priyanka's henchmen) and that paved the way for Kareena Kapoor to walk in to defend her husband against the slightly comic efforts of Paresh Rawal (as the prosecution lawyer). Her defence was impeccable. She used technology to access mobile call records. She contacted a faraway hospital to obtain evidence.

She explained how a woman behaves differently between acts of sexual pleasure and assault. She also managed to call her adversary a 'bitch' in legal parlance and ended with a stirring speech on the perils of blaming the man every time.

After botching up a case in Meerut, Jagdish Tyagi aka *Jolly LLB*—played by Arshad Warsi—moved to New Delhi and opened up not only Pandora's but all the boxes he could find. Frustrated by his lack of success, he filed a PIL and pitted himself against Tejinder Rajpal (Boman Irani), the most hotshot lawyer of the country. The case was similar to one of the most recognized trials of recent times. The scion of a prominent business family ran over a bunch of pavement-dwellers in his Land Cruiser and put together a procession of fake witnesses and dodgy evidence to save him. What started as an effort to make a quick buck soon became a high-stakes moral crusade for Jolly as he contended with bought witnesses, bought policemen, dead witnesses and even live witnesses (who seemed dead). Presiding over this mayhem in the unglamorous, non-airconditioned courtrooms was Hon'ble Justice Sunderlal Tripathi played by Saurabh Shukla in a role that stole the show. Apart from his eccentricities, Judge Tripathi managed to make pithy observations about India's judicial system and even himself, including the iconic 'Kanoon andhaa hota hai, judge nahin.'

The Big B's baritone is the voice most suited to make persuasive legal arguments, but he has made only a few forays as lawyer.[2]

In *Shootout at Lokhandwala*, he was Advocate Dhingra, brought in to defend the three police officers who carried out an encounter against the gangsters and were hauled up for a human rights violation. The entire movie was a flashback as the three officers recounted the events leading up to the shootout in response to some aggressive grilling by Dhingra. Eventually, the lawyer rose in court to eloquently defend the accused officers, arguing it was 'protection' and not 'murder': 'Aapke ghar ke bahaar ek aadmi gun leke khada hai. Aap kya chahenge, ki woh aadmi kaun ho? Maya ya ACP Shamsher Khan?'

> *Bonus Movie*: S. Ramanathan's *Zamaanat* (probably the longest-in-the-making movie ever) had Amitabh Bachchan as a blind lawyer making a comeback to the courtroom to defend an innocent man (Arshad Warsi) on the request of his girlfriend (Karisma Kapoor). This mouth-watering premise looked horrendously dated in the trailers and the movie is yet to see a proper release.

---

[2] In *Mahaan,* he was a lawyer framed by his crooked client and friend (Amjad Khan), and was on the run from the law. In his only major scene as a lawyer, he turned around from defending and argued for his friend's conviction instead.

Focused People: 12 Photographers

Bollywood stars, perennially on the glamorous side of flashing cameras, have occasionally gone over to the other side and played photographers in films. Working for newspapers or freelancing, shooting fashion models or murder victims, falling in love or in ditches, star photographers have lit up our screens with their flashbulbs.

Shammi Kapoor has had two outings as a photographer taking sensational pictures for newspapers.

In *Bluff Master*, he bluffed his way into a reporter's job at *Bhookamp Weekly* (claiming to be the chief reporter of England's 'sensational newspaper'). On the very first day, he snapped Saira Banu slapping an eve-teaser using a modified Kodak Retina camera with a massive flash. Needless to say, the issue sold out like hot cakes. He moved on to other cons, disguises and gags and forgot about photography.

In *Brahmachari*, he was the eponymous bachelor who ran a home for orphaned children. He took on photography only to fund his expenses. His editor asked him for an exclusive photograph for which he would be paid Rs 500. He immediately set out and bumped into Rajshree, who was on the verge of committing suicide. He thought her photo—taken with a Rolleicord II Twin Lens Reflex camera—had given him the needed scoop but she seemed to have other ideas, and thus his photographic career came to an end.

Photographers are nothing if they don't have a swagger. And nobody does swagger better than Dev Anand. In *Heera Panna*, he was the globetrotting photographer who went around in a snazzy car painted with the names of pretty much every world capital you can think of. His gear consisted of a Nikon with never-ending telephoto lenses though he was not averse to using a pocket-sized autofocus camera as well. He devoted an entire song to his pursuit ('*Main tasveer utaarta hoon*') and diligently photographed a bikini-clad Zeenat Aman lounging around in a hammock.

Jaane Bhi Do Yaaro featured the two owners of Beauty Photo Studio ('specialist in modelling photography'). Naseeruddin Shah and Ravi Baswani's newly inaugurated studio got very little business in subsequent months. Work came from the editor of *Khabardar* magazine who was initially mistaken for a model and aggressively flirted with ('*Main photo khnichoonga aur photo ke sivai kuch nahin khnichoonga*'). After the initial tomfoolery, the duo launched a sting operation on the builder–bureaucracy nexus in Bombay, sometimes claiming to be from *Time* and *Newsweek* and sometimes claiming to be Albert Pinto. They also tried to send an entry to the ORWO Photo Contest but their camera caught something suspicious and the two photographers had to blow up the photo to spot a murder, which led to—of course—more tomfoolery.

Bonus Trivia: Naseeruddin Shah used a Nikon camera in the film, which belonged to him in real life. Unfortunately for him, he forgot the camera in a local train station while shooting there.

In *Khoon Bhari Maang*, plain Jane Rekha returned from the dead[1] to become a supermodel, assisted by plastic surgery done abroad. She walked into Kraft Advt. Agencies [sic], whose photographer had become bored with clicking Sonu Walia, the reigning supermodel. The photographer was Shatrughan Sinha, who wore pale yellow jackets with bright yellow scarves, and did not look out of place in a fashion atmosphere at all. His slightly archaic Nikon camera wasn't used much since he was interested more in wooing Rekha with bombastic lines than in snapping her pictures.

We can never be sure if Rishi Kapoor did photography for a living in *Chandni*. What we can be sure of is that he snapped enough pictures of her to completely plaster one (gigantic) wall of his room with them. But then so would you if Sridevi was your girlfriend and you were Rishi Rich.[2] He sneaked into a ladies' sangeet to snap her photographs. He held his telephoto lenses like barrels of bazooka and seemed majorly depressed when unable to handle his cameras after a paralysing accident. However, his affair was with Sridevi and the camera was just a tool to capture her beauty. He made no effort to return to photography later, even when he could.

---

[1] Rekha is one of many people to return from the dead. For a longer list, check out page 448.
[2] Hyuk hyuk.

Deewana Mujhsa Nahin had Aamir Khan as a fashion photographer as well as a passion photographer, thanks to his one-sided love for model Madhuri Dixit. He kept clicking Madhuri for ads, fashion shows and generally everywhere including a song which went '*Ready steady smile*' (in his dreams, though). He worked for an advertising agency (BB Agency) whose owner seemed to praise him to the skies. He used an anonymous camera which sometimes had really long (and seemingly unnecessary) telephoto lenses and did an inordinately large amount of still shoots for ad films.

In *Nishabd*, Amitabh Bachchan was an artistic photographer (not the wedding variety, as his daughter hastily clarified). He shot photos like an artist made portraits and he had been published in many 'international journals'. He was seen expertly cleaning his Nikon gear early in the film. When Jiah Khan went berserk with a hosepipe in the garden watering herself down in a white shirt and hot pants, the photographer—and the dirty old man inside him—couldn't help but fall in lust with her and took a whole lot of snaps though his camera had become a Canon by now. A sixty-year-old man falling in love with an eighteen-year-old girl brings its own set of problems and the camera took a backseat in the rest of the film.

John Abraham is probably the dishiest (male) subject many cameras have seen. In *Dostana*, he went to the other side—in more ways than one—by becoming a gay fashion photographer in ultra-glamorous Miami. As a fashion photographer, he shot an elaborate fashion ensemble for room-mate (and object of affection) Priyanka Chopra who worked for *Verve* magazine. His shoot involved many models in avant-garde costumes and hairdos, set among surreal frames and fluttering leaves of autumn. Priyanka Chopra won many accolades for the shoot and John duly turned up once again to photograph the event celebrating the launch of the magazine's special issue.

In *Click*, Shreyas Talpade played a fashion photographer with a model–girlfriend.[3] The couple ended up killing a girl in a late-night accident and strange figures started emerging in his photographs. As he peered through his camera viewfinder, he could see ghostly figures nobody else could. Sometimes, the apparitions appeared when he developed the photograph in his studio. The main poster of the film had Shreyas Talpade focusing a Nikon camera while a ghostly figure stared at us from the lens. 'Smile. You're on camera'—the tag line happily goaded us.[4]

---

[3] *Clarification*: Not a girlfriend who's perfect but a girlfriend who's a fashion model.
[4] *Cheat Alert*: *Click* is a straight lift from a Thai film, *Shutter*.

Bonus Movie: Speaking of cameras with special powers, Neil Nitin Mukesh—in *Aa Dekhen Zara*—was left a camera by his grandfather which could click pictures of the future. Suddenly stock markets, horse racing and other games of chance became eminently photogenic though we didn't get to know how his girlfriend (Bipasha Basu) would turn out ten years in the future.

Farhan Qureishi of *3 Idiots* wanted to be a wildlife photographer and dreamt of training with the famous Hungarian photographer Andre Istvan. Except his father's ambitions had him landing up at the Imperial College of Engineering instead. In college, he ended up with a maverick genius who egged him on to follow his dreams and his life changed. He dropped out of placements and confronted his father. Finally, his father saw reason and even returned the laptop he had bought for him, getting him a professional camera instead. Farhan started off by being the photographer at his batch's convocation and went on to become a famous wildlife photographer with at least three coffee-table books to his credit—*Panda*, *Snakes Speaks* [sic] and *Life of a Tiger*. He even wrote an account of his adventures—*Tales from the Indian Jungle*.

Shai Edulji (Monica Dogra) in *Dhobi Ghat* was an investment banker from New York, on a sabbatical in Mumbai. She had a research grant to study and photograph small businesses and the shifts in traditional occupations in Mumbai. This called for a very eclectic mix of subjects for her Canon camera. She started off by shooting a portfolio for Bollywood aspirant Munna the dhobi (Prateik Babbar). Her crush on artist Arun (Aamir Khan) also led to a bit of spy photography. For her project, she started off with Dhobi Ghat and went to quaint parts of Mumbai—with *ittar* merchants, flowersellers, fish markets, kebab joints—creating an eccentric portfolio that she developed in her own studio in her apartment. We didn't get to know how Shai's research culminated but the pictures of the city probably formed—as the film's tag line suggested—some sort of Mumbai Diaries.[5]

Bonus Mumbai Photographer: Mumbai attracts many camera-toting lovers. In *Wake Up Sid*, Ranbir Kapoor was the young drifter with an eye for superb photographic composition. Thanks to a friend (Konkona Sen Sharma), he became a photo intern for *Mumbai Beat* magazine and found his true calling through his Nikon's viewfinder. The movie ended showcasing his contribution for a photoessay ('Shades of the Sea') in the magazine, surely paving the way for more.

---

[5] The photographs that were shown as taken by Shai in the film were actually by Jyotika Jain.

Roof over the Head: 10 Homes Bought or Rented

Grand chandeliers to party under. Sweeping staircases to throw villains down from. Round (preferably rotating) beds to cavort on. Gargantuan bathtubs to work oneself into a lather in. Bollywood homes are everything we dream (or dare not to dream) of. The mundane matter of buying and selling houses is left off screen. I mean, somebody asks '*Bhai, tum sign karoge ya nahin?*' and you respond, '*Haan, lekin revenue stamp kidhar hai?*' So *not* cool.

While the abiding memory of *Tere Ghar Ke Samne* is the music by S.D. Burman, the movie's plot was about, well, plots. Of land.

Dev Anand played an architect who was hired by Seth Karam Chand (Harindranath Chattopadhyay) to build a house. The plot was right next to one owned by his arch-rival, Seth Jagannath (Om Prakash), and the house had to be grander. One problem: Dev Anand was Seth Jagannath's son. And yes, he fell in love with Nutan who played Karam Chand's daughter. As each old man dreamt of building a house grander than the other, their common architect had a tough time hiding his construction designs from them and hiding his romantic designs from his lady-love. Eventually, the film ended peacefully with both rivals getting identical houses and the marriage of their children coinciding with the *grihapravesh*.

Mr Agarwal made a good deal for his building in Bombay. After the papers were signed, he told his buyer that he had not bargained enough and paid a couple of lakhs higher than the fair price. His buyer retorted that he would have happily paid 10 lakh rupees more, if only Mr Agarwal had asked for it. When the stupefied Mr Agarwal wondered how the building was so special, the buyer—one Vijay Verma—said his mother's blood and sweat was mixed in the foundation of the building. '*Aaj se bees baras pehle jab yeh building ban rahi thi, meri maa ne yahan eentein uthayi thi. Aaj yeh building main apni maa ko tohfe mein dene jaa raha hoon.*' *Deewaar* was about a little boy's quest to find comfort for his mother. In this quest, he had

140

remembered to buy his mother a skyscraper but had forgotten that the source of the gift was more important to his mother than the gift itself.

In *Trishul*, a construction-magnate's illegitimate son competed with his father in a race to change the landscape of Delhi. Their battles started when Shanti Constructions launched a 'housing development project' on land that R.K. Gupta (Sanjeev Kumar) hadn't managed to clear from illegal encroachment but which Vijay Kumar (Amitabh Bachchan) did in a jiffy.[1] Their battles started with tendered projects from Daaga Shipping Corporation and with Asia's largest hospital commissioned by Maniklal Memorial Trust. It reached a climax over a housing colony to be built on government land and sold at cheap prices. When R.K. Gupta took away the project (by a nasty act of cheating), Vijay Kumar retaliated by buying out all the adjoining land and offering houses at half the price R.K. Gupta was selling for. His plan was to lose tons of money himself in order to bankrupt his illegitimate father. He launched his Shanti Nagar colony at a price point that was going to revolutionize the real estate market. As he said, '*Main iss bazaar ki keematein palat doonga.*'

Thirty-five years on, we are still waiting for the prices to fall.

In *Ghar*—remembered for its wonderful Gulzar–R.D. Burman soundtrack—Vinod Mehra left his father's house after an altercation over his marriage. He got married to Rekha without having a home. In those days, wives and colleagues were both very accommodating—his boss got him a swanky mansion (belonging to an overseas friend). They had to vacate when the owners landed back and Vinod Mehra made a half-hearted attempt at finding a place (while staying at Rekha's house). The rent quoted was Rs 750 per month along with six months' deposit—which he found unaffordable. He finally got an apartment with a parasite neighbour and all was well again. Tragedy struck when Rekha was gang-raped and the trauma was bad enough for her to withdraw into a shell and start believing that she wasn't worthy of their home.

Griha Pravesh was the story of a couple, Sanjeev Kumar and Sharmila Tagore, who were planning to buy a home. The film opened with them talking about their savings of Rs 55,272. The intent was to save heavily and build a home fund—since Sanjeev Kumar wasn't keen on taking a loan. Flats of 650 sq. ft carpet area (two bedrooms with attached baths) in areas like Danda and Worli would elicit deep sighs among home-buyers of Mumbai today. The couple went with a south Indian broker to see flats under construction and were startled by the instalment amounts. Broker Subramaniam was upstaged by Sleeveless Sarika—a younger,

---

[1] I know everybody knows this but I just have to say this again—AB cleared the plot (occupied by Shetty) by landing up at the plot in an ambulance, beating the shit out of his bald head and sending him to a hospital in the ambulance!

sexier colleague Sanjeev Kumar fell in love with, after which the home search took a new turn.

In *Gharonda*, Amol Palekar and Zarina Wahab were seeking a home in 1970s' Bombay. In those days, the price of a 1 BHK flat (with a 15x15 bedroom and a 4x3 bathroom) in Bombay was Rs 50,000. Without any SMSs offering cheap home loans, they made an optimistic saving plan of Rs 1,200 per month that would realize their dream in four years.

But when their promoter died and their savings went with him, their quest for a home took a morally complicated detour leading to Zarina Wahab marrying her boss for the money. The home search took a break. But Gulzar's award-winning lines immortalized their dreams that went beyond food, water and shelter: '*Do deewane shaher mein, abodana dhoondte hain, ek aashiana dhoondte hain . . .*'

Basu Chatterjee's *Kirayadar* opened with scenes of a tenant being unceremoniously thrown out of a house and that set the tone for what was to come. Lucknow resident Raj Babbar landed up in Bombay for a job and was instructed by his father (Utpal Dutt) to stay in their flat—rented out to a mother–daughter family. Flat 701 of Oasis building in Pali Hill was being rented out at Rs 500 per month for the last fifteen years without any deposit. Hey, what happened? Why are you clutching the left side of your chest? Arre, this was in the 1980s.

Anyway, there are no prizes for guessing that Raj Babbar fell in love with the daughter (Padmini Kolhapure) but she fell out of love when Utpal Dutt wanted them to vacate the flat. The story then moved to the courts where the two parties spent tons of money before realizing the landlord and tenant getting married was probably the smartest (and cheapest) way out of the mess.

'*Jahan mere teeno bete khade ho jayenge, wahin mera ghar hai.*' Waheeda Rehman repeated an English proverb in eloquent Hindi: Home is where the heart is.

Om Jai Jagdish was about the attempts of three brothers—Anil Kapoor, Fardeen Khan, Abhishek Bachchan—to 'return home'. Their home was a sea-facing bungalow on the Juhu beachfront in Mumbai called Gulmohar Villa. The interval saw the family fall apart and Gulmohar Villa fell in the hands of Om's unscrupulous business partner (Parmeet Sethi). He had no respect for memories and promptly put the bungalow on the block. In an uplifting climax, the three brothers united to jointly bid in the auction to buy back their palace of memories, with considerable help from India's (then) nascent software industry.

Real Estate Quiz: In 2002, the bungalow went for Rs 20 crore in the auction. What would the price of the bungalow be today?

Ram Gopal Varma's **Bhoot** opened with corporate executive Ajay Devgn looking for a flat in (what looked like) Andheri. His broker tried to avoid a particular building while Ajay insisted on seeing the empty duplex penthouse. The previous resident of Flat 1201 had fallen to her death from the flat and that kept away tenants. Obviously, this also brought the price down. The deal was concluded in a jiffy and the new tenants moved in. Ajay did not tell his wife (Urmila Matondkar) of the death and she was stupefied when strange apparitions started tumbling into their flat. Ram Gopal Varma took the unlikeliest of settings for a horror movie—a Mumbai multi-storeyed building—and populated it with the usual characters (batty maid, insolent security guard, eccentric neighbours) to create terror. (Looking at property prices in Mumbai also has the same effect.)

And the final name in the list has to be the ultimate underdog film about a west Delhi middle-class family and their nest—**Khosla Ka Ghosla**.

Kamal Kishore Khosla put his life's savings (Rs 30 lakh) in buying a plot of land (Plot No. 32) in a soon-to-be-aspirational part of Delhi (New Sapna Vihar), but it was usurped by a shady property dealer, Khurana, assisted by an unholy nexus of property dealers (Vijender of World Famous Properties[2]), the police and lawyers. This sort of land-grabbing by property sharks and releasing it after a hefty payment is a common occurrence in Delhi, of which director Dibakar Banerjee had first-hand experience. But the film was obviously different from real life! The sons of Mr Khosla, theatre director Bapuji, and visa agent Asif Iqbal joined hands and brains to create a super plan to hoodwink Khurana and realize their father's lifelong ambition. As their neighbour said, '*Khosla sahab, aap toh south Delhi wale ban gaye . . .*'

---

[2] Rajendra Sethi, who played Vijender, has made an illustrious career in Bollywood real estate. He was also Ajay Devgn's broker in **Bhoot** (the man who got him the haunted apartment).

Eat to Live, Live to Eat: 11 Roles of Food

Amitabh Bachchan shows us the right way to a woman's heart

Roti, *gaajar ka* halwa[1] and *kasam* are the three things Bollywood eats. While there are many movies and even more songs dedicated to drink, not too many are about food. After all, when a man has just thirteen screen minutes to woo a girl, there's hardly any time left to cook a three-course candlelight dinner for her. It is far easier to sing a song.

The most passionate tribute to food was paid by Amitabh Bachchan in **Cheeni Kum**, as a sixty-four-year-old chef running a restaurant (Spice 6) in London. The owner–chef of 'London's finest Indian restaurant'—as he never failed to remind us—called himself a practitioner of the greatest art form. Unlike any other art, a good dish appeals to all five senses and therefore, ringing cell-phones were not allowed in the restaurant so as not to disturb the world's greatest artists.

His belated love story began when a patron—the ethereally beautiful Tabu—returned a plate of *Hyderabadi Zafrani Pulao*, a first in the history of the restaurant. He insulted the patron. She returned with a perfect version of the pulao. He ate humble pie. And the love story began. The way to a woman's heart is also through her stomach.

---

[1] *Maa ke haathon ka!*

The first Bollywood superstar also had a 'food role'. In **Bawarchi**, Rajesh Khanna was the—well—bawarchi of the constantly squabbling Sharma household. He joined his job early in the morning and cooked up a storm in a jiffy. His opening dishes were *Suran Ka Kebab*, and *Kachche Kele Ka Dum Pukht*—mistaken to be mutton. Soon, he was suggesting Coca-Cola and lime juice to make desi *tharra* tasty, along with dal fry. Not to mention egg kachori with tea. The Bengali director also put in a favourite dish of his region when the bawarchi offered to cook *Shukto*, a bitter mix of vegetables cooked in the traditional style. Net result? The two ladies of the house were discussing the weight they had put on and thinking what work they could do.

Sidhu (Akshay Kumar) worked with his Dada (Mithun Chakraborty) at their paratha joint in Old Delhi. Bajrang Bali Parathe Wale was located in Chhatta Madan Gopal of Parathewali Gali, Lal Qila, Chandni Chowk, Delhi 6! His days were spent in chopping potatoes and onions, kneading the dough and frying the parathas ('*shudh desi ghee se nirmit*'). His machine-like movements were preparing him for bigger battles, which started when he moved from **Chandni Chowk to China**. He was invited to a Chinese village to save them from the villainous Hojo as Sidhu resembled a Chinese warrior of the past. He surely wasn't a warrior in his present birth and in the final showdown, he seemed well and truly beaten. Just then, he remembered his Dada's advice to play to his strengths and he started mimicking the motions of chopping vegetables and imagined the villain to be a (no kidding!) giant potato. This worked brilliantly as he not only beat the villain, but pummelled him into submission—borrowing from his action of kneading the dough.

Before he turned a mafia don in **Vaastav**, Sanjay Dutt was a typical Mumbai *sadak chhaap* tapori staying in a chawl with his family. His education (or lack of it) wasn't enough to get him a job. So he proposed to start a business of *pav bhaji*. His understanding of the business was very clear. He needed 40,000 bucks to put up the roadside cart. His competition did a daily business of 5,000. He planned to trump him by picking up his stock from Byculla instead of Dadar, where everything would be a lot cheaper ('*Aath rupiah ka batata char rupiah mein, chhe rupiah ka kanda teen rupiah mein*'). He planned to price a plate at ten bucks (and make five bucks a plate) while his competition was making less at a higher price. His Jai Maharashtra Pav Bhaji Wala stall kicked off with a bang (a song, actually) and it was just about to '*nikal padi*' when a gangster came to his stall and a brawl broke out over the payment. Pav bhaji–wala Raghu went on to become Raghu bhai.

Shah Rukh Khan did his food act in **Duplicate**. When he was not the manic murderer Mannu Dada, he was the bumbling chef Babloo Chaudhry. Before the mistaken identities could kick in, Babloo got himself a job with a hotel. He held a diploma from Sarla Cooking Classes and *baingan ka bharta* was his speciality. The hotel's banquet manager (Juhi Chawla) dispensed with an interview and asked him to prepare a Japanese dish for a delegation scheduled to arrive in the next twenty minutes. In those twenty minutes, Babloo took charge of the colour-coordinated kitchen, the miniskirted waitresses and the team of chefs to not only prepare a fantastic dish but also sing a 'food song'—'*Dheere dheere pyar ki aag jal gayi / Jitni masti do dilon mein thi ubal gayi / Arre is ka mazaa chakh toh loo main zaraa / Phir kahoonga main ke daal gal gayi*'.

Main Sundar Hoon was a vehicle for comedy king Mehmood, playing a buck-toothed waiter who went on to become a Bollywood star. His career opened in Rasraj Hotel, where his signature act was to reel off the entire menu of the hotel in a breathless burst. It started with '*rasgulla chamcham rasmalai gulab jamun*' and ended about a minute later with '*sambhar idli bonda*'. Stuffed in between were Mehmood antics like balancing six cups one on top of the other, cracking smart-alec jokes with customers and trying to woo the hotel-owner's daughter. While the movie soon shifted gear to Mehmood's film career, the hotel piece probably stuck better. After all, who can forget a waiter with buck teeth bigger than Bugs Bunny's?

Kal Ho Naa Ho had two cute food cameos. When Saif Ali Khan's character was introduced to the audience, his father was said to have made his fortune in the takeaway food business. The name of their business? 'Dial-A-Dhokla'! And then Jaya Bachchan was shown to be running a restaurant that was on the verge of shutting down. It was a nondescript American-style diner (called 'New York'), with no USP and frequented by workmen. With some help from SRK and her neighbours, she transformed it into a traditional Indian restaurant with ethnic decor and—eventually—a never-ending queue. The name? 'New Delhi'.

Saif Cooking Alert: Saif Ali Khan played a chef in **Salaam Namaste** who ran a restaurant called 'Nick of Time' (his name was Nick, you see!) and was famous enough to be invited to a radio talk show, hosted by a pretty Indian RJ.

After ten decades of movies on famine and hunger, *3 Idiots* came and turned around the cliché of the 1950s Bollywood b/w movie. As Farhan and Rancho landed up at Raju's humble household, they were subjected to a dose of a home-cooked meal supplemented by a mother's diatribe. That *bhindi* was twelve rupees a kilo and *gobi* ten, came back again and again in the film, as a recurring joke. All this while, heroes were supposed to support their poor friends in finding a square meal. Rajkumar Hirani made that into the joke—when the friend walked out of the house and the friend's mother was crying, the hero concentrated on the *Matar Paneer* instead.

The largest amount of food in India gets consumed out of a *dabba*.

Stanley Ka Dabba paid an affectionate ode to the humble tiffin-box through a fable about a little boy (Partho Gupte) and his run-ins with a khadoos teacher (played by the film's director, Amol Gupte, who is also Partho's father). The teacher demanded a share from every student's dabba and Stanley not getting one was the reason for the run-in. The reason for the absence of Stanley's dabba formed the crux of the story. Amol Gupte's brilliant understanding of child psychology had already been demonstrated in his screenplay of *Taare Zameen Par*. *Stanley Ka Dabba* only cemented that. And it brought a new facet of his to light—that of being a gourmet. The detail and affection with which he showed food and eating in the film—colour, texture, variety—were something that can only come to someone who loves eating.

While on the subject of dabbas, it is said that Mumbai's much-celebrated dabbawalas make one mistake in eight million deliveries. And when they do, a film like *The Lunchbox* happens.

A wrongly delivered lunchbox was the beginning of a beautiful love story between a neglected housewife and an aged insurance executive. A desire to be appreciated led to her preparing luscious dishes like Paneer Kofta.[2] The lucky recipient was quite cool about the food to begin with, though. 'The salt was fine. Chilli was on the higher side,' he had replied. The two lovers—without meeting—continued their relationship through letters tucked in between the sugar and spice of great food.

What makes a chicken recipe special?

When Omi (Kunal Kapoor) returned from London to Lalton village in Punjab, he realized the secret ingredient of his grandpa's chicken recipe was worth its weight in pounds sterling. As he interviewed almost the entire village for the secret, everyone ended up having a point of view—*heeng*? *kali mirch*? *jeera*? *imli*? what? During the search, he had to contend with his own greed, an annoyed chacha, a madcap *mama*, a TV *sadhvi*, a sentimental cousin, and a lover he had abandoned. And in between all these people, he eventually found *Luv Shuv Tey Chicken Khurana*.

> *Bonus Feast Alert*: A Lucknawi chef – brought up on the city's florid culture – flamboyantly wooed a simple Hyderabadi as food formed a fragrant backdrop in *Daawat-e-Ishq*. Aditya Roy Kapur served up a storm of shammi and sheek kababs, biryani, phirni and

---

[2] Non-vegetarians, please excuse.

kulfi for guests at his restaurant – Haidari Kababs – while flooring Parineeti Chopra with jalebi, chaat and even a cauliflower. Even the lyrics of the songs alluded to 'feasty' words – lazzat, daawat and dastarkhwan.

PRISON FOOD

After all the delicious food, we should spare a thought for those poor souls who were in prisons and thus, had seriously curtailed diets. They certainly didn't stop eating because *jail ki roti todna* seems to be a common enough pastime in Bollywood. The rotis are a natural progression from all that chakki peesing and peesing and peesing that seem to happen in jails.

- *Kaalia*: The master criminal went from prison to prison, lining up for grub everywhere. It is in one of these queues that Kaalia saw a handicapped person being pushed back and decided to fight on his behalf. The fight started with Kaalia's adversary throwing a plateful of rice at him and the standard-issue aluminium plates became the weapon of choice.
- *Satya*: Bhiku Mhatre went in and out of prison so frequently that his wife was frustrated. Though she visited him with his favourite kheer and he gulped it down gleefully while casually talking about bail with his lawyer and royally ignoring the prison guards. After all, *Mumbai ka king kaun?*
- *The Legend of Bhagat Singh*: Sometimes, it is not about eating but about not eating. The freedom fighters took their resistance against the British to a new level when they went on a hunger strike for an astounding 64 days – refusing food till the jail authorities agreed to treat political prisoners better. Food as a weapon acquired a completely different meaning.
- *Ek Hasina Thi*: As wrongly imprisoned Urmila fought for survival in the prison, the prison kitchen was a 'plum posting' where she worked and plotted her escape. But the bigger message was probably that thali of inedible prison food that was set in front of her. She had no interest in it till she saw a rat come up and start nibbling on it. And that incident gave a whole new edge to her plan.
- *Shivaji The Boss*: Rajini was jailed. Rajini was about to be killed. Rajini was given food . . . when suddenly, the mound of rice glowed and vibrated. Woe my Gaad Thalaiva . . . Someone had smuggled in a smartphone, complete with an MMS clip exposing the villains' nefarious designs to Rajini.

6

Never Up to Any Good

Bad man!
—Gulshan Grover in *Ram Lakhan*

Life is not a bed of roses. Even if it was, there would be enough thorns to make life hell.
This section is about bad people and bad things.

Chor, Chor: 11 Thieves

For ages, Bollywood has specialized in stealing *dil* and people have been singing '*Chura liya hai tumne jo dil ko*' or similar declarations of cardiac thievery. But many thieves don't waste time chasing hearts or skirts; they concentrate on hard cash instead. (This is strictly not true because Bollywood thieves are usually good at stealing everything including the hearts of the people who are trying to catch them.) And yes, they are different from conmen. Conmen promise you the world, take money for it, give you Andheri East and run away. Thieves steal things.

*Ek tha **Jewel Thief**.*
   The film opened with images of a gloved hand lifting expensive jewellery off store shelves. Newspaper headlines screamed about his scale ('Biggest jewel theft in twenty years'), his modus operandi ('Locks remain closed—jewellery vanishes'), his frequency ('Fifty jewellery thefts in last two years'), his impact ('We will catch him, Home Minister assures House') and even one in India TV style ('Jewel Thief—*Insaan hain ya pret?*'). He was known as Prince within his gang. His other acquaintances—including a fiancée with a hefty diamond ring—knew him as Amar. And he seemed to have a lookalike, a handsome jewellery expert called Vinay. Midway through the film, the entire world had been convinced that Vinay was the Jewel Thief. And the new Jewel Thief took over in great style through two daringly executed thefts. In one, his gang members passed off Vinay as a French jewellery buyer and used him to make off with a gem-encrusted Bappi Lahiri.[1] And in another, it was again Vinay—now brainwashed into believing he was the real Jewel Thief—who led a dance party into a king's coronation to steal the crown right off his head.

A lost-and-found plot (involving freedom fighter Father Pran) was punched with a Robin

---

[1] You wish. It was a model who was part of the plot to steal the jewels.

Hood one and stapled on to a love-in-the-time-of-choleric-parents story leaving the daredevil thief very little time to pull off big heists. Millionaire Ashok Roy (Dharmendra) by day became *Jugnu* by night, stealing priceless antiques and jewellery (from bad people, obviously) to fund his philanthropic activities of running orphanages and donating money to charitable causes promoted by beautiful women (Hema Malini). The most daring theft was pulled off just before the climax when Jugnu raided a heavily guarded museum to steal a gem-encrusted fish. He hoodwinked hundreds of security men patrolling the grounds by entering from the ceiling,[2] dangling from the chandelier and creating an optical illusion with the fish. Of course, moral sense demanded that Jugnu eventually confessed to his crimes, only to be sentenced to five years of prison. *Aur paanch saal baad . . . Jugnu phir jail se bhaag gaya!* Arre no yaar, kidding only.

Shalimar had Rex Harrison as Sir John Locksley, an international thief (rich enough to have a massive palace on a private island) who was terminally ill and wanted to pass on his mantle. To this end, he called a motley crew of thieves (including Shammi Kapoor and O.P. Ralhan) to his island and challenged them to steal Shalimar—a massive red gem (ruby?) valued at nearly a 2G scam. Simple: steal Shalimar and be known as the smartest thief alive.

Each guest took imaginative shots at the gem and—needless to say—failed. Dharmendra was the last to take a shot at Shalimar and he used his earthy intelligence, the good offices of his ex (Zeenat Aman, who was now Sir John's moll) and a black-and-white-chequered bodysuit to pull it off. Needless to say, he zipped off the booby-trapped island with the gem and his girlfriend before the tribal security could say *Jhingalala.*

As the name **Haath Ki Safai** indicates, the movie was about a pickpocket called Raju Tardeo (Randhir Kapoor), named after his area of operation. There have been many pickpockets in Bollywood and Raju wasn't different from them. This movie stands out for two reasons.

One, Raju was trained in this trade by Usman bhai (Satyen Kappu) who shouted slogans ('*Bolo haath ki safai ki jai*') and sang songs praying for loaded pockets for all humanity. While the song was on, innovative pickpocketing techniques were taught and practised by the trainees. Two, Raju was the long-lost brother of Shankar (Vinod Khanna), a crime boss. Long-lost brothers always meet unknowingly in movies but here they met with *that* dialogue of one-upmanship among thieves. Raju tried to steal Shankar's wallet but got caught. Shankar turned around and said, '*Bachche, tum jis school mein padhte ho hum uske headmaster reh chuke hain.*'

---

[2] Two decades later, Tom Cruise did the same in **Mission Impossible**.

Poignant Detail: Apart from the cash, Shankar's wallet also had his brother Raju's childhood photograph. If the wallet had actually been stolen, then we could have been saved about ten reels of celluloid.

In ***Do Aur Do Paanch***, Amitabh Bachchan and Shashi Kapoor extended their rivalry to stealing Bittoo, son of the ultra-rich Rai Bahadur for whom a couple of crores of ransom wasn't a very big deal. Bittoo's father had created a security ring around his school and brute force wasn't going to breach that. In walked the two thieves posing as teachers in the school and the game was afoot. But all their imaginative attempts to steal the boy ended in disaster since they were hell-bent on pulling each other down. Sometimes it meant putting the little boy in a broken piano and smuggling him out of the school; or chloroforming the poor kid and escaping through a secret passage. Of course, leading actors playing thieves also necessitate a change of heart and the dynamic duo had theirs just in time for the climax.

Anil Kapoor was the King of Thieves aka Romeo aka Ramesh Verma in ***Roop Ki Rani Choron Ka Raja***. One moment, he was making an escape from the scene of crime with a hundred ferocious dogs giving him chase. The next, he had given them the slip and was singing a confessional song ('*Romeo naam mera, chori hai kaam mera*'). Very soon, he had met his match and rival in the Beauty Queen aka Seema Soni who stole diamonds by day and was a supermodel by night. The duo got into a game of one-upmanship in stealing Maharani Yashodhara Devi's diamond necklace (modus operandi very similar to ***Shaan***) and a priceless statue from Egyptian millionaire Abu Aslam Ghanvi (where they appeared as Prince Singh Batata from Matunga and Princess China Cheeni of Chinchpokli[3] respectively). Their rivalry ended in a draw and the two joined forces to steal diamonds worth Rs 100 crore from a train belonging to Kohinoor Diamond Company. Add to this a police officer (Jackie Shroff) who was Romeo's long-lost brother, a philanthropist (Anupam Kher) who had an evil twin and a pigeon called Django—you have a three-hour game of chor–police.

The three films of the ***Dhoom*** franchise are important 'thief' movies because—unlike other movies where the 'hero' is the thief (for noble reasons, usually)—the thieves in this franchise are 'villains', played by strong actors pitted against the heroes (Abhishek Bachchan and Uday Chopra). The thieves have no noble reason behind their actions though they seem to be

---

[3] Chinchpokli, in the movie, was a country sandwiched between China, Chile and Cherrapunji. In reality, it is located somewhere between Lower Parel and Byculla.

honourable guys. John Abraham and his gang were pizza delivery boys by day who turned into a daredevil bunch of thieves also by day (daylight robbery!) as they used the Western Express Highway of Mumbai to make their escapes after looting banks, cash delivery vans and police charity funds before hitting a casino in Goa for their climactic heist. Hrithik Roshan was Mr A, whose ambition was to see his name written across the length and

Sunehri of Andheri: Stealing hearts at a silver screen near you

breadth of the globe. He was the 'smartest and coolest' thief, daring the cops to catch him and leaving clues for the dates of his operations and the pattern of his locations. He took away a Rs 30 crore diamond from the Mumbai Art Museum before stealing a 600-year-old sword from Junagadh Fort. In between, he had picked up a gorgeous assistant called Sunehri before zipping off to Rio to pick up a coin. Not any ordinary coin but the first-ever coins made by man valued at 150 crores. Rupees? Dollars? Mr A never bothered with these trivialities.

Aamir Khan's playground was Chicago where he was taking revenge for a bank's heartless treatment of his father, by robbing them to bankruptcy. Eye-popping bike stunts, ear-popping circus tricks and a brain-popping Katrina Kaif came into play as he ran circles around the American cops, who finally had to call in experts from Mumbai Police to catch the thief.

An IBN7 programme called him a *shaatir, dhurandhar aur hairatangez* criminal with *sansanikhez* thefts under his belt. Abhay Deol as Lucky in **Oye Lucky! Lucky Oye!** used his west Delhi gall and dimpled charm to steal literally everything. He started off with a Mercedes and built his equation with Gogi bhai, who was a party singer by night and a fence for stolen goods even later in the night.

A music system from a teenage girl's room, a TV while *beeji* was lying in the next room, everything from a TV reporter who dared to cross his path, and even a Pomeranian dog! After his arrest, when the police exhibited all the stolen goods, they needed to put up a shamiana in the compound. And that was not enough; they had to travel across India to squeeze out stuff stolen by him in Bangalore and Pune. And yes, he stole female hearts too; when a lady reporter asked the arrested Lucky '*Aage kya plan hai?*', he flashed his dimpled smile and said, '*Bharat darshan. Aaogi?*'

Why would an underworld don wanted for drug-trafficking in eleven countries try to steal Deutschmark printing plates? Search me but that was the premise of **Don 2**. Shah Rukh Khan orchestrated his arrest and incarceration in a Bangkok prison to build his contacts and lay siege on Berlin. All old-fashioned and newfangled implements were brought into play as Don enlisted the support of computer hackers, international mobsters, double agents, old flames and even Hrithik Roshan to enter Berlin's best-guarded building and make off with the plates. In between, there were car chases bang in the middle of Berlin, songs to announce his arrival on to the crime scene, flashes of his past romance and Priyanka Chopra in tight shirts.[4]

STEALING SONGS

While on the subject of lifting, a quick look at the most favourite sources of Bollywood composers.

- 'Macarena': The Los Del Rio hit turned out to be a huge favourite of Anu Malik as he managed to compose two songs in quick succession—'*Dil maka dina*' (in **Dhaal**) and '*Dil le le lena*' (in **Auzaar**)—based on it.
- 'Tama': Mory Kante's 1987 hit inspired two hit composers, of which one did not ever bother to change the lyrics. Laxmikant–Pyarelal took credit for '*Jumma chumma de de*' (**Hum**) while Bappi Lahiri did the same for '*Tamma tamma loge*' (**Pune**).
- ABBA: The Swedish pop group was a big favourite of R.D. Burman's and he based at least two of his massive hit songs on their compositions. '*Mil gaya hum ko saathi*' (from **Hum Kisise Kum Naheen**) was copied from 'Mamma Mia' while '*Kaisa tera pyar kaisa*' (from **Love Story**) was based on 'I Have a Dream'.

---

[4] SRK appeared in the last scene riding a bike with a licence plate reading 'DON 3'. With the 'if' of the sequel settled, we can now discuss: when Don returns, will he be a mafia don or a thief?

Killer Kaun? 13 Clues to Identify Killers

There have been very few true-blue murder mysteries in Bollywood to start with. Some of them got lost in the other subplots that are present almost habitually in every Bollywood film in which the identity of the murderer (or the murdered) is never as important as the next song. A list of murderers can be most intriguing—and even funny—in the Bollywood context but there is the problem of spoilers. So, this list is constructed as a quiz with two parts. The first part is a hint about the identity of the killer and the second part (should you choose to read it) reveals the film from which the killer is taken.

1. The killer wore different-sized shoes (8 and 9).
2. The killer had a bracelet, with a horse emblem dangling from it. The kid hero saw it (only it and nothing but it) as he was peeping from inside a cupboard.
3. The killer had an overgrown toe.
4. The killer was a tiger. No, wait—he was a man. Nope—he was a tiger.
5. The killer got on the train at VT. He got off at Dadar, committed the crime and took a flight to Nagpur, from where he got back on to the train. A perfect alibi of being on the train all the time.
6. The killer had a bandhgala with a button missing. Each button of that bandhgala was a precious stone in an exquisitely crafted setting, worth about a million bucks each.
7. The evil killer had a twin good brother. The evil one killed his brother and set it up as if he had been killed himself. And prepared for a lifetime of respectability.
8. The killer had a slow twin.
9. The killer was the one who was the victim all this while.
10. The killer was the heroine's uncle.
11. The killer was not a killer. Because the victim was not dead.
12. The killer murdered his wife and went to the police to report a case of a missing person.

But a woman turned up, claiming to be his wife.

13. The killer had a cigar. And a hat. And an overcoat in peak summer. And dark glasses in a dimly lit nightclub. Oh wait—he was not the killer. He was 'the CID'.

---

1. Ajit's different-sized feet (and therefore, shoes) were probably the most celebrated physical deformity in Bollywood (apart from Shah Rukh Khan's stammer). In **Yaadon Ki Baaraat**, Ajit played Shaakaal—the goggled super-villain who thought nothing of killing painters who could paint his likeness for the police. But he never bargained for the painter's three sons who would see his different-sized shoes and one of whom would grow up to be the He-est Man in Bollywood. Great music, super dialogue and a breathtaking pace . . . we almost forgot that there was a murderer.

2. It's Ajit again, underlining how pervasive the Loin was as a villain in the 1970s. In **Zanjeer**, he played Teja—the mobster who went on to become the don and had to contend with honest police officers with a bad temper and great lines (written by the hottest scriptwriters of the country). The father who got killed was totally inconsequential in the greater scheme of things while the killer's distinctive bracelet assumed a bigger role by haunting the son throughout his life.

3. Paresh Rawal's gigantic toe gave him away. In **Baazi**, he was the slimy deputy CM Chaubey, who was not beyond harbouring terrorists in his own home and molesting dancers he took a fancy to. He got chopped up by a special branch officer, who realized in the climax that Chaubey's big toe was the same size as his father's killer's (who had also made lewd propositions to his mother, for good measure). To know how that little boy saw the killer's toe but not his face, you have to see the film.

4. It was Rahul Roy, who looked dangerously close to being naked in some scenes. In **Junoon**, he was the ichhadhari tiger (which was such a welcome change after years of ichhadhari *nagins*). As every little child with a very basic knowledge of biology knows, a human turns into a tiger every full-moon night if he is bitten by a cursed tiger. This was exactly what happened to Rahul. The mild-mannered Rahul turned into a Big Cat, only to devour all those he did not like in his human avatar.

5. It was the Big B, in one of his earlier roles as a crazed lover. In **Parwana**, he

was the artist Kumar Sen, who faced the double whammy of being rejected as suitor by his supposed girlfriend's uncle while the girl fell in love with Navin Nischol. He solved both these problems in one fell swoop when he murdered the uncle and framed his girlfriend's lover for the crime. And he did this with extensive help from Indian Railways and Indian Airlines.

6. Prem Nath was the uber-cool Good Samaritan who turned out nothing like he pretended to be. In *Teesri Manzil*, he was Kunwar Sahab, the millionaire with a heart of gold who went all out to help the hero clear his name as a murder suspect. Not only that, he was the ever-smiling elder statesman who supported the latter's romantic pursuits as well. Except that he had had a relationship with the dead woman he pushed from the eponymous third floor. And in the scuffle, the victim wrenched a button off his coat.

7. Anupam Kher was the one zipping between saints and sinners. In *Roop Ki Rani Choron Ka Raja*, he played Jugran—the mastermind of jewel heists who assumed the persona of noted industrialist and do-gooder Manmohan Lal. This latter had fooled everybody because they had given up the villain Jugran for dead. Along came the Beauty Queen and the King of Thieves who realized that the bruises on Jugran's wrists were exactly the same as those on Manmohan Lal's.

8. In **Akayla**, Keith Stevenson played the roles of twin brothers—one mentally retarded and the other, cruel. He was Tony Braganza who was regularly arrested at crime scenes by an alcoholic cop in a yellow Beetle. And every single time, his lawyer managed to get him off the hook by showing irrefutable proof of his presence at a different place at the same time. It was working like a dream till the cop's girlfriend took him to see a film called *Seeta Aur Geeta* (incidentally directed by Ramesh Sippy too).

9. Urmila Matondkar played the girl all alone in a mansion, terrorized by strangers. In *Kaun*, she was forever shivering and giggling as she went traipsing all alone in her house having heard the news of a serial killer on the prowl. A garrulous door-to-door salesman landed up, as did a gun-toting silent type. They were soon fighting to save the helpless girl from each other. And when one of them reached the attic to pacify the girl, there was a body there. Soon, there were two.

10. Anant Mahadevan, known for his studious looks and mild demeanour, was the man out to get his niece's inheritance. In *Khiladi*, he was the insignificant brick in the even-more-insignificant background wall as a group of college kids

played a kidnapping prank that went wrong, with one of them ending up with a knife in the back. There was a brother who was a police officer. A dancer who tried to run down people with her car. A comedian who was hard of hearing. And a 'player' who bet on everything.

11. Well, there was no killer but it was Surendra Kumar who orchestrated his own death. In **Do Gaz Zameen Ke Neeche**, one of the earlier Ramsay Brothers spooks, he was a part-time scientist and full-time millionaire who was 'murdered' by his gold-digger wife and her shady uncle. Burying him in a grave two yards deep (how did you ever guess?), the duo started robbing his mansion and strange things happened. Money and jewels vanished, their plans were thwarted and, finally, the grave turned out to be empty.

12. Rishi Kapoor was the very unlikely wife-killer. In **Khoj**, he was initially the hassled husband—Ravi Kapoor—who reported his wife to be missing. A woman emerged soon after, claiming to be his wife. Ravi went blue in the face telling everybody that she wasn't his wife but she seemed to have every proof including wedding photos and marriage certificates. Very soon, a priest emerged to support the story and there was only one way left for the husband to convince the world that this wasn't his wife—by confessing where he had hidden her body after killing her.

13. Iftekhar—he of the slim build and slimmer moustache—has been playing these laconic roles since eternity. In **Khel Khel Mein**, he appeared on the sidelines of a college prank gone wrong. A group of students had written a letter to blackmail a jeweller, who was killed immediately afterwards. Threatened with the possibility of being seen as murderers, they embarked on an elaborate cover-up mission as Iftekhar the mysterious landed up at every place they tried to hide in. So, if he wasn't the killer, who was the killer? Well, that's one spoiler less then.

Evil Eve: 10 Lady Villains

Bollywood has created several iconic villains who dominate our memories. Vamps have either been relegated to being molls or cruel mothers-in-law. The main villain, around whom the story is pivoted, is seldom a woman. But on the relatively fewer occasions when it has been so, the fun—intended or not—is quite unprecedented.

A dreaded crime boss is apprehended by the police. Instead of publicizing the arrest, the police find a lookalike and infiltrate the gang to find out more. When the crime boss finds out—wait a minute, isn't this the story of *Don*? Well, this was also the story of **Madam X**—starring Rekha in a double role.[1] Rekha's jewel-encrusted shoes, colour-coordinated costumes (from head to toe), monogrammed headgear and even a gold-plated machine gun were straight out of bling heaven. On top of that, if you add the Mogambo-like following ('*Madam X ko mera salaam*') and Macmohan as her right-hand man (imaginatively named Sambha), you have Bollywood's most flamboyant lady villain. Oh—and did I mention her cool signature line? '*Hum hain maut ki woh express, duniya jisse kehti hai Madam X!*'

Getting married to a rich dude for his property is an old trick in Bollywood. Killing him off in the 'Just Married' car is slightly less common. But having to contend with the dead man's reincarnation was something only Simi Garewal did, in Subhash Ghai's **Karz**. The game started at the behest of crime boss Sir Juda (Prem Nath) but the plot was soon taken over by Simi. She aged two decades in the movie, going from seductress Kamini to the regal Rani Saheba. She seduced Ravi Verma and then romanced his reincarnation Monty Oberoi with style. On the one hand, she had to contend with Monty and his cohorts trying to extract a confession

---

[1] The male lead was Pakistani cricketer Mohsin Khan, who married Reena Roy and had a stint in Bollywood. His acting career ended in a resounding thud after a few forgettable flops.

of her crime. On the other, she had to rebel against Sir Juda. It was a role to die for and Simi Garewal put in a stellar performance to become the only Bollywood villain to have a love song dedicated to her in the film—'*Ek haseena thi . . .*'

Bonus Movie: Subhash Ghai's classic was remade as **Karzzz**—tragically starring Himesh Reshamiyya as Ravi/Monty and Urmila Matondkar as Rani Saheba. The twang of '*Tan-tan-tandoori Nights*' only made us realize how much we still love the original.

Urmila Matondkar played the psychotic female stalker to perfection in **Pyar Tune Kya Kiya**. She was the spoilt daughter of a billionaire who fell in love with a photographer (Fardeen Khan). Used to getting whatever she wanted, she was seriously shocked when she found out that her beau was happily married and his flirtatious behaviour towards her was not love. That was the trigger for her to turn into a love-crazed demon—stalking him, threatening him, misleading his wife, trying to commit suicide, and finally trying to kill his wife. The movie—produced by Ram Gopal Varma—did not do very well at the box office probably because Urmila's tragic end was not taken well by the audience. After all, the world loves a lover—even a crazed one.

Rajkumari Suryalekha of Sangramgadh didn't just hate men. Her hatred for men was so strong that she reared an army of gladiators (and leopards and man-gorillas) to fight whoever desired her hand in marriage. Such a role can only be played by an actress anointed Mard Singh after her first movie and it was indeed Amrita Singh who played the androgynist princess. But she was up against a pillar of strength, a mountain of muscle—the descendant of Surya *Suryavanshi* Vikram Singh (Salman Khan).[2] In a transgenerational saga, the body of Suryalekha traumatized medieval India and her ghost traumatized modern India—running into Salman Khan on both occasions. Women and Salman have had violent pasts and this movie was no different. And yes, he won.

Honey Irani's directorial debut featured yet another spoilt brat—Preity Zinta, who was suffering from schizophrenia in **Armaan**. Amitabh Bachchan and Anil Kapoor were a father–son doctor duo, committed to building a state-of-the-art hospital for the poor. When Amitabh died with the wish unfulfilled, Anil decided to marry Preity for the money he would get from her father to complete the hospital. He broke up with his girlfriend—Miss Goody Two-Shoes Gracy

---

[2] Strangely, Salman Khan—in his medieval avatar—had blonde shoulder-length hair and a get-up reminiscent of Thor. Only the hammer was missing.

Singh—for this and ran into a Zinta-sized tornado. Preity turned into a full-time witch as she bullied Miss Goody Two-Shoes, accused Anil Kapoor of infidelity, embarrassed him in public, tried to seduce him with the most un-sexy seduction song ever and slashed her wrists. (Now, where have we heard this before?) For her troubles, Preity Zinta received a Filmfare nomination for Best Performance in a Negative Role.

Preity Zinta did not win the Best Villain Filmfare Award. Kajol did—for *Gupt*. There, I said it. But strictly speaking, the spoiler went off when Kajol collected the award. Kajol's love story with Bobby Deol got soured when Bobby's father (Raj Babbar) announced his marriage to Manisha Koirala. An incensed Bobby threatened his own father at the party and Raj Babbar was duly found stabbed to death. Bobby was sentenced to fourteen years in prison for the crime but he broke out of jail to find the killer and a chase of red herrings began. Rajiv Rai directed this smart thriller—also a huge hit—where Kajol killed several people to keep the suspense alive till the very end. Wait a minute. She murdered all those people for Bobby Deol? Hmm. Not a very smart killer then, no?

SPOILER ALERT

Lady Macbeth is one of Shakespeare's most complex characters and in Vishal Bhardwaj's recreation of the play, Tabu's performance in the role was brilliant if not perfect. In *Maqbool*, she was the lover of the protagonist and egged him on to murder the man whose mistress she was. She was a hot seductress and cold dominatrix by turns, driving Irrfan Khan to a murderous frenzy. She plotted the murder perfectly and was his active accessory in removing the mafia don, which paved the way for Maqbool's ascension. Post the murder, her guilt and hallucinations were hair-raisingly real. Much has been said and written about Tabu's acting talents and nowhere are these it more apparent than in the chilling negative character of *Maqbool*.

Vishal Bhardwaj has a knack for creating memorable lady villains. She had gnarled fingers, matted hair and creepy eyes. She stayed in a dilapidated mansion adorned with skull and bones. She drank the blood of eagles and bats. She was known to have dark magical powers and turned people into animals at a star-shaped altar in her mansion. She was the *chudail* in *Makdee*.

While it was supposed to be a film for children, Shabana Azmi became an evil witch who managed to scare even adults. She met her match in Chunni (child actor Shweta Prasad) after she 'turned' her twin sister Munni into a chicken. The little girl pulled together all her courage, friends and meagre resources to fight the evil witch—who became a metaphor for superstition and blind faith. And in the climax, Shabana Azmi's frenzied performance made us realize once again why she is still India's finest actress.

Villainous women usually use sex as a weapon. Whose body can be a better sexual weapon than Bipasha Basu's? And how can you call the movie anything other than *Jism*?

Bipasha Basu seduced John Abraham to assist her in murdering her husband and claiming his inheritance. In the traditions of Vishesh Films, the movie had extended lovemaking scenes to the tune of hit songs. Bipasha Basu's lithe figure (especially her bronzed back) was lovingly portrayed as were John's dimples and abs, both adding considerably to the on-screen heat. Once the murder was done and panic calmed down John's libido, he realized he had been had—badly. Bipasha Basu was the manipulative queen bee who orchestrated murders to enter her rich husband's life and then, again, to get him to exit hers. There was something about her that caused men to lose all their senses and just die at her command. As they said in the song, '*Jaadu hai, nasha hai . . .*'

Aitraaz was *Disclosure* with a desi makeover, in which Priyanka Chopra's character was nothing like Bollywood had ever seen. She had a romantic liaison with Akshay Kumar, which involved premarital sex (gasp!). When she got pregnant, she went ahead with an abortion (double gasp!) while her beau was mumbling promises of marriage. She then got married to an ageing billionaire (triple gasp!) and became her ex-lover's boss by becoming the chairperson of his telecom company. She promoted her ex-lover so that she could have a good time with him. As she tried to get down and dirty with him, she huskily said a line quite momentous for Bollywood: '*Maine kab kaha ki tum apni biwi ko chhod do? Main toh sirf physical relationship ke liye keh rahi hoon . . .*' And, of course, she accused him of rape when he didn't listen to her demands. She came up against a *sati savitri* in court when Kareena Kapoor decided to become husband Akshay Kumar's defence counsel. And you know what happens when loose women face *pativrataa*s in Bollywood, don't you?

And finally, we have the film named after a lady villain – *Khal-Naaikaa*.

After the mushy debut in *Aashiqui*, Anu Agarwal acted in this remake of *The Hand That Rocks the Cradle* and played the governess from hell. In an attempt to take revenge for her husband's death (who was a patient-molesting doctor, by the way), Anu wreaked havoc on the lady (Jaya Pradha) who complained against the doc. The Devil wore Pradha down through murder of a faithful family retainer, murder attempts on all and sundry and seduction attempts on her husband (Jeetendra). Finally, she got into a suit for the climax and took a baseball bat to the battle before collapsing in a bloody heap.

Jab Tak Suraj Chand Rahega: 10 Politicians

Bollywood rarely goes beyond fisticuffs to solve problems. Televised debate is just not its thing. Two *maharathi*s are more adept at picking up swords than a megaphone. Though occasionally there has been the appearance of khadi and the Gandhi *topi*—both uniforms of the favourite whipping boy of Indian cinema. But while politicians have been all over the place, they have essentially been effete or villainous caricatures, always at the receiving end of bombastic speeches or severe beatings by the hero or heroine. The nitty-gritties of political strategy and the real hurly-burly of political action have been in the limelight fewer times.

Aandhi still remains an iconic film depicting Indian elections in partly realistic, partly airbrushed glory. With the streak of white in her black hair, Suchitra Sen will always be the on-screen Indira Gandhi despite hectic clarifications that the character was based on nobody in particular.[1]

An initially Bohemian daughter of an established and overbearing politician fell in love and married a hotelier. Unable to take the twin pressures of her father's political ambitions and being a wife, she walked out of the marriage and the town. She came back several years later to fight an election (under the symbol of a bird) and rediscovered her love for the estranged husband. All hell broke loose as her rivals started to dig up skeletons and scandals around this 'affair'. People tend to remember this film only for the absolutely stupendous soundtrack (probably the greatest of the Gulzar–RD collaborations), but the entire electoral process was reasonably well sketched—including a satirical song on politicians returning to constituencies every five years. What a pity it was the weakest song in the album.

You cannot talk about elections in films without *Coolie* and *Inquilaab*—and they are obviously connected. Needless to say, these were the most unrealistic films of the lot. But

---

[1] It has sometimes been reported that the character was based on Nandini Satpathy, ex-chief minister of Odisha.

then, if you want reality, you may as well go and watch *Bigg Boss*. Also, the elections were only a small part of the overall package of the two films, in the true tradition of all Amitabh films of the early '80s (where everything, except Amitabh himself, was a small part of the overall package). Given the topicality of Amitabh's entry into politics around that time and that the political subplots in both films were so unconnected to the initial storylines, they might well have been written halfway through the shooting. Or maybe, on the morning of the shoot. In *Coolie*, Iqbal went from being a porter to a trade unionist (for other porters) to an organizer of strikes to an election candidate—who then got blackmailed into almost withdrawing by villains (who had kidnapped his mother). In *Inquilaab*, the transformation was even more dramatic. Amarnath started off as a black marketeer of tickets. He became a police officer. He was promoted to ACP. He killed a dreaded smuggler—Khoya Khoya Attachi—after which he was made the leader of *Garibon Ki Party*. He won the elections in a landslide and became the chief minister. What he did at his first cabinet meeting is something I dare not repeat, lest some Young Turks get ideas.

Aaj Ka MLA Ram Avtar proved anybody—absolutely anybody—could become an elected political representative. Even your friendly neighbourhood barber called—you guessed it—Ram Avtar. Rajesh Khanna played the barber to the minister who got pole-vaulted into politics when his minister's party ran out of candidates. The genial shaver entered the fray with the good wishes and votes of his many supporters who expected the simple do-gooder to push their case. But Ram Avtar transformed into one slimy politician once he got the MLA stamp next to his name. To paraphrase a famous line, since he did not die a hero, he lived long enough to become a villain. But the good thing about Bollywood is that redemption is just a climax away.

It may have been the elections for only a village cooperative, but Shyam Benegal infused it with all the emotion that is normally associated with the general elections in India. *Manthan* saw the sarpanch (Kulbhushan Kharbanda) being pitted against lower-caste candidate Bhola (Naseeruddin Shah) in an election to manage their milk cooperative. This unequal battle was catalysed by the modern-thinking Dr Rao (Girish Karnad, playing a role based on Dr Verghese Kurien's life). Given the social churning that was brought about, the sarpanch, who was used to winning elections unopposed, lost this first election he contested.

One of the most politically charged films in recent times has been *Yuva*. Set against the volatile politics of Bengal, the countryside, the rural elections, the strong-arm tactics of the ruling party and the idealism of college politics were brought out vividly. After a maze of machinations by the villains and some depressing violence, the three young men—led by Ajay Devgn—

managed to win their first elections and walked into the Assembly to become three spots of blue denim in a sea of white dhoti–kurtas. You couldn't help but feel a frisson of happiness at even this obviously unrealistic situation. When you see the film, you wonder, why was it set in Calcutta? But then, where else?

In Anurag Kashyap's edgy *Gulaal*, a college election assumed epic proportions. Hanging in the balance were not just the lakhs that could be siphoned off from the college festival fund but how the winner would impact the separatist movement for Rajputana. Pitting the volatile Ransa (Abhimanyu Singh in a short but brilliant role) against the steely Kiran (Ayesha Mohan), the entire build-up to and conduct of the election was played at a hurtling pace. The campaigning, the abrupt and brutal murder of a candidate, the emergence of a replacement and the subtle rigging to swing the results were paced breathtakingly and filmed in a jagged, realistic style.

Political satires are few and far between in Bollywood. After all the intensity and unrealism of the previous films, we have *Chintuji*—with Rishi Kapoor in the title role. Ostensibly playing himself, the film star landed up in his (semi-manufactured) village of birth with a PR manager in tow to contest an election, and promptly got embroiled in many complications. The film took a caustic look at two of India's most visible careerists—film stars and politicians—borrowing extensively from real-life characters and creating a hilarious mockumentary at the end of it.

Ram Gopal Varma's *Rann* viewed elections and politics through a different prism. It examined how the media looks at politics, how it becomes part of it even without wanting to. Or, how it wants to. With Paresh Rawal as the unscrupulous PM-in-waiting, Mohan Pandey, the film followed the fortunes and dilemmas of idealistic media baron Harsh Vardhan Malik (played with his usual aplomb by Amitabh Bachchan). The two were supported by a very talented ensemble cast as the film did a reasonable recce of politics in the times of 24x7 news cameras. Sting operations, orchestrated riots, moles in the media, the business of politics and the politics of business made for a realistic film that was an almost unceasingly cynical take on our times. And that was probably best brought out by an acidic reprise of our national anthem that was considered too explosive for public consumption and not passed for cinematic release. Sigh—a ban on a film on the media.

Probably the most definitive film on contemporary politics is Prakash Jha's *Raajneeti*. Here, we got to see the whole gamut of dirty politics that included but was not restricted to sex, money and power. The plot was a condensed version of the Mahabharata[2]—the go-to manual

---

[2] See 'The Great Indian Movie: 8 Movies Inspired by Epics' on page 289.

for politics, anyway—packed into the campaigning process for a state's election. Brothers of all kinds—full, half-, step-, illegitimate—lived and died as dynastic politics kicked in at its ugliest. The film climaxed with the entry of Katrina Kaif in the political arena, playing the young widow of the scion of a political family. She went hoarse trying to explain that the role was not based on the life of Sonia Gandhi, but her point would have been a little easier to believe if she hadn't worn those cotton sarees and styled her hair a little differently. And yes—her accent wasn't similar. Wait, why did she have an accent in the film? Well, she has an accent in every film.

BATTLE OF THE STARS

While there are many stars who joined politics, film stars fighting elections against each other are relatively rare.

Rajesh Khanna (Congress) vs Shatrughan Sinha (BJP)

Rajesh Khanna entered politics with a bang as he contested against L.K. Advani in the 1991 Lok Sabha elections in the New Delhi constituency. His charisma almost pulled him through, however, he lost to the veteran leader by a mere 1589 votes. Since Advani had also won from Gandhinagar, he vacated the seat and by-polls were ordered. This time, BJP fielded Shatrughan Sinha to nullify the star power, but that was not enough and Rajesh Khanna won comfortably.

During the 2014 election campaigning, Shatrughan Sinha said that he regretted contesting that election because he lost a very good friend in Rajesh Khanna due to the political battle.

Kirron Kher (BJP) vs Gul Panag (AAP)

While not as high-voltage as the Rajesh–Shatru battle, the 2014 Lok Sabha elections had the two major actresses contesting from Chandigarh. The campaigning was hectic and occasionally bitter. Panag upped the glamour quotient by campaigning on bikes while Kher fell back on her Punjabi mother roles to bring in the sentiment. Eventually, Kirron Kher pulled through quite easily, riding on the BJP wave throughout the country and polling nearly double the votes.

Dawaa Ya Dua: 8 Kinds of Diseases

A doctor comes out of the OT (a red bulb switches off), takes off his glasses and morosely pronounces, '*Inhe dawaon ki nahin, duaon ki zaroorat hai.*' This is the cue for the kin to break for a kirtan (Asha Parekh) or a diatribe against God (Amitabh Bachchan). But what are the diseases being fought? Apart from accidents, and pregnancy (which *is* treated as a disease), what are the other afflictions? In short, what ails Bollywood?

Cancer

The Big C is undoubtedly the most popular disease for the absolute surety it brings to the death of the protagonist. Rajesh Khanna would have to be the brand ambassador of the disease, with deadly performances in two landmark films—*Anand* and *Safar*. These had everything an ideal cancer patient should exhibit—stoicism, joie de vivre and an ability to sacrifice everything on his way out. Anand even had a name for the illness—lymphosarcoma of the intestine. And he was very proud of the regal sound of it: '*Jaise kisi viceroy ka naam ho . . .*'

Amitabh Bachchan got the disease (lung cancer) himself in *Waqt: The Race Against Time*. And he had nine months to make his son stand on his own two feet before he died. In those nine months, his son fell in love, went on a honeymoon and became an action star who did his own stunts. Wow.

Brain Tumour

The other 'fatal' disease in Bollywood is brain tumour.

In two movies—*Kaash* (directed by Mahesh Bhatt) and *Anjali* (directed by Mani Ratnam)—it is a child that has the tumour, making things all the more tragic. While the former had a star couple trying to patch up a marriage for the sake of their son, the latter had a group of siblings starting to accept their terminally ill sister back into their household. Both gut-wrenching.

The Big B had a brain tumour with a bizarre twist in **Majboor**. When diagnosed with the disease, AB was faced with an operation with limited chance of success and potential paralysis. Instead, he chose to confess to a millionaire's murder and redirect the informer's reward to make his mother's and siblings' lives secure. On death row, he had a seizure, was operated upon and had his tumour successfully removed. Now, he was in jail wrongly accused of murder (which he had confessed to, himself) and a healthy life ahead of him. *Kya hua* next?

Heart Diseases

Usually, the extreme form of this is used to dispatch Daddy when the baraat goes back for want of dowry or when the daughter runs away to marry out of caste. Nazir Hussain specialized in rolling his eyes, stopping mid-sentence, clutching the left side of his chest and collapsing in a heap. There are way too many scenes like that to keep count. The long-drawn-out heart disease is used to keep the viewer in suspense over the fate of the patient. This disease is also a money-sink for which the patient's relatives have to adopt desperate measures.

Shah Rukh Khan's tragic act in **Kal Ho Naa Ho** remains the beacon of cardiac plot lines of all time. He cracked jokes with Saif, wooed Preity and generally acted like the Good Samaritan, but when your cardiologist Dr Sonali Bendre leaves you for Sanjay Kapoor, you should commit suicide if not die of a terminal illness.

Sometimes kids get afflicted with these as well. Ajay Devgn's nephew in **Pyar To Hona Hi Tha** had a hole in his heart, for which Ajay went around stealing stuff. Like the adult patients of this disease, this kid also turned out to be good-natured, his part leading to a greater number of wet hankies.

Amnesia

The signature line of this disease is '*Main kahan hoon? Main kaun hoon?*' accompanied by a take on the first question and a double take on the second.

Sadma had a case of selective amnesia, where Sridevi forgot everything between age five and her current age. Evil reviewers commented that there was not too much of a gap between her mental age and that of a five-year-old, anyway. But her act as a little girl in a twenty-one-year-old body was quite good, although all people remember from that film are Yesudas's songs.

Another movie with star amnesia—actually 'retrograde amnesia' (whatever *that* means)—was **Salaam-e-Ishq** (which has also been referred to as Salaam-e-Eeks). Vidya Balan remembered everything in her life except John Abraham. Our dude had to do what he never did before . . . he tried to remind a girl of himself. Maybe Vidya had a secret affair with Hrithik and wanted to forget John. Either that, or women forget their husbands two years after marriage.

The most hilarious amnesiac of them all was Aamir Khan in *Andaz Apna Apna*. He pretended to lose his memory after Raveena Tandon hit him on the head with a stick, and thus became her house-guest. Since he did not even remember his own name, he was christened Teelu (because he was found on a *teela*) and had to be treated by Dr Prem Khurana (who was '*Iss dhande mein bahut purana!*').

Selective Memory Alert: If *Andaz Apna Apna* was Aamir's comic turn, **Ghajini** was his manic turn. A head injury led to him contracting a medical condition last seen in Hollywood (*Memento*, 2000). His memory lasted all of fifteen minutes after which he had to depend on Polaroid photographs kept in his pockets, Post-it notes all over his house, and tattooed instructions all over his body. Good thing he didn't get married in the film. Imagine what havoc he would have played with his wife's birthday?

Blindness

It started off with *Dosti* and has carried on beyond *Fanaa*. Most of the biggies of Hindi cinema—Rajesh Khanna (*Mere Jeevan Saathi*), Sanjeev Kumar (*Qatl*), Amitabh Bachchan (the unreleased *Zamaanat*), Mumtaz (*Jheel Ke Us Paar*), Madhuri Dixit (*Sangeet*), Kajol (*Fanaa*), Naseeruddin Shah (*Sparsh*), Rani Mukherji (*Black*), Akshay Kumar (*Aankhen*), Deepika Padukone (*Lafangey Parindey*)—have played blind people. And some of them have pretended to be blind as well (Amitabh Bachchan in *Parvarish* and Mehmood in *Johar Mehmood in Hong Kong*).

Ship of Theseus told the remarkable story of a blind photographer who got her sight back thanks to a donated cornea—but that created a new problem. Aida Al-Kashef—who is an Egyptian film-maker—played the blind woman with a rare sensitivity and the blindness was shown—well—in new light.

Nirupa Roy turned blind on screen—when a tree descended on her—and then regained her eyesight after she fervently prayed to Shirdi wale Sai Baba. In *Amar Akbar Anthony*, twin flames emerged out of the eyes of the Baba, travelled all the way to the back of the prayer hall and inserted themselves in her eyes. And she saw again! *Zor se bolo jai Baba ki! Phir se bolo jai Baba ki!*

AIDS

One reason why AIDS is yet to catch on as a life-ending disease in Bollywood is because of the doubt it brings about the patient's character. Imagine Bhaskar Banerjee thinking about

Anand, 'Hmmm, the bugger was getting it on the sly . . . that's how he got the virus . . .' Poof! All the poignancy and sympathy would fly out of the window. Hence, it has been seen only in serious movies dealing specifically with the problems associated with the disease.

Phir Milenge (directed by Revathy) had Salman Khan infecting Shilpa Shetty with the virus after a one-night stand, but the movie was so sparsely watched, nobody thought of burning their effigies for promiscuity and moral turpitude.

Onir's *My Brother Nikhil* was probably the first Indian movie to show a gay relationship realistically, without either of the partners being portrayed a pansy, or cracking any jokes about homosexuality. Sanjay Suri delivered a first-rate performance as the award-winning sportsman who got ostracized because of his disease.

Others

Devdas is the poster boy of liver disease (presumably cirrhosis) since he was the pioneer of drinking-to-death. Chhoti Bahu of *Sahib Bibi Aur Ghulam* is, of course, the poster girl.

Sanjay Leela Bhansali was not happy with Rani's triple handicap in *Black* so he gave Amitabh Alzheimer's. Subsequently, Kajol was afflicted with the same disease in *U Me Aur Hum* as her (real-life and filmy) husband Ajay Devgn wooed her afresh every day.

Amitabh Bachchan made progeria famous with his glorious performance in *Paa*, complete with a young boy's shuffle, prosthetic make-up and 'shitty' dialogue.

Not to be left behind on uncommon diseases, Shah Rukh Khan became the Asperger's Syndrome–afflicted Rizvan Khan in *My Name Is Khan* and gave this version of autism a visibility that only he can bring.

Filmi Diseases

And, of course, there are diseases that could not have happened anywhere in the world but in Bollywood. Hyperactive imaginations have come up with some really crazy afflictions.

Like loveria, for example. In *Raju Ban Gaya Gentleman*, SRK and Juhi Chawla had this disease characterized by deep sighs, insomnia and general unease. An elaborate song-and-dance routine was created around it, which soon topped every music chart in town and nobody wanted to get well too soon.

In *Bol Radha Bol*—a maniacal comedy by David Dhawan—Kader Khan turned blind at 6 p.m. every evening. And you thought that was funny? Well, at the climax, his eyesight was restored to 24x7 but his hearing vanished at the same time of day instead. Beat that! Or better still, find a cure for that.

7

All That Connects Us

Connecting people
—Tag line of Nokia

We get news. We get information. We go from one place to another. We share common passions.

This section is about how Bollywood looks at information, broadcasting, transportation and passion.

Stop Press: 10 Filmi Newspapers

Journalists have been beacons of hope in many films. Over many years we had newspaper reporters and photographers chasing crooked politicians and evil businessmen. Now—in the last decade or so—we have had TV journalists coming into the fray as well. A journalist in Bollywood has always been clearly typified—wearing a kurta–pajama (for the Hindi press) or jeans with a photographer's jacket (English)—but their newspapers less so. Which newspapers did they work for? What were their editors like? Their owners? Their editorial policies? Do they ever show anything about the making of the newspaper except the mandatory shot of the printed papers pouring off the press?

Dainik Aelaan / Comrade Daily

Yash Chopra's **Mashaal** was about the passing of the torch of courageous journalism from one idealistic reporter to another. Dilip Kumar started off as a senior journalist who left his job because his paper did not take kindly to his exposés of an influential businessman (Amrish Puri) with political ambitions. Egged on by his wife (Waheeda Rehman) to start his own paper, Dilip Kumar started *Dainik Aelaan* and continued his journalism of courage. Not only that, he even inspired a tapori (Anil Kapoor) to give up a life of crime and become a journalist. Things turned around when Dilip Kumar lost everything—including his wife—and took to a life of crime. His protégé returned and started a crusade to expose his erstwhile mentor. He did this by infiltrating gangs using his tapori connections—giving embedded journalism a filmi twist! His vehicle was a newspaper with clearly Leftist leanings—*Comrade Daily*—which boasted of a bearded man (Alok Nath) as the editor and had another bearded man (Karl Marx) enshrined on the wall.

Daily Toofan

When you had an editor who climbed on tables while talking to his star reporter, who paid extra money to get a scoop on an absconding heiress and who popped pills while trying to tear out his hair, the newspaper he ran was bound to be super-interesting. In *Dil Hai Ke Manta Nahin*, Tiku Talsania ran the aptly named *Daily Toofan* and had explosive tiffs with his smart-alec crime reporter Raghu Jaitley. But he was not beyond consoling the guy when he had a break-up and resembled the Bollywood father figure: a heart of gold inside a tough exterior.

Crimes of India

Do we have so many crimes and misdemeanours going on around us that we have a full newspaper dedicated to it? Of course we do. In fact, the crime situation can be so bad that we would need an invisible hero—*Mr India*—to solve it. The *Crimes of India* had Mr Gaitonde as editor, who continuously got wrongly connected calls (from international smugglers and housewives seeking dry-cleaners), and a vivacious journalist called Seema Soni who hated kids. Annu Kapoor did a superb comic turn as the hassled editor of the newspaper which loved doing interviews with criminals just released from prison. Apparently, the newspaper also carried ads for houses on rent and you had simple people like Arun Verma (played by Anil Kapoor) walking into the office to book an ad. He got mistaken for a thief just released from jail and the mistaken identity was only one of the many states of confusion that the newspaper endured.

Independent / Swatantra Bharat

The meteoric rise of *Guru*—Gurukant Desai—was precipitated by the strong support he got from the upright newspaper-editor and -owner Manik Dasgupta of the *Independent*. Right from the pre-Independence days, this editor had championed causes that were noble. So, when Guru turned truant, it was Manik Dasgupta (aka Nanaji) who let loose his best journalist (Shyam Saxena, played by Madhavan) to expose him. The film's story was believed to have been loosely based on Dhirubhai Ambani's life and his run-ins with Ramnath Goenka of the *Indian Express*; Madhavan's character was apparently based on that of Arun Shourie. Mithun Chakraborty delivered a brilliant performance as the honest and eccentric Bengali editor of the principled daily, and Mani Ratnam's eye for detail

Manik Dasgupta, editor-in-chief, the Independent *and* Swatantra Bharat

ensured that the look of the newspaper was very real—right from the masthead down to the columns.

New Delhi Diary

Jeetendra's few offbeat roles—in between his white-shoe-pencil-moustache-energetic-dance routine—tend to get lost. In *New Delhi*, a songless thriller, he played a journalist who got beaten to paralysis and was then jailed by an evil politician duo. After coming out of prison, he, along with his girlfriend, started a newspaper called *New Delhi Diary* which seemed to have a knack for getting exclusives ahead of everybody else, from its mysterious reporter Vishwanath. In a plot lifted partially from Irving Wallace's *The Almighty*, Jeetendra delivered a restrained performance as the newspaper editor who plotted brilliantly to bring his powerful enemies to their knees. Incidentally, there was a scene in this film where Jeetendra single-handedly made the entire front page of the paper's launch edition. Real-life editors have confirmed that this is a task probably even beyond Superman. But not the Bollywood hero.

New Delhi Times

Written by Gulzar and set in modern New Delhi, the film of the same name traced the experiences of editor Vikas Pande (Shashi Kapoor in a National Award–winning role) as he unravelled the sinister connection between a hooch tragedy and the murder of an MLA against a backdrop of political unrest. The political pressures on a leading daily's editor, the editor–owner relationship, the ambitious and ruthless politician, the perils of idealism, and even the work–life balance of a journalist were brought out brilliantly in the film. The film had a wealth of acting talent—the characters of Om Puri as a politician, Sharmila Tagore as the editor's wife, Manohar Singh as the newspaper-owner and A.K. Hangal as the editor's idealist father were all wonderfully etched.

Samaadhan

What kind of newspaper sends reporters to jail to track convicts who may actually be innocent? That too, lady reporters in bright yellow dresses. But then, the reporter was the jailer's daughter and when she (Raveena Tandon) was attacked by burly goons, there was a burlier hero (Sunil Shetty) to save her. This was *Mohra*. Raveena Tandon worked for a newspaper called *Samaadhan* under the able editorial guidance of Yunus Parvez and she was ever-ready to assist Inspector Amar (Akshay Kumar) on undercover missions, as a cabaret dancer. But except for the first few minutes of the film—in which she embarked upon a crusade to free the wrongfully convicted Sunil Shetty—Raveena did nothing even remotely resembling a journalist's normal work. But then, you did not go to watch her pen an op-ed piece. You went to see her dance in the rain, wearing a clingy yellow saree.

Khabardaar

Two struggling photographers trying to run a studio got commissioned to take pictures by a newspaper out to expose the high and mighty. The sting was to be done on a well-known builder who had a finger in a commissioner's murder, and they all ended up in a live play with a corpse which had become something like a proof of the murder. Those who have seen *Jaane Bhi Do Yaaro* would realize what an inadequate description of the story this is and how every single element added exponentially to the mayhem. Bhakti Barve played the no-nonsense editor of *Khabardaar*, a newspaper which stayed true to its name by being a whistle-blower. The editor was not beyond flirting with her freelance minion (Naseeruddin Shah) to get him to swear undying loyalty to her. Nor was she beyond a few behind-the-scenes dealmakings to get a good price for the pictures.

Nation Today

Page 3 became the first newspaper section to be made into a film and Konkona Sen Sharma played the journalist zipping around high-society parties in Mumbai even as she faced taunts from colleagues about whether her beat was news or entertainment. Madhur Bhandarkar is known for the meticulous research he puts into his films and this one was no exception. Among the characters and newspapers represented in the film as it explored the seamy underbelly of the commercial pressure on newspapers, plenty of real-life parallels were identified. Boman Irani played Konkona's kind but spineless boss with his customary brilliance, and all the people in his office looked totally real. Including the desk editor who cut Konkona's copy beyond recognition.

The Times of Hindustan

Sujoy Ghosh mashed together the names of India's two largest read English newspapers to come up with a vehicle that would carry an agony uncle column by his hero (Viveik Oberoi). As Gyan Guru, he dispensed advice on '*family, pyar, affair, Viagra, vagehra . . .*' and it was supposed to be the reason why people read the newspaper. Since the film was about the hero bunking his office and column to work on a screenplay for Karan Johar, we never got to know too much about the newspaper except that it had an editor (Juhi Chawla) who was always angry and a minion Gokhale who was always trying to get Gyan Guru to come to office.

> *Trailer Alert*: In the film, there was a TV chat show in which Viveik and his heartthrob (Mahima Chaudhary) appeared together called *Hot Seat with Hitesh*, which sets us up nicely for the TV channels that are coming your way in the next chapter.

Idiot Box: 9 TV Channels

Soon after the entry of multi-channel television in the early '90s the cut-throat world of TRPs, aggressive journalism, and the blurring line between entertainment and news became fodder for the story mills of Bollywood. TV channels have now become part of the standard background in movies but there are some in which they *are* the show.

'I am the best': Shah Rukh Khan in Phir Bhi Dil Hai Hindustani
said what TV anchors are always saying

The concept of 24x7 news cameras was just gaining currency when ***Phir Bhi Dil Hai Hindustani*** happened, probably ahead of its time. Shah Rukh Khan played TV news anchor Ajay Bakshi with a cool signature line ('*Jahan na pahuchey insaan pashu pakshi, wahan pahuchey Ajay Bakshi*') and a nifty hand gesture to introduce his channel, K Tea-V. The channel's name was derived from Kakey da TV owned by Satish Shah, an ex-canteen manager of the rival TV channel, Galaxee TV.

To counter Ajay's ubiquitous presence, Galaxee's owner (Dalip Tahil) hired Ria Banerjee (Juhi Chawla). Ria had made her name in TV24 where she covered the Bihar floods by recreating them in a studio. After the initial rivalry, Ajay and Ria joined hands for a serious cause—bringing justice to Mohan Joshi[1] (Paresh Rawal), who had murdered a

---

[1] The name seems to have been taken from the film ***Mohan Joshi Hazir Ho*** directed by Saeed Mirza—who happens to be the brother of Aziz Mirza, the director of ***Phir Bhi Dil Hai Hindustani***.

minister's brother for raping his daughter but was instead labelled a terrorist.

As their own channels turned against them, the lead pair tried to answer a few questions that would become more relevant in the coming years. Which is bigger—an anchor or the channel? How do you raise issues when it is much easier to entertain? And of course, what is the first question to ask in television interviews? When Mohan Joshi walked towards the gallows, a reporter thrust a mike in his face and asked—'*Aap kaisa mehsoos kar rahe hain?*'

When 'reality shows' started to become a rage, *7½ Phere* was about a TV show around weddings. Juhi Chawla played a TV producer trying to film a real wedding for a show. She approached a suitable family with an upcoming wedding but they refused. With bosses on her head, she managed to befriend an 'uncle' (Irrfan Khan) in the extended family and hid cameras in different parts of the house to record the wedding on the sly. The family had more than its share of skeletons in closets and the recordings revealed affairs, horny uncles, the bride's plan to elope and assorted scandals. The dilemma was classic—junk the masala and have your career stuck forever. Or air it on prime-time TV to move up, not caring about the ensuing problems in the subject's family.

In one of the criss-crossing love stories of *Salaam-e-Ishq*, Vidya Balan played Tehzeeb Hussain—a young reporter for Times Now, deeply in love with her husband (John Abraham). On her anniversary, she had to leave her hunky hubby to cover the inaugural run of the Goa–Mumbai Holiday Express, a 'very romantic train'. While covering the train's run, she passed on an unspoken message by wistfully fingering the pendant he had given her and brought a rare touch of pensiveness to the breathless world of 'breaking news'. Of course, the 'breaking news' came charging back when the train met with an accident[2] and Vidya was left with a rare form of amnesia. But that was a story for another channel.

A Wednesday was about a very intelligent man running in circles around in the Mumbai police force as he planted bombs across the city and threatened to detonate them if his demands were not met. Sitting in his hidden perch high above the city, he devised a clever way of monitoring the police. He let a TV journalist loose on them. Naina Roy (Deepal Shaw) of UTV News started off by covering the kind of story that typically makes news channels infamous. In the beginning, she interviewed a man who had survived massive electrocution and was now called 'Electric Baba'. But soon our mysterious man started calling her and giving her leads on the bombs planted, prisoner movements and all key events in his plan so that he could follow

---

[2] Devastating accidents on inaugural runs are hugely popular ever since a ship called *Titanic* tanked on its first voyage. Another Indian 'train' film—*The Burning Train*—was about a, well, train that caught fire on its maiden journey.

what was happening on the ground. The police commissioner soon caught on to this trick and planted a few red herrings of his own. And the battle of wits played out on prime-time TV.

When the makers of **God Tussi Great Ho** decided to base it on *Bruce Almighty*, they gave Salman Khan the same profession as Jim Carrey. He was the anchor of a show called *Mano Ya Na Mano* on Channel One, run by Dalip Tahil (who's the most experienced channel head in Bollywood by now). The show covered astonishing people and their achievements and the first episode was on Loha Singh, who attempted to hold back a helicopter with his teeth. The hero's perennial bad luck meant Loha Singh's teeth broke on national television. Channel One's other show had their star reporter Alia Kapoor (Priyanka Chopra) conducting a sting operation to expose a hospital scam where doctors took money to treat a dead body. Their new show—being developed by our hero—was called *Jhooth Bole Kauwa Kaate*. Salman constructed a lie-detecting chair and planned to invite celebrities and politicians to answer his questions sitting on the chair. (This has, of course, been tried and tested on real television as *Sach Ka Saamna*.)

In the 'season' of farmer suicides, a farmer's announcement that he will kill himself triggers a full-blown media circus. **Peepli Live** was a damning indictment of the media in which TV channels rushed in to cover issues without an iota of understanding or compassion. The film portrayed the desperate attempts of all these channels to squeeze out stories from the small village where the suicide was supposed to happen ('*Aap dekh sakte hain kis tarah Nathaji ke kapde latke hue hain . . .*').

The initial scenes were equally telling as they established the priorities of TV news in India. There was an English news channel (ITV News) with an intellectual air and a Hindi one (Bharat Live) sensationalizing stuff—both with an eye on TRPs. The English anchor wanted to plug a hole in her CV ('Farmer kind of stories are not really my forte') while the Hindi anchor wanted to please the boss. While ITV News interviewed the minister of agriculture (who looked as if he had never seen a paddy field in his life), the Hindi channel found a girl who was kissed by Saif Ali Khan in class 8 ('*Barah saal ka chumban*'). The political lobbies behind the channels ('*By-elections ke pehle kam se kam 15 stories chahiye*') became abundantly clear and the film remained strictly in a world we don't want to face but have to.

Rann played out as a battle for TRPs between India 24x7 run by Harsh Vardhan Malik (Amitabh Bachchan) and Headlines 24 run by Amrish Kakkar (Mohnish Behl). There were easily identifiable real-life parallels as Amrish was shown as Harsh Vardhan Malik's protégé who left India 24x7 to start his own channel. This was probably because their views on news were radically different. While Malik felt that the media was about presenting the truth effectively, Amrish had no qualms in selling it ('*news ko masala banake becho*'). The movie traced a battle for the prime minister's post as bombs exploded and shady political characters fed channels with information that served their purposes. A CD with dubious origins was given credibility because it was presented by Harsh Vardhan Malik, the news-purveyor of unimpeachable integrity. As it turned out, the murky connections between media, politics and business ran very deep and it took a superhero to stand up and solve them all. In the climax, Amitabh Bachchan did exactly that by delivering an impassioned speech on live television.

Love Sex Aur Dhokha pretty much settled it by basing one of its three overlapping stories on a sting reporter, Prabhat (Amit Sial). An obsessive man with a 24x7 spycam, Prabhat was beaten up—in the opening scene—by a woman he accused of pimping her own daughter. In the hope of journalistic fame and a bonus from his employer, he teamed up with an aspiring model to do a double sting (called 'Sting of the Century' by his editor) on Loki Local, India's top pop star. First, Loki was filmed seeking sexual favours from the model in exchange for a role, and then they tried to film him buying the earlier tape. Despite the crassness of this convoluted plan, you could not help feel a twinge of regret for Prabhat, who obviously believed that truth can bring about a change. Before this, his biggest story had involved filming the chief minister's secretary taking a bribe and he was inordinately proud of it ('*Sarkar gira di thi iss camere se maine*'). But that had not brought him fame or fortune. He and his entire team had been hounded by the government with false cases, CBI inquiries and arrests. And so he was left with a failed marriage, a despicable job and an obsession that led him to 'sting' perverted pop stars.

Starting with the title itself (which was a headline in the *Times of India*), *No One Killed Jessica* was a true story. It was India's first televised crusade in which the media and civil society joined hands to bring about change, shaking the political and judicial system in the process. The channel in the film was NDTV and Rani Mukherji played the abrasive, aggressive TV anchor—supposedly based on Barkha Dutt—who didn't stop at anything once she decided to 'break' a story. Though the film did take some cinematic liberties to attribute greater credit to the heroine and the channel than they deserved in real life, it was a reasonably accurate depiction of the events. Her career started by covering the Kargil War and then the IC 814 hijack (interrupting a lovemaking session to go on air), before she stumbled upon the Jessica case. The journalist in her turned into an activist as she planned and executed an elaborate sting to nail the main witness. Incidentally, this sting was conducted by *Tehelka* in real life and it was mentioned in the credits for 'breakthrough journalism'. Eventually it all ended in a message of hope as justice was served after a photogenic candlelight vigil at India Gate.

A few months after his conviction in the real Jessica case, the accused—out on parole for his mother's illness—was seen partying at a swanky Delhi nightclub, where he got caught in a brawl. But yes, we live in hope.

TV STARS IN BOLLYWOOD

Till very recently, very few TV stars made it big in Bollywood and the ones who did were

- **Smita Patil**: One of India's finest actresses, she started her career as a newsreader at the Bombay station of Doordarshan and moved on to the bigger screen. She often returned to Doordarshan to host the occasional show or celebrity interview.

- **Shah Rukh Khan**: Bollywood's King Khan became a major TV star as the dimpled commando Lt Abhimanyu Rai in the smash hit show *Fauji*. He also appeared in another series, *Dil Dariya* (which he had signed even before *Fauji*), and then played the lead role in Aziz Mirza's *Circus*. He also acted in a lesser known show called *Doosra Keval* and Mani Kaul's mini-series *Idiot*. In fact, his first film role was in an English telefilm—*In Which Annie Gives It Those Ones*—written by Arundhati Roy.

- **Vidya Balan**: Before Ekta Kapoor became the queen of soap operas, she produced a superhit comedy show, *Hum Paanch*. In this show about a man and his five daughters, Vidya Balan played Radhika Mathur—the intelligent middle daughter who was hard-of-hearing and did not have perfect eyesight.

You could say Vidya Balan opened a floodgate for TV stars entering films, though none of them have managed to reach the success levels of these three players. Yet.

Lifeline of the Nation: 10 Trains You Shouldn't Miss

Chugging along across the length and breadth of the country, the humble train is a great unifier as everybody seems to have only happy memories associated with rail journeys. Add those happy memories to the beautiful memories of Bollywood and that's the best you've felt in some time. Hindi cinema and trains have crossed paths many times, though trains have been in a 'character' role for most.

The earliest train movie was probably *Miss Frontier Mail* starring the inimitable Fearless Nadia who got into spectacular duels atop (what was then) India's fastest long-distance train. The sinister designs of the villain were surprisingly modern as he was orchestrating train robberies on the behest of an aeroplane company owner so that the general populace's confidence in the rail system was eroded after which they would be compelled to take to air travel as an alternative. Of course, the dashing Nadia put paid to all his plans with fantastic fights and daredevil stunts and the film went on to become a massive hit. It garnered gushing reviews like 'fastest feature of Indian filmdom' and completely wowed audiences with its 'crashes, smashes, fights, dangers, stunts, acrobats'.

In *The Train*, Rajesh Khanna was the CID officer who had to crack a series of crimes that seemed to have a rail connection (pun not intended). Soon, he was climbing on top of train roofs in three-piece suits after taking a break from singing songs with a train beat. People kept getting murdered in first-class compartments as the good officer ran helter-skelter before guiding the film to a suspenseful climax.

Never-forget Alert: The song that effectively ensured Rajesh Khanna's ascendancy to the superstar throne was one involving a train too. Rajesh sang '*Mere sapnon ki rani*' in a jeep running abreast of the Himalayan 'toy' train in which the comely Sharmila Tagore simpered and pretended to read an Alistair Maclean novel.[1]

Disaster movies have never been popular in Bollywood. This is strange because a dysfunctional group of underdogs rising to the occasion—a key aspect of disaster movies—is a very popular theme in Bollywood. One of the very few disaster movies made in India— and probably ahead of its time—was **The Burning Train.**

It was about a super express that was supposed to go from Delhi to Mumbai in fourteen hours.[2] Vinod Khanna was the chief engineer of the project ('brain behind the train', you could say) but a jealous colleague bombed the damned thing on its inaugural run and we had a runaway train on the loose, burning with thousands of passengers from every corner of India on board. To the passenger list, add the chief engineer's son, his best friend, his best friend's ex-fiancée, another star couple who were falling in love, a large contingent of schoolchildren and you have more chaos than you can imagine in a lifetime. The film was packed with more stars than sardines in a tin. Needless to say, three of them—Vinod Khanna, Dharmendra and Jeetendra—got together and brought the train to a screeching halt, though not before a few songs in flashback, reunions of estranged couples and general patriotic bonhomie.

Sholay opened with a train chugging in and it ended with another one going out.

Seven minutes into **Sholay**, there was a train action sequence so spectacular—and so advanced for its time—that it blew (and continues to blow) people's minds. Shooting on the outskirts of the then-uninhabited suburb Panvel, the producer employed international action directors, desi fightmasters and a visionary director to make a scene that set the tone for the rest of the movie. Police Inspector Baldev Singh was returning to his post with two petty criminals in a goods train when a band of dacoits attacked them. The dacoits hadn't bargained for Bollywood's three most iconic daredevils to be on the same train, and after a massive gunfight involving dynamite, guns and country liquor, they were well and truly beaten. The trio went on to fight bigger battles.

---

[1] *Can't-avoid Alert*: Emraan Hashmi got embroiled in his usual extramarital affair and a false murder rap—yet again—in a film known as **The Train: Some Lines Should Never Be Crossed**. There seemed to be no rail connection in the film except that he met his mistress on the Bangkok Metro.

[2] *Fact Alert*: Today's fastest trains—Rajdhani and Duronto Express—take about sixteen hours to go from Delhi to Mumbai.

Bonus Steam Engine Alert: The premise of a platoon of villains attacking a steam engine used by the heroes to escape came back in another blockbuster: **Gadar—Ek Prem Katha**. Sunny Deol made his bid to escape Pakistan with his wife and son in a train as (what seemed like) half the Pakistani army gave chase. Helicopters, hand grenades and machine guns were all brought into the play as Sunny made mincemeat of the hapless soldiers and his wife and son made themselves useful by shovelling coal into the engine.

Basu Chatterjee put Tony Braganza and Nancy Perreira on a Mumbai local from Bandra to Churchgate and showed a romance that must have happened to thousands of Mumbaikars. In **Baton Baton Mein**, Amol Palekar and Tina Munim played the two Mumbaikars who passed notes, cast some furtive glances and exchanged shy smiles before falling head over heels in love with each other. The helpful 'localite' passed on their notes from one end of the compartment to the other as Tony sketched Nancy and made polite conversation with her uncle at stations. Of course, those were less hurried and less crowded times. But when you get on to a local even today, you still come across a young couple or two smiling at each other. And even with iPod earphones on, they can still talk, listen and fall in love—'*Kahiye, suniye, baton baton mein pyar ho gaya*'.

The lifeblood of India's fastest city—the Mumbai local—has been like a character in several films. Except the one in which it is supposed to have a title role. Abhay Deol missed *Ek Chalis Ki Last Local* (that plied between Kalyan and Kurla). The two and a half hours that he had to spend before the 4.10 *ki* first local became the subject of a gripping movie. Among the events that played out in real time, Abhay met a beautiful woman, went into a beer bar, met a mafia don, played some high-stakes teen patti, got into serious trouble and nearly had his ass taken—not your usual whiling-away-time-at-the-station stuff.

It started on Eurail.

Simran Singh was about to leave on a holiday with her friends—and she was late. As she ran through the station towards the only open door of the train, a dimpled smile and a friendly hand pulled her in. That was Raj Malhotra and Simran hated the flirt at first sight; but we all know how these things turn out, don't we? A few months later, Raj was in Punjab—trying to rescue Simran from an impending marriage. And all his efforts finally boiled down to a showdown on a railway platform. Raj was on the footboard of the train about to leave and Simran was being held back by her father. At the last possible moment, her father released her and she ran towards the extended hand in the train once again . . . in one of the most whistle-inducing scenes of Bollywood. Whether it is by Eurail or Indian Railways, **Dilwale Dulhania Le Jayenge**.

Bonus SRK Train: SRK added another train—as successful if not as iconic—to his kitty with **Chennai Express**. Going from Mumbai to Rameswaram to immerse his grandfather's ashes in the sea (while trying to take a Goa detour), he met Deepika (and her bodyguards) aboard the eponymous train and a complicated love story ensued in true Rohit Shetty style.[3]

Riding on the back of the monster success of *Mr India*, **Roop Ki Rani Choron Ka Raja**—with the same producer–actor–actress team—was supposed to be India's answer to Hollywood's technical wizardry, and break all box-office records. In reality, it was a disaster and the world's greatest train-robbery scene was lost in the debris. Master-thief Romeo struck a deal with criminal mastermind Jugran to steal a trainload of diamonds. Romeo's separated-in-childhood elder brother, police inspector Ravi Verma, got a tip and also arrived at the scene. And thus began the spectacularly choreographed sequence where Romeo landed on the train and completed the heist in the three minutes it took to pass through a wilderness. At the time of release, it was one of the most eye-popping displays of action and technical wizardry in Bollywood. It still compares favourably with the best action from anywhere in the world.[4]

In **Ghulam**, Siddharth Marathe was the local Mumbai tough who didn't think twice before getting into a scrap. When he picked a fight with Charlie and his—no, not chocolate factory—biker gang, he was challenged to a different game. Called 'Dus dus ki daud', it was a deadly race towards an approaching fast local train (of 10.10 p.m., which gave the race its name) near Saanpada station. Starting from a predetermined point, it tested how fast one could run towards death before developing cold feet and jumping out of its way. Shot with multiple cameras, the scene put to test Aamir Khan's fabled perfectionism because he did the scene without a double and waited till the very last second before jumping off the track.

The final mention is a film where the train has no connection to the story.

But when Malaika Arora's slim midriff fills up the entire screen and our collective senses, you can do nothing but go 'Chhaiyya chhaiyya' to the tune of A.R. Rahman's rocking music.

---

[3] **DDLJ** has been the morning show at Maratha Mandir for nearly twenty years now. In August 2013, **Chennai Express** became the other three shows, thus making SRK the holder of a rare record of having two of Indian cinema's most successful films running simultaneously at the same theatre.

[4] Train heists are surprisingly common—or many, at any rate—in Bollywood. In recent times, two major films—**Dhoom 2** and **Tees Maar Khan**—had a train robbery as an important plot point.

In *Dil Se*, Farah Khan choreographed this very unusual—but unforgettable—sequence with Shah Rukh Khan and Malaika, using multiple cameras, a massive crane and a toy train chugging through Northeast India. It was a terribly complicated shoot as the train passed through tunnels and an assistant was placed in the front to scream a warning whenever a tunnel approached (so that the crew could duck in time). Her effort ensured that Farah Khan picked up the Filmfare Award for Best Choreography and she called it 'the happy ending everybody wanted from *Dil Se*'.

Dil Se: *The most magnificent train and passenger combination in Bollywood*

This train is not a real train but the most famous human one. In **Aashirwad**, Ashok Kumar—an accomplished singer in his time—returned to playback-singing with what is called the first rap song of Hindi cinema. As a train of little children went around him in a park, he sung to the beat of a moving train. Rhyming stations from all over India came alive as he breezed through Mangalore–Bangalore, Malegaon–Talegaon, Sholapur–Kolhapur, Jaipur–Raipur, Khandwa–Mandwa, Nellore–Vellore—as part of some very crazy lyrics written by Harindranath Chattopadhyay. The joys of those childhood train journeys came alive as scenes zipping past the windows were brought to life once again.

HONOURABLE MENTION

Taking Flight: 10 Aircraft and Pilots

Bollywood heroes are paid to fly high. And they sometimes do so literally by donning the smart uniforms of an air force pilot or a regular pilot. Even a regular guy trying to stop hijackers or generally be cool on a flight gets some extra points in the style quotient.

If we really start at the beginning of civilization and define 'aircraft' loosely, then *Haatim Tai* becomes the first entry for its magic carpet with an invocatory mantra (that sounded somewhat like '*Jan jan jindu jantara*'). Jeetendra was the hero of this fairy tale in which he had to perform seven tasks to release a girl from a curse. This involved locking horns with an evil magician (Amrish Puri) whose *jaan* resided in a parrot. In a double-barrelled climax, fairy Sangeeta Bijlani zipped across the skies trying to catch the squawking parrot while Jeetendra and Amrish Puri wrestled atop a flying carpet. The carpet precariously tilted and tottered before Amrish Puri was thrown off it (and the parrot's neck wrung for good measure) to end the movie.

> *Bonus Movie*: Amrish Puri is clearly Bollywood's official entry to the World Fighting-on-a-Flying-Carpet Championship. In *Ajooba*, he fought Amitabh Bachchan on yet another flying carpet before being bumped off it.[1]

SUV-flying, eardrum-bursting, super-successful director Rohit Shetty made his debut with *Zameen*, loosely based on the IC 814 hijacking. Make that 'very loosely' because the movie was closer to the rescue of Israeli hostages at Entebbe as Ajay Devgn and Abhishek Bachchan managed to free the hostages in an eye-popping defiance of terrorism, common sense and the

---

[1] For details about the superpowers of *Ajooba*, please turn to page 78.

laws of physics. The hijacked aircraft belonged to Indian Airways [sic] with an orange IA logo adorning its tail, looking very similar to our national carrier. The hijackers took the aircraft from Mumbai to the Muzaffarabad army airbase in Pakistan, where it was stormed. Indian Airways had shapely, dutiful air hostesses in the form of Bipasha Basu, and a courageous captain (played by Pankaj Dheer). Finally, the flight dodged a hail of bullets to take off from the enemy airbase and landed in India to ecstatic screams of '*Vande mataram*'.

In *Hijack*, Shiney Ahuja was the maintenance engineer at Chandigarh airport who had to go aboard a hijacked flight with no cabin baggage but with emotional baggage exceeding permissible limits. He was a widower whose daughter was on the flight and he had to sneak in to kill the terrorists on board to rescue her. He was assisted by a comely air hostess (Esha Deol) and, needless to say, the terrorists' goal to free one of their leaders came to naught. The movie borrowed some details from the IC 814–hijacking, but Shiney ended up being more of a Bruce Willis in *Die Hard 2* in rescuing the hostages from the villains.

Border was dominated by Sunny Deol (playing Major Kuldip Singh Chandpuri) who seemed to have pushed back a full armoured division of the Pakistan army almost single-handedly in an episode from the 1971 war. The movie ended with a brief sortie by the Indian Air Force to clean up the last bits of the Pakistani tanks. Wing Commander Bawa (Jackie Shroff) was shown to be waiting till daybreak to mobilize his planes and fly to the army's assistance. The movie was criticized for underplaying the importance of the air force in winning the battle, but then, you have to agree that Sunny with a machine gun is a far bigger box-office draw than Jackie in a plane.[2]

It was Shahid Kapoor's turn to take a leaf out of *Top Gun* and become a fighter pilot in *Mausam*. From a happy-go-lucky bumpkin in rural Punjab, he went on to become an air force pilot as fate made him play hide-and-seek with his lady-love (Sonam Kapoor). The publicity stills of the movie were dominated by Shahid in Aviators and the supercool air force uniform that needs a moustache to go with it to be complete. His love story was interrupted when he was called in to fight in the Kargil War that led to a serious disability. The war scenes were apparently shot with permission and guidance from the IAF but the movie ran into pre-release turbulence when the IAF objected to a thirty-second sequence citing that it was 'unrealistic'. Objecting to a Bollywood movie because it is unrealistic—sigh.

---

[2] J.P. Dutta dedicated *Border* to the memory of his brother, Late Squadron Leader Deepak Dutta of the Indian Air Force.

Heroism was not in short supply in *Agnipankh* either—a love quadrilateral in air force uniform. Jimmy Shergill, Sameer Dharmadhikari and Rahul Dev were the dashing fighter pilots while Shamita Shetty, a combat helicopter pilot. I think the love link went somewhat like this: Shamita was in love with Sameer who was in love with Richa Pallod who was in love with Jimmy Shergill. But then, what do I know? I am just a civilian. Oh—all their planes crashed in Pakistani territory and they were imprisoned and tortured but they escaped with some 1971 POWs, blowing up half of Pakistan on their way out. Never mess with the IAF. Never.

Not all air force officers in Bollywood have been in the glamorous Ray Ban–sporting, slow motion–walking mould. Shashi Kapoor produced Govind Nihalani's *Vijeta* and cast his son Kunal Kapoor in the film, which was a sensitive story of a teenager's growing up—to become a fighter pilot. In between the teenage angst against his father and his budding romance (with Supriya Pathak), Kunal Kapoor's character participated in some serious aerial action in what was supposed to be the 1971 India–Pakistan war. A separate crew for the aerial photography, and inputs from Indian Air Force officers ensured that the battle scenes were realistically exciting.

Not all aircraft in Bollywood involve violence. Some crash peacefully also.

In *Sunny*, Dharmendra—in a guest appearance—ran into a spot of bother with his wife (Waheeda Rehman) about his mistress (Sharmila Tagore) and did an aerial version of drunken driving. He got into his private plane and went round and round till his plane crashed. His mistress's son was usurped (oh—don't ask!) by his wife and the plot moved ahead. The son grew up to be Sunny Deol, who also had a penchant for flying with a cause. When he found out about his 'mother's' deceit, he too hopped on to a plane and went round and round to get to the point. Yeah, I know, I know—it was a silly trick but it did the job. And the movie finally ended.

The easiest way to kill off a dashing hero in an honourable way is to crash an air force plane. And two kinds of crises have been precipitated by such a tragedy.

Sometimes, the crisis is political. *Rang De Basanti* was a searing indictment of the condition of our combat aircraft. Madhavan played a conscientious air force pilot—Flight Lieutenant Ajay Rathore—who was forced to crash his MIG 21 but did so outside city limits in order to save thousands of lives while sacrificing his own. His death opened several cans of worms including shady defence deals, the government's cavalier attitude towards the death, and attempts to cover it up—all of which seemed to merge somehow with the freedom struggle of India. It was also a subtle yet memorable reminder of how our air force is full of idealistic, competent officers whose services we squander.

More commonly, the crisis is romantic. When the hero or a key character is shot down, it leads to a void in the heroine's life and storylines get complicated. Raj Kapoor in **Sangam** and Shashi Kapoor in **Silsila**, for example.

However, the most famous air force pilot to have been shot down was Rajesh Khanna in **Aradhana**. His passionate romance with Sharmila Tagore had one soaring moment when he took her on a flight (but no Mile High Club membership, mind you) and a tragic end when his flight crashed—leaving Sharmila pregnant with their child. The child went on to become an air force pilot as well and **Aradhana** went on to become one of Hindi cinema's all-time classics. Rajesh Khanna's character was so memorable that four decades on, Sharmila Tagore ended her tribute to the departed superstar with an allusion to the film: '*Goodbye, Flight Lieutenant Arun, I will miss you . . .*'

AIRPLANE MEETINGS

- **Khel**: Conmen (con-persons rather) Anil Kapoor and Madhuri Dixit had their second meeting on a flight to Tikamgarh and promptly left the aircraft to sing a song ('*Na hain zameen na aasmaan*') on the clouds, which they called the Badal Nagar Cooperative Society.

- **Dil Chahta Hai**: After Aamir Khan's persistent attempts to woo Preity Zinta at their college farewell came to a violent end, they met again on a flight to Sydney and—as they say—this was the beginning of a beautiful friendship.

- **Hum Tum**: The forever-bickering lead pair (Saif Ali Khan and Rani Mukherji) met for the first time on a plane on their way to New York from Delhi. They spent their time in the flight getting disgusted by each other's habits, Saif trying to flirt with Rani and Rani trying to avoid Saif. Saif's character was a cartoonist in the film and he created his two characters—Hum and Tum—on the flight.

- **English Vinglish**: Sridevi was on her maiden flight abroad to New York and scared out of her wits. The passenger in the next seat got her drinking water, provided Hindi subtitles to the in-flight movie and set her off on her trip with sage advice. We have come to expect these sorts of things from Amitabh Bachchan.

Vrroom, Vrroom: 10 Cars

Bollywood takes us for a ride all the time and we enjoy it thoroughly when it does. Sometimes, literally. Swanky cars, not-so-swanky cars, over-the-top cars, topless cars—they have all been used to woo heroines and audiences alike, and what a ride it has been!

The most memorable title role for a car was the super-hilarious *Chalti Ka Naam Gaadi*. The Ganguly Brothers[1]—who were probably as funny as the Marx Brothers—went on a rampage in their Ford Model A car (licence plate number CPV 65), with the beautiful Madhubala in tow. The story was silly, and fertile ground for great comedy. It was about the two younger brothers' romantic escapades in the face of the elder brother's extreme misogyny. By setting it in a garage, the movie also became about the car(s). It had a car race where the winning strategy included spraying water at rivals. It had a full song about the charges of a late-night car repair ('*Paanch rupaiyah barah anna*'). It had a song about a wet girl stranded in a garage ('*Ek ladki bheegi bhaagi si*'), and of course, the anthem of jalopy-driving: '*Babu, samjho ishaare, horan pukare pom pom pom / Yahaan chalti ko gaadi kehte hain pyare pom pom pom.*'

Taarzan: The Wonder Car was a four-wheeler with a deathless soul and a Tarzan figurine hanging from the mirror.

Car designer Deven Chaudhry (Ajay Devgn) designed a stupendous, futuristic car (eight-cylinder, V-engine, 400 BHP, 500 Nm torque, zero to 100 kmph in 5.3 seconds, *ten* airbags!) and tried selling it to the Four Fox Motor Company. They refused when he wanted 20 per cent royalty and his initials (DC) on the car. And for good measure, they stole his design and drowned him, along with his vintage car (licence plate number BML 1501). Twelve years later,

---

[1] Their names in the film were Brijmohan (Ashok Kumar), Jagmohan aka Jaggu (Anup Kumar) and Manmohan aka Mannu (Kishore Kumar). Fans will remember the second brother's plaintive cry to the third—'*Mannu, tera hua, ab mera kab hoga?*'

his son found the car and remodelled it into one sleek piece (now with a new licence plate number MH 01 M 37). This concept car was designed by noted car designer Dilip Chhabria (thus explaining the DC on the car). The car turned out to be a vigilante as it hunted down the four owners of Four Fox to extract revenge for its owner's murder. When not killing millionaire-murderers, the car did all sorts of cool tricks including driving itself while the hero scratched his skimpily clad girlfriend's back. Wow.

Another car in the title role was *Taxi No. 9211* (full licence plate number MH 01 C 9211) driven by a foul-tempered cabbie (Nana Patekar) on the mean streets of Mumbai. All hell broke loose when he picked up an equally short-fuse passenger (John Abraham) on his way to a contentious inheritance. Soon, both their lives were in jeopardy because of each other and the eponymous taxi was in the middle of it all. Eventually, all ended well and John bumped into yet another car—but that car's driver was considerably more pleasing to the eye than Nana.

> *Bonus Trivia*: The producers of *Taxi No. 9211* executed a product placement in another film of theirs, *Bluffmaster*. When Abhishek had to chase a thief who stole his car, he hailed a cab that was numbered 9211 and the forthcoming movie was well promoted in the chase scene. (The number is, of course, a tribute to Dev Anand's immortal road movie—*Nau Do Gyarah*—where the licence plate first appeared.)

Seven years after *Sholay*, Amitabh Bachchan got his own Basanti.

In *Khuddaar*, he played Chhotu Ustaad, the taxi-driver out to make an honest buck to pay for his brother's education. He called his standard black-and-yellow Mumbai Fiat taxi Basanti (licence plate number MRP 9333) and she was his quasi-human companion. Apart from Amitabh talking to her and her responding in 'auto-matic' ways, she had a crime radar. Whenever people with criminal intent or contraband got into the cab, Basanti refused to start. This was a very handy talent to have except towards the end—when Amitabh got into the cab in a fit of rage, she refused to start and Amitabh smashed her with an iron rod. Of course, there was repentance later on, but think about it—Bollywood's biggest star hitting a 'woman' with a rod?

Though the film was called *Akayla*, Amitabh Bachchan had a trusted partner in Rampyaari in the film. Rampyaari was a canary yellow Volkswagen Beetle (licence plate number MMD 2768) and she seemed to have a mind of her own, or at least a sense of humour. In a song dedicated to her ('*Chal chal re chal meri Rampyaari*'), she was entrusted with the task of making a child laugh and she did exactly that by spraying exhaust fumes on a traffic cop and performing other strange antics. The song had some (horribly tacky) graphics showing her pouty pink lips and fluttering eyelashes. Rampyaari had a deadly side as well. Amitabh used her to trap a gangster in a dead end and crushed him to death under the car while we were being treated to dramatic close-ups of a Durga image on the dashboard.

In *Ta Ra Rum Pum*, Saif Ali Khan played the hotshot racing-car driver—Rajveer aka RV—on the American circuit. He started off as a desi whom nobody was willing to give a chance till he was taken on by a straggly outfit called Racing Saddles and from there, he managed to reach the top of the circuit with skill and daredevilry. His rich and famous life took an abrupt U-turn when his car crashed. After recovering, he developed a strange phobia for driving and lost all his wealth faster than a Ferrari pit stop. The car-racing angle promptly dissipated from here and the film changed gears to become a quasi-comic melodrama (intentionally or otherwise). But Bollywood doesn't allow racing-car drivers to fade into the sunset. The climax involved his return to the track—racing for the Goodyear Cup—when he engaged his biggest rival Rusty in an auto version of fisticuffs and won magnificently. Chevrolet (Aveo) was being endorsed by Saif at that time and they got untold mileage through cars in the movie, on-track branding and Saif's racing uniform.

Talking of races, we can now come to the last race in the career of business tycoon Madan Chopra. Racing was his hobby and he had won every race he had participated in. The off-track vibes he gave were very F1-ish though the slightly dusty tracks, spectators on scaffolding seats, and drivers in Studds helmets left a slightly go-karting impact. Chopra declared that he was retiring from the races to give the youngsters a chance but he was warned that a new driver called Vicky Malhotra was coming up fast. To cut a long story short, Chopra took to the tracks in yellow gear, riding a yellow car (sponsored by JK Tyres) and was almost beaten by newbie Vicky in a red car (sponsored by McDowell). Just when the chequered flag was in sight, Vicky took his foot off the accelerator and let Chopra win.

When questioned about this, Vicky said something that floored Chopra, his nubile daughter and the entire country. That line was the true finale of the car race—'*Kabhi kabhi jeetne ke liye kuch haarna padhta hai aur haar kar jeetne wale ko **Baazigar** kehte hain.*'

Not all racing cars are raced on tracks. In Delhi, we do it on crowded roads and intra-city highways. *Delhi Belly* courted controversy with Hyundai Motors when they showed a car that looked like a Santro (licence plate number DL 3C 6390) being gifted to the hero (Imran Khan) by his to-be in-laws and the hero's friend (Kunal Roy Kapoor) describing it as what results when 'a donkey f***s an auto-rickshaw'. Subsequently, the car was involved in a chase with gun-toting, Scorpio-riding goons hot on the trails of Imran and his lady friend (Poorna Jagannathan). The car was completely trashed (causing lots of grief to his fiancée), but that wasn't the end of the adventure. More chases, back-seat kissing, and getaways from heists were happening all around them and the red car was at the centre of it all.

Apradh was the true-blue 'stylish' Feroz Khan movie set in the world of professional racing and he managed to bring in a lot of adrenaline into it by shooting at real racetracks across the world. It would easily be the best depiction of car racing in Hindi movies. The title sequence itself set the pace by showing a race in Germany called the 'world's most unpredictable auto race'—a Formula Four event—where one had to do five laps in a 100-kilometre track and in which, needless to say, Ram Khanna (Feroz Khan himself)—won handsomely, driving a Volkswagen with his lucky number 7. In the midst of a plot involving the smuggling of a stash of stolen diamonds with the heroine (Mumtaz) being on the other side of the law, *Apradh* depicted some seriously racy (pun intended) stuff on the tracks (and off it as well). In fact, a later race showed Ram Khanna driving a Ferrari. (The car number this time was 60 as the luck of 7 seemed to have worn off.)

How can you forget a car that is the icon of aspiration the world over? How can you forget a car which belongs to God himself? *Ferrari Ki Sawaari* was about Sachin Tendulkar's red Ferrari (licence plate number MH 01 AD 9999) and a young cricketer's father 'borrowing' it to ensure

his son got a chance to play at Lord's. Sharman Joshi played the upright RTO officer who got into a harrowing experience when he took the 560-HP mean machine on a spin. Add to that a politician's son's wedding, an aggro wedding planner, a cantankerous grandpa (Boman Irani as Sharman's father), Vidya Balan's item-ode to a Ferrari, and you get a joyride for sure.[2]

Iconic cars. Iconic owners. Sharman Joshi contemplates a sawaari *in a famous Ferrari*

---

[2] *Blooper Alert*: When the movie released (in 2012), Sachin Tendulkar had already sold his Ferrari to a businessman from Surat.

Swadeshi Alert: If a Ferrari zooms in, can a Maruti be far behind? In a very interesting brand placement, India's largest-selling car maker became the 'title sponsor' of **Mere Dad Ki Maruti**—a cute film about the chaos in a Punjabi family's 'tansions' when the son makes off with a Maruti Ertiga (licence plate number CH 04E 6402) meant to be his sister's wedding gift.

The car was (almost) non-existent. But in **Justice Chaudhary**, Sridevi and Jeetendra performed a complete song around their '*Pyar ki gaadi*' (licence plate number MSC 700) which ran (apparently) to the sound of '*Mamma mia pom pom*', and all the elements of driving—accelerator, brake, horn, main road, turns—were dutifully recapped.

In **Miss 420**, Baba Sehgal screeched an invitation, '*Aaja meri gaadi mein baith ja …*' and followed it up with promises of long drive, full speed, wining and dining—all thanks to the car. The car had some additional features (not part of the standard equipment), e.g. heart-streamers that fluttered out of the boot. Wonder why there was a refrain of 'get lost' in a female voice all through the song?

'*Mannu bhai motor chali pum pum pum*' from **Phool Khile Hain Gulshan Gulshan**, with Rishi Kapoor, Mithun Chakraborty, Asrani et al. stuffed in Mukri's vintage car, told one of all the things to do in Bombay if one had a honking car—e.g. going to Chowpatty, eating bhelpuri and eyeing pretty women. Basically, the same things to do if one didn't have a honking car.

One for the Road: 12 Road Movies

Unlike Hollywood, Bollywood—constrained by the need to have five songs and three mother/sister/uncle subplots—never took to road movies seriously. Once in a while a rich heiress has gone on the run or a beleaguered couple has made a break for it, but then, *road pe aa jana* is not a good thing.

Viveik Oberoi and Antara Mali eloped to avoid her father's wrath in a Tata Safari (licence plate number DL 2CK 7857) and kicked off the first 'official' road movie of Bollywood—***Road***. Their plan was to go from Delhi to Jodhpur (a 600-km drive), get married and return to pacify the girl's dad. This was seriously jeopardized by the motley crew they met on the road. An increasingly demanding hitch-hiker, a helpful trucker, a hotel receptionist prone to PJs and a petrol station attendant with Bollywood ambitions were the characters they came across. Add to that the search party sent out by the girl's dad and suddenly the song on the car stereo made sense. In a nod to the producer's earlier film, the stereo blared '*Khallaas*'.

From the road, you must progress to the highway. Basically if your father made *Sadak*, you act in ***Highway***.[1]

That's exactly what Alia Bhatt did when she went on an unplanned road trip with her kidnappers in ***Highway***. She was the spoilt Delhi brat, who got kidnapped by rustic truck driver Randeep Hooda, and their journey became a complex exploration of the Stockholm syndrome. They went on a run through six states as they encountered sophisticated Delhi, rugged Haryana, barren Rajasthan, lively Punjab, serene Himachal Pradesh and surreal Kashmir. A.R. Rahman's path-breaking tunes and Anil Mehta's brilliant camera framed an unforgettable canvas for the journey, which was neither an adventure nor a social drama nor a love story. Or maybe it was all three.

---

[1] Joke—of unknown provenance—stolen from Twitter.

A rich heiress runs away from home to marry her beau (who's in love with her father's money). She meets a smart-ass reporter on the way. He helps her, smelling an exclusive. They fall in love. They get separated. Eventually, all gets settled and the heiress runs away again—this time from her wedding with the shady beau. Frank Capra made *It Happened One Night* and the template has been adapted by Bollywood in diverse periods. Nargis and Pooja Bhatt jumped off their fathers' ships nearly forty years apart and embarked on a trip to Bangalore.

In **Chori Chori**, Raj Kapoor was a gossip columnist, while in **Dil Hai Ke Manta Nahin**, Aamir Khan was a crime reporter. They got on to a bus to Bangalore, missed it, stayed as a couple in a shady lodge, kept the relation platonic (with help from a wall of bedsheets) and sang hit songs. Shankar–Jaikishan and Nadeem–Shravan added the Indian tadka and made the Bombay–Bangalore trip hummable.

Bombay to Goa—again a 600-km drive—conjures up images of sun, sand and susegad in India's most popular holiday destination. Quite strangely, the movie that immortalized this route was about a girl (Aruna Irani) escaping from gangsters out to kill her for witnessing a murder. She ran from the gangsters' den and jumped on to an MP Travels bus bound for Goa. The bus was full of colourful characters including Kishore Kumar (playing himself) who had to hitch a ride since his car had had a breakdown on the road. A lanky stranger who was following the girl also joined her in the bus and created such a ruckus that we still have his song buzzing in our ears: '*Dekha na hai re socha na . . .*'

> *Bonus Movie*: Three friends took the same drive from Mumbai to Goa in a Mercedes convertible and made promises to make the same trip together many times in the future. Farhan Akhtar made **Dil Chahta Hai**—which isn't strictly a road movie—but it suddenly made Bollywood 'cool' and egged many to get into a car and zip southwards from Mumbai along the Konkan coast.

A perennially depressed business heir was trying to escape his unsuccessful life while an excessively bubbly girl was going home to Bhatinda on the same train in **Jab We Met**. The journey started from Mumbai's Chhatrapati Shivaji Terminus, in a train bound for Delhi. After some hiccups due to missed trains at Bar Nagar and Ratlam, they ended up spending a night at Hotel Decent. Soon afterwards, they had shifted to a Madhya Pradesh Path Parivahan Nigam bus that took them to Kota. Some exotic song locales in Rajasthan later, they had huffed and puffed into Kareena's home in Bhatinda. And just a song later, they were back on the road again. This time, Kareena had eloped. Shahid had helped her elope. The destination was her boyfriend's home in Manali.

Heroes paid a tribute to the glory of the Indian army. Two irreverent young men (Sohail Khan and Vatsal Seth) went on a bike journey from Delhi to Amritsar to Himachal to Ladakh, delivering three letters from war heroes to their family members. As is the case for all road movies, their journey became one of transformation and the two 'boys' changed into 'men' thanks to the lessons from the journey. Some major stars (Salman Khan, Preity Zinta, Sunny Deol, Bobby Deol, Mithun Chakraborty and Dino Morea) had short appearances in the three stories that unfolded.

Dev Benegal's **Road, Movie** was not typical Bollywood fare. An offbeat movie with a lot of festival acclaim, it was the story of a drifting young man (Abhay Deol) who only knew that he didn't want to join his father's hair-oil business. To find out what he did want, he offered to drive an antique truck—also a travelling cinema—from Jodhpur to a museum across the desert, near the Rann of Kutch. On the way, he picked up a gypsy woman, a young boy and an entertainer as the evening stops became show time. A little too stylized and slow for popular tastes, the movie nevertheless managed to pay a sweet tribute to the spirit of cinema and wandering. And when the hit song from *Pyaasa* played on the truck's projector, it was a nod to the business Abhay Deol had left behind. '*Maalish, tel maalish . . .*'

Two fast friends from the Imperial College of Engineering were looking for their best friend from college when a despicable batchmate landed up and claimed that he had found Rancho in Ranchi. Arre no yaar, he had found Rancho in Shimla. Farhan ('*flight chhodke*') and Raju ('*apna pant chhodke*') immediately got into the batchmate's Volvo XC90 (licence plate number DL 3C BA 0778). During the 350-km drive, they reminisced about the great time they had as *3 Idiots*. But the Ranchhoddas Shyamaldas Chanchad they met in Shimla wasn't the man they were looking for. They got an address of a school in Ladakh and zoomed off, only to remember Rancho's college sweetheart who was getting married in Manali that very day. Zipping 250 km from Shimla to Manali was a breeze. Whisking the bride away from the *phera*s and zooming 450 km to Ladakh wasn't too difficult either. What is driving a thousand kilometres when you have to meet a long-lost friend?

Two strangers—**Anjaana Anjaani**—met on New York's George Washington Bridge while trying to commit suicide. After much commiseration and multiple suicide attempts, they decided to have a twenty-day binge that would end with their suicides on 31 December. This meant going to Las Vegas and living it up. To eat up the 4,000+ kilometres between NY City and Sin City, there was the 'third lead' of the movie—a classic red Ford Falcon called Blush with whom Priyanka Chopra had conversations. And the drive became, literally, a song. They went from the snowy, windy climes (Priyanka in woollens) to the sunny, sultry weather (Priyanka in hot pants), giving lifts to all sorts of hitch-hikers and their own moods. Their road trip also included Priyanka Chopra peeing in the open, having their car stolen and then stealing it back before they reached Vegas.

Hey, what happened in Vegas? Baby—whatever happens in Vegas, stays in Vegas.

Lara Dutta was the la-di-da investment banker (with a suitably la-di-da name, Mihika Mukherjee[2]) who was trying to go from Mumbai to Delhi to meet her husband. The movie was predictably called *Chalo Dilli*, and she had a garrulous saree trader from Delhi (Vinay Pathak) for company. She went from full-service airline (missed) to budget airline (diverted to Jaipur) to cab (broken down) to camel cart (rickety) to train (ticketless) to hitched ride (with escaped convicts). The typical clashes between upper-class India and middle-class India happened many times as the odd couple roughed it out in airport terminals, dirty dhabas, crowded train compartments, trucks, a police station and even through an item number.

An investment banker from London, a construction businessman from Mumbai and an advertising copywriter from Delhi met in Barcelona for a pact made in college. The pact was that each would choose an adventure sport and the other two would participate unquestioningly. And we took to the breathtaking roads of Spain in *Zindagi Na Milegi Dobara*. The three friends went from Barcelona to Costa Brava in an SUV[3] before giving in to their impulses and shifting to a sky-blue 1949 Buick convertible. The trio went from Costa Brava to Buñol (for the Tomatina festival) and then to Seville (for a skydiving adventure) and finally to Pamplona (to run with the bulls) through scenic roads, with scenic girlfriends, in their super-scenic car. The exotic land of Don Quixote and flamenco dancers looks the best when seen through the windscreen of an exotic car.

> *Blooper Alert*: The Running of the Bulls in Pamplona happens in the first half of July while La Tomatina happens in the end of August—shown a couple of days apart in the film. But boys—would you give up Katrina Kaif encased in tomato puree? And girls—would you give up Hrithik running ahead of the bulls? No? Let's live with the blooper happily ever after, then!

---

[2] Have you noticed how female executives in Bollywood are very often Bengali? Nishigandha Dasgupta (*Corporate*), Shonali Mukherjee (*Karthik Calling Karthik*) and Ashima Roy (*Vicky Donor*) immediately come to mind.

[3] The car chosen for brand placement was a Land Rover Discovery 4. The practical, comfortable choice was in the movie for a short while and the focus was always on the flamboyant sky-blue 'topless' car.

Hello, Hello: 10 Uses of Phones

Romance. Action. Sentiment. Emotion. Drama. Good news. Bad news. Bollywood—like life—has adopted technology to send messages. Even though people are fast getting on to Facebook, the clunky black telephone and then the sleek mobile have been all over the place. From time immemorial.

Patanga had the first Bollywood song dedicated to a phone call, that too long distance. For a supposed play, a couple enacted an elaborate song about a husband in Rangoon and a wife in Dehradun as the connecting instrument rhymed with both cities—'*Mere piya gaye Rangoon/ Wahan se kiya hai teliphoon*'. It started with the portly gentleman asking the operator to connect the call and ('*Hello, Hindustan ka Dehradun? Main Rangoon se bol raha hoon*') and the song began after that.

> *Bonus Song*: Bimal Roy's *Sujata* had a song—'*Jalte hain jiske liye tere aankhon ke diye*'—sung entirely on the phone with Sunil Dutt singing it for Nutan.

Mafia dons—ever since they shifted base to Dubai—have to depend on the humble telephone to run their empires. *Agneepath* was different. Vijay Dinanath Chavan, kingpin of the Mumbai underworld in the late '80s, hated the instrument with a vengeance, probably due to the constant din of ringing phones in his gang's den. When he first walked into the den (while his bosses were planning to kill him), he made his distrust of the black instrument clear by saying, '*Ghazab cheez banaya hai telephone. Udhar se aadmi sochta kuch hai, bolta kuch hai, karta kuch hai.*' When he walked back into the same office after killing the bosses, he was again confronted by a ringing telephone. The operator at the other end was surprised to hear Vijay Chavan alive. '*Lekin tum ko toh ludkane ke vaaste . . .*' he began, but was cut short by the man—'*Yeh chhe*

199

foot ka body ludkane ke liye chaar inch ka goli kam padh gaya, maloom?' Probably the most explosive line said on a phone? And then, of course, he hurled the phone away.

> *Bonus Telephone Romance*: In **Baghban**, Amitabh Bachchan—the acknowledged Master of Telephone Romance—walked down to a Zip Fone booth in the middle of the foggy, rainy night and called Hema Malini to croon a romantic-sentimental song (*'Main yahaan tu wahaan, zindagi hai kahaan'*). He had sung yet another hit number on the phone to his wife (Waheeda Rehman) in **Mahaan** as well: *'Jidhar dekhoon teri tasveer nazar aati hai.'*

Contrasted against this, the most surreal telephone conversation in Hindi cinema would be the one conducted between Naseeruddin Shah and Satish Kaushik in **Jaane Bhi Do Yaaro**. In a scene that the 'serious' Naseer just failed to understand, he and Satish Kaushik spoke to each other on a supposed 'trunk call' while being in the same room, after dropping their receivers and picking up the other's. If you haven't seen the scene (unlikely), you will not get the insanity by reading about it. But you just might get the in-joke. When asked for the code word, Naseeruddin Shah said *'Albert Pinto ko gussa kyon aata hain?'* and Satish Kaushik responsed by asking *'Woh daadhi wala?'* Just prior to this role, Naseer had played Albert Pinto in a film directed by Saeed Mirza, a bearded gentleman.

In **Haseena Maan Jaayegi**, Govinda was waiting for sweetheart Karisma when he tried calling her using two mobile phones—one yellow and one green. She finally landed up and the duo started dancing with every part of their body vibrating (not unlike a mobile phone). They soon started singing the song that would have warmed the cockles of Sunil Bharti Mittal's heart—*'What is mobile number? What is your smile number?'* Govinda also asked for Karisma's *galli* number, *jhumka* number and *thumka* number before she offered her sandal number. (In 1999, the mobile phone was still a luxury. A phone in the hands of Govinda, the darling of the masses, would have made a major impact and probably won the nascent telecom industry more subscribers than the advertising campaigns of the telecom companies.)

> *Bonus Device*: The first character named after the mobile revolution was undoubtedly Pappu Pager, elder brother of the redoubtable Munnu Mobile in **Deewana Mastana**. Pappu Pager (Satish Kaushik) was an underworld don, prone to getting thumped by the two heroes (Govinda and Anil Kapoor) in turns. In fact, after the first thump, Govinda even made a topical taunt—*'Battery nikal gayi toh pager band padh gaya na?'*

'Kabeera speaking . . .'—with this one catchphrase in his rib-tickling comedy **Hera Pheri**, Priyadarshan brought back the charms of the rotary-dial telephone instrument. Three down-on-the-luck wastrels—played by Akshay Kumar, Sunil Shetty and Paresh Rawal—received a wrong number call from Kabeera. The call was intended for business tycoon Devi Prasad (Kulbhushan Kharbanda), asking for ransom for his kidnapped granddaughter. The trio took advantage of the interception and tried to gain arbitrage by quoting a higher ransom to the real Devi Prasad. Needless to say, schemes like these never go according to plan and the mayhem that followed distinguished **Hera Pheri** from hundreds of comedies that Bollywood (and Priyadarshan) routinely churns out. And to think, it all started with a wrong number printed in the directory which directed a call for Star Fisheries to Baburao Apte's Star Garage.

Bonus Trivia: The number of Star Fisheries was 2624545 and that of Star Garage was 8881212.

In **Biwi No. 1**,[1] Salman Khan tried to be in two places (home and the love nest) with two different women (wife Karisma Kapoor and mistress Sushmita Sen) on *Karwa Chauth* night by playing a mobile phone trick. (*Cheesy Line Alert*: '*Chand nikalne se pehle tumhara chand pahuch jayega*') While presiding over the happy domesticity of his home, Sallu called the landline from his mobile phone and had a faux conversation about a multi-crore deal. Needless to say, his dutiful *biwi* allowed him to leave for the 'deal' and he—being the heartless bastard that men usually are—promptly landed up at his mistress's. Missed calls and false calls were going to be the mainstay of many filmi cons in the coming years. **Biwi No. 1** (1999) was probably the first to go there.

After one Hrithik, two hit songs and three villains completed the climactic fight in **Kaho Naa Pyaar Hai**, prince-pin Malik (Dalip Tahil) offered to reveal the name of the kingpin—'Sirjee', the man behind all the smuggling and killing. Right on cue and with timing reminiscent of Sourav Ganguly in his prime, Malik was shot by Anupam Kher, Amisha Patel's father in the movie—ostensibly to save his daughter and future son-in-law. Hrithik then discarded the Elvis mantle and donned the Sherlock mantle to pick up the clunky Nokia 5110 from the dead Malik's pocket (crime scene sterilization be damned!) and discovered a missed call from the

[1] David Dhawan seems to be the unquestioned king of depicting mobile phone usage in Bollywood as it was just beginning—with this being his third entry on the list.

elusive 'Sirjee'.[2] He pressed the 'call' button and Anupam Kher's phone started ringing. As a later telecom ad went on to say, 'What an idea, Sirjee!'

Karthik called Karthik on a Kyungmin corded phone (model 0-505) and gave him life lessons. The phone (at an introductory price of Rs 1,200) had a host of features—alarm, calendar, self-reminder, speakerphone, text-messaging, lock function and what not. It, of course, had another feature that managed to change Karthik's life—coaching provided on the phone. Whether he wanted it or not, whether the phone was connected or not, whether it was Mumbai or Cochin, it was *Karthik Calling Karthik*.

After a plethora of songs and dialogues, it is important to put together a common con using the phone.

In **Yaadon Ki Baaraat**, when Shaakaal (Ajit) killed a pesky witness, he made the mistake of leaving three more witnesses (the victim's three sons) and one dissatisfied accomplice. The accomplice was caught and sentenced to long years in prison. When he was released, he called up Shaakaal (from a phone booth) to blackmail him. While talking on the phone, Shaakaal heard a train in the background and deciphered the location of the booth to be right next to a railway track. He dispatched his goons (presumably, to all the 12,943 phone booths in this country that exist next to railway tracks) and had his blackmailer killed.

> *Bonus Con*: In **Aakhree Raasta**, serial killer David had kidnapped the DIG's daughter (Sridevi) and called the police to demand ransom. While speaking to him, Police Inspector Vijay Shandelia (Amitabh Bachchan) recognized the sounds of local trains and church bells in the background. He immediately instructed his team to find out churches that were near train tracks in the city. Very smart, except David (also played by Amitabh Bachchan) *uska baap nikla*. When he called back, David revealed that he had played recorded train sounds on a cassette player earlier to send the police on a wild goose chase.

---

[2] Incidentally, Sirjee's number was briefly displayed on screen when he dialled it—9820050391.

Ruby Talkies. Veterinary hospital. Bharat Laundry. Lunatic asylum. Even international smugglers discussing exotic dancers. Everyone wanted to talk with the editor of the *Crimes of India*. You see, Editor Gaitonde's (Annu Kapoor) phone was not a talking instrument. He called it a radio for the wide variety of cross-connections and wrong numbers it gave him (not to mention the aggravation). While the phone has played many roles in Bollywood, it was almost like a character in *Mr India*—not unlike an annoying sidekick. And no, there was no end to it. As it was revealed at the end of the movie, even Mr India was incapable of solving this monstrosity!

TRRING, TRRING: THE RINGTONES OF WASSEYPUR

In the last decade, phones and—by extension—ringtones have become an integral part of our identities. This came out wonderfully well in *Gangs of Wasseypur* where most of the later characters had a distinctive ringtone.

- The film opened with a shootout and a missed call on Faizal Khan's (Nawazuddin Siddiqui) phone when '*Nayak nahin, khalnayak hoon main*' started playing.
- Faizal's main adversary, Ramadhir Singh (Tigmanshu Dhulia), kept his to his pious politician image by having '*Om Bhurbhuvasvaha*' (sung by Anuradha Paudwal) while his son J.P. Singh had the more romantic '*Koyal si teri boli*' from *Beta*.
- Faizal Khan's main henchman Guddu favoured B-grade classics like '*Kya karte they saajna hum tumse door reh ke*' (from *Lal Dupatta Malmal Ka*) and '*Humra hau chahi*' (a Bhojpuri hit by Guddu Rangeela).
- And if Definite's hairstyle gave any hint of his favourite actor, his ringtone made it absolutely clear. He played the title song from Salman Khan's *Tere Naam*.

Gangs of Wasseypur is likely to become one of those trivia-laden cult classics in the near future. This eclectic collection of ringtones just furthers that cause.

(Thanks are due to film-maker Neeraj Ghaywan, assistant director on *GoW*, who was responsible for choosing this list of ringtones and shared it with us.)

Howzzat: 10 Cricketing Movies

In a country that is so obsessed with cricket, it is quite strange that not too many films have been made on the sport. Of course, making cricketing action look authentic is one big challenge—but then lack of authenticity has never deterred our film-makers from attempting anything.

Lagaan is the certified cricket epic of Bollywood—which took our love for the game to the biggest cinematic stage of the world and came back without the trophy, thus keeping the 'choker' reputation of Indians alive. Several elements from the current cricketing world—foreign coaches, coloured clothing, match-fixing, team politics, captaincy tussles and even the *doosra*—were taken back a couple of centuries to give us one of the most satisfying films about sport in any language.

The earliest cricket movie of Bollywood was the Dev Anand–starrer *Love Marriage* in which he played for the Sporting Club of Jhansi, leading his team to a win in the opening scenes of the movie. He then went to Bombay for a job interview and was soon playing a match at the Brabourne Stadium. Mala Sinha—who initially hated his guts—fell in love with him after seeing him bat, and soon, they had a—no prizes for guessing—love marriage. This was not before they sang a cricketing song ('*Usne phenka leg break toh humne maara chhakka, out karta kaun humein hum khiladi pakka*') and Dev Anand waved his bat and took guard with his customary swagger and tilt.

All Rounder had Kumar Gaurav playing a talented cricketer, egged on by his rustic villager brother (Vinod Mehra in one of his many sugary-sweet do-gooder roles). Gaurav's character broke into the national team, only to be framed on some trumped-up charges of *ayyaashi* (an all-encompassing term for smoking, boozing and womanizing) by Shakti Kapoor and thrown out. All of it came to a happy end when the charges were cleared and Kumar Gaurav made a triumphant return to the team—but not before beating Shakti Kapoor to pulp with a cricket bat. [1] This was a cricket film, you see.

Modern Remake Alert: Harman Baweja starred in **Victory**, the story of yet another talented cricketer who lost his place in the national side thanks to (you guessed it) ayyaashi. Needless to say, he redeemed himself and made a thunderous comeback thumping Dale Steyn in the last over of the match. You wish! Even Bollywood is not so delusional. They got Stuart Clarke to get walloped.

In recent times, **Hattrick** was about the stories of three cricket-crazy fans. One of the fans was Danny Denzongpa, an ex-cricketer trying to win one more battle with a deadpan doctor (Nana Patekar), while the other was Paresh Rawal, who wanted to migrate to England. In the third track, cricket-ignoramus Rimi Sen started watching the game at her husband's (Kunal Kapoor) insistence and fell in love with M.S. Dhoni. In a slightly misguided tribute to MSD, one scene had the couple making love and Rimi screaming out the Indian captain's name in ecstasy.

Cerebral Captain Alert: Anil Kumble was the object of Meera Achrekar's affections in **Meerabai Not Out**. Mandira Bedi played the titular maths teacher who arrived late for her own wedding because she was watching Kumble play but eventually saved the day in the climax with her knowledge of the leg-spinner's exploits.

Q: Which three careers were launched with the Natwest Final of 2002?
A: Yuvraj Singh, Mohammad Kaif and Emraan Hashmi.
Well, yeah. In **Jannat**, Emraan Hashmi went from a small-time betting enthusiast to a top bookie thanks to his 'sixth sense' during the epochal match in England. He predicted Ganguly's six, Sehwag's dismissal and India's victory with remarkable accuracy, thus breaking into the top-dollar *satta* league. And all his success came with a backdrop of major cricketing action—culminating into him being framed for the murder of an international cricket coach. Mahesh

---

[1] *Extra Batsman Overs*: Aamir Khan—who was an upcoming boxer in **Ghulam**—beat up a cricketer and broke his bat into small pieces in a cricket ground bathroom when the guy refused a match-fixing proposition. A bat does come into diverse uses, you see.

Bhatt and company brought back the ghost of Bob Woolmer to weave a tale in which Emraan courted Sonal Chauhan and disaster, though not necessarily in that order.

A young cricketer's journey towards the Holy Grail of the Indian national side is fraught with many heartbreaks. And if the cricketer is hearing- and speech-impaired, the journey could well be impossible. A film on this subject could descend into melodrama very easily but the project was helmed really well by Nagesh Kukunoor, with Shreyas Talpade excelling as *Iqbal*, the fast bowler whose actions literally spoke louder than words. The realistic atmosphere of the state cricket matches, with Girish Karnad as the deal-brokering coach, Shweta Prasad as the affectionate sister and Naseeruddin Shah as the alcoholic mentor, made the film an underrated gem. Super-feel-good—just the way cricket matches should be.

Bonus Failed Cricketer Shining Coach: Like Naseeruddin Shah in *Iqbal*, we had Sushant Singh in *Kai Po Che*—the coach who sought redemption through his ward's success. Giving an added twist was the situation of Gujarat 2002 where a bloodthirsty mob stood between success and the talented Muslim boy and it was only the coach who could get him past.

Young people playing cricket or starting to play cricket is always magical. Especially, when the world's greatest cricketer and the world's snazziest car are involved. Arre baba, I am not talking about Bradman in a Rolls-Royce. This was *Ferrari Ki Sawaari*, where a young Parsi boy was inspired by Sachin Ramesh Tendulkar.

Bonus Talented Cricketer: Karan (Zain Khan) played a thirteen-year-old orphan in *Chain Kulii Ki Main Kulii*, who was selected to play for India—thanks to a 'magic bat'. (Apparently, Kapil Dev used it to score 175 not out in the 1983 World Cup.) His friend, co-opener and coach was the Indian captain (Rahul Bose) and much excitement followed as Karan braved bullies and broken bats to take on—you guessed it—Pakistan in an all-important match.

As a direct counterpoint to the many films where Indians took on the world in cricket, we had *Patiala House*. Southall Sikh Pargat Singh Kahlon's teen exploits included getting Nasser Hussain (the former English captain) out in three successive matches. Kept away from playing for England by his jingoistic dad (Rishi Kapoor), he ran a grocery store till he was given a chance to make a comeback at the age of thirty-four. Playing for England, he had a showdown with Andrew Symonds (playing himself) and, in true filmi style, got his redemption at Lord's in front of his cheering family and approving dad. What—did you say 'spoiler'? Arre bhai, what do you expect when Akshay Kumar plays a cricketer? That he will give away sixteen runs in the last over and be dropped, never to be picked again? Then you should also ask why Nikhil Chopra was giving the Hindi commentary in an England–Australia match in London—no?[2]

While on the topic of sardars playing cricket, it would be apt to bring in Veer Pratap Singh who took the fight to the Pakistanis in—*Veer Zaara*, right? Nope. It was ***Dil Bole Hadippa*** where Rani Mukherji alternated between being Veera Singh, who shook a mean leg, and Veer Pratap Singh, who played a mean game of cricket. It was a solid shot for feminism as Rani Mukherji pretended to be a boy to get into the village cricket team (led by the foreign-returned Shahid Kapoor) and partnered with the hero to lead their village to victory against a Pakistani village in an annual cricket match. In between the cricketing action, Shahid Kapoor walked in while she was showering—thus giving a new meaning to 'two fine legs and no cover'.

And the last word in cricket films can only be Dev Anand's magnum opus ***Awwal Number***. Dev Anand's character in the film was an absolute rarity—the police commissioner of Bombay, who was also the chairman of the selectors. And if that was not enough, his brother (Aditya Pancholi) was the top batsman of the Indian team. Dev dropped his brother from the team because he was doing ayyaashi (see definition given earlier) and took a baby-faced boy called Sunny (Aamir Khan in his pre-one-film-a-decade days) in his place. Aditya took grievous offence to this and teamed up with a terrorist outfit to bomb the stadium from a helicopter above it. In a double-barrelled climax, Dev killed Aditya before he could kill anybody. And Aamir killed the Aussies by hitting a six off the last ball. (This was slightly disappointing because one expected Aamir would bring down the helicopter with the same shot which would eventually be the winning six.)

---

[2] *Trivia Alert:* Balwinder Singh Sandhu, a medium pacer in India's 1983 World Cup–winning squad, is credited as 'Bowling Coach' in this film.

Amitabh did a fantastic monologue in *Namak Halaal*—on the partnerships of Vijay Hazare and Vijay Merchant; and Wasim Bari and Wasim Raja—which was elevated to a different level by his accent. Latching on to an India–Australia match in Melbourne 1929, he explained the exploits of Vijay Hazare and Vijay Merchant in elaborate detail. When rudely interrupted, he shifted to Wankhede 1979, where Wasim Raja and Wasim Bari were playing.[3]

Sunil Gavaskar had an extended guest appearance in *Maalamaal*. Naseeruddin Shah played a cricket-crazy tapori in the film who was asked to spend Rs 30 crore in thirty days as part of a bizarre inheritance challenge. And in one of the ploys to blow it all up, he invited Gavaskar to play against his Chawl XI at the Wankhede Stadium.

In the film *Chamatkar*, SRK—assisted by Naseeruddin Shah's ghost—played a college cricket match against a nasty opposing team, which was captained by Ashutosh Gowariker. Maybe the *Lagaan* idea originated then?

The first scene of *Kabhi Khushi Kabhie Gham* (which came a year after *Lagaan*) showed the last ball of a cricket match in an idyllic English field, where Hrithik Roshan invoked the spirit of his parents to hit a towering six as Karan Johar's camera covered the lush fields, palatial mansions and Hrithik's dimples in a magnificent sweep.

No description of cricket in Hindi cinema can be complete without *Hum Aapke Hain Koun* which has the distinction of being the only time a cricket match has been played with a non-human umpire. Salman Khan's entire family gleefully appealed to the Pomeranian as it dutifully displayed 'Out' and 'Not Out' cards. And in a display of cheesy dishonesty, he promptly churned out a 'No Ball' card when Renuka Shahane got out!

---

[3] By the way, Vijay Merchant and Vijay Hazare batted together probably just once—in Delhi 1951 (and not Melbourne 1929—when neither of them had even started playing cricket). The second pairing is more accurate—though not completely—as Wasim Raja and Wasim Bari did play together in Wankhede 1979, but they never batted together.

Beyond the Boundary: 10 Sports

Is there life beyond cricket? Of course. At least, Bollywood seems to think so. Various sports have dribbled and feinted in and out of the silver screen—sometimes with a full film devoted to them and sometimes with just a fleeting sighting. The charm of an underdog winning against all odds goes beyond India's richest sport.

Football

One of Anil Kapoor's earlier hits—*Saaheb*—was a remake of a Bengali film of the same name. The maudlin plot was about a good-for-one-thing youth who played football and had it in him to make it big. He blew it all away when he sold off a kidney to pay for his sister's wedding.

In Prakash Jha's debut feature film, *Hip Hip Hurray*, Raj Kiran was the newly appointed portly sports teacher of a ragtag school with a talented bully in the football team. With his sincere efforts, he managed to regroup the team to eventually beat a rival school in football while he found love in the form of Deepti Naval.

Dhan Dhana Dhan Goal, starring the super-fit John Abraham, was the story of an Asian team (Southall United) in the English league which made it to the top despite their paunches, John's shaky nose and Arshad Warsi's flowing hair. The film was loaded with solid desi jingoism and decent sporting action, supported by also-super-fit Bipasha Basu as the team physio in spandex.

Karan Johar put his SRK obsession on a giant screen in a New York soccer stadium when he showed a close-up of Shah Rukh's eyes as he was about to take a penalty shot. (Filling up a soccer stadium in the USA is something only Dharma Productions can do.) SRK, of course, did not become famous, and ended up being a frustrated coach in the film (*Kabhi Alvida Naa Kehna*) though no football stadium was ever shown again.

Aamir Khan played football without touching the ball in one hilarious sequence in *Andaz*

Apna Apna, where he described his sporting exploits to demonstrate the return of his truant memory. As a star forward for Mohun Bagan, he claimed to have scored six goals in a match and he recreated the magic in a jiffy by rearranging mocktail glasses on a coffee table.

Hockey

India's pride has been completely sidelined in Hindi cinema, except for that one shining mass of patriotism, inspiration and girls in sleeveless vests and miniskirts—*Chak De India*. The film addressed important issues of women's careers, politicking in sporting bodies and the marginalization of Muslims; but when India defeated Australia in a World Cup final led by Shah Rukh Khan in jeans and aviators, everything else paled in comparison. With finely choreographed sports sequences blended effortlessly with the story and in one stroke, SRK launched the careers of sixteen women.

Bonus Desi Game: SRK is one patriotic dude out to prove Indian supremacy in the sporting field. In *Pardes*, he was the saviour in a kabaddi match where he managed to pull off a last-minute victory much to Indophile Amrish Puri's goggle-eyed delight.

Apart from this, there have been very few instances of hockey appearing on the silver screen. It happened once when Rishi Kapoor and Rakesh Roshan (many kilos and lots of hair ago) came in from behind to win their college hockey match in *Khel Khel Mein*. The match was all of five minutes in screen time.

The Indian sports fan's ultimate fantasy—defeating Australia in a World Cup final

In two comedies by Hrishikesh Mukherjee and Basu Chatterjee respectively, hockey matches kicked off the films' comic plot. In *Golmaal*, Amol Palekar got caught watching an India–Pakistan hockey match by his boss and had to invent a clean-shaven twin. In *Lakhon Ki Baat*, Farooque Shaikh played a sports reporter knocked out by a hockey ball, which led to a lawsuit by his lawyer brother-in-law, Sanjeev Kumar.

Athletics

India's rather dismal performance at track-and-field events was matched by the lack of movies on the sport. Till 2012. The stories of two champion athletes—*Paan Singh Tomar* and *Bhaag Milkha Bhaag*—came out in successive years and gave us two heroes who ran like the wind.

At one level, both athletes had a lot in common. Both of them came from disadvantaged backgrounds and joined the army, where their talents were discovered. Both of them took up their respective sports for the same reason—the extra rations reserved for sportsmen in the army! And both of them had to contend with their demons during their race for respectability. Milkha Singh's story is one of success as he came to be recognized as India's foremost track-and-field athlete despite not winning a medal in the Rome Olympics. His demons—born during the brutalities of Partition—were finally exorcised when he ran a famous race in Pakistan and came to be known as the 'Flying Sikh'.

Paan Singh, on the other hand, was a seven-time national steeplechase champion who became an outlaw in the Chambals after a frustrating retirement. Interestingly, they were both part of the Indian squad to the Tokyo Asiad in 1958, where Milkha won gold medals for 200 metres and 400 metres but Paan Singh missed out because he was running in spikes for the first time in his career.

Basketball

Kuch Kuch Hota Hai started with Kajol and SRK fighting it out on a basketball court in the coolest college in India; they followed up their on-court rivalry with a game played by Kajol in a saree, which had her demonstrating some sexy moves instead of smart dribbles.

Aishwarya and Hrithik tried to be hip and cool in *Dhoom 2* as they bandied a basketball around while keeping the banter going but the dialogue was way too flat for the scene to be interesting.

Table Tennis

In *Chhoti Si Baat*, the introverted Amol Palekar was coached by Wilfred Julius Nagendranath Singh on how to gain the upper hand in life, which included a table-tennis session won by upsetting the opponent's rhythm.

In one song sequence in *Maine Pyar Kiya*, Bhagyashree and Salman appeared in full sporting attire to tap a few ping-pong balls here and there. You can count that if you like.

Billiards
Raaj Kumar played it with great style because this is the only game which permits heavy-duty dialoguebaazi while moving around slowly between shots (in *Tirangaa*). Or, flirtatious heroes tried to teach heroines the game by embracing them from behind and trying to steal a kiss or two (in *Janbaaz*). Or, it could be an equal-opportunity flirting, as in *Hum Aapke Hain Koun*, where Salman and Madhuri got to know each other by swapping life stories and pocketing balls.

Rugby/American Football[1]
Whenever Bollywood needs to show the hero as a global hunk, he is thrown on to a rugby field, after which he dodges past millions of burly blonds to score facile touchdowns. *Dilwale Dulhania Le Jayenge* had SRK as the ultimate British jock (but one who respected *bharatiya sanskriti*) racing across a rugby field as the foreigners licked the mud left in his wake.

Akshay Kumar picked up the rugby ball for the first time in *Namastey London* and proceeded to take his lady-love's white suitor to the cleaners on the pitch. Invoking the spirit of *Lagaan*, his strategy seemed largely confined to catching the ball and running like the blazes. But by Jove, wasn't it successful?

John Abraham in *New York* was the all-American rockstar who introduced Neil Nitin Mukesh to the game in a wonderfully leafy New York park, as the World Trade Center and Katrina Kaif vied for attention in the background.

Cycling
'*Veer bahadur ladke kaun? Rajput! Rajput!*' Sanjay Lal Sharma—the perennial last-bencher—rose against this slogan of the elite Rajput College to participate in a cycling race that was last won by his school—Model School—when his father had raced. His brother—who looked set to win it—was put out of commission by the same Rajputs. In *Jo Jeeta Wohi Sikandar*, Aamir Khan played a cyclist who won the race of his life after just two weeks of practice. Did anybody say 'spoiler alert'? Well, did anybody expect Aamir to lose the race?

Boxing
Many years ago, Mithun Chakraborty took a break from his disco-dancing to appear in a film called *Boxer*, which was about swimming across the English Channel in the month of

---

[1] Rahul Bose was a member of the Indian rugby team, where his short height earned him the nickname of Pygmy. He is yet to appear in a scrimmage on screen.

December. Uff oh—joke, joke! It was about boxing, in which a son went back to the ring as redemption for his father, with many bloody noses and teary eyes thrown in.

The boxing plot cupboard in Bollywood seems to be pretty bare, roughly the same as *Apne*—the Deol family enterprise—in which two sons (Sunny and Bobby) enter the ring to prove their father's coaching abilities.

The biggest shot in the arm to boxing came – strangely – from an actress when Priyanka Chopra decided to play *Mary Kom*, a biopic on India's world champion boxer. Even discounting Priyanka's slightly dodgy accent and the obviously different physical features, the film brought a lot of focus on the oft-forgotten sports and the oft-neglected boxer.

Badminton

Of course, no discussion of sports in Bollywood can be complete without the mention of the epic badminton match played by Jeetendra and Leena Chandavarkar in *Humjoli*. It is momentous for several reasons: it gave Jeetu a valid reason—if he ever wanted one—for wearing white pants and shoes; the game was choreographed to the tune of a song; and most importantly, the sounds of the game (the shuttlecock hitting the racket with a 'tuk') were incorporated into the soundtrack. And we had this absolute gem of a song:

> *Dhal gaya din* *tuk*
> *Ho gayi shaam* *tuk*
> *Jaane do* *tuk* *jaana hai* *tuk*
> *Abhi abhi toh aayi ho* *tuk*
> *Abhi abhi jaana hai?* *tuk*

Maybe I put in more tuks than were actually there—but then, great sporting achievements are meant to be exaggerated.

Bonus Intellectual Alert: Chess has always been the preferred choice to depict superior strategy and intelligence. While there may be a stray *Guddi* where A.K. Hangal and Samit Bhanja played the game in a friendly manner, chess is usually a game of one-upmanship as seen in the contest between Anil Kapoor and Amrish Puri in *Meri Jung*.

And of course, there is *Shatranj Ke Khiladi* by Satyajit Ray where two nawabs of Lucknow (Sanjeev Kumar and Saeed Jaffrey) played the game obsessively without letting their spouses, businesses and even a revolution come between them and their passion.

QUIZ: SONGS OF INSPIRATION

At the threshold of a musical section, we whistle our appreciation to those music directors who took a piece of music, got 'inspired' by it, re-created it and forgot to give credit. Here is a three-way matching quiz on the inspiration, the inspired and the reprise.

	Original		Song		Music Director
1	Brother Louie (Modern Talking)	A	*Ae dil hai mushkil jeena yahan* (**CID**)	i	Annu Malik
2	But you love me daddy (Jim Reeves)	B	*But you love me daddy* (**Akele Hum Akele Tum**)	ii	Bappi Lahiri
3	Faith (George Michael)	C	*Chura liya hai tumne jo dil ko* (**Yaadon Ki Baaraat**)	iii	Dilip Sen - Sameer Sen
4	Five hundred miles	D	*Itna na mujhse tu pyar badha* (**Chhaya**)	iv	Laxmikant Pyarelal
5	I just called to say I love you (Stevie Wonder)	E	*Zoo zoo zubi zubi zubi* (**Dance Dance**)	v	O.P. Nayyar
6	If it's Tuesday, this must be Belgium	F	*We love Rocky* (**Aflatoon**)	vi	Pritam
7	Mozart's Symphony No. 40	G	*Pehli nazar mein* (**Race**)	vii	Raam Laxman
8	Oh my darling Clementine	H	*Payal meri jadoo jagati hai* (**Rajkumar**)	viii	Rahul Dev Burman
9	Sarang hae yo (Korean artist Kim Hyung Su)	I	*Maine Pyar Kiya* title song	ix	Rajesh Roshan
10	We will we will rock you (Queen)	J	*Jab koi baat bigad jaye* (**Jurm**)	x	Salil Chowdhury

Homework: Listen to all the songs and decide which is the most 'original inspiration'.

ANSWERS

1-E-ii   2-B-i   3-H-iv   4-J-ix   5-I-vii

6-C-viii   7-D-x   8-A-v   9-G-vi   10-F-iii

214

8

Geet Sangeet

Tumhare saath yeh kavita na hoti toh tum bahut ordinary aadmi hote.
—*Suchitra Sen in* **Aandhi**

Poetry, especially poetry set to music, is what sets Hindi cinema apart. So many stars on and off screen have been making music so well and for so long that life is unimaginable without it.

This section is about music and lyrics.

All Together, Now: 9 Musical Medleys

Every once in a while we have a film that gets together a million stars or a million tunes in one big spectacular sequence of songs. Medley songs—either covers or parodies of earlier hits—have been a regular feature in Bollywood. Sometimes they are competitive, sometimes funny. Sometimes they pass secret messages between the players, and sometimes they are not so secretive. But they are always entertaining.

Ek Phool Do Mali Marriage Proposal Medley

One of the earliest parody-medleys was in the 1969 film where a parallel comic-romance track was played out between Brahmachari and Shabnam. What would have been a passable item got a new dimension with the appearance of the indomitable Manorama as the girl's mother. To make matters even more interesting, David also popped in. Using some of the most popular songs of the time—'*Mere saamne wali khidki mein*', '*Chal chal re naujawan*', '*Dil ke jharoke mein*', '*Jo vaada kiya*'—the motley group played out a crazy argument about the boy wanting to marry the girl but being scared of her ferocious mom. The film is known for its triangular romantic melodrama but this relatively obscure number still manages to evoke a few laughs.

Hum Kisise Kum Naheen Competition Medley

Nasir Husain never did teenybopper romances without at least one musical face-off between the two leads. And for that, he needed a rockstar composer. With the Junior Burman composing, Manjeet (Rishi Kapoor) outsang and outdanced several sissy competitors as his girlfriend (Kaajal Kiran) simpered coyly in the first row. Just when the judges gave only fifteen seconds for the next competitor to turn up, Tariq strummed his way on to the stage and sang '*Chand mera dil, chandni ho tum*'. And what a contest it turned out to be! An unknown lady in tight and sleeveless clothing ran on to the stage to give Tariq (musical) support. Kaajal Kiran commandeered her bevy of bimbette friends behind Rishi. Guitars, trumpets, white shoes, bandanas and R.D. Burman's voice were all called into action as the two maharathis sang to our heart's content and the whole thing stopped only because a heartbroken Tariq conceded the contest.

Why? See the sequence, no?

Chashme Buddoor Courtship Medley

How do you brag to your friends about how great a time you had with a babe? If you are a DU student? If your father is a small-time producer of Hindi films? And if you never really had a great time but only have to make things up? Ravi Baswani showed you how. Rather violently ejected from Deepti Naval's house by her karate-expert brother, he passed three hours in a cinema hall after getting bandaged at a clinic. And then, he went back home to tell his room-mates about the beautiful songs they sang, from Dev Anand to Feroz Khan, from Meena Kumari to Asha Parekh. The hilarity got compounded manifold when we saw Ravi Baswani doing the Dev Anand swagger ('*Chhod do aanchal zamana kya kahega*'), the Dilip Kumar scowl ('*Pyar kiya to darna kya*') and the Feroz Khan shrug ('*Aap jaisa koi*'). Helpfully, the screens changed from colour to b/w to sepia as the songs segued from one to the other. Oh—but how did he explain the bandages? Simple. He got injured fighting goons while his lady-love sang '*Logon, na maaron isse, yehi toh mera dildaar hai*'!

Mr India Football Medley

What did you do as a kid when an irate neighbour confiscated your football? You pleaded with her. You asked your parents to buy you another. You and your friends pooled money together to get another. You played badminton instead. Right? Well, that's why movies were never made on you and you didn't have an uncle who could become invisible. And—most importantly—your neighbour was not Sridevi.

Whenever you hear this sequence, you can almost imagine the twinkle in Javed Akhtar's eyes as he wrote '*Na maangoo sona chandi, hum maange maafi didi*' or '*Topiwale, ball dila*'. Everybody—on screen and off screen—was clearly having a ball as Laxmikant–Pyarelal's old compositions were rummaged through to string together a sequence in which a gang of precocious kids, Anil Kapoor and Satish Kaushik pleaded with Sridevi to return their football. The southern siren—about to become Hawa Hawaii in the film—responded to their entreaties with an equally high dose of creativity and energy.

Maine Pyar Kiya Antakshari

One of the biggest problems of staying in a joint family and having a Satyanarayan Puja at home (attended by about 840 women in ghagra–cholis) is that you can't say 'I love you' to your boyfriend. However, that problem can be easily solved. All you need is a resourceful Manohar bhaiyya and an encyclopedic knowledge of Hindi film songs. This medley—designed to get Bhagyashree to say 'I love you'—was framed like a conversation for the most part. So, when Bhagyashree sang '*Jahan main jaati hoon, wahin chale aate ho / Yeh toh batao ke tum mere kaun ho?*' Salman replied by singing '*Hum toh tere aashiq hain sadiyon purane . . .*' And it covered the whole gamut of Hindi music from *Jewel Thief* to *Himmatwala*, from *Dus Numbri* to *Sharaabi*, from *Rajkumar* to *Mr India*.

To my mind, this song was the biggest draw of the film and it was a very satisfying mix of nostalgia, topicality and Huma Khan (in what was her—probably—only non-B-grade role).

Lamhe Bollywood Medley

A medley must have a theme—be it an antakshari, introduction or entreaty (see above). And it must serve a purpose—be it saying 'I love you', getting diabetes or a football (see above). This medley did not have a theme but a vague motive. Sridevi and Anupam Kher were trying to make the ultra-serious Anil Kapoor laugh and they did so by singing Hindi film songs because the NRI was apparently fond of them (as is half the world—and their landlord). So, you had Pamela Chopra doing a competent job while Sudesh Bhonsle brought the house down with his mimicry of Hemanta, Mukesh, Rafi and—most notably—S.D. Burman. How could you not laugh your guts out when Sudesh Bhonsle sang '*O majhi, mere saajan hain uss paar*' and Anupam Kher floated around in a swimming pool?

Towards the end of the medley, the duo was joined by Waheeda Rehman doing a brilliant reprise of her *Guide* dance ('*Kaanton se kheench ke yeh aanchal*') and it ended reasonably satisfactorily. If only Sridevi had danced to the '*Ta thaiya ta thaiya*' song.

Jo Jeeta Wohi Sikandar Competition Medley

When top colleges like Rajput and Queen's combine forces to participate in a college musical competition, can *pajama-chhap* Model School ever hope to defeat them? Never, one would have thought. Not even if Model's star performer is one Sanjay Lal Sharma. One of the best college films ever made, *JJWS* just rocked the scene with amazing music, brilliant acting performances and an achy-breaky love story borrowed from Archie Comics. And to build momentum for the climax, there was the intercollege music competition featuring three separate songs performed by the three main colleges. Xavier's and Anne's performed a peppy youthy number, '*Hum se hai saara jahaan*'. Rajput and Queen's performed a hip, pseudo-Goan number—'*Naam hai mera Fonseca*'. And the underdog Model came up with '*Jawaan ho yaaron, yeh tumko hua kya?*' Naturally, the best song (though only just) was the last—but was that enough to win?

Hum Saath-Saath Hain Family Intro Song

Buoyed by the tremendous success of *Maine Pyar Kiya* and the stupendous success of *Hum Aapke Hain Koun*, Sooraj Barjatya made *Hum Saath-Saath Hain*, which gave millions of viewers diabetes. The only bright spot in this film was the point where Tabu entered Saccharine Household and was introduced to the entire clan through a series of songlets performed by Saif and Karisma and compèred by Ajit Vachani and Himani Shivpuri. And in an uncharacteristically immodest gesture, Sooraj Barjatya pushed in two songs from *MPK* and *HAHK* as well.

Mujhse Dosti Karoge Sangeet Song

The directorial debut of Kunal Kohli did not go down too well at the box office, despite the power-packed cast of Hrithik Roshan, Rani Mukherji and Kareena Kapoor. And the love triangle predictably checked into Heartbreak Hotel, where Hrithik Roshan was about to get married to the woman he was not in love with. (Note the clever avoidance of spoiler!) The entire extended family of the three lead players as well as the immediate family of the producers (read Uday Chopra) joined in singing hit songs from across the ages. Some of them expressed undying romance and some were hidden hints to lost love. And some of them were plain and simple hilarious, especially when Satish Shah (as a Sikh) sang '*Main nikla gaddi leke*' with his customary gusto.

Medleys are much more fun when they are illogical.

Waak Engliss, Taak Engliss: 16 Lessons in English

You could legitimately ask—why? Why should we talk about the English language in a book on Hindi cinema? You could then also ask, why an English book on Hindi cinema? And that would be the end of the matter . . . or would it?

Well, Bollywood has mostly presented English speakers as caricatures and hence, the need to have well-written dialogues and elegantly composed songs has not been felt often. There have been only a few examples of the sensible, and many nonsensical ones.

The first lesson in English cannot be anything other than what could be called 'A Maharashtrian in Manhattan'. **English Vinglish** was the uplifting tale of Shashi Godbole who learnt English by attending a coaching centre, by watching Hollywood movies with subtitles, by being courted by a Frenchman, and by being Sridevi. First-time director Gauri Shinde (who also wrote the script) got the nuances of an underconfident Indian housewife just right and Sridevi delivered probably the best performance of her career as she went about '*learning vearning English vinglish dheeme dheeme slowly slowly . . .*'

In 1878, British prime minister Benjamin Disraeli gave a speech in Parliament in which he referred to his bitter rival, William Gladstone. So, why is this relevant to Bollywood? Because Disraeli called Gladstone a '*sophisticated rhetorician intoxicated by the exuberance of your own verbosity*'. Exactly a hundred years later, in **Amar Akbar Anthony**, Anthony Gonsalves jumped out of an Easter egg with the same line, probably the most famous use of English in Bollywood. And of course, Mr Gonsalves did not stop there. He backed it up with important theories like 'the coefficient of linear expansion with juxtaposition of the haemoglobin in the atmosphere'. No wonder everybody in Bandra village thought him to be a total dude.

The most famous English song is, of course, the one sung by **Julie** in the eponymous film. It is a beautiful song, written by Harindranath Chattopadhyay and sung by Preeti Sagar. '*My heart*

220

is beating' never fails to lift our spirits with its simple words and tune. Harindranath was the brother of Sarojini Naidu, so you could attribute the poetry to genetics. The tune was composed by Rajesh Roshan, who is the son of veteran music director Roshan. So you could attribute the melody to genetics as well. And while the song was being sung by Lakshmi who played the title role, her on-screen younger sister was hopping and skipping around her. That little sister grew up to become Sridevi, whose adventures in English have already been recounted.

David D'Costa had only one wish—to speak English better than his son. And he promised his wife exactly that. Soon afterwards, he was framed for his wife's murder and jailed for two decades. In jail, he taught himself English and when he came to his wife's grave after his release, he met an upstart of a police officer who looked exactly like him. Amitabh Bachchan had a verbal duel with Amitabh Bachchan, as the younger one spoke with a brashness and casual accent while the older one spoke with the measured caution of a non-native English speaker. This was the first of many showdowns in **Aakhree Raasta** and the way the two men spoke, it seemed as if they were, well, two different men.

Lagaan obviously had lots of English dialogue. It also had a nice English interlude in the 'O rey chhori' song—as Rachel Shelly and Gracy Singh sang their odes of love in parallel tracks. Vasundhara Das sang the English track to perfection and A.R. Rahman majestically merged the operatic flow of '*I am in love*' with the rustic melody of '*O rey chhori*'. Apparently, the English lyrics were written by Farhan and Zoya Akhtar. They were assigned this task by their father—the credited lyricist of the song—to come up with the words very quickly, and they did.

It is generally accepted that speaking English is a prerequisite for a job in a five-star hotel. When country bumpkin Arjun Singh (s/o Dashrath Singh s/o Bheem Singh) was told about this, he immediately proceeded to demonstrate his knowledge of English and the similarities between Bhairon and Byron (along with the aforementioned commentaries on cricket). He got the job—if not for anything else but to just make him stop. And to his *maalik*, he became the **Namak Halaal**.

Zany lines in English come in droves. It started way back when Kishore Kumar and Nutan taught each other English in **Dilli Ka Thug**: '*C.A.T. Cat maaney billi, M.A.D. Mad maaney paagal*'.

Around the same time, in **Howrah Bridge**, you had Helen shimmying in a kimono and announcing her oriental origins to the world—'*Mera naam Chin Chin Choo / Raat chandni main aur tu, hello mister how do you do?*'

In recent times, **Dhoom** and **Dhoom 2**—to get the international feel—zoomed through easy-on-the-ear English lyrics, but somebody should have told them, while Tata Young is fine, Uday Chopra singing '*My name is Ali*' did not really help towards the international marketability of the franchise.

In *Kuch Naa Kaho* (starring Abhishek and Aishwarya—before they got hitched), Javed Akhtar wrote some clever stuff using English letters: 'ABBG. TPOG. IPKI. Tum POG?' For those who haven't got it, read the letters individually.

In *Tashan*—a film which pretty much defined the phrase 'style over substance'—Kareena was asked to put on a blonde wig and wiggle her body as Akshay Kumar complimented her white-white face and confessed that he wanted to advance-book at her '*dil [ka] box office*'. Wow.

In the Annals of the English Bollywood Song (if one such exists in the first place), the person who would get the largest entry would be Anu Malik.

In *Main Khiladi Tu Anadi*, he intoned in the screechy tuneless monstrosity of his voice—'*My adorable darling / I think of you every night, every morning.*' He followed it up with LML and GTH—'*Let's make love*' and '*Go to hell*' respectively—in *Hathkadi* (starring Govinda and Shilpa Shetty). And then, he delivered the knockout punch in the most inane and gratingly bad lyrics of *Waqt: The Race Against Time*—'*Do me a favour / Let's play Holi*'. Why? Why? Why? Why is playing Holi a favour? Why doesn't Mr Malik do us a favour and stop singing?

But nothing—absolutely nothing—can come close to the greatest English lyrics in the history of Bollywood that were written by Indivaar and set to tune by the legendary Bappi Lahiri in a film called *Rock Dancer* (aha—English name too!):

> *You are my chicken fry*
> *You are my fish fry*
> *Kabhi na kehna kudiye bye bye bye*
> *You are my samosa*
> *You are my masala dosa*
> *Main na kahoongi mundiya bye bye bye*

Wait, where are you going? There's more . . .

> *You are my chocolate*
> *You are my cutlet*
> *Main na kahoongi mundiya bye bye bye*
> *You are my rosogolla*
> *You are my rasmalai*
> *Kabhi na kehna kudiye bye bye bye*

What poetry! If he had heard all of these, Shelley (Percy Bysshe—not Rachel) would have drowned himself to death. Oh—he did?

Lines: 9 Poems

Bollywood has never been short of poems—either on screen or off it. Major poets from the world of literature have written evergreen verse for Hindi cinema. Most of these have been set to music and turned into songs we still hum.[1] Comparatively, a much smaller number has been recited as poetry—probably due to the paucity of poets (or people with poetic sensibilities) as major characters. (You surely will not accept Govinda reciting deep, meaningful poetry with philosophical undertones.)

Pyaasa

In-film Poet: Vijay (Guru Dutt)
Actual Poet: Sahir Ludhianvi
Context: After Vijay was mistakenly thought to be dead, his poetry was published to great acclaim. Actually, he was incarcerated in a lunatic asylum and had no idea of his fame. One day he heard a nurse of the asylum reading his verse and realized his own family had cheated him.
Theme: In the shadows of thought and dream, I am adorning your hair with flowers, I am embracing you and placing my lips on yours. While we may never part, I still feel we are strangers, despite our union.

Khayaal-o-khwab ki parchhaiyaan ubharti hain
Main phool taank raha hoon tumhare joode mein
Tumhari aankh masarrat se jhukti jaati hai
Na jaane aaj main kya baat kehne wala hoon
Zabaan khushk hai awaaz rukti jaati hai
Khayaal-o-khwab ki parchhaiyaan ubharti hain

---

[1] None of these poems have been literally translated. Any such attempt would be blasphemy.

Mere galay mein tumhari gudaaz baahein hain
Tumhare honton pe mere labon ke saaye hain
Tumhare yakeen ki hum ab kabhi na bichhdenge
Mujhe gumaan ki hum mil ke bhi paraaye hain
Khayaal-o-khwab ki parchhaiyaan ubharti hain[2]

Anand

In-film Poet: Dr Bhaskar Banerjee (Amitabh Bachchan)
Actual Poet: Gulzar
Context: Anand's terminal disease had rendered his doctor-friend helpless and fearful. The forever cheerful Anand exhorted his friend to look death in the eye. He responded with a poem from his college days.
Theme: Death is a poem. Its lines will reveal themselves when heartbeats sink and the pain starts to ease off. When the sense of time recedes, when the body nears its end and the soul nears its beginning, the lines of the poem promise to come to me.

Maut, tu ek kavita hai
Mujhse ek kavita ka vaada hai, milegi mujhko
Doobti navzon mein jab dard ko neend aane lage
Zard sa chehra lekar jab chaand ufaq tak pahunche
Din abhi paani mein hai, raat kinare ke kareeb
Na andhera na ujala ho, na abhi raat na din
Jism jab khatm ho aur rooh ko saans aaye
Mujhse ek kavita ka vaada hai, milegi mujhko

Aandhi

In-film Poet: JK (Sanjeev Kumar)
Actual Poet: Gulzar
Context: Hotelier by day, poet by night, JK wooed his wife with the poetry that he was writing ever since '*jab main barah saal ka tha*'.
Theme: Instead of the usual moon-gazing, he offered to hoist his lover on his shoulder so that she could kiss the moon with her full lips, for today's night was special. The moon had come crawling to see them up close.

---

[2] These lines were extracted from Sahir's long anti-war poem called '*Parchhaiyan*'.

Aao utha loon tumhe kandhon par
Tum uchak kar sharir hothon se
Choom lena ye chand sa matha
Aaj ki raat dekha na tumne
Kaise jhuk jhuk ke koniyon ke bal
Chaand itna kareeb aaya hain

Kabhi Kabhie

In-film Poet: Amit Malhotra (Amitabh Bachchan)
Actual Poet: Sahir Ludhianvi
Context: Amit was in love with Pooja (Raakhee) but felt that their union wouldn't be possible due to parental opposition. His poetry was deeply pessimistic, deeply apprehensive.
Theme: One often wonders if one could spend life in the shadow of your tresses, if the nectar of your eyes could erase the ink of sorrow. But since that didn't happen, one wanders around in the dark recesses without any hope of direction, light or destination. Life passes by without you, sapping one even of an effort to be with you.

Kabhi kabhi mere dil mein khayal aata hai
Ki zindagi teri zulfon ki narm chhaon main guzarne pati
Toh shaadab ho bhi sakti thi
Yeh ranjo-gham ki siyahi jo dil pe chhayi hai
Teri nazar ki suahon main kho bhi sakti thi
Magar yeh ho na saka,
Magar yeh ho na saka aur ab yeh aalam hai
Ki tu nahin, tera gham, teri joostjoo bhi nahin
Guzar rahi hai kuch iss tarah zindagi jaise,
Isse kisi ke sahare ki aarzoo bhi nahin
Na koi raah, na manzil, na roshni ka suragh
Bhatak rahi hai andheron main zindagi meri
Inhi andheron main reh jaoonga kabhi kho kar
Main janta hoon meri humnafas, magar yunhi
Kabhi kabhi mere dil main khayal aata hai

Ijaazat

In-film Poet: Maya (Anuradha Patel)
Actual Poet: Gulzar

Context: Mahendra (Naseeruddin Shah) ended his relationship with Maya and returned all her things. She sent a letter-sized telegram asking for all the things he hadn't sent.
Theme: You still have the memories of those damp monsoon days we spent together. You have kept the sound of those autumn leaves we saw dropping. You returned the letters but you still have those sleepless nights I spent writing them. You still have my favourite mole on your shoulder, the fragrance of wet mehndi and one hundred and sixteen moonlit nights of my life. You have returned all my things. My memories haven't yet been returned.

Ek dafa yaad hai tumko
Bin batti jab cycle ka challaan hua tha
Humne kaise bhookhe pyase becharon si acting ki thi
Hawaldar ne ulta ek atthani deke wapas bhej diya tha
Ek chawanni meri thi, woh bhijwa do
Saawan ke kuch bheege bheege din rakhe hain
Aur mere ek khat mein lipti raat padi hai
Woh raat bujha do
Aur bhi kuch samaan tumhare paas pada hai
Woh bhijwa do
Patjhad hai
Patjhad mein kuch patton ke girne ki aahat
Kaanon mein ek baar pehan ke laut aayee thee
Patjhad ki woh shaakh abhi tak kaanp rahi hai
Woh bhijwa do
Ek sau solah chaand ki raatein
Ek tumhare kaandhe ka til
Geeli mehndi ki khushboo
Jhoot moot ke waade . . .[3]

Agneepath

In-film Poet: Not mentioned (recited by Alok Nath and Master Manjunath)
Actual Poet: Harivansh Rai Bachchan
Context: Young Vijay (Manjunath) was being brought up by his idealistic father (Alok Nath). When the bright lights of Bombay—across the sea from their village—attracted him, his father reminded him to stay on the path of truth, the difficult fiery path of truth.

---

[3] '*Mera kuch semen tumhare paas padha hai*'—**Vicky Donor** (Joke cracked on Twitter by Avinash Iyer aka @IyerAvin).

Theme: An honest life is a path of fire. You have to forge ahead on this path without stopping, without turning, without asking for help. And when you reach the end of this path, you are covered in blood, sweat and tears. But you make the grandest sight of humanity.

Agneepath agneepath agneepath
Vriksh ho bhale khade, ho bade, ho ghane
Ek patra chhah bhi maang mat, maang mat, maang mat
Agneepath agneepath agneepath
Tu na thakega kabhi, tu na thamega kabhi, tu na mudega kabhi
Kar shapath, kar shapath, kar shapath
Agneepath agneepath agneepath
Yeh mahaan drishya hain
Chal raha manushya hain
Ashru, swedh, rakta se latpath latpath latpath
Agneepath agneepath agneepath

Dilwale Dulhania Le Jayenge

In-film Poet: Simran Singh (Kajol)
Actual Poet: Anand Bakshi
Context: Simran led a cloistered life under her strict father but her imagination flew far and wide. She imagined a stranger who would walk into her life and sweep her off her feet. But then, she was about to get married and was hardly likely to meet a dashing stranger on a month-long European holiday.
Theme: For the first time in eighteen years, a mysterious stranger comes knocking on the thoughts of a beautiful girl. His eyes ask her questions. His breath warms the nape of her neck. His presence becomes almost real, even as he remains unseen and unknown.

Aisa pehli baar hua hai satrah athrah saalon mein
Andekha anjaana koi aane laga hai khayalon mein
Aankhon ki khidki par ek saya sa lehrata hai
Dil ke darwaze par koi dastak de ke jaata hai
Gehri gehri kaali aankhen mujhse mujhko poochhti hain
Haaton ki rekhaon mein ek chehra sa ban jata hai
Uski saanse resham jaisi gaalon ko chhoo jaati hain
Uske haaton ki khushboo hai ab tak mere baalon mein
Haan, aisa pehli baar hua hai satrah athrah saalon mein
Andekha anjaana koi aane laga hai khayalon mein

Udaan

Rohan (Rajat Barmecha) gives Udaan *to his thoughts and they come out as beautiful lines*

In-film Poet: Rohan Singh (Rajat Barmecha)

Actual Poet: Satyanshu Singh

Context: Stuck in a strict missionary hostel, Rohan's poetic output was tried out on his loyal—but uncomprehending—friends. Waiting to be sent back home after expulsion, he reminisced about the stage of life he was leaving behind.

Theme: When you start walking barefoot on the memory fragments scattered on grassy moments, you often lose track of the distance and forget that you were wearing shoes once. Your heels become harder from the long walks, but when you feel the tickle of naughty memories on them, you also realize that you probably don't need the shoes any more.

Chhoti chhoti chhitrayi yaadein
Bichhi hui hain lamhon ke lawn par
Nange pair un par chalte chalte
Itni door chale aaye
Ki ab bhool gaye hain
Joote kahan utaare they
Aedi komal thi, jab aaye they
Thodi si naazuk hai abhi bhi
Aur nazuk hi rahegi
In khatti meethi yaadon ki shararat
Jab tak inhe gudgudati rahe
Sach, bhool gaye hain
Ki joote kahan utaare they
Par lagta hai
Ab unki zaroorat nahin

Zindagi Na Milegi Dobara

In-film Poet: Imran Habib (Farhan Akhtar)
Actual Poet: Javed Akhtar
Context: Three friends—during a road-trip-cum-bachelor-party in Spain—came face to face with their fears as they attempted three different adventure sports. Investment banker Arjun (Hrithik Roshan) had a fear of water but was cajoled into the sea by the diving instructor (Katrina Kaif). It was a life-changing experience for him.
Theme: In the stillness, in the solitude, in the blueness of an ocean, the sky and the earth merge as one. And when you hear every breath and every heartbeat, you believe in yourself again. And you live again.

Pighle neelam sa behta yeh samaa
Neeli neeli si khamoshiyan,
Na kahin hai zameen na kahin aasmaan,
Sarsaraati hui tehniyan pattiyan,
Keh raheen hain bas ek tum ho yahan,
Bas main hoon
Meri saansein hain aur meri dhadkanein
Aisi gehraiyaan, aisi tanhaiyaan
Aur main, sirf main
Apne hone par mujhko yakeen aa gaya

> *Nursery Rhyme Alert*: After all that heavy duty poetry, let me end with a bit of *tukbandi* from **Khubsoorat**. Rekha's family spoke in rhymes when fancy struck them and they built in food and current affairs into their lines.
>   'Ae Ashrafilal, zara dhyaan se.'
>   'Arere, yeh ummeed nahin thi Shri Y.P. Chavan se.'
>   'Kyun daddy, kya hua?'''
>   'Unhone Indira-ji ko chhod diya.'
>   'Haan, sabne milke Congress ko tod diya.'
>   'Waise Reddy-ji ki achhi proposition thi.'
>   'Lekin daddy, unki bhi toh opposition thi.'
>   'Nahin beta, sawaal hai ekta ka.'
>   'Kyun bhai Ashrafi, yeh haal hain nashta ka?'

Sitar Aur Guitar: 12 Stringed Instruments

If you took music out of Bollywood, you would only be left with Hollywood. And if from the music, you took the dashing guitarists and soulful sitarists out, you would have only the melodious sounds left. Errr, which is not a bad thing . . . but hey, how can you have a rocking song without the manic guitar-strumming by the hero?

Guitar

Manmohan Desai's **Kismat** opened with the Scorpion gang blowing up bridges and trains. The owner of Twist Musical & Photo Shop claimed to have evidence about the gang but the gangsters reached him before the police. But by then, the music shop—owner had slipped the evidence (a microfilm) inside the guitar of a club singer. Cue hit song. Make that 'songs' as Biswajeet hopped, skipped and jumped to O.P. Nayyar's soundtrack wielding the guitar like a tommy gun. Soon, the Scorpion gang was after his life as he and his guitar (along with girlfriend Babita) dodged bullets, knives, pythons and what not. Guitars got exchanged, spies were unearthed and that guitar managed to have a movie-full of characters in a tizzy.

The transgenerational theme music of **Karz** sounded best on Monty Oberoi's guitar. He first played the tune at the HMV Golden Jubilee celebration and collapsed on stage after getting visions from an unseen life. He was referred to the 'Neurology and Psychiatry Department', where a hundred electrodes were fitted to his head as an EEG output blipped on the screen. When the blips did not move on normal questioning, a guitar was requisitioned and Monty, again, played the 'high notes', getting back the same visions. The doctors were clueless about the diagnosis but we have clear empirical evidence that guitars do bring back old memories, you know: '*I got my first real six-string / Bought it at the five-and-dime / Played till my fingers bled / Was the summer of '69 . . .*'

Very little of **Disco Dancer** was about the guitar; it was almost entirely about Mithun's sinewy dance moves that drove audiences crazy. Mithun climbed the shiny, sequined stairs of disco-success but made more than his fair share of enemies on the way.

The First Guitar Appearance happened when he was on the way to his first public performance and a bunch of hired goons tried to stop him. He tried to reason with them and they responded by smashing his guitar. This was the trigger for Mithun the Disco King to turn into Ninja King. He thulped them into porridge for breaking his guitar and rushed off to his performance.

The Second Guitar Appearance was more tragic and heralded a major turning point. Mithun's enemies hired an international hitman (Bob Christo) to kill him, who managed to put a 'current' through his electric guitar. Since even silver bullets always dodge the hero, the hero's mother managed to reach the concert in the nick of time and snatch away the guitar. She was fried red-and-green as Mithun (literally) broke apart, thus making his enemies' plan at least partially successful.

A guitar is supposed to be a key fixture in a film about a musician, but in **Rockstar**, it was a metaphor for his anger. As Janardhan Jakhar slowly became Jordan, his guitar also transformed into a weapon against the world which misunderstood him. He sang '*Jo bhi main kehna chahoon*' in a college social, holding the guitar gingerly and strumming it lovingly. He was more confident in the Prague Music Festival. But when his resentment had peaked and he demanded '*Sadda haq*', he twanged the guitar with a murderous rage and looked as if he was venting his anger on it. This anger reached a crescendo when he showed the world his middle finger in front of Patiala House Court. The song was '*Nadaan parindey ghar aaja*' and it culminated in the surreal scene of a guitar burning as Jordan sank helplessly in a bathtub.

As final entries in the severely restricted guitar list, it might be apt to list out three very diverse songs by three very diverse stars from three different eras—all using the guitar to stunning effect:

1. As a maverick composer made music through clinking glasses, Zeenat Aman positioned her guitar in front of her parted legs and sang '*Chura liya hai tumne jo dil ko*'. Sigh . . . the heart-stealing bit was 100 per cent true.
2. At a farewell function, Aamir Khan stole the show with his casual style and a guitar slung from his shoulder. He proceeded to sing the anthem of the youth—'*Papa kehte hain*'—and strummed his way into our hearts. He still hasn't left.
3. Amitabh Bachchan redefined 'cool' after he turned sixty as he sang '*Jhoom barabar jhoom*' in a Jack Sparrow costume and a double-necked guitar.

What do you do with two guitar necks that you can't do with one? You jhoom twice. Amitabh Bachchan in Jhoom Barabar Jhoom

Sitar

Sometimes a brief appearance leaves a deep impact. *Tahalka* was that kind of movie. Dong was that kind of villain. In an entrance that is usually reserved for heroes, Dong—Bollywood's only multi-musical villain—enacted a full-fledged musical show that included (among other things) a sitar. Of course, Dong—being the rockstar that he was—didn't play it like a regular sitar but like an electric guitar with riffs and headbanging. And he got two of his molls to hold the sitar while he played it. 'Shom shom shom shom shaamo sha sha . . .'

In Hrishikesh Mukherjee's *Alaap*, Amitabh Bachchan rebelled against his father to marry a prostitute and immersed himself in music. During the course of his musical journey, he was seen playing the tanpura during his *riyaaz*.[1]

---

[1] For the purposes of entertainment and longer lists, the sitar is being interpreted a little loosely here to include tanpuras as well.

Bonus Film: In **Abhimaan**, AB was a singer whose on-screen singing was only marginally supported by a bit of piano-playing. However, he was shown with a sitar in one of the many photos that hung in his house.

The sitar seems to be a symbol of rebelling against authoritarian parents. In **Parichay**, Sanjeev Kumar wanted to pursue his passion for music while his businessman father was dead against it. He was seen practising his ragas with a sitar as his father envisaged other plans. Even after his death, his musical instruments—including the sitar—were seen lying around his room and his photo adorned the walls. Jeetendra briefly fiddled around with the sitar to reveal his own musical bent.

Other Stringed Instruments

As token entries, one has to look at some of the other stringed instruments which make short but impactful appearances.

Celina Jaitley's debut movie was **Janasheen**. Cast opposite the producer's son, she had to do something really eye-catching to get noticed. She did catch our eye when she stood knee-deep in the sea and played a violin wearing a bikini. That is to say, she played the violin, wearing a bikini. With that one scene, Celina sealed her image in Bollywood and remained the 'hot babe' throughout her career. All thanks to a violin!

In **Dilwale Dulhania Le Jayenge**, cool dad Anupam Kher told his son, '*Maine tujhe yeh tuntuna bajane ke liye paida nahin kiya*' and SRK had to abandon his banjo and make a gallant attempt to win back the love of his life. The banjo had made occasional appearances during his Europe holiday and it looked cutely romantic then. Anupam Kher made it look a bit of a sissy.

It is neither a sitar nor a guitar. In fact, it does not even make an appearance in the movie. And yet, the *iktara* has such a haunting presence in the song from **Wake Up Sid** that you cannot ignore it. '*Goonja sa hai koi iktara iktara . . .*'

HONOURABLE MENTIONS

QUIZ: MAKING A SONG AND DANCE ABOUT MOVIES

The transition from a musical section is always smoother when you do a quick recap of some cool songs where people were watching/making/talking about movies. Can you match which movie was watched in which song?

1	*Coolie No. 1*	A	*Woh Ladki Hai Kahan*
2	*Dil Chahta Hai*	B	Unnamed film starring Govinda and Madhuri Dixit
3	*Judwaa*	C	*Tezaab*
4	*The Dirty Picture*	D	*Andaz Apna Apna*
5	*Toofan*	E	*Love and Love Only*

ANSWERS

1D When Govinda and Karisma were singing *Main toh raste se jaa raha tha*, they did several things including going for a film that was Housefull and they ended up sitting on the theatre stairs just like the two heroes of *Andaz Apna Apna*.

2A Saif and Sonali Kulkarni went to watch a fictional film called *Woh Ladki Hai Kahan* and ended up imagining themselves on screen, doing the now-famous flappy bird dance. Incidentally, a fleeting shot of the poster indicated WLHK was written, produced, directed & edited by Ritesh Sidhwani.

3B Salman Khan invited Karisma to come with him for a 'nau se barah' show and promised to take her to what seemed like a David Dhawan trademark—'*Yeh filmon mein No. 1 hai, Govinda hain hero uska aur Madhuri heroine hai*'. The film was never seen though we would have liked to!

4E As Silk panted and heaved her way up the steps of stardom during the *Ooh la la* song, we saw glimpses of her movies' posters: *Kashmir, Gauri, Madras Star*, and—of course—*Love and Love Only*.

5C Amitabh Bachchan and Farooque Shaikh sang 'Don't worry, be happy' on the streets of Mumbai and slipped in a message against video piracy when they saw an empty theatre showing *Tezaab* and a 'video parlour' showing a grainy print of a random movie.

9

Undivided Attention

What she's looking, yaar!
—Anil Kapoor in **Tezaab**

This section is about the things that grab our attention and don't let go.

Inked: 10 Tattoos

Body art in Bollywood is not merely of cosmetic value. Apart from giving an extra sheen to a toned body, tattoos in Hindi movies have united families, identified long-lost friends and relatives, exuded attitude and menace, and sometimes even helped people remember phone numbers.

The most clichéd use of a tattoo in Bollywood is to identify long-lost siblings. Usually, two maharathis locked in a near-fatal battle reveal identical tattoos when their clothes get torn in fisticuffs. And . . . bhaiyya!

In *Zameer*, this standard formula received a twist in the tale. Shammi Kapoor's son—who had a *trishul* birthmark on his shoulder—was kidnapped by dacoits as a child. To usurp the parents' massive wealth, an unscrupulous family retainer tattooed a similar trishul on a random-handsome-guy (Amitabh Bachchan) and sent him to Shammi's estate. AB scissored his own shirt's stitches and angered Shammi. Shammi manhandled him and—true to Bollywood tradition—tore his shirt to reveal the crescendo-music-inducing trishul. Soon, he was being feted as the heir, his 'mother' had regained her speech (hitherto lost due to the shock) and the world was at his feet. One second—if he was the fake son, there must have been a real son with a real birthmark wandering about somewhere. Oh damn, yes!

After a brutal attack left his brain battered and memory erased every fifteen minutes, Sanjay Singhania (Aamir Khan) had to devise an elaborate plan to catch the man behind it all—*Ghajini*. He got his body sculpted and used it pretty much like a Post-it note with phone numbers and to-do lists tattooed all over it. The most prominent one—'KALPANA WAS KILLED'—was, of course, the raison d'être of his life and was spread across his chest. There was a question ('Who is Ghajini?'), a licence plate number (MH02 KA 6038), a date (16/04/07) and a phone number (Anthony 9820189743[1]), and several other scraps of information inked all over his body (including a 'Take Camera' on his left foot). And just in case he needed help, there was also 'Emergency 2384702'. When Ghajini found these 'cheat notes' on his enemy's body, his reaction wasn't too different from exam invigilators finding similar notes on examinees!

Tattoos are all about an exhibitionist attitude. A guy who sports a tattoo is also giving a not-so-subtle look-at-me vibe. That pretty much describes the gangster wanted in eleven countries—Don. The opening scenes of the sequel, **Don 2**, hovered over a white motorboat zooming through the inland waterways of Thailand. As we came closer to the boat, we saw the familiar stubbled jaw, the matted hair, the Ray Bans, the cigarette and the forearm with a distinctive D. And we knew—the King was back. SRK and the production house had the tattoo design registered with the intent of using it on the merchandise planned around the film.

Decorative tattoos have been the order of the day in a few recent movies. Body art is fast gaining currency in swanky tattoo studios and more stars are getting on to the bandwagon faster than we can say **Dum Maro Dum**. That was the movie where Deepika Padukone[2] adorned her midriff with a 'cobra' tattoo and engulfed our entire consciousness with it. The posters of the film adapted the tattoo into the title of the film as well.

> *Bonus Design*: In **Matru Ki Bijlee Ka Mandola**, Anushka Sharma came out of a village pond wearing *kachchha banyan* and gleefully displayed the truck-inspired quote on her lower back—'*Dekho magar pyar se*'. Of course, we obeyed her.

Decorative tattoos are not restricted to sexy midriffs of leggy lasses. Keeping the other half of the audience in mind, they can be seen—as prominently—on the waxed and toned chests of leading men as well. In **Singham**, Ajay Devgn gave substantial footage to the Shiva tattoo he has on the left side of his chest in real life. But how do we get to see the tattoo on the chest

---

[1] Incidentally, this mobile number belonged to one Dr Surekha Verma of Mumbai. Needless to say, she was deluged with phone calls asking for Anthony, and Aamir had to placate her by gifting her a new number, some chocolates and flowers!

[2] During her relationship with Ranbir Kapoor, Deepika got an 'RK' tattoo done on the nape of her neck. She re-inked it to something else after their break-up and eventually removed it completely.

of a police officer, who is always on duty and wearing a uniform all buttoned up? Well, the scene of his introduction had him emerge out of a river bare-chested (having just completed a ritualistic bath where hundreds of men and women in pink dhotis or sarees *utaro*ed his arati). Stylish. Classy. Subtle. And a solid blow for women's rights!

Real-life tattoos of stars sometimes become part of the scenery of a film as well. Sometimes, they are apt. Sometimes, they are not. Either way, it seldom affects the enjoyment. In *Agneepath* (2012), when we saw Kancha Cheena for the first time, his tattoos were also lovingly introduced to us. A combination of Om and the zodiac sign Leo appeared just under his (non-existent) hairline. And we were subjected to Samurai soldiers, Lord Shiva, Tibetan shlokas, lions and dragons on various other parts of his anatomy.

> *Bonus Movie*: While the aggressive warrior tattoos seemed quite appropriate on the psychotic criminal Kancha, they seemed wildly out of place when Sanjay Dutt played an author in *Shabd*. All his tattoos were displayed when he was shown cavorting bare-chested with Aishwarya Rai in a bathtub.

Why would the villain of a video game have a tattoo? Or more specifically, why would it have a tattoo when it stepped out of the game into the real world? Good questions. It came out of the game in order to kill a little boy who had beaten it at the game. Duh. Happens all the time, right? It had the tattoo because it 'stole' the persona of a model in an advertisement for a perfume/deo/purported chick magnet. That guy had the tattoos—all over his body—which were a mixture of Chinese-looking calligraphy and the test page of a dot-matrix printer. Of course, you know that the film in question is *Ra.One* and the actor is Arjun Rampal. There could be many questions about the suitability of tattoos on video game characters but when a hunk like Arjun tones up his body, any amount of body art gets fully justified.

> *Bonus Movie*: Arjun Rampal, playing a Bangkok badass in *Ek Ajnabee*, inked his left forearm and right bicep with some wavy motifs. And he proceeded to display them to great effect with rolled-up sleeves and a swaggering gait.

Tattoos are reincarnated too. Junior artiste Om Prakash Makhija had an Om tattoo on his right wrist. In Bollywood style, it could have been the identifier if he ever got lost in the Kumbh Mela. He got lost in a transgenerational mela instead. He died and was reborn as top Bollywood star OK (Om Kapoor). And as superstar OK waved to the hundreds of fans outside his mansion's gate, we got a close-up of the same wrist and it had a birthmark in the shape of Om. As we repeated the name of the film to ourselves—**Om Shanti Om**—we also got goosebumps in the shape of Om. Thrilling!

When a traitor is discovered—rightly or wrongly—in Bollywood, scriptwriters go crazy trying to cook up imaginative ways of punishing the fellow. If rightly, then we all feel vindicated at justice being served. If not, we all wait eagerly for the villains to get their just deserts! In **Soldier**, when an honest soldier was framed on charges of arms-smuggling, the entire village went berserk. Like Berserk, with a capital B. First, they disallowed his cremation (and let the desert sand bury him instead). Then the bad guys—responsible for the smuggling in the first place—got hold of his widow (Raakhee) and tattooed '*Mera pati deshdrohi hai*' on her forehead. Imagine, on the forehead. And for two decades, she waited—in a temple with the pallu covering her forehead—for her son (Bobby Deol) to return and take revenge. And when he did, what an explosion it was!

And finally, we come to the most iconic tattoo of Bollywood. It was what the film was based on and it shaped the course of the boy's life after he got it. Honest union leader Anand Babu was the signatory for the labourers. He was coerced by the management to sign on patently unfair terms and he did so in order to save his family. When the news of this betrayal came out, the entire workforce turned against him. He couldn't take his own fall from grace and absconded. His family became the target and the labourers decided to teach his elder son a lesson. On his left arm, they tattooed a line that he would never forget. A line which got imprinted on his soul. It was the line that defined **Deewaar** and Amitabh Bachchan's Angry Young Man persona: '*Mera baap chor hai*'.

Mera baap chor hai: Bollywood's most iconic tattoo

After a Bath: 9 Towel Scenes

A towel is about the most massively useful thing an interstellar hitchhiker can have.

—*The Hitchhiker's Guide to the Galaxy* by Douglas Adams

Bollywood has developed a code book for depicting various situations not suitable for family viewing on erstwhile Doordarshan. Colliding flowers in place of kissing. Hands with interclasped fingers in lieu of sex. Spilt milk to depict rape. That makes it almost logical to have a heroine in a towel to depict post-bath coitus. Or at least the hero's desire to indulge in some.

The most iconic towel scene is also accompanied by an iconic towel song. In **Aradhana**, Rajesh Khanna and Sharmila Tagore got married (*bhagwan ke saamne*, not *registrar ke saamne*), got caught in a downpour and were completely drenched when they found shelter in a dilapidated guest house. While Rajesh was building a fire in the fireplace, Sharmila took off her wet clothes and put on an orange towel to set the whole industry on fire. And as the roving camera slithered around the couple,[1] Kishore Kumar's voice sang '*Roop tera mastana*' and you forgot everything in the world—except the orange towel. Well, not exactly, but you know what I mean . . .

> *Cheat Alert*: Strictly speaking, Sharmila wasn't wearing a towel but a blanket which Rajesh had picked up from the bed. Tell me, gentlemen, what should I have done? Removed this from the list?

A whole lot of diamonds had disappeared, leaving behind several dead bodies and **Victoria No. 203**. The driver of the Victoria was arrested for murder and his daughter (Saira Banu) was

---

[1] The whole song was shot in one continuous take.

willing to do anything to catch the real killer and find the diamonds. In Bollywood parlance, this means getting drenched in the rain, changing into a—you guessed it—towel, and trying to seduce a lascivious person (Ranjeet) into divulging information (which we were never sure the person had in the first place). Anyway, to get to the point—Saira Banu got into a blouse–sarong ensemble crafted out of an orange (again?) towel (or two), a huge safety pin and a Boy Scout's knowledge of knots. She sang a song ('*Thoda sa thehro*') before Ranjeet got all horny and tried to jump her. That was the cue for the unlikely heroes of the film (Ashok Kumar and Pran) to jump in and save her. End of towel song.

Two thieves—or at least, two people accused of thieving—formed the story of the imaginatively named ***Do Chor***. Tanuja was out to steal back her inheritance for which she was ably assisted by known thief Dharmendra. As they fell in love and the mandatory showers caught them unawares, they had to take shelter in a bamboo hut and the lady quickly changed into a white towel with pink patterns. Needless to say, they also sang a song on how a *chorni* was trying to steal a *chor*'s heart ('*Kaali palak teri gori, khulne lagi hai thodi thodi / Ek chorni ek chor ke ghar karne lagi hai chori*').

All towel scenes don't have songs to go with them. Some towel scenes don't linger either. They come for a fleeting moment in the movie and get etched on our memories forever. But for that, you need a star like no other and a director like no other. Dimple Kapadia was that kind of a star. Ramesh Sippy was that kind of a director. And *Saagar* was that kind of a film.

Rishi Kapoor was wandering along the beach early in the morning when he saw a mermaid in a black swimsuit going for a swim. With a subject as voluptuous and vivacious as Dimple, voyeuristic tendencies tend to engulf basic human goodness. Rishi ogled shamelessly as the nymphet had her swim and emerged out of the sea, glistening in the early morning sun. She came out and narcissistically wiped herself with a striped towel and changed from her swimsuit into a sarong. No male viewer of *Saagar* could have refused to trade places with the towel right then.

Inder (Rishi Kapoor) aka Eena, Meena (Juhi Chawla) and Deeka (Vinod Khanna) were the three unlikely constituents of ***Eena Meena Deeka***, one of those David Dhawan potboilers of the mid-'90s you were supposed to find funny but didn't. The entry of this eminently forgettable film into this list is because of probably the only song in which the humble towel had a title role. As Juhi sauntered out of her house in a towel, Rishi advised her against it by singing '*Towel mein bahaar jaogi toh hulla mach jayega*' and assured her that the consequences would be dire ('*Tumko aisa dekhke har ek ladka sharmayega*'). Yeah, right! Since we got so excited about this 'title song', it might be useful to dampen our enthusiasm by saying that—

on closer inspection—the towel wasn't really a towel but more like a yellow shawl with large white tassles on the sides.

The towel comes handy in many situations—especially if you are a bachelor. In Sai Paranjpye's *Chashme Buddoor*, Siddharth Parashar (Farooque Shaikh) was in a major fix when a detergent saleswoman (Deepti Naval) appeared at this doorstep and wanted to give a demo. His flatmate had covered an entire wall of their flat with pictures of semi-naked women, with a nude silhouette being the pièce de résistance. Showing tremendous alacrity, our good-natured hero did two acts of towelling. He placed one towel on a hook on the postered wall to strategically block the main offending poster. He produced one more towel for the beautiful girl to complete her demo of the detergent's efficacy. As one thing led to another, one could attribute the beginnings of the love story to a towel. Or two.

Simran led a cloistered existence under her dictatorial father. But that did not stop her from imagining the man of her dreams and singing odes to him. Kajol's not-so-svelte figure in *Dilwale Dulhania Le Jayenge* (and in most movies for that matter) wasn't very conducive to towel songs or songs in the rain. But the ecstatic abandon with which she sang '*Mere khwabon mein jo aaye*' wearing a cream towel was an uplifting experience for all. Using the towel as a screen to shield her freshly bathed body from the audience, she danced with verve in her room and the song was one of the million reasons why *DDLJ* went on to become such a massive hit.

With two beauty queens (Miss Universe Lara Dutta and Miss World Priyanka Chopra) and Akshay Kumar, *Andaaz* was a major casting coup and the movie utilized the charms of the leading ladies to the hilt. In one scene, Akshay Kumar was 'stranded' in a room with Priyanka Chopra who had come out of the bathroom wearing a towel. The sexy lady flirted outrageously with Akshay by offering to show him more than what was on display. Eventually, she 'hid' him under the towel when a bhabhi walked in unannounced. Yes, you read that correctly: Akshay Kumar hiding under Priyanka Chopra's towel. Somehow, the movie managed to make it look tamer than it just sounded though the gossip magazines managed to make it wilder. And due to domestic pressures, Akshay had to soon give up working with Piggy Chops.

Singer and hopeless romantic Ranbir Raj found out the name of the woman he was pining for—Sakina—and went into raptures. *Saawariya* unleashed a gem of a song ('*Jab se tere naina*') as the young man danced about in his room, wearing nothing but a white towel. The scene opened with our hero standing on a window ledge wearing the towel and swaying seductively. As the opening bars of the music played, he opened the towel's knot and—for want of a better word—aired his private parts. The camera lovingly caressed his body and moved away in the nick of time as the towel was dropped, only to return with Ranbir's modesty protected again. After decades of gratuitous female nudity, we were treated to a display of luscious—and of course, gratuitous—male nudity. And it was a towel which accentuated it!

BATH-ON BATH-ON MEIN

While on the subject of towels, it might be a good idea to recap some of the famous bathing scenes. (Bath = presence of at least one of the following: tap, bucket, shower, bathtub. Don't look for *Ram Teri Ganga Maili*, perverts!)

- *Pati Patni Aur Woh*: Sanjeev Kumar's substantial girth encapsulated in a striped chaddi was the star of the most iconic 'bath song' in Bollywood: '*Thande thande paani se nahana chahiye*'. He was joined enthusiastically by his son, an assortment of buckets and lotas and eventually his wife (Vidya Sinha).

- *Silsila*: In a strange display of sibling bonding, brothers Amitabh and Shashi bathed together—displaying their muscular shoulders and hairy chests (much to the delight of the female audience). And they also had a private joke: they never bent down to pick up a dropped soap. Why? Let your imagination run wild.

- *Khiladiyon Ka Khiladi*: When you wrestle in the mud, you have to take a bath. Rekha and Akshay Kumar totally followed this childhood advice as they sang a seductive song ('*In the night, no control*') that took them through progressive degrees of filth before they cooled down (actually, not!) under a shower.

- *Shabd*: When you are lovers, you bathe in the rain, in the jungle, in the pool, under the waterfall—always in full public view. When you are husband and wife, you have a bubble bath. This seemed to be the message as spouses Aishwarya Rai and Sanjay Dutt cavorted in the tub and did a lot of rub-a-dub-dub.

- *Gangs of Wasseypur*: After a century of heroines bathing for the visual pleasure of heroes, Manoj Bajpai took off his shirt and got under the tap to seduce a woman (Reema Sen) he fancied. A skimpy langot and red gamchha were his accessories as the lady ogled him hiding behind haystacks.

Hot! Hot!! Hot!!! 10 Stars in Swimsuits

Every now and then, we have a heroine burning up the screen in a swimsuit and the country goes nuts examining every curve and pore of the display. We love to discuss the scene, the heroine's sashay, her figure, her diet to reach that figure, and everything else in between. And then of course, the images are immortalized in the form of glossy posters on hostel walls across the country. We are a religious country, that way.

In 1938, Master Vinayak made a movie—***Brahmachari***—about a young man (played by the director) who was trying to follow the radical teachings of the Rashtriya Swayamsevak Sangh and become a celibate, eschewing worldly pleasures (that included junking his collection of movie posters). His steely resolve met the charms of Meenakshi, who threw off her saree and jumped into a pool—thus becoming the first Indian heroine to wear a swimsuit on screen. She sang a song ('*Yamuna jal khel kheluya Kanhaiya*') while swaying seductively in the water. It would be opportune to mention here that the heroine's full name was Meenakshi Shirodkar and she was the grandmother of two girls by the name of Shilpa and Namrata. In the 1990s—sixty years after their grandmother scorched the screen—these two girls conclusively demonstrated the strength of genetics in human traits.

Raj Kapoor and Nargis brought a smouldering sensuality to Bollywood that was quite radical in the 1950s. *Awara* had the iconic scene in which the lead pair flirted and cavorted in a natural pool. While Raj Kapoor dived in wearing regular shorts, Nargis created a flutter in her swimsuit. Nargis also turned out to be an expert swimmer, diving smoothly and cutting into the water while Raj Kapoor was a bit clumsy. He, of course, got to say the line that was said in the literal sense but is usually used figuratively—'*Hum toh doobenge sanam, tum ko bhi le doobenge*'.

Bonus Actress: Raj Kapoor's love for the female form manifested again in **Sangam** when the voluptuous Vyjayanthimala appeared in a red swimsuit. In a scene built like Krishna's stealing of the *gopis*' clothes, Raj Kapoor played the bagpipes atop a tree while the actress swam in the river.

Nutan donned a swimsuit in **Dilli Ka Thug**—a typical Kishore Kumar comedy famous for the '*C.A.T. Cat maaney billi*' song. She played a rich girl who was also a swimming and diving champion. She first participated in the diving event of the Inter-Provincial Swimming Competition and beat Miss D'Souza of Dehradun. She then participated in the swimming competition and won by a mile. She was finally seen in the swimsuit on a podium and exited from the swimming pool in a robe to the applause of the (predominantly male) audience.

Sharmila Tagore played a globetrotting heiress in **An Evening in Paris.** And true to the image, she waterskied wearing a blue swimsuit as Shammi Kapoor hung from a helicopter, singing '*Aasmaan se aaya farishta*'. The coolness with which she pulled off the skimpy costume—first lounging in the sun and then skiing—signalled her arrival as a Bollywood diva. She also appeared on the cover of the August 1966 issue of *Filmfare* wearing a bikini, and did a full photo-feature for the magazine. It is said that she walked into the photographer's studio with only a small purse. When asked about the clothes she intended to wear, she simply took out the bikini from the purse.

After the debacle of *Mera Naam Joker*, Raj Kapoor came back with a vengeance to make a blockbuster—and the movie was **Bobby**. Dimple Kapadia was unleashed on the world and she became the new pin-up queen. In the famous scene around a swimming pool, Dimple became among the first bikini-clad heroines of mainstream Bollywood.[1] As the chubby Rishi Kapoor tried to spoil the scenery with his goggles and see-through shirt, Dimple was just lava-hot in the red bikini. Since the times were simpler, no protests were lodged against the position of her rosary nestling in the bikini top. **Bobby** went on to become a monster hit and the heroine had even the nation's reigning superstar smitten.

Feroz Khan's **Qurbani** had all of his trademark devices—stylish costumes, great music, breathtaking locales and him getting the girl in the end. However, when the girl is Zeenat

---

[1] A little before **Bobby**, Mumtaz appeared in a bikini for Feroz Khan (another connoisseur of the female form) in **Apradh**.

Aman in a bikini, you couldn't really blame Feroz for scripting himself in the girl's arms. In a white bikini, Zeenat ran out of the sea and (unfortunately) towards Feroz Khan instead of us before breaking our hearts and putting on a sarong. While the bona fide bikini scene was a short one, the entire movie flaunted Zeenat's many (ahem) talents, leaving the audience gasping for more.

With early bikini scenes in **Heera Panna** and skimpy scenes in **Satyam Shivam Sundaram**, Zeenat had pretty much sealed the sex symbol tag in her favour. The woman who gave Zeenat serious competition—and some say, who even overtook her—in the sex symbol department was Parveen Babi. In **Yeh Nazdeekiyan**, she played a model doing a Coca-Cola ad directed by Mark Zuber, with whom she eventually had an affair in the movie. She ran out of the sea wearing a bikini (though toned down by a sarong) and went straight into a male model's arms. As per the ad film director's instructions, she had to run 'like a tiger' with 'desire, longing'. Since it was a shoot, her run was rather artificial, but when Parveen Babi wears a bikini . . . sigh!

N. Chandra created an aquatic casting coup when he had two top heroines get into a swimsuit for **Tezaab**. Mandakini had created a white-hot (pun intended) reputation with **Ram Teri Ganga Maili** and Madhuri Dixit had just begun to scorch the scene with **Uttar Dakshin** and **Dayavan**. Together, they appeared on the sides of a swimming pool vying for the attention of instructor Anil Kapoor. Mandakini's black and Madhuri's blue costumes had the entire nation in a tizzy. While the two ladies were much ogled at, Anil Kapoor also appeared in swimming trunks in the same scenes—but nobody was really sure if he was wearing a black full-sleeved T-shirt or not.

In 2003—three years after the Y2K scare and nine years before the Mayan calendar scare—Jackie and Ayesha Shroff produced a movie called **Boom**. Of the three lead heroines—launched with much fanfare—only one could survive the debris of the nuclear flop and act in Bollywood again. Katrina Kaif not only acted again but went on to become its top heroine. However, **Boom** was momentous because it was the film in which Katrina appeared in a bikini (and wore super-skimpy clothes for most part of the film).[2]

> *Bonus Actress*: Priyanka Chopra's bikini appearance in **Dostana** was much hyped but she had already done a bikini scene in her very first film, **Andaaz**.

---

[2] Sex symbol Bo Derek—who had appeared in an iconic golden bikini scene in a movie called *10*—was part of the cast as well: she came out of the sea in a golden saree in **Boom**.

In the worthy tradition of her grandfather, Kareena Kapoor set off a tsunami of debates when she announced that she would become 'size zero' and flaunt her figure in a bikini. The movie was *Tashan*. For all her seductive purring and the much-touted scene where she emerged in a green bikini, the movie flopped. Kareena's figure was analysed less by hormonal teenagers and more by dieticians and social scientists, who apocalyptically claimed that an anorexia epidemic was scheduled to hit the country very soon. As a happy ending, it may be noted that Kareena regained her Kapoor chubbiness and her fitness trainer went on to write a bestselling book on looking good *and* staying healthy. All thanks to the bikini!

In a desperate attempt to balance out the blatant sexism of choosing ten women in swimsuits, one can only present uber-hunk John Abraham and his yellow swimming trunks from *Dostana*—trunks which he tantalizingly pulled down.[3] He set half a billion hearts on fire when he sauntered across the beach in his briefs to the accompaniment of swooning females. He gave serious competition to hot-pants-clad Shilpa Shetty in the gratuitous display of the body, though nobody was really complaining.

Keeping John company in the hunk-in-trunks category is Big B when he dived into a swimming pool in *Don* in a striped pair of swimming trunks. The *kachha* feel of the trunks just paled away when he cavorted with Zeenat Aman in the pool, just as an international smuggler should do. Except that the real Don was dead and this was *Ganga-kinarewala* Vijay.

Two not-so-mainstream actors in two not-so-mainstream films – Rahul Bose in *Thakshak* and Sanjay Suri in *My Brother Nikhil* – also dived in, wearing sexy bikini shorts. One was a fitness-freak billionaire and the other was a national swimming champ, making it quite natural.

HONOURABLE MENTIONS

---

[3] Tusshar Kapoor repeated the same scene for *Kya Super Kool Hain Hum*, causing such serious distress that most people even forgot to laugh (which was, presumably, the intended reaction).

QUIZ: LOST AND FOUND

After looking at tattoos and before heading into the interval, this is the right time to look at the ways lost families are reunited in Hindi films. A quick quiz on how lost souls are found:

1	*Amar Akbar Anthony*	A	Trishul birthmark on shoulder
2	*Coolie*	B	Photo in a wallet
3	*Haath Ki Safai*	C	Family song
4	*Johny Mera Naam*	D	Letter written by mother
5	*Waqt*	E	A unique lock and key combination
6	*Yaadon Ki Baaraat*	F	Photo in brother's bedroom
7	*Zameer*	G	Boxing style
8	*Roop Ki Rani, Choron Ka Raja*	H	Club-shaped birthmark on sole of foot

ANSWERS

1D Bharati wrote a suicide note to her husband, which ended up with her second son (who was brought up by Christian priests) and the note emerged when the father and the son was about to clash. 2H A boy got lost in a flood and the villain adopted him and the birthmark emerged when the boy—now as a drunken adult—stepped on a glass shard and all eyes were on his foot. 3B The elder brother had the photo in the wallet and the younger brother (now a pickpocket) tried to steal it but couldn't. 4G When two junior champion boxers spar as adults, they repeat the childhood exhortations ('*Yeh aaya left* etc) and find their long-lost brothers. 5F Brother 1 goes to kill Brother 2, sees his childhood photo and has a change of heart. 6C Every family should get a unique tune composed so that when you sing it at functions, other brothers can rush and get reunited. 7A Caveat: When family retainers know you have lost a son with a birthmark, they get impostors with tattoos and try to hoodwink you. 8E One brother had the lock while the other had the key. One brother was a police officer while the other was a thief.

248

10

Half-time

Humne ek set of characters liya. Humne ek khaas haalaat dikhaye jo seedhi chalte chalte ek jagah kahin aisi ghoomi ke ab samajh nahin aa sakta ki yeh ab kidhar jayegi . . . woh moment interval ka hona chahiye.

—Javed Akhtar

The interval was invented to sell popcorn and soft drinks but film-makers and writers have turned it into a critical point in the Indian film story.

This section looks at the momentous things that happen around the halfway mark of a film.

Half-time Hero(in)es: 6 Appearances at the Interval Point

How confident must a film-maker be to reveal his ace after half his film is over? He creates tension, and builds up anticipation to reveal the star who is going to take the pitch of the film even higher in the second half. Sometimes, he is a supporting character, played by a star bigger than the lead actors. Sometimes, he is the lead actor in a new and improved avatar. Either way, he is a truckload of adrenaline.

In *Kasme Vaade*, Professor Amit (Amitabh Bachchan) was the good-natured academic who loved his fiancée (Raakhee) and brother (Randhir Kapoor) to a fault. Amit's brother got into a bad brawl with a classmate, and as things turned ugly, Amit came to rescue his brother—only to be knifed down. Halfway into the movie, we had a dead hero, a reformed hero's brother and a slightly unhinged hero's fiancée. The hero's brother went to another city, bought a garage and started to lead a peaceful life. Except we got to hear about a 'rowdy' called Shankar, now in jail for his misdemeanours but expected to land up soon as it was the testimony of one of the garage mechanics that had landed him the jail term. And sure enough, a long pair of legs appeared and their owner started giving the mechanic a major thrashing till Randhir intervened, and he was also given a punch for his troubles. And we all stared into the face of Shankar the goon and realized he looked identical to the soft and sweet Professor Amit. *Dhan te nan!*

India was reverberating with the slogan of Quit India. People were laying down their lives with a smile. It was the best time to fall in love—with your country. It was the worst time to fall in love—with a beautiful woman. It was *1942 A Love Story*. Naren Singh (Anil Kapoor) was the happy-go-lucky son of an Anglophile diwan, who fell in love with Rajeshwari (Manisha Koirala), daughter of an undercover revolutionary. As the love story unfolded, the team of revolutionaries awaited the arrival of Shubhankar, who would assassinate General Douglas,

250

the British tyrant. One thing led to another and the revolutionary's cover was blown. Soldiers surrounded his house. Just when they moved in to arrest him, he pulled out his cache of explosives and blasted the whole area around him. The screen exploded in a 'magnificent' ball of fire with never-before audio effects.[1] Rajeshwari, who had been instructed to escape by her father, turned around on hearing the explosion and an overcoated figure pulled her back. As we processed the images of the explosion, Manisha Koirala's grief and the imposing figure, the Intermission sign came on. Shubhankar had arrived. As had Jackie Shroff.

So, how do you solve a problem like *Bunty Aur Babli*? They went from one location to another, as two Robin Hoods who stole from the rich (think slimy resort-owners, used car–salesmen, crooked insurance agents) and gave to the poor. No city in Uttar Pradesh and Uttarakhand[2] was spared from their onslaught and their signature of a double B within a heart, connected by an arrow, usually left behind on a mirror using a lipstick. Until a man was called in, who was literally their *baap*. Amitabh Bachchan was DCP Dashrath Singh, who smoked beedis and wore a *gamchha* around his neck as he went after criminals. The entire first half of the movie was dedicated to chronicling the thieving exploits of this duo. As they became more confident, Dashrath Singh entered in his typical jagged style. He puffed on his beedi, observed their signature with great interest and announced in his trademark accent that the game was afoot.

In *Taare Zameen Par*, Ishaan Awasthi was a wreck. His parents—having raised a super-disciplined, obedient elder son—did not know what to do with him. His teachers constantly complained about his academics. He painted but not the usual dog–cat–village–mountain stuff kids of his age did. His uniform and his handwriting were both in different stages of disrepair. When teachers of his school in Mumbai threw their hands up, his parents enrolled him in a boarding school in Panchgani. Away from his family and constantly persecuted even by this new set of teachers, Ishaan withdrew into a shell and even gave up the one thing

Aamir Khan orchestrates his entry scene in Taare Zameen Par

---

[1] *1942 A Love Story* was the first Indian film to have Dolby sound.

[2] To know about this and other movies set in UP, do check out the chapter on 'Uttam Pradesh' (page 318).

he loved—painting. Just before the interval, the students had assembled in the art class. And instead of the regular teacher, a replacement walked in. Make that, stormed in. Okay, tornadoed in. Sporting oversized ears, an exaggerated moustache and a clown's costume, we had Aamir Khan literally tumbling on to the screen, doing backflips and jiggling his bum. Only an actor supremely confident of his craft and a director totally committed to his vision could ignore the box office to hold himself back for half of the film. But when he did—singing '*Bum bum bole*' with the kids—it was almost a cathartic experience for the audience. And for Ishaan Awasthi.

A geeky video game–developer was told by his son that the villains were the coolest part of a video game. And he came up with the father of all villains—**Ra.One**. Muscular, deviant, relentless—it was the villain nobody was supposed to be able to beat. Except that the game developer's son—code name Lucifer—managed to take him on. In the initial levels of the game, Lucifer beat Ra.One comprehensively. Just as the game was reaching the dangerous higher levels, Lucifer was called off the game and he left behind a terribly mad Ra.One who decided to exit the game and enter the real world to extract revenge on Lucifer. The form-shifting Ra.One left behind a trail of devastation as he tried to reach Lucifer. Tragedy struck when he encountered Lucifer's geeky dad and killed him. He then chased Lucifer and his mother across London till he cornered them at a car pound. He was about to unleash destruction on them when all the cars he threw at them met a wall of resistance. The point of interval in **Ra.One** was marked by the arrival of the 'real hero' of the film—Shah Rukh Khan as the blue-eyed, blue-suited, blue-hearted hero who was everything that the good-natured geek bearing his resemblance was not. After all, SRK wasn't destined to be the geeky, curd–noodles eating Shankar Subramaniam. He was needed to save the day as The Good One—G.One.

Sometimes, the appearance happens on the other side of the interval. The Greatest Film Ever Made had its half-time bell at the very moment when the retelling of Thakur's history with Gabbar ended. When the film reopened, we had a changed Jai–Veeru who promised to get Gabbar without money, in solidarity with Thakur's cause. Right on cue, the news of Gabbar's next rendezvous came in. Thakur egged the duo on: '*Loha garam hai, maar do hathoda.*' And a lilting twanging of a mandolin came on as the scene changed to welcome the sexiest interval appearance of all times: Helen, in a skimpy green outfit, shimmered on to the screen as Jalal Agha yodelled '*Mehbooba mehbooba*'. It is a common Indian affliction to leave for a smoke during the interval and return well after the second half has started. As the word-of-mouth around **Sholay** spread, no hot-blooded male could afford to be out of his seat when the film resumed. Testosterone is thicker than nicotine.

Face-off: 11 Legendary Confrontations

One beautiful thing from the good ol' days of Hindi cinema was the Battle of the Middle Reels. In films starring two leading characters (usually male), there used to be a fight to (almost) the finish after which the two leading characters discovered one of the following: (a) mutual respect, (b) blood relations, or (c) a change of heart. Usually, this high-octane, crackerjack scene laid down the expectations for the climax. When you watched this scene, you got tense because two heroes would be at each other's throats, but you also felt reassured that when these two would join forces, what an explosion it would be!

Johny Mera Naam, one of Dev Anand's biggest hits, was the quintessential Bollywood story of two brothers growing up on opposite sides of the law—with Pran playing the brother gone astray. The film kicked off with a school boxing match where the two brothers pummelled each other, much to their policeman-father's exaggerated ecstasy and their mother's sobbing agony. And the opening sequence ended with the declaration that, like every year, there had been two winners. This boxing set-piece returned later in the movie as Dev Anand and Pran engaged in some solid knuckle-baazi, only to realize that they were both unbeatable. Given that the only unbeatable person each had met in his life was the other, a conclusion was drawn about their blood(y) relationship. Simple![1]

Anil Kapoor and Sunny Deol starred in *Joshilaay*, a Western-style revenge film shot in the rugged terrain of Ladakh. Originally supposed to be directed by Shekhar Kapur, this film had a laconic Anil and a garrulous Sunny fighting each other to catch an elusive bandit—Jogi Thakur (played gleefully by Rajesh Vivek). As they constantly clashed and the bandit escaped repeatedly, they made a pact. They would start fighting each other at nightfall and the man who

---

[1] As an aside, it should be mentioned that the names of the two brothers were Mohan and Sohan. So, who was Johny?

would remain standing at daybreak would get to nab Jogi Thakur. Needless to say, after the night of bare-knuckled daredevilry, both managed to stagger to their feet when the sun rose.

In *Khudgarz*—loosely based on Jeffrey Archer's *Kane and Abel*—Jeetendra and Shatrughan played foes-turned-friends-turned-foes-turned-friends. The first time they met (as foes) was when they were both kids. Jeetu was being driven to school in his father's Mercedes which splashed mud on Shatru, who promptly shattered the windscreen with a stone. A very kiddish fight promptly broke out, post which Sushma Seth (Shatru's mother in the film) brokered a truce and they—even more promptly—became fast friends. Of course, they grew up to face the evil machinations of Kiran Kumar and became foes again. Only to kiss (not literally) and make up in the climax.

Saudagar was again a film about two guys who oscillated between being friends and foes but concentrated on the enmity to keep the dialogue writers and action directors employed. Dilip Kumar and Raaj Kumar's pairing as Veer Singh and Rajeshwar Singh was massively publicized. What was not publicized was Kamlesh Pandey's outing as a dialogue writer, who gave the duo at least three Middle Scene Battles, without a single fist being thrown or a single bullet being fired. For example, when Veer Singh offered Rajeshwar a gun to kill him, the reply was measured and regal. '*Hum tumhe marenge. Aur zaroor marenge. Lekin . . . woh bandook bhi hamari hogi, goli bhi hamari hogi. Aur waqt bhi hamara hoga.*' In another scene, he explained the scale of his emotions by intoning, '*Rajeshwar jab dosti nibhaata hai, toh afsaane likkhe jaate hain. Aur jab dushmani karta hai, toh tareekh ban jaati hai.*' *Taaliyan!*

Shah Rukh and Salman came together in *Karan Arjun,* a reincarnation drama. First, they were dhoti-clad brothers killed by Amrish Puri's goons, and then they were denim-clad city slickers. Salman ended up becoming the henchman of SRK's lady-love's (Kajol) father and they engaged in a really bloody battle, which was stopped only by divine intervention (a clap of thunder, and lightning spread across the screen). Contrary to popular belief, the heavy punches they landed on each other were not enough to bring back memories of their previous birth simultaneously. That happened later—when they joined forces to fight the transgenerational crooks at the theatrical exhortations ('*Mere Karan Arjun aayenge*') of their mother (Raakhee, in the most irritating role of the century).

Not all confrontations were violent, though. Take the one between the dames of *Devdas,* for example. This sequence was invented by Sanjay Leela Bhansali for the film as Saratchandra Chattopadhyay did not imagine that his characters would—one day—be played by Bollywood's Reigning Queen on Her Way Out and the Crown Princess on Her Way In. Madhuri Dixit and Aishwarya Rai pulled out all stops in the Saroj Khan–choreographed number '*Dola re*', whirling like dervishes and sparkling like diamonds—satisfying all Bollywood lovers with a smooth passing of the baton.

Amitabh Bachchan is the acknowledged master of these Mid-film Mayhems as he has encountered countless villains, anti-heroes, side-heroes and brothers in breathless displays of *dhishoom-dhishoom*.

In *Zanjeer*, Amitabh Bachchan took on Pran—the leading character-actor of the times, who got almost equal billing in the posters because he was a bigger star when the film released. They met in a police station, where Police Inspector Vijay Verma kicked away the chair when Sher Khan tried to sit down. '*Jab tak baithne ko na kaha jaye, sharafat se khade raho. Yeh police station hai, tumhare baap ka ghar nahin.*' Sher Khan taunted him back, saying it was the uniform speaking those angry words. In response, Vijay Verma landed up at Sher Khan's den in plain clothes and had a fight so amazing that when the Pathan gangster praised his adversary in another sher ('*Aaj zindagi mein pehli baar Sher Khan ki sher se takkar hui hai*') it seemed almost like an understatement.

Of the many legends, only one film—*Deewaar*—had the privilege of having two confrontations between its lead stars that have gone on to become Bollywood folklore. The first confrontation of *Deewaar* was not a duopoly in the strictest sense since the mother (Nirupa Roy) weighed in towards the end. The battle of the Good Son and the Bad Son was marked by Shashi's indignant demand—'*Bhai, tum sign karoge ya nahin?*'—and Amitabh's poignant refusal to sign the confession unless his whole life was somehow rewound. And the second—and even more famous—face-off happened when the Bad Son tried to save his brother from his own gang. To explain the futility of a police officer's battles, he pointed out his many riches. He had everything in the world. Except for a mother. Probably Hindi cinema's most iconic line, '*Mere paas maa hai*', has now been quoted at the Oscar ceremony by A.R. Rahman, no less.

In *Amar Akbar Anthony*, Amar Khanna was the dutiful inspector, looking for a smuggler who almost killed his foster-father. Anthony Gonsalves was the bootlegger in Bandra village who helped the smuggler escape to make a quick buck. They met in front of Anthony's booze shop. They played a game of verbal one-upmanship. And then, they decided to go at each other with fists, headbutts, chickens and goats. After an unseen explosion inside a poultry coop, Vinod Khanna carried Amitabh Bachchan out on his shoulders—unconscious. As a seven-year-old Amitabh Bachchan fan, I remember being devastated by that scene as it was inconceivable for me to imagine my hero getting beaten. Even by his elder brother.

The scene from **Mard** was nearer to the climax but the situation was perfect. The two people who could rub the British Empire's nose in the dust were not Mahatma Gandhi or Subhas Bose. They were Raja Azaad Singh (Dara Singh) and his long-lost-son Raju (AB). The devious British had imprisoned both of them and realized the only way they could be killed was by each other in a duel. But of course, the father and son would not fight each other. So, they convinced each of them that the other one in the arena would be a masked impostor. And that set up the two titans for an epic battle after which they realized their blood relationship and proceeded to polish off the British Empire. Whose bright idea was it to let the real father and son in the same arena, so that they could find out about each other? Bob Christo's. As they say, blood is thicker than water but not as thick as Bob Christo.[2]

The underrated Yash Chopra classic **Kaala Patthar** had three superstars of its times—Shashi Kapoor, Shatrughan Sinha and Amitabh Bachchan. Amitabh played the silent and angry young man who was being constantly riled by escaped convict Shatru. After a super sequence at a chai stall where Shatru's verbosity and Amitabh's silence caused sparks to fly, came the lighting of the fuse. Shatru insulted Raakhee, who was Amitabh's love interest. The simmering build-up was so fantastic that it was almost a relief when the fighting actually started. And the two nearly killed each other before Shashi came and separated them. And at the exact moment—Amitabh holding a spade, Shatru a chain and Shashi pushing them apart—came the interval slide. Battles don't come any bigger or middler than this one.

A shooting still of Kaala Patthar, filming of the exact Interval scene

---

[2] When I say Bob Christo, I obviously mean the character played by him. For Bob the person—God bless his soul—I have nothing but the deepest respect.

11

Acting Talent

Koi hero yahaan, koi zero yahaan, koi star hai, koi bekaar hain / Main kaun hoon tumse main kya kahoon, hai sach toh yeh doston—I am the best, I am the best, I am the best

—*Shah Rukh Khan in* **Phir Bhi Dil Hai Hindustani**

Bollywood is full of magicians. They whisk away awards. They steal the thunder when we are least expecting it. They walk into our hearts. They appear in many effortless avatars. Sometimes, we wonder what we would have done without them.

This section is about stars and their adventures in Bollywood.

Three's a Crowd: 13 Actors Who Played Three Roles or More

Even before Bollywood discovered special effects for creating doubles, it had stumbled upon the brilliant plot device of long-lost twins. And double roles lived happily ever after. Literally, hundreds of actors and actresses have played twins, siblings, parent and child, or simply lookalike strangers. Triple roles have been fewer in coming. And triplet roles, even more so. Triplets—as plot device—are a little too fantastic even by Bollywood's standards. Amar, Akbar and Anthony are bad enough. Now if Nirupa Roy had to give birth to them all together, probably under a statue of Mahatma Gandhi while Jeevan was coming after them with a shotgun, it might have been a tad difficult for all concerned (not least of all the screenwriter). Therefore, whenever an actor or actress has played multiple roles, there has been an element of vanity around it. The story could have done without it but the box office probably wanted it.

12: Priyanka Chopra—*What's Your Raashee?*

As of now, the record for the highest number of roles played by a single actor in a single film is twelve, held by Piggy Chops—unfortunately in the film which everyone refused to believe was by the director of *Lagaan*, *Swades* and *Jodha Akbar*. NRI Gujju Harman Baweja zipped in from Chicago and went bride-hunting in Arranged-Marriage-Land, only to bump into twelve avatars of Priyanka Chopra—one for each sign of the zodiac. Keeping in mind Linda Goodman's sun sign traits as well as home-grown Indian astrology funda, the Priyankas turned out to be bubbly, balanced, bashful, brash, brazen, bizarre or *behenji* in turn. The story, already unwieldy for a film, was not helped by the lead actor's rather wooden acting and the usually sensitive director's uninspired helming of the project. Priyanka tried valiantly to rescue the disaster but even twelve of her could not salvage it! So, which sign did the guy eventually get married to? At last count, not too many more than twelve people cared.[1]

10: Kamal Haasan—*Dashavatar*

When Kamal Haasan is not getting intimate with heroines half his age, he is playing multiple roles in the same film, including those of a woman, a leper, a dwarf, triplets, and a gas cylinder. Okay, maybe not the last one. But Kamal did appear in ten roles in a film named after the ten incarnations of Lord Vishnu, no less. George W. Bush, a CIA agent, a Punjabi pop singer, and a giant were some of the zanier avatars Kamal Haasan appeared in, clearly having a ball in the process of creating the (then) world record of the maximum number of roles in a single film. A terribly convoluted story of a chemical weapon being delivered to Tamil Nadu around the time of the 2004 tsunami was only an excuse for creating ten roles for Kamal. While at it, even lead actress Asin slipped in a double role of her own and the other actress, Mallika Sherawat, played a pole dancer (where the pole looked suspiciously like Kamal in prosthetic make-up).

9: Sanjeev Kumar—*Naya Din Nayi Raat*

Sanjeev Kumar reprised a role made famous by the legendary Sivaji Ganesan in Tamil cinema and became something of a legend himself in the process. Modelled around the nine rasas— *shringar* (love), *hasya* (comedy), *raudra* (anger), *karuna* (compassion), *bibhatsa* (disgust), *bhayanak* (horror), *veer* (heroism), *adbhut* (amazement) and *shaant* (peace)—the nine roles popped up in the life of Jaya Bhaduri, who was on the run to escape getting married off by her father. A leper, a dacoit, an effeminate actor, a macho hunter, a drunkard, an elderly widower, a doctor and a two-faced priest landed up with a life lesson each, before the girl met the love of her life in yet another similar-faced symbol of shringar rasa. And of course, it all ended with the mandatory last scene of happy-ending Bollywood where all the nine rasas—with their trademark gaits, moustaches, guffaws and deformities—appeared for a group photo.

6: Govinda—*Hadh Kar Di Aapne*

Playing a bumbling detective on the trail of a supposedly adulterous woman, Govinda pulled off something like what Eddie Murphy did in *The Nutty Professor*. He played his entire family of six. Apart from Raj Malhotra the detective, he was also Raj's father, mother, sister, grandfather and grandmother in one manic scene with horrendously bad make-up that got

---

[1] The same story was also made into an extremely popular 1980s TV serial—*Mr Yogi*—where each holder of the zodiac sign was played by a different actress.

partially redeemed by Govinda's comic genius. He managed to infuse a different tic in each character, and despite all of them looking similar, the characters explained perfectly well why audiences lapped up everything Govinda dished out in the 1990s.

3: I.S. Johar—*Johny Mera Naam*

The perennially funny man, I.S. Johar joined the already packed cast of **Johny Mera Naam** three times over and added to the mayhem. He was the simply named Pehla Ram, Duja Ram and Teeja Ram—three brothers who popped up in different uniforms in a film which already had the audience flummoxed about two brothers, Mohan and Sohan.

So Pehla Ram was a police constable (known for his shift-based honesty—'*Hum duty pe rishwat nahin lete*'), Duja Ram was an airline steward (known for his logic—'*Pehla duje ka judwa aur duja teeja ka judwa ho to . . .*'), and Teeja Ram was a barman in Kathmandu (known for serving liquor in Coca-Cola bottles).

3: Mehmood—*Humjoli*

The first comic superstar of Bollywood was not Govinda but Mehmood. In a film famous for Jeetendra playing badminton, not only in white shoes but in a white T-shirt and trousers as well, Mehmood stole the show with a triple role. He did a killer mimicry of three generations of the Kapoor *khandaan*—Prithviraj, Raj and Randhir. In a song, he picked up a sitar, a *dafli* and a guitar to belt out a song in the trademark styles of the three Kapoors including even their voices. His spoofing of the Prithviraj baritone (made famous by the iconic 'Saleeeeem' as Mughal-e-Azam) laid down the blueprint that is used by comedians even today.

> *Bonus Comedians (x3)*: You see, comedians have a thing for doing things in sets of three—especially when they are at the helm of affairs themselves. When Deven Varma directed the Amitabh Bachchan–thriller **Besharam**, he managed to squeeze in three roles for himself—that of a father, mother and son.
>
> When Asrani wielded the megaphone in **Hum Nahin Sudhrenge** (a subtle play on his famous lines from **Sholay**), he gave himself three roles as well.

3: Amitabh Bachchan—*Mahaan*

Father and twin sons—finally, Bollywood of the 1980s cracked the code. With Vinod Khanna taking sanyaas and Mithun Chakraborty not getting his disco shoes on yet, there was a serious dearth of action heroes that could have only been solved by having many Amitabh Bachchans in the same film. Add to that the standard mixture of the characters having varying shades of grey, different levels of silliness and the same baritone to create box-office gold. Papa Bachchan was a lawyer, on the run from the law. Middle Bachchan was Inspector Shankar, looking to catch old lawyers on the run from the law. Junior was the all-singing, all-dancing comic relief. The superstar—who started his reign in the 1970s—went through the 1980s in inertia. The box office was somewhat guaranteed and movies like these were horrible clangers. He was always accused of getting caught in his formulae though you've got to admit three formulae in the same film is not a formula any longer.

> *Bonus Superstar Triple*: Amitabh Bachchan was not the first Bollywood superstar to go triple in a film. Thespian Dilip Kumar essayed three roles in *Bairaag*, playing a father and his two sons—one of them a playboy, and the other a blind simpleton. The roles were set for an all-round Dilip Kumar performance but the film didn't do too well and became the last film in which the legendary actor acted as a conventional hero.

3: Rajinikanth—*John Jani Janardhan*

Non-believers (usually found north of the Vindhyas) would say that this film copied not only the premise (father plus twin sons in a triple role) of an Amitabh Bachchan film (see above) but even took its name from the hit Bachchan song from *Naseeb*. That's all rubbish. True believers know that Rajini had done an 'Inception' in the minds of *Mahaan*'s writers to see how the audience accepted this triple-role concept before he appeared in it himself. Inspector John got killed. The wife delivered twins. One was adopted by a childless Hindu couple. The other was brought up by a Muslim maidservant. The spirit of the father took over the Hindu son, who then got framed with the help of the Muslim son. I could go on and on about Rajinikanth's *apaar mahima* but then that needs a book of its own.[2]

3: Shah Rukh Khan—*English Babu Desi Mem*

What Amitabh Bachchan does, SRK can't be too far behind in doing. In a film that came in the wake of *DDLJ* and was supposed to stamp SRK's stardom on the industry, Shah Rukh played three different roles—and bombed the film spectacularly. He was the NRI industrialist. He was the rebel son, who died after leaving a son of his own. And he was the youngest scion of the family out to look for his elder brother's son. He was also hamming it like he had done in

---

[2] *Issued in Public Interest*: The director of this movie was T. Rama Rao and *not* Trauma Rao, as often referred to by frivolous people.

no other film (and that's saying something). Add to that some bad wigs, worse moustaches and worst costumes and accessories (designed by Gauri Khan, no less), and here was a disaster you'd like to avoid at all costs. Achha, in this inheritance saga, where did the Desi Mem fit in? Well, what else can you call Sonali Bendre?

3: Paresh Rawal—*Oye Lucky! Lucky Oye!*

As the father of India's biggest thief, he was a Sikh middle-aged man who had an edgy relationship with his son. As part-time wedding singer and part-time fence for stolen goods, he was the henna-haired Gogi bhai. As a smooth-talking doctor not beyond fleecing even India's biggest thief, he was Dr Handa. Paresh Rawal's super-prolific career as comedian, villain and actor had an interesting confluence in *Oye Lucky! Lucky Oye!* in which he played three completely unconnected (no twin/triplet/lookalike funda) roles with aplomb. He was the perfect foil to the glib-talking handsome thief, Abhay Deol, playing the exasperated father figure, the slimy associate and trustworthy expert—sometimes all three in the same character.

3x3: Saif Ali Khan, Riteish Deshmukh and Ram Kapoor—*Humshakals*

Sajid Khan—not known for subtlety or small budgets—has taken the humble triple role to a new trippy level altogether. In *Humshakals*, three sets of triple roles—played by Saif Ali Khan, Riteish Deshmukh and Ram Kapoor—wreak havoc, unleash mayhem and spawn migraines in an unabashed, unapologetic, unadulterated series of gags, jokes and tricks. And just in case you didn't get that it was a slapstick comedy, the three actors (and Satish Shah) slapped each other three times to make it clear. Wow! Wow? Wow!

Show Stealers: 6 Roles That Became Bigger
than the Movie

Quite a few characters have outshone the main characters of a movie. This underlines the unpredictability of Hindi cinema, where people get together to make a movie in which the protagonist is so important that the film is named after him—and then comes a Lone Ranger, who steals not only the hero's thunder but all the memories associated with the film as well. Imagine how difficult it is for a character to become bigger than the title role.

Loin—*Kalicharan*

Ajit's signature role was of the deadly smuggler, Lion aka Loin. The Punjabization of Lion became a catchphrase of the MTV generation as copywriters, VJs, screenwriters and magazine editors jumped on to the bandwagon of Ajit jokes. In the movie, a bombastic Shatrughan Sinha was relegated to the sidelines as Ajit threw his lines around with aplomb in Subhash Ghai's earliest hit. It had a pretty interesting plot, with Loin killing off a police officer (Shatru 1) on his trail and the officer's superior replacing him with a lookalike criminal (Shatru 2) (for spoiler, see below[1]).

Babumoshai—*Anand*

Raj Kapoor's term of endearment for buddy Hrishikesh Mukherjee was immortalized by the latter in a film dedicated to Raj Kapoor and the city of Bombay. Apparently, the characters of the two protagonists were modelled on their real-life counterparts as well. What was supposed to be an out-and-out Rajesh Khanna film turned out to be the first step to stardom for Amitabh

---

[1] On his deathbed, Shatru 1 left behind a note for his boss which got misread as 'No 17'. Only at the climax, when a rotating disc with 'LION' written on it was seen, did the not-so-bright boss realize that 'NO17' was nothing but 'LION' written upside down. But he can be forgiven; after all, he was looking for Loin.

Bachchan, with his understated yet intense portrayal of the Bengali doctor. Amitabh was more than a little unhappy with the script as he believed that the dying characters always got the audience's sympathy, but nevertheless, his character came out real like no other. Anand's lilting call of 'Babumoshai' added to the role—and the title became something of an epithet for all Bongs (till Sourav Ganguly became 'Dada' to the nation).

Bhiku Mhatre—*Satya*

The poker-faced Chakravarthy had the meaty title role of Satya—the rootless, amoral guy who rose to the top of the Bombay underworld. But Manoj Bajpai, after a string of obscure bit parts in Ram Gopal Varma films, hit pay dirt as the unkempt, unapologetic Bhiku Mhatre. His violence, his love, his grunting grin, his hysterical sobs, his domestic squabbles and his crazy gang entered cinematic lore as Ramu pulled off what he does best—great gangster movies. This one role was enough to get Bajpai into starring (*Shool*) as well as negative (*Aks*) roles but he was never able to repeat the manic energy he exuded with the '*Mumbai ka king kaun?*' line. Even now, the character rules mindspace with a Wikipedia entry, nickames on Yahoo, Orkut and MSN, thousands of results on Google, and Isha Koppikar's role in *Shabri* (yet another gangster flick produced by RGV) in which she wanted to be a 'female Bhiku Mhatre'.

Bhiku Mhatre gets his place in the sun. And an Amul hoarding.

Mogambo—*Mr India*

An obscure Hollywood film became the name of the second-most famous villain in the history of Hindi cinema. In the last film of Salim–Javed as a team, Anil Kapoor had the dubious distinction of being a hero where both the villain and the heroine (Miss Hawa Hawaii) completely overshadowed him.

An interesting story around its making is about when Shekhar Kapur asked Javed Akhtar to explain the character of Mogambo to him and Akhtar replied with 'Mogambo khush hua'. The explanation was that it was the line of a megalomaniac who used verbal approval to reward his gang. To convince an incredulous Shekhar, Javed Akhtar told him, 'Shekhar sahib, when Kapil Dev hits a six over the ground, people will shout Mogambo khush hua. When people play teen patti and if they get three aces, they will say Mogambo khush hua. Trust me on that.'[2] He was bang on with this prediction as Mogambo became the newest icon, and his signature line—performed by Amrish Puri with almost an orgiastic relish in the film—rivalled the best lines of Gabbar, with almost as much repeat value.

Genie/Genius—*Aladin*

Aladin Chatterjee was not the most nondescript of names. Khwaish was not the usual name of a city in a Bollywood film. And a resident genie at your beck and call was not your usual perk of college days. Riteish Deshmukh had all that in **Aladin** and he lost it all to—but of course—Amitabh Bachchan doing a comic turn as Genius. The film did quite disastrously at the box office and all the interesting possibilities of modernizing a well-loved fairy tale were squandered. Nor was it that Amitabh Bachchan earned kudos for the film. But it was one of those films where you never asked about Aladin and wanted to know who was playing Genie.

Auro—*Paa*

Amitabh Bachchan has made this into a bit of a habit—being the most important person in a film that is not named after him. Abhishek Bachchan as the Paa of a progeria-afflicted teenager put in a sincere performance; but when a child dies in a Hindi film, the tears blot out everything around it. Add to that a powerhouse performance by Vidya Balan in the role of the mother and you have a clean sweep at the award ceremonies. But to be fair to Abhishek, the film was never about the father.

---

[2] Interesting details of the Mogambo character can be found on Shekhar Kapur's blog (shekharkapur.com).

Ghajini Dharmatma is probably the first villain[3] in Bollywood to have a film named after him. But then, how do you remember him in a story which has Aamir Khan in six-pack abs and a crew cut? Of course, after the mind-numbing violence, very few people even remembered the name of Aamir Khan's character.[4] And it has been more than fifteen minutes since the movie got over.

No One Killed Jessica and almost no one noticed the actress playing the 'title role' either. Here you get featured in a film on one of the most controversial topics of recent times, with a solid star cast that gets very good reviews—and you get killed even before the first scene starts. Like Rani Mukherji in the film, life can be a bitch too!

---

[3] He certainly wasn't the last since **Ra.One** burst out of a video game soon afterwards and took on G.One.

[4] Aamir Khan's character in the film was called Sanjay Singhania.

Pride of India: 14 Miss Indias

They say that if you're not born in the filmi fraternity, the only way to get in is to become Miss India. In fact, for the female Bollywood aspirant, that's the more common way in. Over the years, many Miss India winners have made their way into Bollywood with varying degrees of success. And it has been happening for a very long time. In the earliest days of the Miss India contest, the winners usually hit the ramp, but from the 1980s onwards—when there was increased visibility for the winners—Bollywood lapped them up.

Persis Khambatta

Year of crowning: 1965

Early mark: Her debut was a rather intriguingly named movie called ***Bambai Raat Ki Baahon Mein***, directed by K.A. Abbas.

Biggest claim to fame: Not in Bollywood. She moved to Hollywood as probably the first Indian crossover and starred in a shaven-headed role in *Star Trek: The Motion Picture*. She acted in several other films, though none was very high-profile.

Other notables: Wrote a coffee-table book *Pride of India* on the Miss India pageant down the ages.

Currently: Unfortunately, she died of a heart attack in 1998.

Swaroop Sampat

Year of crowning: 1979

Early mark: Hrishikesh Mukherjee's ***Naram Garam***, where she was part of a really unusual love triangle involving Amol Palekar and Utpal Dutt . . . don't ask, just see the movie.

Biggest claim to fame: Her most-loved role came in the TV serial *Yeh Jo Hai Zindagi*, which entertained middle-class India for a long time and still lives on in reruns and DVD sets.

Other notables: None really unless you count a bikini scene from the movie ***Karishmaa*** that went 'viral' and still logs in many views on YouTube.

Currently: Married to Paresh Rawal and settled into happy domesticity. No plans of returning.

Sangeeta Bijlani

Year of crowning: 1980

Early mark: As one of the three leading ladies in **Tridev**, she got noticed because of the sheer magnitude of the film's success if not for the length of the role.

Biggest claim to fame: Sadly, not quality but quantity. She had an astonishing twenty releases in her seven-year career and nine in one year (1991) alone. Actually, her moment in the sun—if you can call it that—was when the married Mohammad Azharuddin ditched his first wife to marry her.

Currently: Divorced from Azhar. Seen often at Page Three parties.

Juhi Chawla

Year of crowning: 1984

Early mark: Didn't get noticed in her first film, **Sultanat**. Her second Hindi release was **Qayamat Se Qayamat Tak**, which marked the resurgence of romance in Bollywood and sealed her place as an A-list heroine.

Biggest claim to fame: Probably **QSQT** but Juhi has a whole lot of very big hits to her credits, going all the way from David Dhawan (**Bol Radha Bol**) to Nagesh Kukunoor (**3 Deewarein**). She's easily the most successful Miss India in Bollywood.

Other notables: Along with Shah Rukh Khan and her husband Jay Mehta, she is a producer (though not majorly successful yet) and businesswoman (owning the two-time IPL winner Kolkata Knight Riders).

Currently: Ads for snack food and cheering at KKR matches. And occasional 'interesting' roles like the ones in **Luck By Chance** or **Gulaab Gang** (in a negative role in the latter, pitting her against one-time rival Madhuri Dixit).

Sonu Walia

Year of crowning: 1985

Early mark: **Khoon Bhari Maang**, where she was a top model and the villain's moll (with a heart, though). She was 'defeated' by Rekha in a modelling competition as well as in securing Kabir Bedi's advances.

Biggest claim to fame: Again, quantity over quality. She acted in fifteen indistinguishable films in her three busiest years (1989–91) and twenty-six overall.

Currently: Settled in the US with her hotelier husband. No plans of returning.

Madhu Sapre

Year of crowning: 1992

Early mark and biggest claim to fame: The one and only film she has done—*Boom*. Katrina Kaif, Padma Lakshmi and Madhu Sapre had their collective professional obituaries written with this one film (and for good reason too). Only Katrina was able to rise after that. Madhu has never acted in a film again.

Other notables: Highly controversial ad for Tuff shoes that featured her and (then beau) Milind Soman wearing only sneakers, a python and each other.

Currently: Lives in Italy with her husband. Hopefully, she's not planning anything like *Boom* again.

Namrata Shirodkar

Year of crowning: 1993

Early mark: If you call *Mere Do Anmol Ratan* and *Hero Hindustani* that.

Biggest claim to fame: As the golden-hearted prostitute in *Vaastav*, opposite Sanjay Dutt (whose career was resurrected after the film).

Other notables: Sister of Shilpa Shirodkar, Namrata has been eye-candy in several not-so-notable movies.

Currently: Married to Telugu actor Mahesh Babu. No plans of returning.

Sushmita Sen

Year of crowning: 1994

Early mark: Her debut film, *Dastak*, was about a Miss Universe being stalked by an obsessed fan. It generated an unprecedented buzz but did not do too well.

Biggest hit: *Main Hoon Na*, where she appeared like a typical Yash Chopra heroine.

Other notables: Mainly off-screen romances and assorted gossip haven't really helped us focus on her body of work. The occasional comic role (*Maine Pyar Kyun Kiya*) and 'acting' role (*Chingaari*) have got noticed.

Currently: Has a long-standing ambition to produce and star in a film on the Rani of Jhansi, which may have some autobiographical shades if she has her way.

Gul Panag

Year of crowning: 1999

Early mark: *Dhoop*—a short and strong performance in a serious film.

Biggest hit/claim to fame: Has acted in mainly offbeat films, the most acclaimed of which is *Dor*. She played a woman whose husband stood accused of murder and only an impossible task could free him.

Other notables: Another realistic performance in ***Manorama Six Feet Under*** and a sassy role in ***Turning 30***.

Currently: Looking forward to a happy married life and some more interesting roles, apart from an active career in politics. She was the Aam Aadmi Party candidate for Chandigarh in the 2014 general elections and did some seriously cool campaigning on Royal Enfield Bullets. Incidentally, at her wedding the *baaraat* arrived on Bullets too.

Lara Dutta

Year of crowning: 2000

Early mark: Her debut film, ***Andaaz***, pitted her against Priyanka Chopra (whom she beat to become Miss India). Not a huge commercial success, it was in the news for the casting and costumes.

Biggest hit: Probably David Dhawan's ***Partner***, opposite Salman Khan.

Other notables: Hysterical roles in comic capers like ***Bhagam Bhag, Masti, No Entry***, etc.

Currently: Looking forward to a happy married life with Mahesh Bhupathi, and more films from her production house, Bheegi Basanti, whose first release was ***Chalo Dilli*** (where she starred opposite Vinay Pathak).

Celina Jaitley

Year of crowning: 2001

Early mark: Skimpily clad as Fardeen Khan's arm-candy in ***Janasheen***. Got completely overshadowed, as is the norm in home productions of male stars.

Biggest hit/claim to fame: Probably ***Golmaal Returns***.

Other notables: Smallish roles in multi-starring comedies like ***No Entry, Thank You***.

Currently: Happy married life with hotelier Peter Haag and her twin sons, Winston and Viraaj.

Neha Dhupia

Year of crowning: 2002

Early mark: In ***Qayamat***, where she was the woman from Ajay Devgn's past and did a bikini scene (as she was probably expected to, with her Miss India 'background').

Biggest claim to fame: ***Julie***. Her dare-bare act as a prostitute on a mission got a huge number of eyeballs. This was amplified by her comment—'In the industry, only sex and Shah Rukh sell.'

Other notables: Some roles in offbeat films like ***Phas Gaye Re Obama*** and ***Dasvidaniya***. Large number of small roles in multi-starring comedies.

Tanushree Dutta

Year of crowning: 2004

Early mark: **Chocolate**, a faithful and yet uneven remake of *The Usual Suspects*.

Biggest hit: Probably **Aashiq Banaya Aapne**—which also got a lot of publicity because of her clinches with Emraan Hashmi.

Other notables: If that's what you call the usual glam-girl in thrillers or comedies.

Puja Gupta

Year of crowning: 2007

Early mark: An obscure offering—**Kehtaa Hai Dil Baar Baar**—which didn't get her fame or fortune.

Biggest hit/claim to fame: **FALTU**, which was famous for the ultimate party anthem '*Chaar baj gaye lekin party abhi baaki hai*'.

Other notables: None yet.

QUEENS OF THE WORLD

While Miss Universe is the higher honour, Bollywood's two most successful actresses were Miss Worlds – Aishwarya Rai and Priyanka Chopra.

Ash shrugged off criticism about her wooden acting to debut with master director Mani Ratnam's *Iruvar*, where she played a role allegedly based on Jayalalithaa. She built her commercial equity with films like **Taal**, **Devdas** and **Dhoom 2** while did several critically acclaimed roles in **Hum Dil De Chuke Sanam**, **Guru**, **Raincoat** and **Chokher Bali**. She finally settled into happy domesticity with Abhishek Bachchan though the rumours about her impending return are rife.

PC started off as a femme fatale in **Andaaz** and **Aitraaz** (though her official debut was also in a Tamil film—*Thamizhan*) but after some super-successful films like **Don**, **Dostana** and **Agneepath**, she became an all-rounder and received lots of praise for her roles in **Fashion**, **7 Khoon Maaf** and **Barfi**. She looks to be ready for some more kickass roles (including a literal one—**Mary Kom**).

Baar Baar, Lagataar: 16 Stars with Hat-tricks at Filmfare Awards

The Filmfare Awards have been around for six decades. They have had their share of controversies amid allegations of favouritism towards various stars at different points of time. Also, without the benefit of hindsight, the jury has sometimes chosen poorly, making the awards list look quite awry a few years on. But for its sheer longevity, Filmfare is still the prize every filmwala aspires to. It is also a great indicator of the extent to which certain people ruled the roost in a certain era. The biggies of Bollywood are all on that list. But how does one identify the real doyens in each category? One criterion is to find people who have done hat-tricks. Only a fantastic mix of talent, speed and luck allows you to win three years in a row. But thanks to the exclusive star system of Bollywood, there seems to be a pretty large number of people who have been there, done that.

Best Director

Given the prolonged involvement a director has (or should have) in a film, churning out one award-winning film a year for three years should be quite impossible. As surprising as it might sound, this is the category where we have not one, but two hat-tricks! Iconic director Bimal Roy did his first trio in the first three years of the awards as *Do Bigha Zamin*, *Parineeta* and *Biraj Bahu* won (between 1953 and 1955). There was a gap of two years when V. Shantaram and Mehboob Khan put a foot in the door but Roy returned in 1958–60 with *Madhumati*, *Sujata* and *Parakh*.[1] To put his achievement in perspective, no other director has won it in even two consecutive years. Very soon, we won't have directors who make even six films in their entire careers.

---

[1] Inertia must surely count for something because Bimal Roy won it for *Parakh* (clearly not one of his best films) in 1960 by beating K. Asif who was in the running with a certain film called *Mughal-e-Azam*.

Best Actor

This one is expected since Dilip Kumar ruled the Best Actor category like his own backyard in the early days of the award. In the first ten years, he pocketed the Best Actor trophy five times including a hat-trick (1955–57) for *Azaad, Devdas* and *Naya Daur.* In doing this, he beat off stiff competition like Raj Kapoor in *Jagte Raho* and Dev Anand in *Munimji.* In fact, the stiff competition carried on for quite some time as the trio of Raj–Dev–Dilip comprised the three Best Actor nominees in five different years. Four superstars—Rajesh Khanna, Amitabh Bachchan, Naseeruddin Shah and Shah Rukh Khan—have won the Best Actor Award twice in a row. But we are still awaiting the hat-trick.

Best Supporting Actor

Bollywood's forte seems to be the theme of the underdog. The guy who gets hammered for a large part of the film returns to beat the shit out of his tormentors. And for a large part, life imitates art. Abhishek Bachchan seems to have followed in the footsteps of his illustrious father in this regard. The Big B waited for his thirteenth film (*Zanjeer*) to hit box-office gold. Junior B waited till his fourteenth film to get commercial and critical acclaim in Mani Ratnam's *Yuva.* After *Yuva* in 2004, he did the supporting act to his father in *Sarkar* and to King Khan in *Kabhi Alvida Naa Kehna*—to complete the hat-trick. The Big B has won three Supporting Actor awards in all (his first in 1970 for *Anand*). Junior B equalled him in three years. And what about Best Actor in a leading role? Well, the Big B leads 5–0 on that one.

Best Music Director

The music categories see the most number of reigns. Music, lyrics and voice—all categories have winners of three consecutive awards. And the big daddies of Bollywood—the music directors—have won the most. Two have won four in a row. No surprises when I say Laxmikant–Pyarelal did it in the late 1970s. LP, the longest playing record in the industry, won it for four rocking tracks—*Amar Akbar Anthony, Satyam Shivam Sundaram, Sargam* and *Karz.* And Rahman sealed his supremacy with *Rang De Basanti, Guru, Jaane Tu Ya Jaane Na* and *Delhi 6.*[2] Shankar–Jaikishan, known to be the melody-makers of RK Films, ironically have *Mera Naam Joker*—the studio's biggest failure—in their hat-trick. Their other two films were *Pehchaan* and *Beimaan.* In the early 1990s, when purists were lamenting the death of melody and originality, in walked Nadeem–Shravan. And for several years, they could do no wrong. They manufactured hit songs by the dozen throughout the decade, but their hat-trick happened in the first three years of their careers with *Aashiqui, Saajan* and *Deewana.*

---

[2] As of 2013, Rahman has won the highest number of Filmfare Awards for Best Music—ten. And it is going to be some time before his record is broken as none of the current crop of music directors is even close.

Best Lyricist

Gulzar has won the Best Lyricist prize eleven times. Javed Akhtar has won eight. Neither has managed to win three times in a row, though. The person who did it never won a Filmfare Award again. Shakeel Badayuni's trio of hits—running from 1960 to 1962—was a swansong like no other. The title song of *Chaudhvin Ka Chand*, 'Husnwale tera jawaab' (*Gharana*) and 'Kahin deep jale kahin dil' (*Bees Saal Baad*) were the three offerings of Shakeel that became award-winning songs.

Best Playback Singer (Male)

The quirky genius with a curious record at the Filmfare Awards.

It seems a little unfair that Kishore Kumar does not have the longest-winning streak in male playback singing. His longest unbroken reign was four awards when he won for 'Pag ghungroo' (*Namak Halaal*), 'Humein aur jeene ki' (*Agar Tum Na Hote*), 'Manzilein apni jagah' (*Sharaabi*) and 'Saagar kinare' (*Saagar*) between 1982 and 1985. But it sounds almost providential that he also won the prize in 1980 (for 'Hazaar rahein' from *Thodisi Bewafaii*) and would have had a double hat-trick if his own son hadn't beaten him in 1981 with *Love Story*. (Amit Kumar never won again.) Poetic? Tragic? You decide.

So, who does have the longest winning streak? Nope, it is not Mohammad Rafi either—he doesn't even have a hat-trick to his name. The only singer to have five—five!—continuous awards is Kumar Sanu. And quite ironically, he earned his early bread by doing covers of Kishore Kumar classics. He shrugged off jokes about a nasal voice and his winning graph became identical to Nadeem–Shravan's with 'Ab tere bin jee lenge hum' (*Aashiqui*), 'Mera dil bhi' (*Saajan*) and 'Sochenge tumhe pyar' (*Deewana*). He added two more to his kitty with 'Yeh kaali kaali aankhen'(*Baazigar*) and 'Ek ladki ko dekha' (*1942 A Love Story*). What we don't know for certain is whether he stopped winning or—as he claimed—withdrew from competitive awards. What we do know is that he was grateful enough to name his bungalow Aashiqui.

Best Playback Singer (Female)

The ultimate diva—Lata Mangeshkar—competed in a general playback singing category for both male and female singers. She withdrew from competitive awards soon after. Among the rest, four singers have done hat-tricks. Three of them can be considered absolute equals—in talent and in popularity. Anuradha Paudwal won for *Aashiqui*, *Dil Hai Ke Manta Nahin* and *Beta* (1990–92). Kavita Krishnamurthy did it for *1942 A Love Story*, *Yaraana* and *Khamoshi*

(1994–96). Alka Yagnik came to the party last with **Taal, Dhadkan** and **Lagaan** (1999–2001). And the fourth one? She is a little ahead of these three . . . also, she has won four awards in a row for **Caravan, Hare Rama Hare Krishna, Naina** and **Pran Jaye Par Vachan Na Jaye.** She is the one and only—Asha!

Best Actor in a Comic Role
This award has had a patchy stint. For a character as regular as the Bollywood comedian, this award was given regularly only from 1989 onwards and was wound up after 2006. In 1989, Anupam Kher converted the solo award into a joint one. Awarded for **Ram Lakhan,** he called his on-screen partner Satish Kaushik on stage and shared the prize with him. Two years later, he started a hat-trick and picked up awards for **Lamhe, Khel** and **Darr.** He returned for a fifth time to pick up an award for **Dilwale Dulhania Le Jayenge** and to be remembered as one of the greatest comic actors of Bollywood. And to think the role that brought him fame (and his first Filmfare) was a tragic one—the bereaved headmaster of **Saaransh.**

Best Choreographer
The Dancing Queen's crown has been hotly contested—among stars and choreographers. If there has to be a first among equals, it has to be the one who has a hat-trick, the maximum awards *and* is the first recipient of the award. In the first three years of the award itself, Saroj Khan had her threesome by winning for **Tezaab** ('*Ek do teen*'), **Chaalbaaz** ('*Na jaane kahan se*') and **Sailaab** ('*Hum ko aajkal hai*'). Over the years, it has been a see-saw battle between her and Farah Khan, with both ladies breaking each other's hat-trick streaks several times.

Did you notice the composition of heroines in Saroj Khan's hat-trick? Madhuri Dixit: 2; Sridevi: 1. Would you agree that's a fair representation of their standing in the industry in the '90s? Or wouldn't you?

Yo Yo: 10 Famous Casting Flip-flops

Commercial cinema depends on stars to get the cash registers ringing right from Day One. Many a time, the job is considered half-done once the star is in place. And consequently, there is major heartburn and agony when these stars come and go—for a variety of reasons. Sometimes, the stories are too good to be true. Sometimes, the stars are too big to be ignored.

The Greatest Film Ever Made had a massive list of memorable characters. Of the five major ones, Veeru, Basanti and Thakur were finalized easily, probably because the director repeated the three stars from his previous hit, *Seeta Aur Geeta*. Gabbar Singh went through a very well-known ping-pong when Danny Denzongpa was signed on but had to drop out because he was already committed to Feroz Khan's *Dharmatma*. Another tussle went on for the role of Jai. Shatrughan Sinha was the upcoming star. He had started off as a villain but was looking at positive roles, having tasted success with his flamboyant dialogue delivery and screen presence. The distributors were sold on him too. Quietly on the sidelines, an unknown actor was also lobbying for the role. He had a track record of spectacular failure and though he was in talks for some unusual lead roles, his box-office pull was zilch. Dharmendra, who liked this new actor a lot, put in a word with Ramesh Sippy. The Sippys were themselves a little wary of having too many stars in a film and Shatru was not the easiest to work with. Weighing all the pros and cons, they decided to take on the unknown actor for the role of Jai. And the rest, as they say, was history.

In the late '60s, two young boys—Salim Khan and Javed Akhtar—formed a team and started writing screenplays. Sensing the undercurrent of anger and frustration in the country, they created a character which embodied the anger and exploded against the system. The Angry Young Man was an idea whose time had come—but in formula-driven Bollywood, no major star was willing to break out of the prevailing social–romantic mould to play this role. Salim–

Javed's first 'angry' film was *Zanjeer*, sold to an upcoming film-maker called Prakash Mehra. He took the script to three major stars and was refused for various reasons. Dev Anand wanted a few songs to sing. Dharmendra had no dates. Raaj Kumar—being Raaj Kumar—did not like Prakash Mehra's hair oil. (No typos there. He did not like the smell of the hair oil. Jaani, why is that so difficult to believe?) Pran—who had already been signed—got to know of a new actor through his son and asked Prakash Mehra to go and see *Bombay to Goa*, starring this new actor called Amitabh Bachchan. Prakash Mehra saved a lot of money on his lead actor's fees and India got its most durable icon.

Anil Kapoor made his first bid towards the No. 1 slot—hitherto belonging to Amitabh Bachchan (along with Nos. 2 to 10)—with *Mr India*. It was the last film by Salim–Javed as a duo and was written with their favourite actor in mind. An invisible hero had to make a phenomenal impact with his voice, and Salim–Javed believed that only the Big B could carry it off. The megastar politely declined since he felt that in cinema, the audience came to *see* the hero and not merely to hear him. The role then went to Anil Kapoor, who was satisfied with a big idea for his first big-budget home production and *Mr India*'s success set him up for superstardom.

> *Bonus Movie*: Even *Meri Jung*, where Anil Kapoor had a very powerful role as a lawyer, was written with Amitabh Bachchan in mind. The good-natured Anil Kapoor has been modest enough to admit that his success has a lot to do with his accepting AB-rebounds.

Khuda Gawah's next-gen love story featured Amitabh and Sridevi's daughter (Sridevi in a double role) along with a younger star. This role was initially being played by Sanjay Dutt and some scenes—including a high-voltage action sequence to introduce him—were even filmed. However in 1990–91 (when the shooting had started), Amitabh Bachchan's *Hum* and Sanjay Dutt's *Thanedaar* had both released with two songs with a very similar tune[1] and it was never clear who had copied whom. The clash of tunes had soon transformed into a clash of egos and it was rumoured that Sanjay Dutt dropped out of *Khuda Gawah* for this reason. Eventually, the role was played by Nagarjuna who had gained some amount of national recognition thanks to *Shiva*.

---

[1] For the record, both composers (Laxmikant–Pyarelal for *Hum* and Bappi Lahiri for *Thanedaar*) lifted the tune from a song by Mory Kante (an African singer). *Thanedaar*'s song's (rather inane) lyrics also had the same start as the original ('*Tama tama*')!

After Mahesh Bhatt's critically acclaimed and commercially successful *Arth*, his next film was widely anticipated. It was being bankrolled by Rajshri Productions,[2] known for their commercial acumen. The film—also written by Mahesh Bhatt—was decidedly unconventional as it was the story of a sixty-five-year-old retired headmaster, B.V. Pradhan. For this role, he had chosen a new actor called Anupam Kher[3]—very talented but totally unknown. When he communicated this to the producers, they insisted on a more saleable name and suggested Sanjeev Kumar. When Anupam Kher got to know of this decision, he was heartbroken and decided to return to his hometown. But before he left, he went to Mahesh Bhatt's house and exploded, calling him a fraud for going back on his word. It is said that in Anupam Kher's outburst, Mahesh Bhatt saw the climax of **Saaransh** where B.V. Pradhan stormed into a minister's room and gave him a piece of his mind. He went back to Rajshri and had the original actor reinstated.

Yash Chopra started work on an extramarital drama called **Silsila** when Bollywood was abuzz with rumours of an affair between the super-successful box-office *jodi* of Amitabh Bachchan and Rekha. Initially, Padmini Kolhapure was cast as the wife and Parveen Babi as the lover. But Padmini Kolhapure couldn't give dates and was replaced by Smita Patil. It is said that just before the first outdoor shoot, Yash Chopra came to Amitabh and asked for his help in casting Jaya and Rekha to make the film really special. Too much speculation has happened on the whys and hows of this casting since the trio were obviously not oblivious to the gossip mills around them. The fact remains that the two leading ladies were convinced to participate in the casting coup of the century and they performed their roles to perfection.

In the mid-'80s, Subhash Ghai was the director with the Midas touch with superhits like *Karz*, *Hero* and *Karma* to his credit. Though all his earlier movies had Laxmikant–Pyarelal as music directors, he chose R.D. Burman for **Ram Lakhan**. RD had started composing while Ghai was working on *Devaa*, a mega-project starring Amitabh Bachchan. However, when *Devaa* was shelved, Subhash Ghai started work on **Ram Lakhan** and shockingly announced Laxmikant–Pyarelal as the composers. This was done without even speaking to RD, who was devastated. RD's long-time team-member Manohari Singh recalled, 'Till the evening before, we were composing for **Ram Lakhan**. Next morning, we got the news that we were not in

---

[2] The younger scion of the Rajshri family—Sooraj Barjatya—was an assistant director in the film. The editor of **Saaransh** was David Dhawan, making it a film which can count in its crew three of India's most successful film directors.

[3] Anupam Kher had acted in **Jaane Bhi Do Yaaro** as a character called Disco Killer but his role got edited out of the final cut.

it.' In a later interview, Pyarelal said they had told Subhash Ghai that they would never work with him if he gave **Ram Lakhan** to R.D. Burman. RD was at a professional low when this happened and the whole incident was a huge blow from which he never really recovered.[4]

With *Fire*, Deepa Mehta had already attracted the ire of several right-wing groups. But the critical reception also ensured that her next film was much awaited by audiences and major Bollywood stars were willing to work with her. In early 2000, she started shooting her next film—**Water**—with Shabana Azmi, Nandita Das and Akshay Kumar in Varanasi. No sooner had it started than protests began alleging disrespect towards widows in the script, and the shooting had to be given police protection. But the situation went

Shabana Azmi, Deepa Mehta, Akshay Kumar and Nandita Das address the press before a shoot of Water *that never got completed*

out of hand and the administration had to eventually advise Deepa Mehta and her crew to leave Varanasi. Both Shabana Azmi and Nandita Das had shaved off their hair to play nineteenth-century widows. They had to go around with their new hairstyles for quite a while after that. Eventually, **Water** was shot nearly three years after these incidents in Sri Lanka (under a false name to avoid attention) with Seema Biswas, Lisa Ray and John Abraham.

Madhur Bhandarkar's **Heroine** was launched in Cannes in 2011 amidst great fanfare with Aishwarya Rai in the lead role, who also clarified that the movie wasn't based on her life. She started shooting immediately after her return to India. After about a week of shooting, the news of Aishwarya's pregnancy came out. Madhur Bhandarkar claimed that he wasn't aware of Aishwarya's pregnancy at the time of the film's announcement. Aishwarya stated that she thought she would be able to complete the shooting before the pregnancy became visible. Madhur Bhandarkar countered that the movie would require a lot of physical exertion that cannot be safe for a pregnant woman. And Aishwarya made a graceful-if-controversial exit

---

[4] A detailed account of this incident—and indeed, R.D. Burman's entire life—can be found in the award-winning book *R.D. Burman: The Man, The Music* by Anirudha Bhattacharjee and Balaji Vittal.

from *Heroine*. Soon afterwards, Kareena Kapoor was signed on to play the lead and rumours circulated that she was paid a record Rs 8 crore for the film. And the media dutifully started asking Kareena if *Heroine* was based on *her* life.

Anurag Kashyap broke into the big league after nearly a decade of being a pariah. His unconventional vision started to fit into the Bollywood definition of *hatke* and he started playing on a bigger canvas. He launched *Bombay Velvet*—a thriller set in 1950s Bombay about how the city became a metropolis. Initial rumours were that Aamir Khan was to play the lead. The breathless speculation peaked when it was heard that Aamir *and* Shah Rukh would both act in *Bombay Velvet*. Finally, Ranbir Kapoor was officially announced as the male lead for the film—rendering all the passionate discussions redundant. Anurag Kashyap stated that he had never considered either superstar for the role but the media almost completely ignored this. Since it came from the director, it was the truth. But how can you let truth spoil a good story?

HONOURABLE MENTIONS

Several movies made in movies have had interesting casting flip-flops too.

In *Rangeela*, supporting dancer Mili Joshi got a chance when heroine Gulbadan eloped with her driver.

In *Luck By Chance*, newcomer Vikram Jaisingh came in when superstar Zafar Khan dumped Romi Rolly's film to work with Karan Johar.

But the most audacious casting flip-flop was part of *Om Shanti Om* when junior artiste Bela Makhija (Kirron Kher) had to refuse K. Asif's offer to play Anarkali in *Mughal-e-Azam* because she was expecting her son, Om. '*Waise Madhu ne theek thak sambhaal liya*,' she conceded gracefully later on.

CASTING COUP-FLOPS

- *Awwal Number*: Dev Anand approached Imran Khan (to play Aditya Pancholi's role). Imran had just retired from cricket but did not agree despite Dev Anand's best attempts, citing his political ambitions.
- *Gangster*: Mahesh Bhatt approached Shoaib Akhtar for the title role as he believed that the cricketer had 'a lot of raw emotion, animal magnetism and the vulnerability of a child'. Shoaib initially thought the offer to be a joke but understood the seriousness after meeting Mahesh Bhatt. But he also refused, citing his cricket commitments.

12

Inspirations and Tributes

Kala toh kala hoti hai chahe apni ho ya parayi. Bas, lakshmi aani chahiye chhan chhan chhan chhan chhan chhan . . .

—*Anil Kapoor in* **Taal**

Indian cinema is rather cavalier about recycling. Turning established plots and well-worn situations into fresh scenes has now become something of an art form. And the durability of the proven ones extends well into our future. The sources are varied. And before you call them ungrateful, they pay the occasional tribute too.

This section looks at the most 'inspiring' people, books, plots and movies.

Inspiration + Perspiration: 6 'Lifted' Plots

On one episode of *Koffee with Karan*, Javed Akhtar recounted a story from his salad days. He had gone to a producer to narrate a script and the man had listened to it without interruption. After finishing, a nervous Javed Akhtar asked, '*Sir, kaisa laga?*' To young Javed, the producer explained the risks of being original in Bollywood—'*Darling, story toh teri achchi hai. Lekin ek bada risk hai . . . Yeh kahani kisi bhi film mein aayi nahin hai ab tak!*'

'Inspiration' is a—well—inspired word in Bollywood. There are a million films to make but only a few tried-and-tested themes. And even fewer Hollywood movies to look at for stories.

Many directors have taken inspiration from films—some with credit and some without. Sometimes, the inspiration has taken the form of scene-by-scene replication and sometimes, the film has grown bigger than the original plot.

Plot: A spoiled heiress runs away to be with her lover and meets a reporter, who helps her just to get an exclusive story, but ends up falling in love with her.

In 1934, *It Happened One Night* made a clean sweep of the box office and the Oscars with a heart-warming tale, and it was only a matter of time before the Gods of Parental Opposition and Runaway Lovers made it into an Indian story. Raj Kapoor and Nargis starred in **Chori Chori**, which added the only thing that was missing in the original—superhit songs. Shankar–Jaikishan provided an eminently hummable score to make the film complete. The charm of the story was not lost even six decades later as Aamir Khan and Pooja Bhatt got together in **Dil Hai Ke Manta Nahin.** And again, the plot was brought alive by crackling dialogue and great music.

Plot: Terrorized by bandits, a village enlists the help of mercenaries to protect itself.

It started with Akira Kurosawa's *Seven Samurai*, which was followed by the Hollywood version (*The Magnificent Seven*). Again, the terror of dacoits, the visual delight of their rocky dwellings and the bravura of a small group taking on a large one were too much for Indian film-makers to resist. In India, two films—***Mera Gaon Mera Desh***[1] and ***Khote Sikkay***—had very similar plots. And later, it continued with Rajkumar Santoshi's ***China Gate***. The same simple tale was remade as the Greatest Story Ever Told, which is still considered to be the pinnacle of Indian cinematic success. The finesse with which the entire concoction was served differentiated this offering from any other mishmash of borrowed plots and devices. *Sholay*, with its perfect orchestration of characters and emotions, rose above the ordinary and became an epic, many times the sum of its parts. *Sholay* borrowed not only its plot but a few catchy devices from other films as well. For example, the double-sided coin was borrowed from a film called *One-eyed Jack*. And no, the title wasn't original either. B.R. Chopra had already made a film of that name, though he'd spelt it differently, as *Shole*.

Bonus Claim: The strongest claim to *Sholay*'s story came from B-grade cult icon Joginder, who sued G.P. Sippy for lifting the story of his ***Bindiya Aur Bandook***. Released in 1972, the film was a pretty big success and had exactly the same plot of a village's fight against a cruel dacoit.

Plot: A geek falls in love with a beautiful girl and enlists the help of a date-coach to woo her.

This seemingly innocuous plot came under fire when Sony Pictures sued the makers of ***Partner*** for lifting the plot of their hit production *Hitch*. It was very embarrassing for the Indian film industry but if one stepped back a bit, one realized that the story had been in circulation long before *Hitch* hit the screens, in ***Shagird*** (starring Joy Mukherjee, Saira Banu and I.S. Johar).[2] You only have to discount the details of whether the love guru trained one geek or many, whether the geek was a young man or old, whether there was a love triangle or a quadrilateral, etc., and you are looking at two more similar films—***Chhoti Si Baat*** (starring Amol Palekar, Vidya Sinha and Ashok Kumar) and ***Shreeman Aashique*** (starring Rishi Kapoor, Urmila Matondkar and Anupam Kher). So, who copied whom?

Plot: A man goes on the hunt for his wife's killer, who also injured him so badly that he now has short-term memory loss and forgets everything after every fifteen minutes.

This came first in *Memento*—the film which made a cult hero out of Christopher Nolan—and had all kinds of film-making stunts like going forward and backward in time as the hero hunted for clues and tattooed them on to his body to help him remember later. A few years

---

[1] Incidentally, ***Mera Gaon Mera Desh***'s villain (played by Vinod Khanna) was called Jabbar Singh.

[2] See chapter on Transformations (Page 414).

after *Memento*, posters of Tamil superstar Surya—with phone numbers and names tattooed on his muscular body—came up in Chennai for a film called *Ghajini*. This was subsequently up-starred to Hindi, when Aamir Khan got his six-pack to do the remake. In response to allegations that the film was a copy of *Memento*, Aamir Khan said in his blog that apparently the scriptwriter (Murugadoss, who's also the director) heard about the story of *Memento* and wrote his own version of the script. When he saw the film later, he found that his version was very different from the original so he went ahead and made *Ghajini*. Aamir calls this a genuine instance of being inspired by something, and nothing beyond that. I guess we will have to take his word on that.

Plot: A man is imprisoned in an anonymous room for fifteen years and abruptly released. He puts together clues from those years to find out who was behind his fate.

Based on a manga comic, Korean film *Oldboy* took on a unique theme and fashioned a gruesome tale of violence, passion, forbidden emotions and heartbreaking loss. Critics across the world lauded director Chan-wook Park's achievement but none flattered him as much as Sanjay Gupta. Since imitation is the sincerest form of flattery, Mr Gupta ripped off the film almost frame by frame, costume by costume. *Zinda* was even set in Bangkok like the original, and Sanjay Dutt's character was fed Chinese dumplings—exactly as in *Oldboy*. One Indian hunting for another is far easier in Bangkok (and that was the exact opposite of the film's premise) but that didn't stop the director, who was also the scriptwriter (nudge nudge, wink wink).

Plot: Two people from warring families fall in love.

William Shakespeare wrote the source code. Scions of the rival families of Verona—Romeo Montague and Juliet Capulet—fell in love and their story became the benchmark of doomed romance. *West Side Story* transported this story to the gangs of New York in an exuberant musical. The Jets and Sharks fought in the streets as the siblings of the two gang leaders fell in love. Mansoor Khan was obviously fascinated with this story because he made not one but two films around it. The first one starred his debutant cousin, and its freshness—despite a tragic end—gave romance a new life in Bollywood. *Qayamat Se Qayamat Tak* was *Romeo and Juliet* revisited and an all-time classic. The second starred another superstar and was extremely similar to *West Side Story* in terms of the love interests, gang codes and structure. *Josh* did not do too well—despite a stellar cast—but still manages to evoke a smile or two for its style and chutzpah. And for SRK singing his first song.

The durability of the plot is obviously fantastic because one of the biggest hits of 2013—*Goliyon Ki Rasleela: Ram Leela*—had the eponymous lovers fall in love despite ear-splitting, finger-chopping opposition from their families.

Reboot: 8 Decades of Reincarnation

While on the topic of formulae in Bollywood, reincarnation probably beats even the most popular formula—family lost and reunited—in terms of sheer longevity. While the familiar device of having a song to reunite a family is slowly falling out of favour with the multiplex crowd, star-crossed lovers from different lives still pop up every now and then. In fact, there has been an iconic[1] reincarnation story in every decade since the 1940s.

1940s

Abandoned palace. Old portrait showing a likeness to the hero. Ancient caretaker who has seen it all. Haunting tune wafting in from the beyond. Unnatural death (at the hands of a tyrant). One of the first films on reincarnation, *Mahal* set the rules that film-makers followed quite religiously for many decades. Kamal Amrohi put a touch of Allahabadi noir to the film in which Ashok Kumar was the new occupant of a mansion and had an uncanny similarity to one of the previous occupants. A beautiful woman (Madhubala)—seemingly from his earlier birth—sang an unforgettable tune ('*Aayega aanewala*') to call him to the same lake where two lovers had met a tragic end. The tune was well and truly unforgettable as it made a superstar out of the young girl called Lata Mangeshkar who sang it.

1950s

The story of *Madhumati* was written by Ritwik Ghatak. It is ironic that this supremely talented director who made starkly real films wrote a story that was clearly in the realm of fantasy and the supernatural. Stuck in an old mansion due to a landslide, Dilip Kumar listened to the story of his previous birth when he had fallen in love with a tribal girl, Madhumati (Vyjayanthimala). Unfortunately, his horny boss (Pran) lusted after Madhumati and the girl disappeared. Dilip

---

[1] Terms and conditions apply. Definition of iconic may vary from person to person. Please read offer document carefully.

Kumar then discovered a lookalike of Madhumati and devised a plan to bring the lookalike face to face with Pran to extract a confession. If you have seen **Om Shanti Om,** you know what happens next and if you haven't, you should see both as soon as possible.[2] Back in his current birth, Dilip Kumar reached the station (where he was going before he got stuck) to receive his wife who was coming. When the wife got off the train, we realized it was Lady Gaga. (Aww, come on . . . you know who it was!)

1960s

In **Neel Kamal,** Raaj Kumar was Chitrasen of Chitrapur[3]—a sculptor in a king's court who fell in love with Princess Neel Kamal and was sealed behind a wall (evidently a punishment devised by a feminist seeking revenge for Anarkali). Many centuries later, Waheeda Rehman v2.0 started to sleepwalk towards his final resting place whenever she heard his plaintive cries. One of her somnambulism sorties led her to walk on a railway track and she was saved by a knight in a shining suit (Manoj Kumar). They got married but the marriage promptly ran into problems since his mother wasn't about to accept a bahu who vanished in the middle of the night. The communion finally happened when the heroine finally reached the resting place of Chitrasen, saw statues in her likeness and had a transgenerational conversation to finally rid herself of her 'affliction'.

1970s

Rajesh Khanna took shelter in a bungalow during a rainstorm . . . oh hell, is that how all these stories start? Well, at least in **Mehbooba**—that's how it did. Rajesh Khanna saw a portrait of a beautiful woman and realized he loved this woman (Hema Malini) in his previous birth (no shit, Sherlock!) when he was the royal singer and she was a courtesan (wow—what originality!). Soon, he had bumped into the same woman (reborn) in his present birth and managed to lure back her memory as well. Just when you didn't think it would all end easily, it didn't. Two suitors (Asha Sachdev and Prem Chopra) from their present incarnation popped up and they were not ready to take this para-psychological bull—would the duo please return to their present birth and get real? Of course, it all ended happily for most (if not all) as the star-crossed lovers united in their present birth.

1980s

Subhash Ghai garnished this tried-and-tested formula so well with memorable characters,

---

[2] If you are hell-bent on learning the trick, see the chapter 'Not-so-Scary Movies: 10 Ghosts in Non-horror Movies' on page 105.

[3] Why are you laughing? You haven't heard of Juhi from Juhu and Bindra from Bandra?

mind-blowing music and a breathtaking pace that *Karz* became *the* reincarnation movie of Bollywood. Ravi Verma came back as Monty Oberoi, a haunting tune and an enigmatic woman uniting the two births. Unlike the other where one lover 'called' the reincarnated lover, this tune did the 'calling' here. (That made it the world's best 'caller tune'.) To cut a long story short (or not to flog a dead horse), Monty remembered the plight of his metaphysical ancestor and took the fight to the extremely well-preserved Rani Saheba and then to her backer, the silent Sir Juda, while falling in love with Tina 'next-birth-Mrs-Ambani', saving his mother and sister from the previous birth and furthering his pop-singing career. Whew!

1990s

Most reincarnation stories have a romantic motive. One pair of the romantic jodi 'calls' the other. In *Karan Arjun*, the motive was revenge. The 'caller' was the mother (Raakhee) from the previous birth—who hung around for nearly three decades. Shah Rukh and Salman went around in dhotis buying bangles for their mother and spreading dimpled joy, till the swordsmen of Amrish Puri (helpfully named Durjan Singh) slashed them to death. Maa Kali—unable to take Raakhee's exhortations—engineered the duo's rebirth as denim-clad city slickers. Very soon, SRK followed his love interest (Kajol) to his past-life village and memories of his past birth followed suit. Salman followed SRK's memories but his memories didn't come till the two were attacked—with swords—by Durjan's aforementioned cohorts and Salman's memory too made a timely comeback. The dynamic duo then put the villains in a transgenerational blender and pressed the Max Power button. Well, not literally, but you get the picture—right?

2000s

No other film in this list contests the 'iconic' word as strongly as *Love Story 2050*. The debut vehicle of Harman Baweja (son of producer Harry Baweja) was as close to unmitigated and extravagant disaster as we will ever get to, since the *Titanic* hit an iceberg. Nevertheless, it deserves an entry because it was a reincarnation story with a twist. Instead of past lovers meeting again in the present day, it had present-day lovers meeting again in the future. In the future, a perfectly sweet and sexy Priyanka Chopra turned into badass pop star Zeisha (rhymes with geisha, but for no apparent reason) with spiky red hair, furry costumes (where's PETA when you need them?) and irritating walky-talky toys. If that doesn't make you turn off the future forever, you deserve to live till 2050!

2010s

Strictly speaking, *Makkhi* is not a Bollywood movie, but when a reincarnation drama as inventive and crazy as that appears in Hindi (however bad the dubbing might be), you have to appropriate it. The dubbed version of S.S. Rajamouli's Telegu hit *Eega*, it was the story of a love-struck, jugaadu youth who got killed by an unscrupulous businessman and was reborn as a fly. *Karz* met *The Fly* met *Honey I Shrunk the Kids* as our spunky hero took revenge against his billionaire adversary by enlisting the help of his human girlfriend who was—quite conveniently—a miniature artist. Gunpowder, micro-goggles, matchsticks, needles, bulb filaments and black magic combined in a roller coaster of stunts that took reincarnation to a different—well—scale.

REBIRTH OF HOLLYWOOD

A selection of five Hollywood films that are based on our favourite theme:
- *The Reincarnation of Peter Proud*: Often called the film *Karz* was inspired by, it was a thanda film about a college professor remembering his previous birth where his wife had drowned him in a lake. *Na ek haseena thi, na mere umar ke naujawan they . . .*
- *On a Clear Day, You Can See Forever:* Barbra Streisand played a woman who regressed into her past lives when hypnotized and the doctor (who performed the hypnosis) fell in love with one of them.
- *Little Buddha*: Bernardo Bertolucci's epic drama about a group of monks landing up in Seattle to meet a boy who they think is the reincarnation of a great Buddhist lama, incorporating the story of Buddha (played by Keanu Reeves).
- *Kundun*: Martin Scorsese also made a film on the hunt for the new Dalai Lama, who is always believed to be the reincarnation of the previous Dalai Lama. (The title refers to the name by which the first Dalai Lama was called.)
- *Birth*: Nicole Kidman met a ten-year-old boy who seemed to be the reincarnation of her deceased fiancé because he knew intimate details of their life together—causing her to re-examine the relationship with her present fiancé.

The Great Indian Movie: 8 Movies Inspired by Epics

To paraphrase a proverb—what isn't there in the Mahabharata isn't there in Bharat either.

The Mahabharata and the Ramayana comprise a large part of the stories we listen to, the advice we heed and the dilemmas we face as individuals. Many people of India—business families as well as political dynasties—are natural set-ups for tales of brotherly angst and violent power struggles. Needless to say, these dens of intrigue are fodder for movies as well. So, if epics are found in family feuds and family feuds are found in movies, it naturally follows that the epics will be found in movies. Bollywood has drawn extensively on these two canons to devise interesting stories as well as life lessons for the masses.

Shyam Benegal's **Kalyug** had a stellar star cast from theatre and parallel cinema backgrounds, playing the Pandava and Kaurava brothers. The film did not go literal at any stage and did interesting, modern takes on the plot points of the Mahabharata. There was the secret help of technology from a foreign collaboration, which winched up enactments of the Brahmastra mantras. Instead of Draupadi's disrobement, there was an income-tax raid, with officers sifting through lingerie drawers as helpless husbands looked on. There were family gurus who came in when the couples remained childless for long periods. And there was a driver's son called Karan Singh, who was the differentiator between the feuding sides. In the only literal scene that happened near the end, Karan Singh chose to travel through a deserted road—despite threats to his life—and got a flat tyre. He got down from the car to change it, and . . . we all know what happens to tragic heroes when their chariot wheels get stuck, don't we?

Prakash Jha's **Raajneeti** saw one of the biggest assemblies of stars in recent times, and a story around the Greatest Indian Epic required no less of a cast. Played out in the divisive political landscape of present-day India, it had all the key elements of the Mahabharata. The reprisal in the modern context had to be easily identifiable and yet fresh, given the average Indian's familiarity with the epic. The film started with a young girl's infatuation with a leader named

Bhaskar and an illegitimate child was sired, who got adopted by a low-caste driver. The sons of two brothers fought for control of a political party and its attendant riches. A canny adviser named Brij Gopal guided the good guys, though, towards the end, we were never quite sure who the good guys were. In that respect, the film was closer to the present-day Indian political scene than to the Mahabharata.

One of the least known but most faithful retellings of the Ramayana was a film called *Haisiyat*. Lost in the mayhem of dancing among clay pots, nobody noticed this film in which Jeetendra played Ram, a union leader in the plant of businesswoman Seeta, played by Jaya Prada. Ram sided with the labourers in a battle with the 'management' (thus abandoning the wife in response to complaints from the masses) and even went on a hunger strike. Of course, the misunderstandings were amicably settled but the bad guy (Shakti Kapoor, who else?) kidnapped Seeta and held her hostage in a mansion that had—hold your breath and your laughter—a minefield all around it. Our valiant hero crossed this metaphorical sea by tiptoeing between the mines, and razed the metaphorical Lanka to the ground.

Raavan's premise was very interesting—the exploration of Ravan's love for Sita and the retelling of the epic from the villain's point of view. Add to that a legendary film-maker like Mani Ratnam and an A-list Bollywood cast supplemented by the best of Tamil cinema, you are supposed to have one hell of a film—right? Wrong. *Raavan* managed to break every expectation and not one box-office record. The eternal story of good triumphing over evil was given a modern and ambiguous twist. Mani Ratnam turned the war to rescue one's wife and honour into one in which the 'god' committed atrocities on innocent villagers to catch Robin Hood Raavan. The ambivalence of the director in taking sides would have made for a great retelling if not for some childish dialogues and scenes. Abhishek Bachchan played Beera Munda—a character supposedly based on the life of Naxalite Kobad Ghandy—who was the villain. But his mannerisms—instead of being fearsome—only ended up being a hindrance to understanding his complex character. A screeching, shrieking Seeta (Aishwarya Rai) and overly stoic Ram (Tamil superstar Vikram) did nothing to push the epic quotient.

We tend to lose ourselves between the songs and sacks of sugar of *Hum Saath-Saath Hain*. We completely overlook that it's a near-perfect rendition of the family compulsions of the Ramayana. The ageing patriarch (Alok Nath) was coerced by his second wife (Reema Lagoo) to sideline her virtuous stepson (Mohnish Behl) and promote her son (Salman Khan) instead. When the oldest son accepted this decision, the youngest son (Saif Ali Khan) joined him in the back of beyond while the middle one—now the heir apparent—refused to accept the inheritance. Seen through this prism, it is now easy to fit in every character into the Ramayana cast. True to the Barjatya tradition, there was no villain and Lanka was not part of the plot. Instead, there were elaborate feasts, gushing praise for all, traditional values and songs for all the characters.

Gol Maal is arguably the funniest Hindi film ever. The extremely durable comic duo of Amol Palekar and Utpal Dutt made the film unforgettable with their zany capers. But there is also a very strong Ramayana connection to this film. We, of course, had the two (?) sons of Dashrathprasad Sharma—Ramprasad and Lakshmanprasad (aka Lucky). Apart from that, we also had Urmila, who was wooed by both the brothers but fell in love with the clean-shaven Lucky. This was ordained since the times of the original epic for Lakshman's wife was indeed Urmila.

Raavan Leela was a re-enactment of the Ramayana in an operatic style—directed by a new-age theatre director who was also the lead actor. Stylized acting, over-the-top costumes, special effects and operatic music formed a new template for the age-old plot and the epic was afoot in a posh south Mumbai theatre. Ayushmann Khurrana played the actor-director in Rohan Sippy's *Nautanki Saala* and he was saddled with a suicidal Kunaal Roy Kapur who was co-opted to play Ram in the production. What started off as a love triangle in the epic ended up being a love triangle (or was it a quadrilateral?) in the movie as well.

Any discussion on the influence of the epics on Bollywood has to, has to, *has to* talk about the climax of *Jaane Bhi Do Yaaro*.

No amount of logic or analysis can succeed in understanding this iconic scene. Draupadi leant on Duryodhana. Duryodhana—in turn—decided to 'drop the idea' of disrobing her. But the Pandavas tried to convince the Kauravas to go ahead with it. One bespectacled Duhshasana was chased by another in underwear. Bheem emerged in sunglasses and announced his 'shareholding' of Draupadi in a Punjabi accent. Drupad called Bheem '*durachari, atyachari, bhrashtachari*' and ended that diatribe with a '*bol sorry*'. Eventually, Jalaluddin Mohammed Akbar entered and tried to pass judgement on the fate of Draupadi. All this while, Yudhishthir was trying to pacify his burly younger brother with the most cult dialogue of them all—'*Shaant gadadhari Bheem, shaant!*'

The inventiveness of the scene and its manic energy is something that never comes across in description. Even after being seen a million times (that's about the cumulative views of the scene on YouTube), it still manages to make you double up with laughter. And when you do manage to stop laughing and get up from the floor, you share Dhritarashtra's plaintive query that is repeated throughout the scene, '*Yeh kya ho raha hai?*' Yes, what *was* going on? And more importantly, what was the writer smoking when he wrote this scene?

Jaane Bhi Do Yaaro: *An epic scene on the epic*

An Offer You Can't Refuse: 6 Remakes of *The Godfather* or Parts Thereof

Ever since Francis Ford Coppola brought that Italian mob boss called Vito Corleone to the screen, it forever changed gangster movies in particular and movies in general. The plot, the characterization, the acting style, the mood—all of these became benchmarks for generations of film-makers, whether working on gangster films or not. The impact of *The Godfather* has spread far and wide, India not being an exception. In any case, Indian film-makers are quite liberal with their sources of inspiration and this one was just too good to miss. The rise of the small-time crook to the highest rungs of gangland. The benevolent anti-hero handing out jungle justice. The heir apparent with a fatal flaw. The prodigal younger son. His love for a modern girl and marriage to a traditional one. All these themes have appeared in many films.

First off the block was **Dharmatma**.

Three years after the original, Feroz Khan directed the first Bollywood remake and played the Michael Corleone role himself. Grand locales in Afghanistan came to replace Sicily, and Hema Malini sizzled as a gypsy dancer. The traitor in the family, the refusal to get into narcotics, the level-headed consigliere (played by the dependable Iftekhar), the beating up of rapists (by the voluminous Dara Singh)—were all there. Feroz Khan reduced the number of Corleone brothers to one—himself—and made it all into a tussle between the father's (played by Prem Nath) illegal ways of doing good and his own straighter intentions. He replaced the broody characterizations with dazzling dances, the sombre background score with a *dhinchak* one, and had games of buzkashi in the Afghan plains instead of shoot-outs in seedy New York bars. In the original, Michael Corleone came into the limelight only towards the end. But when that role is played by the uber-stylish Feroz Khan, it would have been a crying shame to waste him like that—no?

After Part I's remake, it would be interesting to look at a remake of *The Godfather Part II*. An immigrant in a big city excels in many ways, crime probably being the most interesting of those. Like the Sicilian Vito Corleone, Velu came from the southern part of India to Bombay and rose to become the messiah of the masses—*Dayavan*, the benevolent one.

Feroz Khan's *Godfather* fetish was completely satiated when he remade Kamal Haasan's *Nayakan* in Hindi, with Vinod Khanna in the title role. The desi Robin Hood, who becomes the champion of his people (immigrants in an alien land) on his way to the top of the underworld, is a theme no one tires of.

In *Aatank Hi Aatank*, Aamir Khan was the son who returned to take charge of his father's underworld empire after his elder brother (Rajinikanth in one of his last Hindi roles) was killed. Aamir took a leaf out of the Italian mob boss's sartorial style with gelled-back hair, a moustache and waistcoats. Occasionally, he wore suits and wielded AK-47s to kill his father's enemies. In between, he romanced Juhi Chawla and Pooja Bedi (in yawn-and-miss and blink-and-miss parts respectively). Before he decided to cut down on his assignments and concentrate on working in one film at a time, Aamir Khan did some unbelievably ruinous movies, of which this is one.

Virasat was the story of Anil Kapoor returning to his native village for a holiday with his leggy, near-firangi girlfriend (Pooja Batra) and getting caught in inter-clan rivalry. The transformation of Anil Kapoor from a US-returned rake to a responsible chieftain was quite remarkable.[1] The film was about his growing emotional attachment to the village post his father's death and as that happened, his mannerisms started to resemble his father's. If *The Godfather* is the story of an initial outsider who eventually sacrifices many of his ideas to discharge responsibilities expected of his family, *Virasat* was exactly that. Complementing Anil Kapoor was Tabu who delivered a fantastic performance as the village belle who got married to the new thakur. Overall, a beautiful film from the time when Priyadarshan actually put some thought into his films.

Dynastic politics—the subject of *Raajneeti*—is best exemplified by India's greatest epic. But in a story built around the Mahabharata, Prakash Jha incorporated distinct shades of *The Godfather*. Arjun Rampal as the volatile elder brother who had no respect for anything except his younger brother was manic. On the other hand, Ranbir Kapoor put in a brilliant performance as the outsider who got reluctantly sucked into the cesspool of politics in an attempt to protect family honour. The hospital scene—a father lying badly wounded and a

---

[1] *Virasat* was based on yet another Kamal Haasan film, *Thevar Magan*, leading one to wonder whether the south Indian thespian is also a *Godfather* devotee.

boorish police inspector thrashing the son when he raised doubts about the security—was a direct replica. Even the severed horse-head scene returned in a modified avatar as a stubborn adversary was scared into submission.

The Godfather is the symbol of extra-constitutional power—a parallel justice system which offers remedies where governments fail to. We have many such power centres in India of varying degrees of influence. Irrespective of their power, the title accorded to these satraps is the Hindi word for government—*Sarkar*.

Ram Gopal Varma declared in the film's opening frame that this was his tribute to Francis Ford Coppola. Closer home, he previewed the film with Shiv Sena supremo Bal Thackeray and sought his 'blessings' as the lead character was said to be based on the life of the Maratha chieftain. And he created a godfather like no other. Amitabh Bachchan's silences and stares spoke volumes as he dispensed justice through his durbar. He kept chief ministers on a tight leash and controlled trade—both legal and illegal—in the city. His power was challenged by a troika of gangsters, politicians and godmen—supported by his treacherous older son. His power was multiplied by the emergence of his younger son who gave up his US business plans to take on the Mumbai underworld. And as the second generation took over the reins of power, the man became weaker but the sarkar became stronger. As they said in the film, '*Subhash Nagre ek aadmi ka naam hai aur Sarkar ek soch. Aadmi ko maarne se pehle uski soch ko maarna zaroori hai.*' *The Godfather* is, after all, not a person but an idea, an image, an inspiration.

Hats Off: 7 Tributes by Film-makers

Bollywood is always reviled for imitating, and quietly lifting without telling. However, there have been several instances of film-makers being genuinely impressed by people whom they consider idols and paying an affectionate tribute to them. These tributes are always subtle and always original. And they are usually very clever—weaving a simple but telling detail into the narrative. It is a lot of fun to discover them, for it is very heart-warming to see open acknowledgement of an inspiration.

Main Hoon Na

Farah Khan is a self-confessed Bollywood addict, with a softer corner of her heart reserved for humour and the Hindi film 'formula'. Her directorial debut was a tribute to both these things as she made a film on the much-loved, much-hated formula of long-lost brothers. And in a special tribute to one of her favourite films, she named the lead characters after the two brothers in Hrishikesh Mukherjee's *Gol Maal*—Ramprasad and Lakshmanprasad Sharma. Even the nickname was not spared. The anglicized Lakshman preferred to be called Lucky in both films. In addition to *Gol Maal*, her tribute to Yash Chopra came in the form of a heroine called Chandni Chopra (Sushmita Sen) who only wore shimmering chiffons.

Om Shanti Om

See above for Farah Khan's love of 'formula'. In her second film, she took up yet another formula—reincarnation. Projecting Bollywood stardom as 'a dream so big that one lifetime is not enough' to fulfil it, she had her hero coming back for more and built the entire film around the most famous reincarnation film—*Karz*. The title was obviously from the biggest hit song of the film. Her film opened with a scene in which *Karz* was being shot, and in the shooting, two characters got into a fight over a jacket which Rishi Kapoor had thrown into

296

the crowd. One of them was Om Prakash Makhija, played by Shah Rukh Khan. The other was a nameless woman, played by Farah Khan.

Kabhi Khushi Kabhie Gham

KJo's respect for the Yash Raj banner is well known. Aditya Chopra is one of his best friends. Yash Chopra was a much respected 'uncle'. And Johar's film-making style—especially his locales and sets—is unabashedly YRF-ish, sumptuous and larger than life. His tribute to his guru came through the title of his second film—*Kabhi Khushi Kabhie Gham*—which used a slightly unusual spelling in the second 'Kabhie'. This was taken from Yash Chopra's classic love story—*Kabhi Kabhie*.

Johnny Gaddaar

Sriram Raghavan is a fan of crime thrillers as a genre—both in books and films. In his second directorial venture, he doffed a cap to established masters of the genre in varying styles. The title was an allusion to *Johny Mera Naam*, Vijay Anand's taut crime caper. In fact, the film was 'dedicated to Thriller Maestros Vijay Anand and James Hadley Chase'. When the hero Neil Nitin Mukesh walked into a hotel, the film was playing in the hotel reception and in a small bit of misunderstanding, his name in the hotel register became 'Johnny G'.[1] The thriller's writer entered the film as Neil Nitin Mukesh read a book (*The Whiff of Money*) by him. The other homage paid in the film was to *Parwana*, from which an important plot element was taken, but the director—instead of hiding the fact—actually showed the character getting the idea when he saw the film on TV.

Jaane Bhi Do Yaaro

The beginning of India's craziest comedy film (also the most trenchant satire) was rooted in a classic film by Italian director Michelangelo Antonioni—*Blow Up*. A photographer unknowingly shoots the scene of a murder and only realizes it when he is back in his studio and enlarges—'blows up'—the negatives. This was exactly what the owners of Beauty Photo Studio did when they were at the scene of Commissioner DeMello's murder. Now the average Indian viewer wouldn't have heard of Antonioni—but the director had to acknowledge his debt. So, the murder and the photo shoot happened at Antonioni Park—prominently displayed on a signboard at the location.

---

[1] Director Sriram Raghavan said that he decided to include this scene because Nitin Mukesh had told him once that the title made no sense.

Namastey London

The plot of the Akshay Kumar–Katrina Kaif starrer was a modern-day reprise of Manoj Kumar's *Purab Aur Pachhim*, where a son of the soil married an anglicized girl in an effort to bring her to appreciate the wonders of Incredible India. While the modern-day version did not have the bombastic patriotism of the first, it had to play the India Shining tune often enough. And when Akshay Kumar had to lecture a group of posh Englishmen on Indian culture, he gave them an earful and concluded by telling his interpreter (Katrina) that the rest of the lesson could be gleaned from a DVD of *Purab Aur Pachhim*.

Jhankaar Beats

Sujoy Ghosh's debut film was an affectionate tribute to 'Boss'—R.D. Burman—to the extent that the two heroes' names started with 'R' (Rishi) and 'D' (Deep). When a third member—Neel—joined their band, he made it R'N'D. In fact, they inducted this new member with a song about their hero ('*Boss kaun tha, maloom hai kya?*'). And in the climax, they played music by 'Boss' ('*Humein tumse pyar kitna*') for 'Jhankaar Beats', a music contest they wanted to win very badly. Apart from RD, the film paid homage to the Greatest Film Ever Made. The two heroes asked each other **Sholay** trivia ('*Gabbar ke baap ka naam kya tha?*'). They wondered about the characters ('How did Thakur eat?'). And they mouthed **Sholay** dialogue ('*Bahut yaarana lagta hai*') to describe regular situations.

If we start including all the films that have paid tributes to **Sholay**, we will be here till eternity. There should be a separate chapter on that.

Jhankaar Beats: *A film-length tribute to the 'Boss'*

The Greatest Film Ever Made: 10 Tributes to *Sholay*

There has never been a more defining film on the Indian screen. [The] Indian film industry can be divided into Sholay *BC and* Sholay *AD.*

—Shekhar Kapur

The impact of **Sholay** on the Indian audience has been amazing. The impact of **Sholay** on the Indian film-maker has been even more amazing. An unbelievably large number of tributes, spoofs and hat tips to **Sholay** are strewn all over the history of Bollywood.[1] Interestingly, none of the movies seems to have lived up to the original while the short tributes are all quite heart-warming and interesting.

The grandest—and, tragically, the most disastrous—tribute to *Sholay* is **Ram Gopal Varma Ki Aag**. Ironically, the whole rigmarole started when the Sippys invited Ram Gopal Varma to make a sequel of *Sholay*, taking the germ of a story they had. RGV recounted on his blog that G.P. Sippy wanted him to make a sequel with Gabbar's son (conceived with Helen's character after the '*Mehbooba mehbooba*' song) kidnapping Veeru and Basanti and their sons coming to save them. Apparently, there was also a request to incorporate a role for Jackie Chan (!) in the sequel. Having heard this story, we can debate which one would have been the worse movie—this one if it got made, or the one that actually got made.

What does not need any debate is the absolute unanimity with which critics and the audience panned **Ram Gopal Varma Ki Aag**. They even agreed on the jokes! Rajeev Masand

---

[1] Apart from movies, TV channels have created an avalanche. Channel V did a series of spoofs involving duplicates of the actors, ringing phones in the vicinity of Thakur and Simpoo Singh. Stand-up comedians have made careers out of *Sholay* sketches. Even south Indian cinema has not been spared. A recent Telugu blockbuster was Pavan Kalyan's *Gabbar Singh*, where the hero's nickname was taken from *Sholay* because he was extremely fond of the villain as a child.

(CNN-IBN) called it '*RGV ka daag*'. Raja Sen (rediff.com) called it '*Ram Gopal Varma ki Aargh!*' Khalid Mohamed (*Hindustan Times*) called it '*Ram Gopal Varma ka Ugh*' before giving it 'this Lifetime's Worst Ever Movie Award'. More serious reviews were by Anupama Chopra (NDTV) who called it 'an exercise in futility' and Nikhat Kazmi (*Times of India*) who felt the director 'ends up axing the soul out of the cult film'. But—even the original had opened to poor reviews, hadn't it?

Jagdeep, after acquiring cult status by acting in *Sholay*, decided to make a film on the character he played. He managed to rope in both Amitabh Bachchan and Dharmendra to make guest appearances in *Soorma Bhopali*. Even Rekha—who was willing to do *any* film with Amitabh then—came in for a bit role. As it turned out, these three megastars were incidental to the plot as it was all about Jagdeep in a double role (Soorma and his twin brother Dilawar Khan Dilwala) in a strange fracas over their inheritance. A priceless diamond necklace, two characters called Kaalia and Sambha and some inane jokes and songs later, everything ended in a messy heap (as it was probably expected to). The only reason to remember the film is probably because even a minor character from *Sholay* managed to create a full-length feature film around himself.

Ramgarh Ke Sholay put together an assembly line of duplicates as lookalikes of Amitabh Bachchan, Dev Anand, Anil Kapoor and Govinda joined the real Gabbar Singh (Amjad Khan) in an absolute farce of a plot. Two of Gabbar's henchmen—called Lamba and Goriya—were the least of the problems as Gabbar's foreign-returned daughter joined the fray, as did an impostor who pretended to be the super-*daku*. Add to that a character called Kajal Bhopali and we had a cracker of a Hindi thesaurus instead of a film. Nevertheless, if you are willing to play along with how the village mistook the duplicates for the real stars and got them to fight the hugely bloated Gabbar, you may just enjoy it more than Ram Gopal Varma's film.

Kanti Shah is the king of the so-bad-it's-good genre and his cult classic *Gunda* is considered to be, well, a classic. Kanti Shah paid his tribute to *Sholay* through the not-so-imaginatively named *Duplicate Sholay*. And the movie lived up to the name by having more duplicates than the original had stars! The duplicates of Amitabh, Dharmendra, Mithun, Sunny Deol, Sanjay Dutt and Anil Kapoor locked horns with Gabbar's three henchmen—Mangal, Jangal and Dangal Singh. If you are missing Basanti in all this, let me assure you that her sister (Lajwanti) was there seeking revenge, because Gabbar had raped her and turned her into Daku Chutiya. (Yes, yes, I know. Don't ask. Let us just quietly move on.)

Apart from the full movies based on *Sholay* (or parts thereof), there have been many small—but significant—tributes in major movies.
    Karan Johar's debut *Kuch Kuch Hota Hai* had all the ingredients that make a Hindi movie

successful (except maybe a scraggly-bearded dacoit—but we didn't miss that too much). Johnny Lever's character—Almeida—was an Anglophile who ran a summer camp for kids. To explain the huge portrait of Queen Victoria in his office and the Union Jack in the camp premises, he revealed that '*Mera baap angrezon ke zamane ke tailor tha*'—a non sequitur that cannot be explained by anything except a desire to include a *Sholay* reference!

Bollywood clichés are Farah Khan's favourite and she thulped a whole lot of them in **Om Shanti Om**. Her first film, **Main Hoon Na**, had a major reference to The Film. In a pivotal chase scene, Shah Rukh Khan commandeered a cycle rickshaw and set off behind the villains. The rickshaw that performed this stellar duty was called Dhanno—Bollywood's most famous animal.

Many of the *Sholay* references are gender-neutral. Dharmendra's iconic tank-top monologue has been reprised by—of all people—Katrina Kaif in **Mere Brother Ki Dulhan**. In the movie, she played an oft-drunk free spirit ping-ponging between two brothers (Imran Khan and Ali Zafar). In one scene, she jumped on Imran Khan's jeep's bonnet and started off by screaming 'Soocide' while Imran tried in vain to shush her. Her accent was a little—ahem—inauthentic and the acting was a little—cough cough—wooden, but hey! When an iconic movie scene is re-enacted by the top heroine from three decades later, it deserves a mention—right?

The Greatest Bit Part in Indian Cinema—Sambha—has also been immortalized in Zoya Akhtar's **Luck By Chance**. Daughter of one of the writers of *Sholay*, Zoya got Macmohan to give away the certificates at the graduation function of an acting school in her film. Given that almost the entire industry was rounded up for cameos in the film, Zoya could have got anybody to do that bit—but then, a star-struck student couldn't have requested 'Mac' to say 'those three words'. Macmohan stood up and said '*Pooray pachaas hazaar*' as applause broke out in the room.[2]

Ram Gopal Varma's **Daud** didn't do too well at the box office but he managed to pack in a series of crazy characters and jokes—including the Good Samaritan Chacko (played by Neeraj Vora). In love with Urmila, he popped up every now and then trying to help the lead couple, who were always on the run. In a pre-climax fight—when Urmila and Sanjay Dutt got trapped by the villain's gang—Chacko landed up with a gun and repeated what another man with a gun on a cliff said in *Sholay*: '*Agar kisi ne hilne ki koshish ki toh bhoon ke rakh doonga*'. We burst into applause at the reference and in laughter at the comical differences between the two men who said it.

---

[2] There is a belief that Sambha uttered just three words in **Sholay**. Actually, he had one more line of dialogue to his credit. When Sachin was leaving the village, he was one of the four dacoits playing cards and he challenged one of his colleagues with '*Chal be Janga, chidi ki rani hai!*'

In jokeathon ***Andaz Apna Apna***, Rajkumar Santoshi kept serious cinema aside for a bit as Amar and Prem assaulted our funny bones with their antics. In a scene to decide who would get a shot at wooing millionaire heiress Raveena first, Javed Khan suggested a tactic from *Sholay*. '*Tum ne* Sholay *picture dekhi hai?*' he asked the two heroes. Prem jumped up. '*Haan, dus baar!*' he said enthusiastically. Amar was sarcastic—'*Iske baap ne likkhi hai.*' This would have passed unnoticed if Prem hadn't been played on screen by Salman Khan, whose father is one Salim Khan.

HONOURABLE MENTIONS

The only other film that has a comparable number of tributes is probably ***Deewaar***, with the highest concentration of memorable dialogues. Avoiding the iconic '*Mere paas maa hai*', we can go with another line that has featured in at least two humorous tributes.

In Sujoy Ghosh's ***Aladin***, the Genie offered to get Aladin's (Riteish Deshmukh) dreamgirl to fall in love with him. When the boy felt it would not be right, the exasperated Genie borrowed the line he said himself three decades back and intoned, '*Uff, tumhare usool, tumhare adarsh . . .*'

A few years later, two ***Desi Boyz*** were arguing about the ethical and economic dilemmas involved in being strippers. One raised the minor issue of cheating his girlfriend and his friend repeated the same line—'*Uff, tumhare usool . . .*'

SHOLAY REVIEWS

When it released, Sholay's reviews ran the entire gamut from gushing to scathing.

- *Hindustan Times*: 'Sholay is the costliest attempt to make dramatic capital out of this rather inglorious premise [that the defence against violence must always be more violence].'
- *Filmfare*: 'A major trouble is the unsuccessful transplantation it attempts—grafting a Western on to the Indian milieu . . . the film remains imitation Western, neither here nor there . . . could have gone easy on the depiction of violence . . .' [Rating: **]
- *Trade Guide*: 'The excessive length and the slack pace of the film is [sic] is the main drawback . . .'
- *Blitz*: 'The best film made in India.'

Coming Soon: 7 Clichés That Are About to Happen

It would be interesting to do a count of the number of times '*Main tumhare bachche ki maa banne wali hoon*' has been said on screen. Because this is probably the most clichéd use of a cliché. This phrase has been demonstrated as a cliché in real life more times than it has been actually said on screen. The true-blue cliché is actually '*Sab kuchh theek ho jayega*'[1] as there was a time till the end-'90s when I had not seen a single movie where this line was not spoken.

One good thing about clichés is that you start missing them when they stop happening. For example, one of the evergreen—but unsung—clichés is the hemming and hawing around a lip-to-lip kiss. It goes something like this: The leading pair is in—what the newspapers call—a compromising position, more often than not after the hero has dispatched a few goons. They murmur sweet nothings as the hero tries to get the heroine to do things that would allow the directors to show flowers touching. Eventually, the hero points to a body part (say, shoulder) where he is hurt. The heroine demurely kisses him there. A bulb lights up somewhere. He points to another body part (say, wrist). The heroine kisses him there as well. Now (usually with a mischievous smile), he points to his lips and indicates pain. Bingo![2]

Since books and websites have already been devoted to listing the biggest clichés of Bollywood, we could turn the cliché around and do a bit of crystal-gazing to figure out which are the dialogues/scenes that are going to become clichés in a few years from now.

Exposing a Gay Relationship

Konkona Sen Sharma is to this what Nirupa Roy was to motherhood. She has already done it twice (*Page 3*, *Life in a . . . Metro*) and is looking good for more. With more and more films being made on realistic gay relationships, it is only natural that closet homosexuality will have

---

[1] This dialogue received a new-age non-literal translation in *3 Idiots*—'*Aal izz well!*'

[2] Note for directors: for best results, use at least two non-sexual body parts before the lips.

to be depicted pretty regularly. What will make it tiresome is the way it will be shown. In both the films mentioned above, the scene unfolds in exactly the same manner in which the hetero partner (cuckold?) arrives at the apartment of the closet-gay for a celebration (Konkona was even holding exactly the same things—a bottle of wine and some flowers) and sees her lover in bed with another man. How long before a man walks in on a lesbian couple? I can bet the expression would not be the aghast one the woman had.

Signs of Suicide

More and more dysfunctional relationships on screen can mean only one thing: more and more suicide attempts. And as in the socials of the 1960s, where a close-up of the *mangalsutra* signified a married woman, we will keep getting close-ups of sutured wrists to show the harried woman . . . The cliché will probably not be the fact that people try to end their lives but that these characters are always women. I guess men just choose a more leisurely way of ending their lives (see **Devdas**) but a slashed wrist is much more amenable to cinematic drama than an X-ray of a bloated liver. Kangana Ranaut has tried both options (**Woh Lamhe**, **Gangster**) and she appears perennially poised on the edge of a parapet about to jump off.

Thirty-plus

Rajesh Khanna took almost fifteen years to get out of college. He started as a college student in one of his first hits—**Do Raaste** (1969)—and stayed on right till **Souten** (1983). The scenario of a sixteen-year-old heroine falling in love with a nineteen-year-old hero continued till Rishi Kapoor just could *not* fit into the benches of the colleges that were hired for a film shoot. This cliché's last rites were performed when the only crib against **Rang De Basanti** was about the forty-year-old Aamir Khan hovering around the gates of Delhi University. Although we never raised an eyebrow when Mithun jumped around college campuses in his mid-forties.

Now, of course, the age combos have just multiplied with old-man–old-woman (**Baghban**, **Pyaar Mein Twist**), older-woman–young-man (**Leela**, **Oops**), young-woman–old-man (**Nishabd**, **Cheeni Kum**) all elbowing out the teenybopper romance. The cliché around this is the forced ridiculing of the elderly member(s) of the family, which brings about a (temporary) realization of the difference age makes. '*Aapko toh abhi bhagwaan ka naam lena chahiye*' is usually the unsolicited advice for the couple to go to a temple instead of a disco. And it produces an equally stereotypical angry reaction, followed by doubts on the future of the relationship . . . and remorse. Of course, sometimes the line is as funny as '*Uncle ko Durex chahiye*' (in **Cheeni Kum**) but the situation is a cliché (about an old man pursuing a physical relationship) and threatens to become bigger.

Old Man + Young Woman = Durex. Amitabh–Tabu's
sugar-free romance

For Adultery Only

Finally, Hindi cinema has managed to have people survive premarital or extramarital sex. Till as late as the '90s, the lead players of Hindi cinema either died or got widowed or got tuberculosis or took to prostitution or had to smell an anaconda's fart even if their shadows touched during a song on a rainy night. And of course, they got pregnant. Not any more! Mallika Sherawat (in *Murder*) neither died nor got pregnant for having an extramarital affair (but she had to repeatedly kiss Emraan Hashmi, which is probably a fate worse than death). Jokes apart, the cliché is the way in which a married woman and man approach a liaison. The married woman is guilty and has pangs of conscience. She pulls away from the man and even exits the room. And then she comes back for a reason (or an excuse?) and is pulled into the whole 'mess'. She usually cries after the first time. The married man—on the other hand—is an unmitigated bastard who has no such qualms. In an ironic way, this is the Sati-Savitri cliché and it will take some time to be junked.

The Jehadi Recruitment

Post 9/11, there is a new villain in cinema, and Bollywood adopts it as well—the Muslim terrorist. Sometimes he is a cardboard composition of villainy and bombast, sometimes he is the chocolate boy dealt with unjustly. Either way, he is about to do an awful lot of collateral damage. And he has recruited/is recruiting a group of jehadis for a suicide mission. The cliché here is the recruiting process. You give the prospective jehadi a gun and ask him to shoot an innocent target. He pauses, he sweats, he trembles and eventually takes a shot. Entrance test passed! What happened to the body of the innocent? You see, the shot was a blank one. The intention was to test whether the motivation of the recruit was strong enough to make him take a shot at an innocent unknown.

The Flunked Hero

What Rajesh Khanna and Shashi Kapoor were to *Maa-main-pass-ho-gaya-le-beta-mooh-meetha-kar-le-yeh-kya-tum-ro-rahi-ho-yeh-to-khushi-ke-aansoo-hain-beta-kaash-tere-pitaji-aaj-zinda-hote*, Ranbir Kapoor is to the failed metrosexual. In two successive films—**Wake Up Sid** and **Rocket Singh: Salesman of the Year**—he either flunked or passed with grace marks, winning millions of hearts outside the campuses of IIT, AIIMS and SRCC. He is the *number-kum-hain-dimaag-nahin* guy who's forced into academics (weren't we all?), while his true calling lies elsewhere. And of course, like all underdogs, he manages to score very satisfying victories for everybody including his distributors and producers.

Intel Inside, Bollywood Outside

The first Hindi film to mention a computer was **Trishul**[3]. When Shashi Kapoor returned from abroad, he called Raakhee (his father's super-efficient secretary) a 'computer' (*'ek aisi machine jo har sawaal ka theek jawaab deti hai'*)! Clearly, this 'computer is always right' notion was before GIGO (Garbage In, Garbage Out) was coined.

We have come a long way from that to the point that it is probably becoming mandatory for Bollywood stars to have an active virtual life. First, it was supposed to be in their real lives. But now—thanks to Himesh Reshammiya—even film characters must dodge in and out of Facebook and Twitter. In **Radio**, RJ Vivaan Shah chatted on Facebook while his less-enlightened colleagues were still figuring it out (*'Yaar, yeh Phesbuk hota kya hai?'*). His relationship status was 'complicated'. His listeners complained about boyfriends on porn sites. All he didn't have was a Twitter handle. I am inclined to believe this casual weaving of online stuff into filmi conversation is about to become a trend. And right on cue, full-fledged movies on themes of online relationship (**Mujhse Fraaandship Karoge**) and hacking (**Mickey Virus**) are coming up with increasing frequency.

We have to wait only a little bit before the original cliché is turned on its head and the hero is compelled to ask—'*Kya main iss bachche ka baap hoon?*' Do you remember the first film that happened in?[4]

---

[3] Computer Science made its first Hindi film appearance in **Hamrahi** (1974) where Randhir Kapoor and Tanuja were both toppers in the subject from Lucknow and Allahabad universities respectively.

[4] KK's character in **Life in a ... Metro** was a gent suspicious of his own paternity, who asks his wife (Shilpa Shetty) this. The exacts words he used were '*Bachcha toh mera hai na?*'

13

Location, Location, Location

Bambai se gayi Poona, Poona se gayi Dilli, Dilli se gayi Patna . . .
—*Juhi Chawla (in the voice of Alka Yagnik) in* **Hum Hain Rahi Pyar Ke**

Kashmir. Goa. Europe. Dharavi. Bollywood moves in strange ways, across many lands. Some locations come out of the writers' imagination. Some of them become part of our imagination.

This section looks at the many places—real and fictional—movies have been set in.

Office, Office: 10 Corporate Settings

You use bullets for your presentation. You fire a print. You shoot a mail. Real life is boring.
—Publicity line for Wave Cinemas

When you have ravines, havelis, kothas, police stations and bars to conduct your business in, why would any Bollywood hero (or heroine) with half a brain walk into an office? But they do. Offices are also venues for romance and redemption, success and seduction, tension and, well, termination.

In *Chhoti Si Baat*, the middle-class corporate romance between Arun Pradeep (Amol Palekar) and Prabha Narayan (Vidya Sinha) was given centre stage as the film's opening credits appeared on a typewriter, with a telephone operator's voice in the background.

Arun's love story was given a context by the romantic history of his colleagues in Jackson Tolaram Pvt. Ltd. He was a supervisor (grade 2) in the sixty-year-old firm located in the large heritage offices of south Bombay. While it was only vaguely hinted that it was a trading firm, the romantic traditions of General Manager Noshirji Bomanji Batliwala, Chief Accountant Heerji Nanji Parekh, Executive Officer N.K. Vasudevan Nair and even the peon (Pandurang Ganpat Dhonde) were explained in detail.

For jobs at Urmila Traders, freshers, traditionalists and mustachioed men got preference. But if you cracked the minefield of an interview with the proprietor Bhawani Shankar, you could expect a princely salary of Rs 850 (while the norm was Rs 550 for a fresher). In *Gol Maal*, Urmila Traders (named after the proprietor's daughter) seemed to be engaged in trading and the organization consisted of new joinee Ramprasad, nose-hair-pulling Bade Babu or Head Clerk (played by Yunus Parvez), some faceless employees and the hapless receptionist who had no choice but to observe the nose-hair-pulling. Ramprasad established his competence by pointing out that the short-term loans Urmila Traders took from Ahuja & Ahuja Company were given after deducting the interest amount, thus raising the effective interest rate. He threw numbers at his boss and finally negotiated with the lender to get the amount refunded.[1]

In *Trishul*, R.K. Gupta and Sons was the largest construction firm in Delhi. The chairman—R.K. Gupta—presided over the operations in an office almost the size of a football ground, assisted by a super-efficient secretary (Raakhee) and Bhandari (Yunus Parvez). Soon, his son returned from abroad and joined the company. His minions were nameless, voiceless people who reminded him about steel and cement quotas and did the physical bidding at auctions when he clicked his fingers. The adrenaline of the construction industry kicked in when a young upstart came and took away a contract by filing a tender value that was just one rupee lower. Vijay Kumar of Shanti Constructions was not beyond corruption when it came to taking away business from R.K. Gupta. And like a true entrepreneur who had to do in one year what his rivals had done in twenty-five, his offices had difficult operating hours: '*Khulta hai saadhe dus baje. Lekin office bandh hone ka koi waqt nahin hai.*'

In *Om Jai Jagdish*, youngest brother Jagdish (Abhishek Bachchan) was a hacker, who was expelled from college for leaking exam papers. He moved to Bangalore to get closer to his ambition of working with Softcell Technology. His dream was to make the ultimate anti-hacking software that 'will be bigger than Windows'. When Softcell's website was hacked, he walked into their office and asked for a hundred seconds to track the hackers. When he did the seemingly impossible task, the CEO—a bit of a geek himself—took him on board to develop the commercial version of the software. And in true Bollywood style, Jagdish named his software Om.

Parts of the film were shot in the sprawling Infosys campus in Bangalore, including their futuristic auditorium where Jagdish gave demonstrations of his software. The CEO of Softcell was a splitting image of Narayana Murthy (including the name—Narayan Pillai) and suddenly the Indian software boom came alive on screen.

When a generation of Indians started working as per Pacific Standard Time and answered queries of people sitting thousands of miles away, it was big enough to inspire a Chetan Bhagat novel—*One Night @ the Call Centre*, which was made into *Hello*. The spacious offices of Connexions Call Center did not look like the usual cubicle farm of call centres. While Shyam became Sam and a terribly annoying boss (Dalip Tahil) kept repeating 'God bless America'

---

[1] For the commercially inclined, Urmila Traders took a short-term loan of Rs 25,000 at 1.5 per cent monthly interest. But they received Rs 22,750 after deducting the interest amount, thus increasing their effective interest rate to 2.29 per cent. While the principle is valid, the effective interest rate may not have been as high as Ramprasad calculated.

at every stage, realism wasn't high on the agenda. The boss from Hell managed to bring in 'realism' by stealing his team's website design and passing it off as his own. All got resolved in true filmi style when the desi call centre employees put together a completely improbable plan that 'increased the call volume by 400 per cent'. And yes, they executed it too. All with the help of their indigenous brains and a little more help from God.[2]

Madhur Bhandarkar's succinctly named and sprawlingly filmed *Corporate* was about the rivalry between two Indian conglomerates—Sehgal Group and Marwah Group. It kicked off with the Sehgals backing the right party for the Central government and getting a finance minister of their choice, which—in turn—led to a lucrative JV with a US food giant, Friscon. The subsequent wheeling-dealing to take over a government bottling plant and launch a brand of soft drinks formed the bulk of the movie. Real events like the discovery of pesticides in the soft drink were part of the script. The landscape was littered with CII conferences, shady ministers, business journalists engaged in award-broking, babas dispensing business advice and corporate surveillance behind philandering CEOs. All this was punctuated with exultations of 'deal closed' and pseudo-motivational statements about how people do their best under pressure. Oh—all that and office sex with bosses advising employees to say at home, '*Subah presentation hai. Saari raat kaam chalega.*'

Karthik Narayan worked in a construction company called ACL, where his designation was likely to be Chief Doormat. His boss ran roughshod over him. His colleagues took all the credit for his work. He had 5,287 unsent mails addressed to the office bombshell, Shonali. Mukherjee@ACLconstructions.com. Everything was just terrible till he got a call from himself and it was a strange case of *Karthik Calling Karthik*. The Chief Doormat became a cool dude and the movie became a wet dream for those desirous of negotiating better terms at work. He got a raise, a cabin, a designation and his boss's balls on a platter.

And for those desirous of an office romance, the movie was also a primer on persistent wooing: Yahoo chat, customized nameplates (Coffee Tonight?) and requests stuck in reverse on photocopiers (which would appear on the wooee's copies).
STATUTORY WARNING: Stunts were performed by handsome individuals on people working on a pre-decided script. Don't try any of these at office.

When Harpreet Singh Bedi joined AYS Corporation, he had dreams in his eyes and a spring in his step. He didn't envisage the corruption and one false step got him sidelined in a jiffy. That's when he set out to change the way the computer sales and service industry works

---

[2] To fully understand the importance of God in Bollywood, turn to page 101.

and became ***Rocket Singh: Salesman of the Year.*** The almost exclusively male world of chasing sales targets— sometimes unscrupulously—with all its review meetings and drunken office parties came out real and raw. The travails of an idealistic young chap in this world were distressingly real as were the characters—the devious owner, the abrasive boss, the slimy colleague, the horny maintenance guy, the shady purchase manager, the eye-candy receptionist and even the jaded peon seemed to have walked out of the

Bad bosses. Cold calling. Paper planes. Sluggish sales. Just a regular day at office for Rocket Singh

nearest office. Even the arbitrary macho statements—'*Risk to Spiderman ko bhi lena padhta hai. Main toh sirf ek salesman hoon*'—you seemed to have already heard somewhere.

All businesses have to start from zero. When Delhi University students Shruti Kakkar (Anushka Sharma) and Bittoo Sharma (Ranveer Singh) started their wedding planning company Shaadi Mubarak in a single shop-cum-mezzanine in the DDA Market of Paschim Vihar, they made Janakpuri cool. ***Band Baaja Baaraat*** traced the exponential growth of this start-up which promised personalized weddings with the distinctive jovial flavour of the West Delhi locality. Their business plan (start small before targeting the posh Sainik Farm weddings), role definitions (Shruti handles creative, Bittoo handles logistics), partners (florist, caterer and DJ), and investments (in trucks, in business development) were all wonderfully real.

At the centre of ***Hate Story*** was Cementec Infra, run by the young son (Gulshan Devaiah) of a tycoon, with offices in the glass-and-steel environs of DLF Cybercity in Gurgaon. The movie opened with a sting operation exposing the bribery of a judge by the company. The company got off the hook by convincing the employee to admit that he acted on his own accord—which was straight out of real life. On the other hand, offering a corporate role to a journalist at three times her current salary was not. But then, you went to see Paoli's bare back and not bare reality—didn't you? As a story of revenge unfolded, corporate espionage, corruption around government lobbying around FDI in key sectors, leaked files, fictional assets and honey traps took over. And a seductress (also a murder suspect) bagged a board membership in a major bank by sleeping with a minister[3] leading to a climactic revelation at the company's AGM. The sex overdrive in the movie must have led many head honchos to believe that they are clearly on the wrong end of the average.

Organization structure. Cross-functional teams. Targets. Motivation. Rewards and recognition. Calculated risks. Terminations. Succession battles. Ownership splits. Ram Gopal Varma equated the Mumbai underworld with the corporate world in his now-legendary *Company* about mafia kingpin Malik (Ajay Devgn) and his lieutenant Chandu (Viveik Oberoi).

OFFICE SPACE OF THE MEGA-VILLAINS

- *Parvarish*: Amjad Khan's den had silhouettes of dancing girls on red walls. If that doesn't blow your mind, there was the circular pit in the centre which had retractable spikes on its walls (just in case you needed to puncture a business rival). When the international baddie Supremo arrived on the scene, he went one better. He operated out of a submarine . . . Beat that, happiest companies to work for!
- *Shaan*: An island far off the coastline of India. CEO's office with sharks swimming in the background. Revolving chairs with a hungry crocodile under them. Lots of automatic sliding doors. All secured by armed guards and hunting dogs.
- *Mr India*: Again an island, from where India is just within the reach of Mogambo's nuclear missiles. With a fully functional nuclear command centre. A laboratory with sizzling chemicals and a robot. And a central hall with a vat of red human-melting acid under the floors. And of course, a prison to lock pesky trespassers in.
- *Andaz Apna Apna*: When Teja decided to kidnap his twin brother to control the brother's wealth, he came prepared. He had a prison cell to keep the brother in. He had a pleasure cell to entertain himself. He also had a ramshackle 'conference room' to ideate with his cronies. For the climax, we shifted to Gogo's den. Gogo, being Mogambo's nephew, seemed to have got a crash course in den-making from his uncle.

---

[3] Or rather, by not letting the minister sleep!

Oh, Calcutta: 12 Movies Set in Kolkata

For years, Hindi movies remained steadfastly within Bombay and ventured out only to find a *Kashmir Ki Kali* in Shimla. All other cities—except probably Delhi—have remained largely out of bounds. Calcutta aka Kolkata has had the misfortune of featuring in international productions, which hardly ventured beyond its slums. *City of Joy*—ostensibly a tribute to the spirit of Calcutta—and, more recently, *The Avengers* had white messiahs doing their bit for the downtrodden in Calcutta slums. Bollywood, though, has had some interesting forays in this city. Some of them featured Calcutta in a starring role and some had the city in a guest appearance.

For a lilting start, we have to bring in two major hit songs set on a boat that ambled on the river. In **Amar Prem**, Anand babu took his beloved Pushpa on a boat cruise and sang '*Chingari koi bhadke*' as the shimmering skyline of Calcutta and the Howrah Bridge formed a majestic backdrop. (Incidentally, the song was shot in Mumbai's Natraj Studios, in stagnant water with a horrible smell. The expressions on the lead players' faces didn't give that away, though.) And in **Khamoshi**, Rajesh Khanna took Waheeda Rehman on the same boat ride, passed right under the Howrah Bridge and serenaded the lady with '*Woh shaam kuch ajeeb thi*'.

> *Bonus Trivia*: Apart from having Rajesh Khanna's presence and Kishore Kumar's voice, both the films were remakes of extremely popular Bengali films (*Nishi Padma* and *Deep Jeley Jai* respectively).

Howrah Bridge has got to be the most iconic emblem to signify that you have arrived in the city. The anonymous highways outside Calcutta airport just don't have the human drama and atmosphere of the bridge across the river Hooghly. And Shakti Samanta immortalized **Howrah**

313

Bridge with his 1958 film. A murder mystery (about Ashok Kumar coming to Calcutta from Rangoon to search for his brother's murderers and bumping into a Chinese villain named Chang), it is best known for two famous songs featuring two divas of Bollywood. Helen sang '*Mera naam Chin Chin Choo*' with verve and Madhubala sang '*Aaiye meherbaan*'—both unforgettable songs. There was another song in the film—sung on screen by Om Prakash driving a tonga—that could be to Calcutta what '*Ae dil hai mushkil*' is to Bombay. A full-fledged ode to Calcutta by Bollywood, it summed up the city thus:

> *Chowringhee ki chowk mein dekho matwale bangali*
> *Rasgulle si meethi baatein inki shaan niraali*
> *Kahin Banerjee kahin Mukherjee kahin Ghosh kahin Dutta hain*
> *Suno ji yeh Kalkatta hai . . .*

Probably the first Indian film to win substantial international recognition was Bimal Roy's **Do Bigha Zamin**. The germ of the idea—of a poor farmer's land getting usurped by a zamindar—came from a Rabindranath Tagore poem, although the film added a strong message of socialism into the basic story. Here, Calcutta was depicted as the 'Holy Grail' for Bihari landless labourers and the heartless city took away your spirit in exchange for money. Calcutta was full of unhelpful citizens, unscrupulous middlemen, pickpockets and thieves as a poor farmer tried to earn money by pulling a rickshaw on its mean streets.

In **Raincoat**, Manu came to Calcutta from Bhagalpur in search of money and ended up meeting his ex-girlfriend, Neeru. Ajay Devgn and Aishwarya Rai turned in sincere performances as the estranged couple in what was essentially an indoor film though the geographical markers of the film were made very clear by the clothes, atmosphere and lingo. Directed by noted Bengali film-maker Rituparno Ghosh, **Raincoat** was based on a famous O'Henry short story and diehard Calcuttans say that the story could only have taken place in their city.

When the Naxal movement was ignited in north Bengal, Calcutta was soon engulfed in its flames. Noted Bengali author Mahashweta Devi wrote the story on which **Hazaar Chaurasi Ki Maa** was based and it was a searing portrayal of a generation that was lost to the movement. Jaya Bachchan played the title role under Govind Nihalani's direction as we tried to come to grips with the fact that there were 1,083 people dead before the one we were seeing in the film. The film worked on very sparse settings and no overt imagery of Calcutta was used but given the historical context of the Naxal movement, the location couldn't have been anywhere else.

True to its message about the increasing filth of the Ganga as it makes its way from Uttarakhand to the Bay of Bengal, *Ram Teri Ganga Maili* chose Calcutta to be the place of the final desecration of the heroine (as a symbol for the river).[1] Mandakini started off in virginal white in the foothills of the Himalayas as she cavorted under waterfalls. When Rajiv Kapoor impregnated her and decamped, she started off to look for him. During her trip along the river Ganga's path, she was subjected to increasing levels of dirt-efaction. Molested in Hrishikesh, raped in Varanasi, she reached Calcutta only to be turned into a prostitute and recruited to dance at her lover's wedding. Calcutta was not really a major presence but more of a symbol of the last stop in the Ganga's path to the seas.

Parineeta opened in 1962 Calcutta. As the familiar sights of the Howrah Bridge and trams flitted past, the baritone of Amitabh Bachchan took us through the faith of the city ('*Kalibari ke vishwas ka*'), the food of the city ('*rasgulle ke mithaas ka*'), the sport of the city ('*football ke uchhaal ka*'), the passion of the city ('*adde ki behes ka*'), the politics of the city ('*siyasat ke tahes nahes ka*') and—of course—love of the city, which brought us to Lolita and Shekhar. Director Pradeep Sarkar painted this period love story really well; he had grown up in the city and presented its contrasts very effectively. From the Durga Puja *arati*s to Moulin Rouge cabarets, there was never a false step in glamorizing Calcutta. The city was never like that outside of romanticized nostalgia but then, that was exactly what everyone wanted to see!

From the first scene which had Ajay Devgn falling off the Howrah Bridge to the last, where four denim-clad young Turks walked into the West Bengal Assembly as a symbol of change, *Yuva* did not leave Calcutta for a second. Presidency College—the city's premier educational institution—was the hotbed of student politics and the harbinger of revolution. Narrow bylanes and crowded tenements were scenes of unlikely romance. Calcutta nightclubs and nearby sea beaches became the setting for rocking songs. And the characters—the idealistic student leader, the Bihari tough, the apolitical drifter, the slimy politician—were all picked off the streets of Calcutta. The only unreal thing was Om Puri's Bengali accent.

The location of Abhishek Bachchan and Rani Mukherji's dingy flat in *Yuva* offered a majestic view of the Howrah Bridge. When the deaf and mute Barfi escaped to Calcutta with the autistic Jhilmil Chatterjee, they also took up residence in the same area—with an identical view of Calcutta's most enduring landmark. The young couple lounged on the lawns of the Victoria Memorial and Ranbir got into the mood wearing a batik kurta for the most part. Anurag Basu's

---

[1] The Ram of the title is actually Ramakrishna Paramahamsa—who was told that his Ganga had turned dirty while cleaning the sins of all. Interestingly in this context, the name of Rajiv Kapoor in the film was Naren—which was Swami Vivekananda's birth name.

lyrical *Barfi!* moved between Calcutta and Darjeeling, with both cities of the 1970s coming to life. A wall painting with the young 'Comrade Jyoti Basu' asking all and sundry to join the revolution was a classic touch.

Bonus Bridge View: When the gang of fake CBI officers in *Special 26* checked into a hotel in Calcutta, Howrah Bridge again formed a majestic backdrop to their plans of raiding an unscrupulous trader's office. They pulled off their heist in the serpentine lanes of Burra Bazar, one of the few areas in the city which has not changed a bit in twenty-five years and can be the perfect setting for a period film.

In recent times, Calcutta has hosted some very high-profile films—even though some of them have entailed only guest appearances. *Bullett Raja*, for example, zipped in and out of the city (with the mandatory shots of the yellow Ambassador cabs) as the main action happened in the badlands of UP.

The film that was entirely set in the dirt and grime of Calcutta was Ali Abbas Zafar's *Gunday*, in which two Bangladeshi refugees grew up to become coal bandits in the city. Their rippling muscles, oiled bodies and bombastic dialogues seemed quite out of place in a city known for its intellectual airs. Their object of affection was a Bengali bar dancer (Priyanka Chopra as Nandita) and their nemesis was a Bengali police officer (Irrfan Khan as Satyajit Sarkar) though all of them remained steadfastly Hindi-speaking in the capital of West Bengal.

Bong-Rage Alert: When Bengalis from across the border heard a fleeting mention of Bangladesh's formation in a somewhat dismissive manner, they decided to register their protest by giving *Gunday* the lowest possible rating on popular movies site IMDb. com. Their mass campaign has led to a 1.5/10 rating and *Gunday* is the Worst Rated Movie on the site!

'*Madam, e Kalkatta mein Bidda Vidya shob ek, same hai . . .*'

The moment Vidya Venkatesan Bagchi stepped into Kalighat Thana and registered a complaint about her missing husband, Calcutta took over the atmosphere of *Kahaani*. The film revisited some existing landmarks (like Mocambo restaurant). It gave cult status to lesser known places like Mona Lisa Guest House.[2] It took the most important festival of the Bengali calendar and imbued it with mystery. It let killers loose in the Kolkata Metro. It took some delightful talents from the Bengali film industry and made the supporting cast look very real. While everyone has been gushing about Vidya Balan, it would be unfair not to acknowledge the bewitching presence that deserved all the Best Supporting Actress awards in town. This is one film that couldn't have worked without the hypnotic setting of Calcutta. You sexy thing.

Enjoying the Howrah Breeze. Saif Ali Khan and Vidya. Balan in Parineeta

---

[2] In the lane behind Mona Lisa Guest House in Calcutta, there is a hair salon called Bob.

Uttam Pradesh: 10 UP Towns in Movies

Kanpur ke joote de rahe hain sazaa / Pehenne se zyada khaane mein aayega mazaa
—*Kabira (Pran) in* **Karz**, *while beating up villains with shoes*

Uttar Pradesh[1] has appeared often in Hindi movies in location, characters and—as Pran showed us in the line above—memorable dialogues. It started with India's biggest superstar, who was from the banks of the Ganga, and with many young film-makers coming from the state, the flavours of UP have only become stronger.

Banaras

It started with a song. Amitabh Bachchan is a *Ganga kinare wala chhora* in real life and he celebrated it with gay abandon in **Don**, making '*paan Banaras wala*' deliriously famous. The song, originally written for Dev Anand's *Banarasi Babu*, has been the anthem of UPites ever since.

In **Laaga Chunari Mein Daag**, Rani Mukherji's impoverished family was based in Banaras before she became a 'high-society call girl' in Mumbai. The ancient ghats and dilapidated havelis made an interesting backdrop[2] to the story as an entire song was affectionately devoted to the quirks and idiosyncrasies of being a Banarasi ('*Hum toh aise hain bhaiyya*').

A priest's son fell in love with a Muslim professor's daughter and the all-consuming passionate affair that ensued could have only started in Banaras. **Raanjhanaa** captured the essence of the small-town romance perfectly as a brilliant Dhanush stalked the object of his affection (Sonam Kapoor) on the ghats, the galis, the *chabutaras*, the cycle rickshaws, the railway platforms with a confidence that was simultaneously silly and touching. When warned of a

---

[1] For the purpose of this chapter, Uttarakhand is also considered to be a part of Uttar Pradesh.
[2] Director Pradeep Sarkar had made a magical music video for Euphoria's '*Dhoom*' that was set in Banaras.

potential heartbreak due to the appearance of a better qualified rival, Dhanush's answer was illustrative of the city's attitude: '*Yeh Banaras hai. Launda yahan bhi haar gaya toh jeetega kahan?*'

Lucknow

A girl from Faizabad was brought to Lucknow, trained in the fine arts of music and seduction and transformed into **Umrao Jaan**. The Lucknawi *tehzeeb* and the *nawabi andaz* were intrinsic to the tale of the legendary courtesan, portrayed by two of Bollywood's biggest stars. Rekha's legendary enigma was superbly exploited by Muzaffar Ali—buoyed by Khayyam's music—and Lucknow seemed as bewitching as its beautiful resident. J.P. Dutta's version with Aishwarya Rai fell flat, though.[3]

The modern-day City of Nawabs came out wonderfully well in **Main, Meri Patni Aur Woh**, where Rajpal Yadav was the head librarian of Lucknow University. As the under-confident husband of the beautiful Rituparna Sengupta, he was perennially under threat from the handsome yet honourable people of Lucknow around him. The city formed an unobtrusive yet beautiful backdrop to the imaginary love triangle.

Most Honourable Mention: While he remains resolutely outside Bollywood, Satyajit Ray's **Shatranj Ke Khiladi** has to be mentioned in any context of Lucknow and its nawabs. Set during the rule of Wajid Ali Shah, two chess-playing nawabs went about their hobby obsessively in the film as a larger tale of political intrigue played out in their city.

Kanpur

Kanpur has an aura of rough and tumble about it. Though it is located only ninety kilometres from genteel Lucknow, the city is far from the mindspace nawabs inhabit.

Tanu Weds Manu opened in the Chamanganj locality of Kanpur, where a typical UP household was in a tizzy over a visiting boy coming to 'see' their girl. The Kanpur girl (Kangana Ranaut) was a woman of the world having studied in Delhi and snagged a boyfriend from Lucknow. And Delhiite Manu (R. Madhavan) also seemed to be from the UP appendage—Noida.

Bollywood's paean to Kanpur was sung by **Tashan**—in ballistic, bombastic style. Akshay Kumar played Bachchan Pandey, the Kanpur toughie who burst on to the screen as Raavan of the Ganga Kinare Ramlila Mandal. His style, his chutzpah, his brazen menace found an

---

[3] In an interesting twist, Shaukat Azmi played the brothel madam Khanum Jaan in the earlier version while her daughter Shabana played the role in the later one.

admirer in city slicker Jackie Mawana (Saif Ali Khan), who paid the ultimate tribute to Kanpur by saying, '*Ab zinda rehne ke liye mujhe kuch aur banna hoga, khatarnaak banna hoga, chaalaak banna hoga, Kanpuriya banna hoga.*'

The *khatarnaak, chaalaak* Kanpuriya came alive in ***Dabangg 2*** when Inspector Chulbul Pandey got transferred to the city and proceeded to wreak havoc in his trademark style. The murder and mayhem perpetrated by Bachcha bhaiyya (Prakash Raj) was countered with Pandeyan panache as politics, police and petty crime played out a sequence of events which were said to be picked out of the real Kanpur.

> *Bonus Town*: Chulbul Pandey's earlier escapades (***Dabangg***) were based in a fictional UP town—Lalganj—which was also suffused with red-towelled aggression. You could say Lalganj was the younger sibling of Kanpur.

Gorakhpur

Two absconding criminals—Naseeruddin Shah and Arshad Warsi—went all across UP before finding sanctuary in Gorakhpur. The don they had come for was already dead and his widow (Vidya Balan) became their unlikely partner for an operation. *Ishqiya* was a tale of love and lust garnished with the colourful language of eastern UP. Ch***yum sulphate was the compound that emerged from the heady chemistry of the three lead players who went about the cottage industry of Gorakhpur—kidnapping. As the city had grown bigger, it spawned many an industrialist. And for every industrialist, there was a plan to kidnap him for ransom. *Kattas*, stolen Maruti Omnis, corrupt policemen, shady politicians and even kinky sex were all part of the landscape—completely real and rugged.

> *Bonus Town*: The sequel ***Dedh Ishqiya*** moved into a dilapidated palace in the UP hamlet of Mahmudabad, where small-time crooks met *shayeri*-spouting begums and gun-toting nawabs. The flamboyant craziness of the characters contrasted wonderfully with the regular worn-out settings and we were never sure if the on-screen Mahmudabad was the same as the real-life one.

Dehradun

Whenever the students of the elite Rajput School and the *pajama-chhaap* Model locked horns on a race track and beyond, we got so caught up in their rivalry that we forgot where they were located. *Jo Jeeta Wohi Sikandar* opened with a commentary about *pahadiyon ke beech mein ek khubsoorat jannat*—Dehradun, a 'heaven on earth' which also had some of the best schools and colleges in the country. The Mall area of any hill station, the dangerous winding roads where cycle races happened and the inevitable tension between locals and outsiders were eminently identifiable zones and the film became a classic building on these.

Cheat Alert: The climactic cycle race was shot in Mumbai and a lot of shooting happened in the hilly climes of Kodaikanal instead of the real Dehradun.

Still-Going-Strong Alert: Dehradun's academic creds haven't dimmed in the last twenty years as St Teresa of *Student of the Year* was also located there.

Bareilly

Apart from the paan of Banaras, the *jhumka* of Bareilly gained nationwide (if not worldwide) fame because of another classic song performed—on and off screen—by legendary stars. In *Mera Saaya*, Sadhana popped up as a street performer in a crowded marketplace and complained she had dropped her ear ornament in a Bareilly market. Asha Bhonsle's spirited rendition of '*Jhumka gira re*' went on to immortalize the western UP town.

Agra

Two conmen tricked an American tourist into buying a venue for his wedding. A nice, marbled building called Taj Mahal. The crowning glory of *Bunty Aur Babli* came when they pulled off the iconic heist. Posing as a minister of tourism (bearing more than a passing resemblance to a lady chief minister of the state) and a broker, the two cons managed to lease out the Taj Mahal for five years (at a measly sum of $250 million and a Rs 50 lakh commission). The bazaars and band parties of Agra provided a raucous reception for the baaraat.

Apart from this, Agra has been the backdrop to many a Taj setting, from *Taj Mahal* (which didn't leave the sets) to *Delhi 6* (in which the NRI was taken on a mandatory Golden Triangle visit).

Fursatganj/Pankhinagar

While *Bunty Aur Babli* carried out their capers all over UP, they were not from any real town. And yet they were from every town. As residents of Fursatganj and Pankhinagar, they inhabited the world of railway colonies, river ghats, crowded bazaars, seedy hotels, upright parents and the lure of success that is part of the fabric of every town in UP.

Kanpur Alert: Kanpur made a special appearance when Gulzar adapted a line from Kanpur's most famous sweet shop, Thaggu Ke Laddoo. '*Aisa koi sagaa nahin, jisko humne thagaa nahin*' was world famous in Kanpur all along. With the title song of **Bunty Aur Babli**, it became world famous all over the world. Shaad Ali, the director, is a Kanpuriya himself.

Nishatganj

The badlands of western UP were ruled by Bhaiyyaji (Naseeruddin Shah), whose trusted lieutenant was **Omkara** (Ajay Devgn). While the town and region were not explicitly named, there were posters and banners behind dance performances that highlighted the location of the performers. The dialect of the land, the law of the land (or lack of it) and the nuances of the land were brought out accurately by the director. It was easy for Vishal Bhardwaj as he hails from Meerut himself.

Almore

The bloody rivalry of the Qureishi and Chauhan clans was played out in a typical small town called Almore. The details of the fictional small town were alarmingly real as shady political goons, petty hooligans and flamboyant local heroes held centre stage with countrymade revolvers and disarming smiles. The violent love story of **Ishaqzaade** received the sharp edge of reality as Habib Faisal got the details down bang on. Make that bang bang on. The language Parma and Zoya spoke, the places they inhabited, the clothes they wore and the honour code they followed were quintessentially UP. Including their passionate response to everything, be it guns or roses.

'Brandish guns so that people miss your crazy dress sense'—*Old UP saying, as seen in* Ishaqzaade

Yen Dollar Pound Lira:
10 Movies in Foreign Cities

Bollywood orgasms over foreign locales so much that Switzerland gave their version of the Bharat Ratna to Yash Chopra for services rendered towards disrupting Swiss lives with dancing Indian stars. Sometimes, foreign locales in Hindi movies have been nameless picture postcards to dance in. Sometimes, they have a more active role in the story, often indicated by the presence of their name in the movie's title.

In **Johar Mehmood in Hong Kong**, the two cons were recruited by a 'millionaire' to woo a beauty queen (Miss Bombay, though the sash only revealed 'Miss Bomb'), who was the daughter of a scientist with a *faarmoolaa* worth Rs 10 crore—for which they landed up in Hong Kong. There were songs sung in what looked like Kashmir. There were cons and counter-cons played by Johar and Mehmood on each other. There was a Chinese jail which was full of Indian prisoners and Chinese guards speaking in Hindi. And the climax involved doing the garba on Hong Kong's streets.

Joy Mukherjee went to Japan to find his elder brother's (now orphaned) son. He found **Love in Tokyo** instead. The love was Asha Parekh, who was being forced to marry a villainous rake (Pran, who else?) by her uncle. Joy's nephew had no intention of returning to India with his uncle. The boy and Asha Parekh formed UAUA (United Against Uncles Alliance) and Asha promptly put on a kimono pretending to be Japanese. So, she sang a song in Japanese. (It started with '*Sayonara, sayonara*' but some words sounded like *vaada nibhaoongi* and *kal phir aaoongi*—something must have got lost in translation). Joy responded (joyfully) by surrendering his heart to this Japanese doll ('*Le gayi dil gudiya Japan ki*') and dancing on the busy streets of Tokyo, colliding with many polite Japanese in the process. What else? After such delightful songs in Japanese locales, does anything else matter?

Trivia Alert: The opening credits of the movie (drawn as picture postcards in Japanese style) included the country ('and Japan') among its lead players.

A millionaire's daughter—tired of greedy suitors in India—landed up in Paris to find out about the legendary French lovers. No sooner had she landed in Paris (and put on a ghagra–choli to look 'poor'), than she had bumped into a batty Frenchman and his dashing Indian friend.

Shammi Kapoor wooed Sharmila Tagore on the Champs-Élysées and atop the Eiffel Tower, singing wonderful songs and claiming to be a Frenchman who knew Hindi. Sigh. Anyway, ***An Evening in Paris*** lived up to its name when a twin Sharmila emerged as a Cancan style dancer in a Parisian cabaret: The dazzling locales of Paris were used to brilliant effect and French extras moped in the background as Indian stars ruled the roost.

Visa Alert: The film moved from Paris to Switzerland for a quick song break, then to Beirut for another song break before pushing off to the USA for a climax at the Niagara Falls!

Close on the heels of Tokyo and Paris came London where Biswajeet and Mala Sinha spent a night. ***Night in London*** turned out to be one of the many inexplicable successes of Biswajeet, buoyed by the music of Laxmikant–Pyarelal. A *majboor ladki* ('*tumhara baap humare kabze mein*', etc. etc.) was forced to steal a necklace to save her father and met the hero while on the run from the bad guys. They abandoned the father, sold the necklace and had sex all night atop a red double-decker bus in London. Sigh, of course not. You think this is *Last Tango in London* or what? They did all sorts of honourable and clever things to solve the mess, including singing hit songs in and around major landmarks of London.

British Bonus Movie: Vipul Shah got Punjab *da puttar* Akshay Kumar to romance Jazz (aka Jasmeet played by Katrina Kaif, who finally got a valid excuse for her accent) in ***Namastey London***. The sights and nights of the British capital were well exploited as Akshay went about taming his anglicized shrew among the familiar landmarks.

Kabul Express did not spend too much time in Kabul but travelled all over the Afghanistan countryside with two Indian TV journalists, an American journalist, their Afghan guide and a Pakistani soldier who had become part of the Taliban. Based on director Kabir Khan's experiences as a documentary film-maker, the film had a unique take on the war-ravaged country from diverse viewpoints. The events in the film took place in the two days it took for the group to go from Kabul to the Afghan-Pakistan border where the Pakistani soldier wanted to reach using the other four as hostages.

Title Alert: The ramshackle Toyota jeep they went around the country in was affectionately called Kabul Express by its owner.

After chasing Osama in Kabul, director Kabir Khan made John Abraham the Indian-American jock in *New York*. After the initial song, dance and romance, the film shifted gears to the aftermath of 9/11 as John Abraham—being Muslim—became a victim of racial profiling in the USA and was subjected to inhuman torture and questioning. New York, a city that symbolized the Great American Dream for millions of immigrants, became a living nightmare for John Abraham as he sought revenge from his adopted country for persecuting him without reason. The Big Apple started off as a luscious backdrop for John and Katrina to frolic in but ended as a place where bombs were planted.

An Indian journalist (Zayed Khan) was offered a high-paying job at Al-Johara, a TV channel in Istanbul. He landed up in the Turkish capital to discover shady goings-on within the channel that seemed to have terrorist connections. In walked a 'freedom fighter' called Rizwan Khan and *Mission Istaanbul*[1] was afoot. Neither the names of the channel (Johara is an Arabic word and the Al prefix is not used in the Turkish language) nor the people (Abu Nazir, Rizwan Khan, Owais, etc.) were Turkish. The film had some aerial shots of the landmark locations of Istanbul (Blue Mosque, Sultanahmet) as well as whirling dervishes, while the chases happened in the labyrinthine lanes of the city. And of course, all the reviewers labelled the film a turkey!

An Indian kick-boxing team went to Pakistan for a tournament and unlocked all the conflicting

---

[1] Why the extra 'a' in Istaanbul? Arre yaar, I haven't even been able to explain why the movie was located in Istanbul. How would I know about the extra 'a'?

emotions typically associated with Indo-Pak rivalry. Newcomer Aanaahaad[2] played Virender Singh, a cricketer, who saw his brother getting killed in a kick-boxing bout with a Pakistani player, Noor Mohammed (Mukesh Rishi). When the death was declared an accident, Virender gave up cricket, trained to become a kick-boxer and joined the team to Pakistan. In the diplomatic backdrop of making friends with Pakistan, he wanted 'revenge' for his brother's death. The battlefield was not the Gaddafi Stadium, but it was still **Lahore.**

Love gives you wings. So you go around the world

Frothy, romantic comedies in which the lead pair meets in Chile, hates each other in Chinchpokli and falls in love in Cherrapunji[3] was super-popularized *When Harry Met Sally.* Ali Zafar and Aditi Rao Hydari did the same in **London Paris New York.** Two young people bumped into each other in London, roamed the streets of the beautiful city and went their separate ways despite feeling the beginnings of a relationship. They bumped into each other again in Paris—probably the most romantic city in the world—and as they roamed the streets, they felt their love grow stronger. When they met again in New York, the girl was about to get married. They—you guessed it—roamed the streets, found the courage to express their love to each other and lived happily ever after.

The final film is named after a city, in which it was *not* based.

An all-too-familiar Indian state capital—Bharat Nagar—was the setting but the political machinery of the state was hell-bent on turning it into **Shanghai.** Dibakar Banerjee's political thriller was about the inherent contradiction of not having clean water but giving subsidized land to investors by selling an illogical dream. The film had no images of China's largest city. The chief political players had no plan. The masses had no hopes either. Instead, it had a slogan that obliterated all logic, bringing a jingoistic fervour to the aspiration of finding an unseen Holy Grail—'*Kasam khoon ki khaii hai, shehr nahin Shanghai hai*'.

---

[2] Oh God—more names with extra 'a's!

[3] *Hat tip*: To Javed Akhtar, who used these places to explain a country's location in **Roop Ki Rani Choron Ka Raja.** See page 150 for a context.

Here and There: 7 Filmi Places

Bollywood film-makers seldom bother with geographical accuracy. Usually, they end up choosing locations for their scenic beauty and not for their connection to the screenplay. Occasionally, very occasionally, we have films that name fictional places as a part of the script, and even more rarely, they get a life of their own.

The first name on the list has to be one that doesn't exist, at least not on the map of India. In Shirish Kunder's *Joker*, Paglapur could not be found on the map of India. In a cartographical error, it was neither in MP nor UP and thus received no government support. All it had was a huge mental asylum whose inmates had taken over the village. To get out of the anonymity, the village's worthy son—Akshay Kumar, playing a NASA scientist—hatched a plot to put the spotlight on the village. He created fake crop circles to show an alien invasion, assisted by the madcap villagers and Sonakshi Sinha. Soon, the entire world's media had landed up to see the fake aliens. Or were they fake?

One of the infinitesimally few examples of punning in Hindi cinema, Dongri-La was the antithesis of the idyllic Shangri-La since it was ruled by the always-cruel, always-correct Dong ('*jo kabhi wrong nahin ho sakta*'), played with great relish by Amrish Puri in *Tahalka*. Dong had a Chinese get-up (complete with pigtail) while the opening voiceover intoned that the country was located on the snowy boundaries of India as the camera focused on a crudely drawn map showing Pakistan and China. Since much of the action in the film was on snow-clad peaks and mountain slopes, one can conclude with a shiver that Dongri-La was probably perched on the outer reaches of the Siachen glacier.

Dhanakpur was where it all started. Thakur Dhanraj Singh killed Ratan Singh to avenge an injustice to his sister. And then, a couple of decades later, his son Raj came back to this place and fell in love with his arch-enemy's daughter, Rashmi. This *Qayamat Se Qayamat Tak*

Dhanakpur was a place close to Delhi, possible to visit on a day trip by bike. That was how Raj went there. It also had a sessions court where Ajit Vachani played a paan-spitting lawyer. And if you were lucky, you could see Rashmi Singh—in a yellow dress—riding a horse. But then, the guy who saw her like that died in her arms at the stroke of sunset. Lucky did we say?

Rakesh, son of T.C. Trivediji, stayed in Fursatganj. Vimmi Saluja, whose parents wanted her to marry a head clerk, stayed in Pankhinagar. Their nicknames were **Bunty Aur Babli**.

Pankhinagar was in the Lucknow district (as a Miss India organizer of Kanpur said) and Vimmi got off at Lucknow from the Jhansi Mail.[1] So, Pankhinagar was probably somewhere around where real-life Sultanpur exists. Fursatganj remained steadfastly coordinate-less. From the pictures of the towns, the mindscapes of their residents and their trajectories after they left, it seemed that these could be Anytowns in Uttar Pradesh—where walls do not constrain dreams, where Mumbai is the Holy Grail and where Himesh Reshammiya is God.

Champaner was the village[2] where a ragtag band of eleven Indians defeated the British in a game of cricket to escape **Lagaan**. In 1893, a guy called Bhuvan went up to one Captain Andrew Russell and challenged him him to a game of '*firangi gilli-danda*' and, to borrow a Ravi Shastri cliché, set a cat among the pigeons. The drought and the landscape seemed to indicate a mid-western location for the village. There was an English cantonment posted nearby. The raja of the princely state had his palace very close to the English barracks. The forest outside the village did not have game, only tame animals. The crew shot near Bhuj and the language was a happy mix of central Indian dialects of Hindi.

Dhaulia. Imam Sahab. Ahmed. Basanti. Mausi. Radha. Ramlal. Even without the main players, the village of Ramgarh was well populated and had a life of its own. The ironsmith's shop. The village well, where the dead body of Ahmed arrived. The thakur's house on a hillock. The famous water tank. The mango orchard. The *talao*. The Shiv mandir. The Holi maidan. We have been subjected to these set-pieces so many times that if we were dropped off in the village, we could easily find our way around. And since the entire village was actually mapped and constructed, there is not a false step or geographical inconsistencies either. When the Imam's son Ahmed was offered a job in a beedi factory in Jabalpur, Basanti mentioned the two 'large cities' close by—Meerut and Moradabad. So, the badlands of central UP was where **Sholay**'s Ramgarh has to be located.[3]

---

[1] *IRCTC Fact Alert*: Incidentally, there is no Jhansi Mail which stops at Lucknow. Maybe it was Gwalior Mail.

[2] A real Champaner exists in Gujarat, about 50 km from Vadodara.

[3] Wikipedia lists ten real-life Ramgarhs in India and there could well be more.

While we are looking at fictional places, it would be interesting to look at two obscure places that have achieved a mythical state due to movies set in them.

Mandwa is a short boat ride away from Mumbai but it is also the place where baddies like Kancha Cheena and Dinkar Rao rule and which Vijay Dinanath Chavan covets. The tourist brochures tell us it has a nice, secluded beach. Bollywood tells us it has paths of fire—*Agneepath*.

Just a few kilometres from Dhanbad station is a locality that was earlier a suburb but is now considered to be part of the city itself. Zeishan Qadri, a boy who grew up in the suburb, went to Mumbai to try his luck in films. In the free time between auditions, he wrote a story about his hometown where the crimes 'would put *City of God* in the shade'. The story was about the lords who ran the *Gangs of Wasseypur*.[4]

THE GEOGRAPHY OF *SHOLAY*

Apart from the legendary Ramgarh, there were several other places mentioned in *Sholay*. Here is a selection:

- *District Jamalpur*: Where Thakur arrested Jai–Viru and had to take them to Damli (police station) before sunset
- *Daulatpur*: Where Viru remembered that Inspector Baldev Singh had arrested them earlier (for stealing from Laljibhai bania's shop)
- *Kheda village*: Where Viru and Jai landed before taking a tanga to Ramgarh
- *Belapur, Naopur, Fatehgarh*: Where Basanti's tanga offered its services, though Basanti quoted a rate only for Belapur (Rs 2) and Ramgarh (Rs 1.50)
- *Belapur*: Where Baldev Singh was once posted and arrested Gabbar (who had planned to loot Haripur village)
- *Haripur*: Where Gabbar's gang had gone to Jamnadas's wedding and had seen Basanti dance
- *Pipri village*: Where Heera and his gypsy caravan set up camp to sell Gabbar arms and entertain him. Presumably no connection to Pimpri near Pune.
- *Purani tekri*: The place outside Ramgarh where Gabbar wanted Jai–Viru to be handed over to him.

---

[4] Zeishan himself played a small but significant role in the film, as Definite (in *Gangs of Wasseypur Part 2*).

QUIZ: BRAND BATAO!

Before you take the Marketing in Bollywood section, here is a quick quiz on the 'branded lines' from dialogues from Hindi films. Identify the films they are from.

1. *'Bread ka badshah aur omelette ka raja – Bajaj. Hamara Bajaj . . .'*
2. *'Yeh Rooh Afza bahut bekaar hai.'*
3. *'Agarbatti Kachhua chhap / Aag pe baitha paani taap / Taap chadhe toh kambal taan / VIP underwear baniyan . . .'*
4. *'Aur kahin chot lagi?' 'Nahin. Dettol wali koi chot nahin.'*
5. *'Zara Dunhill nikaliye, poora carton . . . Ek carton Gold.'*
6. *'Arre, woh khidki kudne lagi thi na, pair mein moch aa gayi.' 'Thehro, main Iodex laga deti hoon.'*
7. [Ad heard on radio]: *'HMT ghadiyan hamesha waqt ka saath deti hain. Iss samay HMT ghadi ke mutabik aat bajkar pachees minute hue hai . . .'*
8. [Song]: *'Caron mein ek car chuni hai, car chuni hai Impala / Impala mein tujhe bithakar ghumega dilwala . . .'*

ANSWERS

1. The man who wanted to launch a billion omelettes was, obviously, Teja of *Andaz Apna Apna*.
2. Ranbir Kapoor expressed his disgust for India's favourite 'soft drink' in *Yeh Jawaani Hai Deewani* and the company (Hamdard Laboratories) was miffed enough to get the line removed when the film played on TV.
3. Gulzar directed this mayhem of a song in *Kitaab*, where Master Raju and his cohorts performed it with a glee that is only seen when teachers are absent for a period.
4. Juhi Chawla as Rashmi won hearts all over the country when she said this line in *Qayamat Se Qayamat Tak* though not the one she wanted to win.
5. The connoisseurs of Dunhill and Gold Flake were Omi (Rakesh Bedi) and Jomo (Ravi Baswani), who plied their debts at the hapless Lallan Mian's (Saeed Jaffrey) kiosk in *Chashme Buddoor*.
6. Dina Pathak sprained her ankle in *Gol Maal* when she squeezed herself in Amol Palekar's house through the kitchen window and was suggested this handy remedy.
7. 8.30 was the time for breakfast in Dina Pathak's household in *Khubsoorat* and that was advertised on radio, no less!
8. Kishore Kumar sang this paean to the classic Chevrolet model in *Holi Aayee Re*, which was picturised on Rajendranath in the song *Meri lottery lag jaane wali hai*.

330

14

Of Advertising and Marketing

Yeh Mumbai hai. Yahan har cheez mein dikhawa hai jisse hum showmanship kehte hain. Sajaavat hai jisse hum publicity kehte hain. Aur banaavat hai jisse hum marketing kehte hain.

—*Anil Kapoor in* **Taal**

If you think about it, Bollywood is one big advertising industry. Smart one-liners, great-looking models, strong brands and enticing promises make up the industry. And quite appropriately, Bollywood has inspired iconic brand messages. It has created some iconic advertising as well, both real and fictional. And Bollywood is home to some of India's strongest brands.

This section looks at advertising in and around movies.

Hype and Buzz: 10 Marketing Campaigns

While every film appoints a PR firm to float rumours of an affair between the lead pair and stories of the actors doing their own stunts, very few manage to cut through the clutter. And surprise of surprises—even doing that successfully is no guarantee of success. What? You have to make a good film for the marketing to succeed? What rubbish!

One of the earliest films to 'engage' the audience before its release was ***Rehnaa Hai Terre Dil Mein***. Remaking a Tamil smash hit (*Minnale*), producer Vashu Bhagnani took out the music album well before the release of the film with multiple versions of the title track in order to promote the soundtrack. The listeners were invited to vote for the best version, which would then feature in the final film. As a strategy, it seemed fine because people were expected to go and see the movie to see if the track they voted for indeed featured in the film. Except that Hindi film audiences are notoriously star-focused and a Saif Ali Khan–Madhavan–Reema Sen combination was not enough to get them to a theatre.

In ***Hum Tum***, Saif Ali Khan played a wisecracking cartoonist initially in hate and eventually in love with Rani Mukherji. In the film, the Hum (guy) and Tum (girl) characters were actually part of a comic strip that was ostensibly his creation depicting the 'battle of the sexes'. Yash Raj Films launched the promotion of the movie with an unprecedented presence in India's highest-read English newspaper. As part of a nine-week campaign, the *Times of India* carried a daily comic called *Hum Tum* in eight of its editions across India. Each of the strips had a man–woman joke written in Hinglish, as the two characters poked fun at each other and built tremendous curiosity while bringing out the sassy tonality of the film.[1]

---

[1] The animation of the comic characters in the film was done by Kathaa Animation and the company's animation director, Vijay Raibole (along with his wife), did the art for the comic strip.

When Sanjay Gupta directed *Musafir*, the plot (lifted from Sean Penn–starrer *U Turn*) was not original but the promotional strategy was. For the first time in the Indian film and television industry, a hunt for an item girl was launched. In association with Zee Music, the producers of the movie put together a full-fledged reality show (called *Musafir Item Bomb Hunt*) to choose a girl who would star in an item number along with Sanjay Dutt. The prize didn't seem too attractive considering the song would play during the end-credits of the film—which is not something people hang around to gape at. Probably this is why there was a profusion of non-Indian participants, one of whom went on to win the contest. Tantalizingly called Tatsania (from Belarussia), she appeared in *Musafir* but in nothing else in Bollywood after that.

Dibakar Banerjee's first film, the cult classic *Khosla Ka Ghosla*, almost didn't get a release till UTV stepped in. And before word of mouth kicked in to make the film the sleeper hit of the year, they had a cute strategy to get some initial viewers in. In Delhi, they offered that anybody with the surnames of Khosla and Khurana could watch the film for free in the first week. All they had to do was to walk in with an identity proof and take sides with either Khosla (Anupam Kher) or Khurana (Boman Irani). It was unlikely that too many people would go with the latter but this was a sure-shot way of getting some people to sample the product for free and say great things about it.

Vishal Bhardwaj's *Omkara* was a dark, brooding and inspired retelling of Shakespeare's play though the Indian audience has only a passing acquaintance with the Bard. The draw of the film was always going to be the star cast (Ajay Devgn, Saif Ali Khan, Viveik Oberoi and Kareena Kapoor) and the lyrics and music (Gulzar and Vishal himself). To build on the allure of the music and the intrigue of the plot, three names for the film were proposed and a contest was launched for viewers to vote which name they wanted. *Omkara*, *Issak* (the UP dialect version of *Ishq*) and *O Saathi Re* were the three names (all of which were rooted in the songs of the film) and the public voted overwhelmingly in favour of *Sheikh Peer Ka Karnama*. Sigh.

Mukhbiir, a thriller (directed by Mani Shankar) about a police informer in the underworld, offered to return the ticket price if a viewer didn't like the movie and this became a first in the history of Bollywood. This 'Satisfaction Guaranteed' offer came with some fine print, though. The offer was valid to the first 5,000 claims in the first week of the film's release. To get back the ticket price (minus the entertainment tax), the viewer had to write an 'application' explaining why he didn't like the movie along with a self-addressed envelope to get a demand draft mailed back to him. There is no information on how many people actually sent in refund requests. The bureaucratic procedure seemed complicated enough to be a deterrent.

For his supernatural thrillers *Phoonk* and *Phoonk 2*, Ram Gopal Varma offered the natural challenge that we do with friends around scary movies. He promised to pay Rs 5 lakh to whoever managed to watch the full movie in a theatre—all alone! The challenge came with its set of regulations—the film had to be watched without a break, the viewer would be observed through cameras fitted inside the hall and his heart rate (which would also be monitored) had to remain constant throughout the film. While there is no record of anybody taking up this challenge for *Phoonk,* it surely generated a lot of buzz because for *Phoonk 2*, one intrepid cinefan (called Ritesh Sharma) took up the challenge in Mumbai. But he flinched at a scary scene quite early on in the movie and was disqualified.

The toy given along with McDonald's Happy Meal is one of the most well-distributed and much-awaited toys. Typically, the figurines are chosen from global franchises (like *Shrek*, *Batman,* etc.). For the first time, in October 2011, an Indian action figure was given out with the Happy Meals. And the character which managed this coup was the One which was being promoted in the most breathless burst of film advertising ever—G.One. The McDonald's tie-up was one of the (literally) hundreds that Shah Rukh Khan did for *Ra.One* and it stood out for being the first time someone did it in India.

In December 2008, more than a hundred employees of Big Cinemas in Mumbai shaved off their hair in the distinctive style of Aamir Khan in *Ghajini.* For two weeks before the film's release (on 25 December), cinegoers were served popcorn and ushered into seats by these eye-catching people. On 11 December, a movie called *Rab Ne Bana Di Jodi* starring Shah Rukh Khan had released and the film press was aflutter like never before about Aamir's hijacking his rival's big release. Even if we keep aside the rivalry of the two Khans, unleashing a sea of shaven-headed people in what was going to be the two busiest weeks of a multiplex chain was a really noteworthy marketing gimmick.[2]

Exactly one year later, Aamir returned to promote his next release—*3 Idiots*. Calling it an 'alternative reality game', he repeated the plot of the film in real life by going missing and inviting the press to find him (just as Madhavan and Sharman Joshi would do in the film). The only difference was that he left clues for the press to follow, the first of which was read out by Sachin Tendulkar in Mumbai. His *Bharat Darshan* in disguise included seven Indian cities in the itinerary—Varanasi (which is his mother's hometown), Kolkata (where he landed up at Sourav Ganguly's house), Chanderi in Madhya Pradesh (where Kareena Kapoor joined him

---

[2] The website for the film (rememberghajini.com—now defunct) also had a cool gimmick. Just as the film's protagonist lost his memory every fifteen minutes, the site returned to its homepage every fifteen minutes.

to buy the famous sarees), Palanpur in Gujarat (where he spent time at a school), Faridkot (where he attended a wedding), Chennai (to do some sightseeing) and an unscheduled stop at a Jaipur doctor's clinic for some medicines. Controversy dogged one leg of his visit when it was discovered that he had stayed in a nondescript Varanasi hotel using a false name and some people filed a case against the hotel owner for allowing a guest in without verifying his identity.

WAH, KYA LINE MAARA!

The first step of marketing a film is to have a kickass tag line that would create a bhelpuri of excitement and curiosity in the audience's minds. A look at some of the popular ones:

- *The Greatest Star Cast Ever Assembled*: Except for the debutant villain, each one of **Sholay**'s stars was a huge star when the film released. Many reviews complained that while this tag line is true, the other one (*The Greatest Story Ever Told*) was not since the story was derived from several popular films.
- *Who's Aamir Khan? Ask the girl next door*: **Qayamat Se Qayamat Tak** launched its unknown but extremely good-looking hero with a teaser campaign that created unprecedented buzz.
- *The most powerful film ever made*: **Parinda**, Vidhu Vinod Chopra's classic, was certainly not short of confidence in promoting their film.
- *Never before a love story with 7 songs and 11 murders*: **Aa Gale Lag Jaa**, which saw the adult debuts of Jugal Hansraj and Urmila Matondkar, certainly knew how to mix things up.
- *It's all about loving your parents*: **Kabhi Khushi Kabhie Gham** had a tag line that institutionalized Karan Johan's brand of saccharine sweet family saga and launched a thousand spoofs.
- *Can you fall in love with someone you've never met?*: **The Lunchbox**, Ritesh Batra's debut film, won rave reviews and was promoted with a line Karan Johar (who presented the film) came up with.

Marketing in Bollywood: 10 Brand Placements

Brand placements in movies are common enough across the world though slightly less in India. But some really cool and some not-so-cool brands have made their mark in the movies. Some of the placements have been quite clumsy while some have been seamlessly merged. Some connection with the plot is preferred, but not considered essential!

The most interesting brand placement did not involve watches, cars or liquor. It was a brand placed on the name of the hero of the film. For **English Babu Desi Mem**, Shah Rukh Khan's name was sponsored by the Bhilwara Group—owners of Mayur Suitings. As part of a very visible campaign kicked off at that time, the star was called 'Shah Rukh Mayur Khan' and this was extended to the movie where the lead character was called Vikram Mayur, the chairman of Mayur Industries. The film's poor box-office collections did not do too much for the brand. But Mayur is still going strong and their latest campaign involves Virender Mayur Sehwag.

In one of the biggest hits of all time, **Dilwale Dulhania Le Jayenge**, we had a beer brand making an appearance—which is a rarity since alcohol brands are subject to strict advertising restrictions and there is always a chance that family audiences might balk at the placement. Nevertheless, Stroh's beer was consumed around a bonfire as Shah Rukh bonded with Parmeet Sethi. When asked why he had come to India, SRK gave a quizzical glance at the can in his hand and claimed his ambition was to set up a beer plant. Stroh's beer cans and large posters were also displayed in Amrish Puri's departmental store, from where SRK hijacked a crate.[1]

---

[1] Originally, the script had SRK asking for condoms at Amrish Puri's store but that was changed to beer to keep it more palatable for Indian audiences.

In *Baghban,* Amitabh Bachchan extended his endorser role for ICICI Bank right into the film. He played the loving husband, the dutiful father and a loyal employee of the bank. The bank's branch was the setting for some key scenes—including one where Amitabh withdrew his entire PF savings for his sons. The Big B's boss behaved like a perfect banker and solemnly advised him not to. It would have done the bank a world of good to have a handsome, credible gentleman manning their branch instead of, say, Emraan Hashmi who would have probably flirted with the customers at peak hour.[2]

Shah Rukh Khan has been one of the best marketed Bollywood stars. And he was one of the first people to get into product placement in a big way. His attic in *Dil To Pagal Hai,* for example, had a prominently branded Pepsi fridge (usually seen only in supermarkets).

For his first home production, *Phir Bhi Dil Hai Hindustani,* he managed to weave in a Hyundai Santro car into the story—a brand he was endorsing then. SRK and Juhi Chawla escaped from a villainous gang in a Santro when we were nearing the climax in the film. In the chase sequence that ensued, the car's superior handling, brake efficiency, quick pickup and spacious interior were all aptly demonstrated. However, considering that the film was supposed to be an attack on the commercialization of the media and how sponsorships have invaded every space, the product placements looked more than a little odd.

Bonus Promotional Car: Maruti Swift made its Indian debut in *Bunty Aur Babli* as the car was seen in the film even before its market launch. Coincidentally or otherwise, the car's launch coincided almost perfectly with the film's release. So before honest people could buy the car with their hard-earned money, two thieves took it out for a spin!

When Shashi Kapoor fell in love with a voice in the 1970s, it involved hiding behind bushes and listening to a scantily clad Zeenat Aman on the sly. In *Lage Raho Munna Bhai* of the 2000s, all the lovable goon had to do was to switch on the radio. Munna bhai fell in love with RJ Jahnavi—who worked for WorldSpace Radio in the film. It was a small matter of detail that the satellite radio service did not have interactive programming in India, unlike the FM channels. But that did not stop the producers from putting up large branding all around the studio, where many of the film's pivotal scenes took place. Vidya Balan, the effervescent jockey with a signature 'Good morning', apparently trained with real-life RJ Malishka of the Red

---

[2] *Trivia Alert*: In *Aankhen* too, the Big B played a bank manager with Vilasrao Jefferson Bank. He was sacked from the bank but returned to take revenge and rob the bank with the help of three blind men.

FM network to get the nuances right. But for all the efforts, WorldSpace did not continue in India and shut shop in 2009.[3]

Weaving a brand into the story is never easy but it happened quite neatly in *Luck By Chance*. Lovers Konkona Sen Sharma and Farhan Akhtar went shopping in a supermarket, discussed Konkona's erratic fridge and her lack of money to replace it. Almost casually, branded material of Godrej Eon Fridge appeared, and at the checkout counter, Farhan wrote out a slogan for the brand (something about 'no frost, low cost') that could win them a new fridge. This small episode passed off almost unnoticed in the film until a brand-new fridge reappeared—this time, in her house—as the promised prize. Godrej followed up this brand placement with a 'Luck By Chance Contest' where all buyers of their products within a certain period were eligible for a lucky draw. Prizes included meeting the stars of the film, CDs of the film's music and even an all-expenses-paid trip abroad to see the shooting of the producers' next film.

In *Gardish*, directed by Priyadarshan before his teaming up with Akshay Kumar, we had a relatively obscure but surprisingly blatant placement—of all things—of mosquito repellents. Before the heroine ascended the stage for a song (a rousing medley scored by R.D. Burman), the audience (in a hand-clapping style reminiscent of '*Ek do teen*') chorused—'We want hit song, we want hit song'. This would have been quite innocuous if the heroine hadn't emerged from a dummy aerosol of Hit Cockroach Killer and large neon signs of Hit hadn't been revolving all around. This was explicable because the producer, R. Mohan, was popularly known as Good Knight Mohan for creating the brands Good Knight and Hit (which were later sold to Godrej). He was making an ad film free within the price of a feature.

In *Hero*, a reformed Jackie Shroff was released from prison and required to be rehabilitated. He was put up for a job at Rajdoot Motorcycle Company. And from then on, he popped up both inside and outside the factory to plug the Yamaha Rajdoot 350, then the flagship bike of the Escorts group. He called it the 'best bike in India' and even rode it to participate—and obviously win—in a Mumbai–Panvel motorcycle race. And apart from the race and factory, logos of the company and advertisements of Escorts Shock Absorbers were strewn around liberally throughout the film. The Hero-on-Rajdoot not only beat his romantic rival, Shakti Kapoor, who was riding a Honda bike in that same race, but even a trashing couplet was produced by Jackie's mentor (Madan Puri) in his favour—'*Honda ho ya Fonda, jeetega hamara munda.*'

---

[3] In *Radio*, Himesh Reshammiya played Vivan Shah, a RJ with Radio Mirchi. The film was promoted heavily by the network as the RJs kept aside their Himesh jokes for a while and said good things about the man who became their 'colleague' on screen.

From Rajdoot at the beginning of their careers, Subhash Ghai and Jackie Shroff moved on to Coca-Cola towards the end, and it is almost unanimously agreed that *Yaadein* was one of the most in-your-face examples of product placement. Jackie sang soulful ballads holding a Coke can. His dying wife gave him a Coke keychain. Hrithik swigged Coke at parties, taking care to display the full logo. It was a triumph for Coca-Cola as the brand was not woven into the story but the story and situations seemed built around the brand. And Ghai did not stop at Coke. Pass Pass mouth freshener ('*Pass Pass khilakey pass pass aane ki koshish kar rahi hai*') and Hero Cycles ('*Hero Cycles ki heroine Isha Puri*') made suitably cringeworthy appearances in the film.

Coke Buy One Get One Alert: *Yaadein* was not Subhash Ghai's first flirting with a bottle of Coke. In *Taal*, Akshaye Khanna and Aishwarya Rai sipped alternately from the same bottle of Coke in a misguided depiction of increasing friendship.

In *Koi Mil Gaya*, Hrithik Roshan played an adult with slow brain development, who had a fully mature body but with the mind of a twelve-year-old. And that quasi-kid, Rohit, was a walking-talking endorsement for Bournvita. He routinely asked for Bournvita when offered tea or coffee and did not desist from attributing his '*chusti aur phurti*' to the health drink. (Unfortunately, the subsequent beefing up of his muscles and the sharpening of his mental faculties were not credited to Bournvita but to an alien called Jadoo.) The association with the brand and the franchise did not end here. In the sequel *Krrish*, the focus shifted to Rohit's son Krrish who was born with supernatural abilities and thought nothing of running ahead of horses. Even he attributed his abilities to Bournvita, and quite fittingly, a jar of the drink was a permanent fixture on his dining table.

The best unplanned plug for any brand in a Hindi movie must be the one for Black Dog whisky in *Shahenshah*. To explain the lusty feelings he had on seeing 'fair butterflies' like Meenakshi Seshadri, Amrish Puri intoned '*Jis din main koi gori titli dekh leta hoon, mere khoon mein sainkro kaale kutte ek saath bhaunkne lagte hain. Uss din main Black Dog peeta hoon.*' Wow—what articulation of brand benefits.

The second best unplanned brand plug of Bollywood landed the makers of *Dabangg* in a bit of a soup when Malaika Arora shook her hips and claimed '*Main Zandu Balm hui, darling tere liye*'. Emami—the makers of Zandu

HONOURABLE MENTIONS

HONOURABLE MENTIONS

Balm—sued the producers for uauthorized use of their trademark even as the superhit song sent sales through the roof. The company reported Zandu's sales had zoomed by nearly 40 per cent after the release of the song. Eventually the company (Emami) and the producers settled the dispute amicably.

Dabangg 2 repeated this lucky formula by invoking India's favourite adhesive to stick a beloved's image on one's heart, but in this case, it was better orchestrated with a co-promotion deal, though there is no data on the impact of the song on the sales of Fevicol.

HISTORY OF COCA COLA IN BOLLYWOOD

Long before *Taal* and *Yaadein*, Coke had made its presence felt in Hindi cinema—especially in the '50s and '60s.

- *Shree 420*: When Raj Kapoor entered Bombay for the first time, a huge banner of Coca-Cola was fixed on an overbridge, visible right above him.
- *Chalti Ka Naam Gaadi*: Kishore Kumar and Madhubala carried on their romance with sips from a bottle of what they called 'Coco Cola'.
- *Miss Coca Cola:* 1955 hit featuring Geeta Bali and Shammi Kapoor had hit music by O.P. Nayyar and an amazing example of a brand featuring in a movie title.
- *An Evening in Paris:* As Shammi hopped around Sharmila in the streets of Paris, she coolly picked up a bottle of Coke from a vending machine in a river ferry.

Coca-Cola exited India in 1977, returned in 1993 and restarted its Bollywood sojourn soon thereafter.

Ad Space: 10 Advertising Campaigns

While many admen have become directors, lyricists or pundits, advertising as a profession is relatively underrepresented in the movies. Professions like rowdies, Roadies, roadside Romeos and Rapchik Rajnis far outnumber creative directors and copywriters. But when they do, Bollywood does a bloody good job of developing interesting advertising for the in-film brands.

In **Benaam**, Amitabh Bachchan was the marketing manager for Glaxose D, who got caught in a dangerous web of blackmail and crime after he witnessed a murder.

His workday started by asking his secretary about news from Punjab and Andhra. Presumably he was asking for sales reports but seemed to be reasonably happy when 'no news' was reported. He took a cursory look at the 'new design' (a green cylindrical tin) and brushed it off as 'interesting'. He assembled a massive audience for the screening of an ad film. The film called the brand 'National Energy' and claimed that Indians of every race, caste and creed got their energy from Glaxose D. AB informed his boss that he had chosen this from all the advertising shorts that had come in and the boss was quite happy to hear that. When he asked the audience about their feedback, they screamed 'very good' and 'very nice' in unison. Immediately after that, AB rejected a poster layout because it had a skimpily clad model on it and his was a 'family product'. Such unanimous approval and quick closures on a marketing campaign are things lesser mortals don't even dream of, but we were not talking of lesser mortals here.

Sai Paranjpye's **Katha** had a fictitious brand of shoes that was the centre of attraction. Naseeruddin Shah was the sincere 'accountant' at Footprint Shoes while Farooque Shaikh was the flashy 'consultant'. Footprint Shoes made an ad film ('*Joota ho to aisa*') starring Jalal Agha as a tapori who teased a young lady before he got whacked by her sandal. '*Sandal pehno toh Footprint, joota ho toh aisa*,' purred the lady while Jalal Agha pointed to the wound on his cheek and proclaimed, '*Joota khao toh Footprint, joota ho toh aisa.*' As the one-minute film ended and the lights came on in the projection chamber, the owner of the company announced,

341

'Jolly good film.' The serious Naseeruddin pronounced that it was a childish film leading to poking fun towards the brand. The owner of the company promptly dismissed this feedback and uttered the words that every creative director longs to hear—'Order the prints.'

Smart-alec creative guys. Sexy babe from rival agency. Clueless client. Jhankaar Beats *packs in the ad agency essentials.*

Both the lead actors of *Jhankaar Beats* were admen—presumably an art and copy team—though they were more gainfully employed in the pursuit of Boss's[1] music and *Sholay* trivia. They worked for Hyphen Advertising and were required to put together a campaign for condoms. The competitor was Zippo Condom ('Will cover *all* your mistakes') and they needed to come up with a tag line that would convince the client to give them the business.

Their first pitch ended in disaster since it happened forty-eight hours ahead of when they thought it would happen! The one-liner (remember, it was for a condom) was '*Haan, mujhe yeh pasand hai*'. In the true tradition of the advertising industry, they regrouped, wasted a lot of time, cracked silly jokes, played some great music, won back a wife, had a daughter and used a neighbour's spontaneous reaction to come up with a winning one-liner: 'Better safe than worry'.

Madhur Bhandarkar is one great fan of the advertising industry. Three of his movies had extensive sequences dedicated to making ads and selling stuff.

In *Page 3*, Konkona Sen Sharma took a break from party reportage and dropped into an ad shoot for underwear. Her soon-to-be boyfriend turned out to be a model among several other topless (male) models who dropped their towels and posed slinkily on a beach chair to demonstrate their waxed bodies and (obviously) their underwear. When Konkona asked the director—in a Prahlad Kakkar–style get-up—why they were shooting in Madh Island and not in some international location, the director replied with utmost sincerity that it was a 'very low-priced' brand and was therefore being shot locally. It was meant for the common man and the slogan was '*Aam logon ki shaan*—Janata Underwear'. You can get five Abbys for a line like that!

In *Corporate*, business rivalry played out in the soft drinks market, when Sehgal Foods launched

---

[1] R.D. Burman, not their reporting manager!

a mint-based soft drink. Bipasha Basu and Kay Kay Menon anchored the launch with some nameless (and almost faceless) minions. There were hectic meetings with the advertising agency (identified by the presence of a long-haired creative director). There were rejections of a brand name ('Chill') and the quick acceptance of another ('Just Chill'). The brand name magically metamorphosed into an ad layout ('I wanna Just Chill'). There was some pseudo-marketing jargon ('Just Chill is a mass-based product . . . identification among all age groups') but that quickly gave way to shooting the ad film (by the even longer-haired Prahlad Kakkar). The jingle was as catchy ('*Jab pyaas ban jaye swaad, Bei-beh tumko aaye woh yaad*') as the launch event was flashy. And we had a full-fledged launch with branded trucks zipping across to quench the thirst of the country. Soft drinks in India are never too far away from controversies. But that is a different story altogether.

Fashion—in a way—was all about ads. Apart from the fashion shows, Meghna Mathur (Priyanka Chopra) became a top model riding on the back of some meaty brand endorsements.

To start with, she was the face of Panache ('fashion clothing') and was soon atop giant billboards that said 'Blow Me Away', which was probably the tag line for the brand. When she moved into her apartment, her drawing-room window overlooked the curve of Marine Drive and the giant Panache billboard—which was something even supermodels would kill for.[2] From the fictitious Panache, she went on to become the face of Kimaya, Sunsilk and Jimmy Choo. When the Sunsilk ad was being shot, some serious-looking people in suits appeared, ostensibly, to represent the company that was footing the bill for the giant billboards.

In *Ghajini*, Asin was a small-time model in ad films. Her 'boss' and director was Tinnu Anand, who was always as exasperated as ad film-makers usually are. They were shown shooting a commercial for Kite Detergent—with an army of beleaguered housewives (in blue-bordered off-white sarees) complaining about the poor quality of cleaning ('*Ragad ragad ke saaf karo, mere haathon ko maaf karo—pilaapan jaata hi nahin*'). The lead model in a gleaming white saree offered the solution ('*Isi liye le aao Kite, sab kuch milega white*') in front of a gigantic rupee coin, which was the price of the *chak chak chakachak safedi*.

Amidst the mayhem of *Delhi Belly*, we had an advertising guy. Vir Das worked in an ad agency, that too with a Bengali boss. He was obviously an art director who roamed around with large portfolio bags and drew smiling bananas for ad campaigns. His bananas were complete with

---

[2] A few decades back, a smuggling don offered a coolie from Bombay's docks lots of money to come and work for him. When the coolie had looked out from nearly the same window as Priyanka did in *Fashion*, he had visions of his helpless mother and brother eking out a living in the city. What better proof of India Shining do you want?

a tophat, a dress suit and a cane. His boss first wanted the banana to smile more because 'he had achieved his ambition to be in a banana split'. With all the sarcasm of an ad agency creative person, he photographed his boss's manic grin and reworked it immediately (because the client wanted it *immediately*). '*Kelon ne meri g**** maar rakkhi hai,*' he muttered. Next day, his boss wanted the banana to be 'less happy' (because the client wanted it 'less happy'). Welcome to advertising.

> *Diamond Biscuit, Diamond Biscuit, jab bhi mood ho kha lo*
> *Diamond Biscuit, Diamond Biscuit, healthy swaad ko pa lo*
> *Mummy Papa jab bhi laatey, saare bachche khush ho jaatey*
> *TOING TOING*
> *Diamond Biscuit, Diamond Biscuit, healthy swaad ko pa loooooooooooo*
> (*Ab naye coconut flavour mein bhi . . .*)

Imran's wonderfully evocative poetry in **Zindagi Na Milegi Dobara** was given a quick burial by his two friends when they sang his most famous ad jingle for a girl he was trying to impress. Imran defended his creative output: '*Karna padhta hai, saalon.*' Cannot disagree with that, really! But even after this put-down, Imran tried a valiant recovery by bragging that the brand had gone from no. 4 to no. 1, thanks to his jingle.

'Come on, flirting is fun. This is an advertising agency.' Arjun Rampal played the flirtatious CEO of ad agency KK & Boyle in **Inkaar**. As we saw his dalliances with the agency's national creative director (Chitrangada Singh), we were also offered a ringside view of the agency's creative pursuits. We got to see some very real characters, events and ad campaigns. Fictional brands like findkaam.com, Chameli soap, Prima One Insurance and Mistair Fashion Fabrics seemed to have some real-life roots. The rise of small-town talent in agencies, the politics of awards, the sexual politics, and the travails of working women were well portrayed as were some of the campaigns which had some very memorable punchlines. Pearly White toothpaste was sold with a catchy '*Daanton ke bhoot baaton se nahin maante*' while a brand of Korean bikes had a sentimental '*Raaston ko hi nahin, rishton ko bhi jodein*'. And of course, the sly one was for Zest condoms which borrowed a line from the director's earlier film—'*Is raat ki subah nahin*'.

Incidentally, the movie was shot in the offices of two well-known ad agencies (Leo Burnett, Grey Worldwide) in Mumbai but they refused to be named in the credits as the movie's topic could have had a negative rub-off on them. So much for fun and flirting in an ad agency!

Utterly Butterly Bollywood: 35 Amul Ads

The Amul advertising campaign is one of the best barometers of society and culture in India. Anything that is in the news or touches our lives gets captured by Amul. Bollywood has always been on Amul hoardings, with the frequency increasing sharply in the last decade or so. From the 1970s to the mid-1990s, very few Bollywood stars made it to the ads but the presence has been much more regular lately.

Part 1: New Releases

Pati patni aur wah. One of the earliest films to be featured in the Amul creative, it was the extramarital comedy twisted into a paean for the butter.

Khaike pav Amul wala, khul jaye bandh akal ka taala. This was probably Big B's first appearance on an Amul billboard with the superhit song from *Don*. He became the most regular filmstar to appear in Amul ads.

Rich taste se hum sabke baap lagte hai. Naam hai Amultabh Makkhan. Amitabh created mass hysteria with *Shahenshah* and his signature line came up in all sorts of places.

Utterly butterly de de. Humul. Again, Amitabh. This time, it was for his all-dancing-all-fighting avatar opposite Kimi Katkar in *Hum*. The '*Jumma chumma de de*' song became almost the national anthem at the time the movie released.

Little Bhatt-er goes well with Aamir Khan-a. Amul Butter: Dil hai ke mangta hai. Aamir Khan and Pooja Bhatt starred in one of the biggest hits of the day and Amul did a cute pun on the actress being the director's daughter.

Aati kya, makhan dala! Amul: On everyone's lips. Aamir Khan's first foray into playback singing was the hit song of the day and Amul couldn't resist having a line with both of them being on everyone's lips.

Roti ke neeche kya hai? Amul: Asalnayak. Sanjay Dutt's controversial turn as the *Khalnayak* (while terror charges were being framed against him) was made doubly so by the double-meaning song from the same film.

Saif, for all Anaris and Khiladis. Akshay-ly brat-erly delicious. Akshay Kumar and Saif Ali Khan's jodi in *Main Khiladi Tu Anari* was a big box-office hit and Amul doffed a cap at the ad-line of the film: The Brave and The Brat.

Super Hit-ik Roshan. Amul: Kaho na bhookh hai. Hrithik Roshan burst into the industry with his monster-hit *Kaho Naa Pyaar Hai* and everybody was floored with this new sensation.

Dish chahta hai. Akhtarly butterly delicious. Farhan Akhtar's ultra-cool buddy flick, *Dil Chahta Hai*, gained a cult following across the country.

Amul lagaan-a. Upon every slice in India. Once upon a time in India, there was a film which took on the British Empire, broke box-office records and went on to make an attempt at Oscar glory.

Lagate raho maska bhai. Amul: Khole toh. The affable gangster's return was marked with new words (Gandhigiri) being added to our vocabulary and older words gaining currency. Bole toh, the ideal setting for Amul to take out an ad.

Chakh Le India. Shah Rukh Khan's inspiring brand of patriotism in the backdrop of Women's World Cup Hockey had everything going for it, including a cute pun.

Savour-iya. Amul: Eat at Om. Two of India's biggest stars and biggest directors faced off at the Diwali box office and the entire country could not speak of anything else but *Saawariya* and *Om Shanti Om*.

Himesha khao. Aap kaa Ammuuul. People either hated Himesh Reshamiyya, or they loved him. But sure as hell, they couldn't ignore him. Amul made a clever play on his debut film— *Aap Kaa Surroor*.

Kabhi Amulvida naa kehna. Amul: For your mitva. Karan Johar walked into 'serious' territory with his take on incompatible couples and infidelity. As the '*Mitva*' song played across the country, *Kabhi Alvida Naa Kehna* was the subject of talk shows, magazine covers and advertising billboards.

Masake le. Amul: Belly fix. Oscar-winner Rahman's best album in some time, *Delhi 6* had the hugely popular '*Masakkali*' song—both of which got a punny avatar in the Amul ad.

Bake up, Sid. Amul: No apologies. Karan Johar's production, starring Ranbir Kapoor, ran afoul of Shiv Sena sentiments and the producer had to apologize to let his film run uninterrupted. The butter remained unapologetically good.

Khaa! Big A for small B. The Big B's brilliant performance in R. Balki's *Paa* was a departure and a talking point.

Ibn-e-butter-tha. Amul: Dishqiya. Vishal Bhardwaj's rustic romantic thriller, *Ishqiya*, had a quirky script and quirkier lyrics, both of which Amul used to great effect!

Part 2: Stars in the News

Khalnayak nahin, nayak hoon main. Amul: Utterly Dutterly delicious. Sanjay Dutt was acquitted of terrorism charges by a court after years and Amul celebrated his return with a triumphant line from his most controversial film.

Heroine addiction. Amul: Fida on you. M.F. Husain's obsession with Madhuri Dixit was not restricted to paintings and film viewings only. He made a film (*Gaja Gamini*) with the actress in the lead and Amul felt his obsession was almost a drug addiction! Soon after, when Madhuri tied the knot, Amul returned with another billboard which had the actress doing her *saat pheras* as the artist stood by morosely. The caption read **Madhuri's fixed it! Amul: National dish**.

Aby to main jawaan hoon! Amul: The Big A. Amitabh Bachchan launched a company, went through an image makeover and launched a snazzy music video. The entire country thought he was much younger than he should be.

Tu hai meri Kiran. Amul: Super cop. Super taste. Kiran Bedi took over as the jailer of Tihar Jail and brought in widespread reforms, earning herself accolades from different quarters. Amul borrowed a line from *Darr* and gave a thumbs-up to her efforts.

Mallika Shararat. Amul: Chan reaction. Sex-siren Mallika Sherawat grabbed eyeballs wherever she went and whatever she said. Her naughty pronouncements and her role in a Jackie Chan film were impossible to ignore.

Part 3: Obituaries

Amar Akbar Anthony & Amul. Bid you farewell, Manji: Bollywood's biggest entertainer, Manmohan Desai, passed away and Amul's tribute went around his three most famous characters.

Hum tere tere tere chaahanewale hai—Mehmood (1932–2004): Bollywood's most iconic funny man, Mehmood, was remembered with his superhit song from the film *Gumnaam*.

Aye dil hai mushkil . . . Johnny bina yahan: Johnny Walker's passing away was remembered with a song he performed on screen in the massive hit *CID*. The ad had a visual of his *tel-maalish* avatar from *Pyaasa*.

Zindagi badi honi chahiye, lambi nahin! Hrishida (1922–2006): Hrishikesh Mukherjee made a point in *Anand* and Amul returned the favour with the same line in this tribute.

An utterly heartfelt obituary

Mogambo . . . dukh hua: Only one word from Amrish Puri's most famous line from *Mr India* was changed to make a very touching tribute.

2012 and 2013 were two particularly bad years for Bollywood, with several stalwarts passing away. We could have done with fewer obituaries.

Bolo Rustam-e-Hind ki Jai!—Dara Singh (1928–2012): India's favourite strongman finally lost a bout and Amul referred to his most famous title.

Chala jaata hoon kisiki dhun mein . . .—Amul prem (1942–2012): Rajesh Khanna's death was marked by the recollection of a happy-go-lucky number in his trademark style.

Freedom fighter. Rahim chacha. Masterji. Shambhu kaka—A.K. Hangal (1917–2012): Probably the only instance of an error in an Amul advertisement. A.K. Hangal did not play the role of Rahim chacha. Amul probably meant Imam Saab of *Sholay*.[1]

Main har ek pal ka shayar hoon, har ek pal meri kahani hai—King of Romance (1932–2012): Yash Chopra, at the end of the day, was a poet.

Yari hai iman mera, Pran meri zindagi . . .—Pransaab (1920–2013): The villain with a heart of gold had many admirers.

Amul's tribute to the legendary A.K. Hangal

---

[1] A.K. Hangal was Shambhu kaka in *Lagaan* and Masterji in several films including *Balika Badhu* and (a cameo in) *Deewaar*. While the more famous Rahim chacha was played by Yunus Parvez in *Deewaar*, Hangal did play a character by that name in *Khud-daar*.

Dream Factories: 10 Production House Mascots

MGM has a roaring lion. Twentieth Century Fox has a spotlight atop a tall building. Paramount has a row of stars circling a peak. Columbia has the lady with the glowing beacon. Indian producers too have their own logo sequences that have stood out and in some cases, have become as memorable as some of their iconic films. Some similarities are striking—the religious (or inspirational) chant, the smoke effect, the background of the great cosmic void or a memorable piece from an earlier film.

RK Films

Probably Indian cinema's most iconic banner—RK Films—earned that position through five generations[1] of Kapoors who have been in films. Their opening sequence has Prithviraj Kapoor performing a puja in the light of dawn. The soundtrack is an extended version of '*Om namah Shivaya*'. In *Awara*, he was facing right and worshipping a smallish idol. But in *Henna*, he was facing left, worshipping a giant shivling and ending the puja with a flourish of sprinkling flowers. This scene gives way to the famous icon—Raj Kapoor holding a violin in one hand and supporting a fainting Nargis—taken from a scene in *Barsaat*. This 'statue' of RK's most durable pair changed over the years as it went from direct likeness in the earlier films to more abstract stick-like figures in the later ones.

BR Films

Thanks to many weeks of *Mahabharat* on television, the opening sequence of BR Films is probably the best entrenched in the collective Indian memory. The soundtrack is in the mellifluous voice of Hemanta Kumar, who sings the famous lines from the Bhagavad Gita

---

[1] Starting with Prithviraj Kapoor's father, Diwan Baseswarnath (who had a cameo in *Awara*), Karisma, Kareena and Ranbir are part of the fifth generation of Kapoors in cinema. The sixth generation has probably started practising their lines in front of mirrors by now.

that advise us to work without the thought of reward ('*Karmanye vadhikaraste ma phaleshu kadachana*'). The visual is of a couple perched on a globe which rotates to reveal the name and a Latin motto over it (*Ars longa vita brevis*, literally meaning 'art is long, life is short') to the accompaniment of smoke coming from all corners. In true socialist tradition, the man atop the globe is seen carrying a hammer and a gear wheel (huh?) while the woman carries a sheaf of grain.

Nasir Husain Films

Their first frame has always been a United Producers nameplate. In the later films, this had become slightly frayed but remained nevertheless. Then, to the accompaniment of lightning and thunder, a comet comes down and starts doing circles to reveal the letters NH on a pedestal with the top of the N resembling a royal face kissing the H. While this goes on, the soundtrack of a baritone voice reciting lines from Jigar Moradabadi (who was a mentor to Majrooh Sultanpuri, Nasir Husain's standard lyrics writer) continues: '*Kya ishq ne samjha hai, kya husn ne jaana hai, hum khaaknasheenon ki thokar pe zamana hai*'.

Trimurti Films

Gulshan Rai's banner has some historic films like **Johny Mera Naam**, **Deewaar**, **Trishul** under his stewardship and **Tridev**, **Mohra** and **Gupt** under son Rajiv Rai's watch. Their opening sequence starts with twinkling stars in the background and three divine symbols appearing—Vishnu's hand holding the Sudarshan chakra, Shiva's trishul and Brahma's feet—in a red triangle on a deep blue background. The soundtrack announces the emergence of the holy trinity with the standard hymn—'*Mangalam bhagwan Vishnu, Mangalam Shiv Shankara, Mangalam Brahmadevascha*'—and ends with blessings for all. Eventually, the name Trimurti Films appears in English over and below the mast of Shiva's trishul, cutting diagonally across the red triangle, while the Hindi version appears under the triangle.

Mukta Arts

Subhash Ghai's banner (named after his wife) for the longest time churned out only superhits. Their sequence has a bright Om lighting up in the centre of the screen followed by the sequential lighting up of concentric circles around it. The final concentric circle has Mukta Arts Pvt Ltd written on top; when fully lit, it reveals a pair of headphones around the Om circles. A male and a female devotee (who seem to be Jackie Shroff and Meenakshi Seshadri) then appear with folded hands and kneel down to reveal Mukta Arts written in cut-out letters in the front as well. The soundtrack is of phased male and female voices reciting the Gayatri mantra.[2] Later films of Mukta Arts had the same Om-wearing headphone motif appearing in a futuristic hologram-like style—in the horizon with a moon above a shimmering lake.

Dharma Productions

Till Karan Johar took over the reins, Dharma Productions had a zero-frills-banner with the name written in shiny letters which vanished quickly. After the success of **Kuch Kuch Hota Hai,** the opening sequence became longer, snazzier and more demonstrative (not unlike Karan Johar's films themselves). The soundtrack became the plaintive chorus of the **KKHH** title song. In the initial films, a Ganesh idol appeared on the left of the screen as the artistically written name appeared on the right. Later, the visual became a rotating circle of flames that eventually formed a sun-like structure. After Yash Johar's death, this sequence was followed by his photograph and a handwritten 'we miss you' message.

For the new **Agneepath**, the soundtrack of the opening sequence changed to 'Deva Sri Ganesha' (from the movie's soundtrack), probably because the violence of the film was a complete antithesis to the romantic–melodramatic mood brought on by the **KKHH** chorus.

Excel Entertainment

A picture of Lakshmi, Ganesh and Saraswati in the typical calendar art style appears first. In the later films, the picture went on to become framed, probably in gratitude to the gods for bringing success and fame. For their first film, **Dil Chahta Hai,** some psychedelic animation—like the visualizations on a media player—became the small 'e' of Excel Entertainment, which appeared boxed in bright boundaries. From their second film (**Lakshya**) onwards, the sequence became the animated image of a man with a sculpted body waving a flag, who finally froze in a semi-abstract depiction of a flag-bearer. The music was inspirational but abstract. The music has now become the theme music of **Lakshya** and the flag-bearer has become more sculpted and stands on a pedestal in the great cosmic void.

UTV

Of the many corporates in Bollywood, few have been as successful or as diverse as UTV. One of their first opening sequences started with a shot of three brass bowls of colour—blue, green and red—and a hand taking the colours on fingers and tracing a line on a glass surface, which turned to reveal UTV Motion Pictures in a flash of light. Eventually, that gave way to a more flamboyant version of three figures in silhouettes dancing across the expanse of a white

---

[2] The Gayatri mantra is a very popular choice among production houses for their opening sequences. Eros International, for example, uses it on a band that runs around a globe and eventually carries the house's name on it as well.

desert throwing colours—green, blue and red—as the dancers merged and the three streams of colour became strands in the word UTV.[3]

> *Bonus Sequence*: For their division working on more experimental ventures—UTV Spotboy—the sequence has a suited-booted-hatted cartoon character sitting atop the word 'boy' on a red screen when the entire red gets sucked in to become the word 'spot' in front of boy. The cartoon character twirls an umbrella and sucks in some more red to 'switch on' the letters UTV along with the familiar three lines in red, blue and green.

Red Chillies Entertainment

Colour + Masala = Red Chillies. The perfect name for a Bollywood production company

Shah Rukh and Gauri Khan's production house has become increasingly large and important in the scheme of things. Their opening sequence starts with a camera's shutter slowly opening as 786 and Om appear around the rim (written in English and also depicted as emblems), symbolizing the two owners' religions. As the shutter opens fully, the writing on the rim changes to 'Red Chillies Entertainment' in circular style. Finally, a red blob appears across the top of the circle that looks (somewhat) like a red chilly.

Three's Company

This company gets featured in the list only because of their name and cute montage. Farah Khan and Shirish Kunder named their production company after the triplets they had and their opening montage shows three foetuses cooing and gurgling before turning into two girls and a boy. The three children then grow angel wings and spread stardust all around them. Which becomes whorls and vortices around them before forming the name of the production company.

---

[3] A very rare version of the UTV opening sequence can be seen in *Lakshya*, where petals of a flower opened to reveal a svelte woman in harem pants and a bikini top with mountains in the background as 'UTV Motion Pictures' appeared in a golden font in front of this ensemble.

QUIZ: EQUAL AND OPPOSITE TITLES

After looking at opposite lengths of titles, here's a quirky quiz of movies which are antonyms of each other.

1. [A TV journalist accepts a challenge to become the CM for a day] / [A lady police officer chases a terrorist who had escaped from her boyfriend's charge]
2. [Cult classic written by Anurag Kashyap and Saurabh Shukla] / [Rajat Kapoor directs a failed actor's attempt to impersonate a crime boss]
3. [Ramsay classic starring vampire Neola who lured women to Kali Pahari and sucked their blood] / [Psychiatrist Amjad Khan tries to cure a peeping Tom with whom his daughter is in love with]
4. [The estranged daughter of an alcoholic singer tries to rehabilitate him] / [Mother-in-law and daughter-in-law battle it out while the slow son looks on balefully]
5. [A nurse pretends to be in love with a mental patient to cure him but actually falls in love with him] / [A mill worker tries everything to save money for an operation that would make his mute son speak]
6. [A boatman teaches one of his passengers a song and corrects her pronunciation] / [A millionaire's daughter buys a woman's husband]
7. [Dharmendra tries to woo Anita Raj, whom he had married as a child] / [Sudha Chandran watches tearfully as her husband Shekhar Suman is wooed by Dimple Kapadia]
8. [A story involving villains like Pasha, Billa and Jimmy Thapa] / [Copy of Korean film *I Saw The Devil*]
9. [Six Indians attempt to rob a bank in LA] / [A computer engineer is kidnapped by militants in Kashmir]
10. [Saratchandra Chattopadhyay's most famous novel] / [A poet is only understood by a sex-worker and a masseuse]

354

15

Very Interesting Names

This section is about the names we will never forget.

Lamboo-ji Aur Tingoo-ji: 10 Movie Titles of Extraordinary Length

This could be the shortest list . . . or the longest. Or the most controversial. With no definitive filmography of Hindi cinema, any list based on film titles is absolutely open to debate, dissent and bloodshed. But the subject of Bollywood is never too far from controversy and anybody who can't disagree shouldn't be discussing Bollywood, of all things.

Short Names

(aka film titles of two letters or less. There seems to be a wealth of three-letter names, so we will stop just short of that)

99 was the comic story of two collection agents (Kunal Khemu and Cyrus Broacha) working for a don in Mumbai, who came to Delhi chasing defaulters.
  Why the name? The film was set in 1999, around the betting scandals that rocked Indian cricket. And the main characters all missed out on their goals—a century—in life by a whisker.

Om was the handiwork of the redoubtable Ashok Honda (maker of Sunil Shetty classics like *Rakshak* and *Krodh*), and was about a young man avenging his sister's rape and murder, through blood, gore and long-handled swords.
  Why the name? The aforementioned young man's name.

Ek was about a hitman who accidentally killed a rogue politician when he was hired just to injure him (and help him garner sympathy votes).
  Why the name? Search me.

Cheat Alert: The full name of the film is actually ***Ek: The Power of One***. Since Ram Gopal Varma never did make his terrorism saga *Ek*, this two-letter film name strictly doesn't exist.

D—the ultimate shorty—was the story of a constable's son who got into the underworld and eventually rose to the top with his hard work, intelligence and guts.

Why the name? Ostensibly from the initial of the lead character's name—Deshu. But when a guy with a name starting with D starts a company, we all know what that means—don't we?

Long Names

(aka film titles of thirty letters or more; all these whoppers have their stories almost completely embedded in their names)

Aamdani Atthanni Kharcha Rupaiya was allegedly a comedy about three couples whose coats were not cut according to their cloth, because of which the wives eventually had to start working to augment the income. The MCP husbands took offence and devised elaborate schemes to keep them at home. The only thing longer than the title was the list of complaints against the film.

Albert Pinto Ko Gussa Kyoon Aata Hai was the story of motor mechanic Anthony Gonsalves finding his two long-lost brothers. Of course not! Played by Naseeruddin Shah, Albert Pinto was a motor mechanic (that part was correct) in textile strike-infested Bombay and frustrated with everything around him.

Trivia Alert: All of Saeed Mirza's films have titles longer than the films themselves, e.g. ***Arvind Desai Ki Ajeeb Dastaan***, ***Mohan Joshi Hazir Ho***, ***Salim Langde Pe Mat Ro***, etc.

Main Madhuri Dixit Banna Chahti Hoon was the ambition of a million Indian girls exemplified by Chutki, who came to Mumbai to become a star. They didn't come from filmi backgrounds. They don't have beauty queen titles. And still—despite a million hurdles—they soldiered on.

Ab Tumhare Hawale Watan Sathiyon was supposedly a film to promote Indo-Pak friendship. It was made by Anil Sharma whose earlier credits include *Gadar: Ek Prem Katha*—which is about as chummy as we could have got with Pakistan. Akshay Kumar in a guest role, Bobby Deol in a double role and Amitabh Bachchan in a what-am-I-doing-here role did not help the cause too much.

Andheri Raat Mein Diya Tere Haath Mein was the title of a Dada Kondke film you don't want to hear too much about. You just have an inkling of the title's double meaning and you want to run away.

Netaji Subhas Chandra Bose: The Forgotten Hero is the forty-letter behemoth about one of the bravest names in India's freedom struggle. Based on the last five years of Bose's life, it traced his attempts to seek German and Japanese help to launch an attack on British India. Even without a judgement on Netaji's controversial death, the film was rebuked for calling him a 'forgotten hero'.[1]

CHUTKULE KA BAKSA

After long and short titles, a quick look at the short titles that are made long by the addition of a subtitle. This started with *Daag: The Fire* and has continued unabated ever since. The basic format of the hyphenated name is Hindi Name – The English Explanation. But there are variations:

- Hindi/English: *Dhund – The Fog, Rocket Singh – Salesman of the Year*
- English/Hindi: *Double Cross – Ek Dhoka, EMI – Liya Hai to Chukana Padega*
- English/Hinglish: *Rules – Pyaar Ka Superhit Formula*
- English/English: *Encounter – The Killing, Commando – A One Man Army, Don – The Chase Begins Again*
- Hindi/Unconnected: *Aan – Men at Work, Ei8ht – The Power of Shani*
- Hindi/Deep Meaningful Thought: *Waqt – A Race Against Time*
- Hindi/WTF: *Chitkabrey – Shades of Grey*

---

[1] Some people still believe that Netaji is alive because he disappeared after a mysterious plane crash and his body was never found. It is another matter that he was born in 1897, so, if alive, he would be 117 years old now.

What's in a Name? 10 Stars Appearing on Screen with Their Real Names

Amitabh Bachchan's Vijay and Shah Rukh Khan's Raj (or is it Rahul?) are two iconic names that have become inseparable parts of their star personae. And indeed, many stars have been identified with a character on screen that has evolved far beyond the running time of the film it is from. For example, Manoj Kumar as Bharat is known far and wide for his patriotic roles (starting with *Upkar* and ending with *Clerk*). But quite a few of the stars have also been appearing on screen with their real names. Some are quite famous while some aren't.

Prem Chopra

'*Prem naam hai mera, Prem Chopra*'—when he said these lines in *Bobby* with his trademark leer and usual floppiness, he immediately established that he was certainly not the Good Samaritan the eloping couple was hoping him to be. It was not the first time he was appearing on screen as Prem but it was certainly the most famous, and his track record as an ace bad-man was cleverly evoked with the utterance of his full name.

For the statistically inclined, Prem Chopra appeared as Prem in twenty-four films (out of the 300 or so he has acted in) including the recent *Golmaal 3*.

Ranjeet

Just when you thought Prem Chopra was the King of the Look-Ma-same-name game, in walked yet another ace villain, Ranjeet, and almost topped him with twenty-three same-named roles (out of his nearly 250 films till date). For the mathematically inclined, that's a higher strike rate than Prem's. In 1977, he appeared in two of the biggest hits—*Dharam Veer* and *Amar Akbar Anthony*—with his real name as screen name, establishing himself as one of the top villains of the time. Both were Manmohan Desai–directed blockbusters, which had more stars than anyone could possibly remember. It certainly made the screenwriter's task easier.

Raj Kapoor

And if you have started to think that villains are the usual suspects to saddle unimaginative (read: real) names with, we have Raj Kapoor appearing with his real name in nearly a quarter of the films he acted in. Be it as the perennial do-gooder or the tycoon with a heart of gold, Raj Kapoor was Raj on screen as much as off it. All his iconic roles—most of them his own productions as well—have him as Raj. Starting with *Awara*, *Shree 420* and *Anari*, right down to his magnum opus *Mera Naam Joker*, audiences knew and loved him as Raj or Raju. Of his sixty-seven films as actor, seventeen are as Raj, and while many of them are bunched around 1950–51, the aura stayed till well afterwards.

Amitabh Bachchan

Amitabh Bachchan has not appeared as Amit as many times as Vijay has. But if Vijay was his angry young avatar, Amit was his sweet, poetic persona. The professor in *Kasme Vaade*, the poets in *Silsila* and *Kabhi Kabhie*, and the householder in *Do Anjaane* were all Amits. Of the nine times he played Amit, there were a few action heroes as well (*Parvarish*, *Mahaan* and *Suhaag*) but even they were not the typical angry vigilantes. In *Benaam*, his name was Amit Srivastava—which is actually his real name because 'Bachchan' was a title taken by his father Harivansh Rai, and Srivastava was their original family surname.

Rekha

When Amitabh is here, can Rekha be far behind? In *Do Anjaane*, Rekha played Amit Roy's wife Rekha Roy, thus making the film one of the very few where the lead pair appear with their real first names. In seven films (out of her total output of 167), Rekha was Rekha—the biggest hit probably being *Rampur Ka Lakshman*.

Sunny Deol

Now, here's a twist. Here is an actor whose screen name is not his real name. But he has acted in several films with his real name. Sunny Deol was christened Ajay Singh Deol but like most Punjabi boys, he came to be known by his nickname. He was Ajay the young boxer out to avenge his brother's death in *Ghayal*—the film that launched him as the Angry Young Hulk and set box-office records across his home state. He ended up being Ajay in eight films—*Right*

Yaaa Wrong being one of the last. And by the way, he was Sunny in two of his earliest films as well—*Betaab* and *Sunny*.[1]

Kumar Gaurav

Rajendra Kumar produced his son's lavish debut vehicle—*Love Story*—and keeping in mind that it was a 'home production', the hero's name was his real-life nickname (Bunty) too. The film became a massive hit and the industry celebrated the arrival of a new chocolate-box star. Except that Kumar Gaurav could never replicate the success of his debut. It may have crossed the mind of someone in superstitious Bollywood that maybe the name 'Bunty' was the lucky mascot and the name was brought back later in a film called *Hai Meri Jaan*. Yes, you are right—that film flopped as well. Sigh.

Pooja Bhatt

Pooja Bhatt debuted—literally and figuratively—as Daddy's girl. Her short acting career (twenty-six films) started and (almost) ended with playing characters called Pooja (in about ten of them). If there was a story to be told through the name, there was none—at least in her biggest hits (*Daddy, Dil Hai Ke Manta Nahin, Sadak, Sir, Phir Teri Kahani Yaad Aayee*). Whether she played a spoilt brat, a psychotic actress or a reluctant prostitute, Pooja Bhatt was always Pooja. But Anupam Kher—her most frequent screen dad—said her name in a variety of ways.

Aamir Khan

Sometimes, there are no numbers. But a fact has to be recognized for its trivia value. Aamir Khan appeared in his second starring role with his real name on screen. In *Raakh*, he played Aamir Hussain,[2] a young man out to take revenge on his fiancée's rapists. The film did not make too much of a mark except that this was the only time—yet—Aamir's screen name was his real name.

Salman Khan

What was it that I said about numbers being too important? Well, if Aamir can use his name once, so can Bhai. *Sniffs, thumbs nose*.

---

[1] Dharmendra's he-man persona became bigger and bigger till he was referred to as Garam Dharam by the filmi press as well but he was hardly ever named Dharam in his films. Among his many hits, he was Dharam Singh in only *Dharam Veer*.

[2] In his first role as an adult for Ketan Mehta's *Holi*, Aamir received screen credit as Aamir Hussain.

In *Sanam Bewafa*, the actor known as Abdul Rashid Salim Salman Khan played a character known as Salman Khan. As in real life, he was the scion of a Pathan family out to balance his dynasty's honour with his lady-love. Reel or real, there's nothing that Salman Khan cannot do.

HONOURABLE MENTIONS

In a very curious mix, the names of the four main characters in *Parvarish* were very similar to their real names. Amitabh Bachchan played Amit Singh, Shabana Azmi was called Shabbo, Neetu Singh's name was Neetu while Shammi Kapoor essayed the role of DSP Shamsher Singh (and his real name is Shamsher Raj Kapoor).

REAL NAMES, UNREAL PEOPLE

There have been a few instances of actors using their real names on screen and borrowing a few details from their real life too but the setting is clearly fictitious.

- *Johar and Mehmood*: The two comedians appeared in a series of comic capers in Goa and Hong Kong among others. They retained their real names and probably their real-life chutzpah but the elaborate cons they played on the police and the public alike were obviously fiction.
- *Guddi*: Dharmendra played a fictionalized version of himself, somewhat distinct from a regular star guest appearance. Though he seems to be the good-natured Punjabi who would want to help out a professor and his niece he would probably not go to the extent of dressing up as a goon to show his niece's fiancé in good light.
- *Khamosh*: Amol Palekar, Shabana Azmi and Soni Razdan all retained their names, playing Bollywood actors. Amol had political ambitions, which he doesn't seem to have in real life. Shabana had four national awards, which she does seem to have in real life. And Soni Razdan got murdered, which she doesn't seem to have suffered in real life.
- *Dastak*: Sushmita Sen played Sushmita Sen, a Miss Universe winner who started getting stalked on her triumphant return to India. While Sushmita may have got a few crazed fans leaving passionate messages and expensive gifts for her, they certainly didn't go to the extent of kidnapping her and trying to marry her.

Name's in a What? 17 High-profile Names

Bollywood keeps using the same names for its characters over and over again—probably for good luck. In the ocean of Vijay, Raj and Poojas, there have been some funny, inventive names. Some of them make socio-cultural points. Some of them make a statement. And all of them are bloody memorable.

1: Names in Movie Titles

Saeed Mirza made films on five fictitious personalities, who were part of the titles themselves. He told us about:

- How Ghasiram became the police chief (*kotwal*) of Pune by making a deal
- How strange the tale (*ajeeb dastaan*) of Arvind Desai was, who didn't know whether to be a capitalist or a Marxist
- How garage mechanic Albert Pinto became increasingly angry in the wake of the collapse of Bombay's textile mills
- How Mohan Joshi was finally summoned during his court battle with his landlord
- How we shouldn't waste our tears on a goon like Salim Langda, even if he tried to reform

Ricky ko Bahlane ke liye Ghalib ye plan achha hai . . . Ladies conning a conman.

Three women were swindled by an ace conman and they hired a fourth woman to execute an elaborate countercon. The guy was very smart, very handsome and very difficult to deal with. But the four women weren't about to give up easily. The game was on—*Ladies vs Ricky Bahl*.

Be it as railway minister or Bihar chief minister, Laloo Prasad Yadav never ran short of attention. Mahesh Manjrekar directed **Padmashree Laloo Prasad Yadav**, about a girl called Padmashree and her boyfriend Lalchand aka Laloo who met a lawyer called Prasad and also a Yadav. Laloo himself appeared in the movie briefly to lecture the gang to follow a life of honesty (without the cast collapsing into laughter around him).

Two Delhi *laundas* made their debut in quick succession in recent films. *Kuku Mathur Ki Jhand Ho Gayee* was the adventure of the forever-hassled youngster who found his calling in kooking, or more specifically in his eatery, *Kuku's Kwalti Khana*.

Rakesh Sharma (no relation with the astronaut) was a chubby child and his friends quickly named him after the world's most famous egg. Not disheartened by this nickname, this desi dude went looking for his life partner and we all got to know about **Humpty Sharma Ki Dulhania**.

2: Names in Songs

Manmohan Desai, it is said, prescribed that a movie should have an item every nine minutes. In his biggest hit about three long-lost brothers, they probably came faster than that. For example, at an Easter party, a Christian tapori jumped out of an egg and reminded the world (as if the world needed reminding): '*My name is Anthony Gonsalves*'.

Anthony had a kindred soul (and I avoid the word 'sister' here) in Jummalina. She appeared in a movie called *Hum* about thirteen years later, springing out from behind a curtain in a dockyard bar. Anthony—by this time—had become a goon called Tiger and was her brother Gonsalves's best buddy. He screamed out her name and asked for kisses every Friday as beer foam overflowed all over the place.

Shalimar opened in Ferguson's Dance Studio, where Aruna Irani (in the husky voice of Usha Uthup) taught every one Cha Cha Cha. Of the students, she paid special attention to a south Indian gentleman by saying, 'This is not the Bharatanatyam. This is the Cha Cha Cha,' and followed it up with the warning that the training won't get over in a jiffy: '*Mr Naidu, gir mat jaana / Yahaan tumhe kal bhi hai aana.*' Since *Shalimar's* records sold a record-breaking 500,000 copies, Mr Naidu was probably the most well-known 'Madrasi' for a while in the late '70s.

As if the scatological references in the script of *Delhi Belly* were not enough, they introduced a Bengali gentleman into the music score and unleashed a storm. (Literally, '*Aandhi aayi*'.)

D.K. Bose was always quite well known in boys' hostel corridors and he made an explosive entry into mainstream Bollywood as the makers did full *paisa vasool* of the A-certificate they were given.

3: Names of Real People

Andaz Apna Apna, Rajkumar Santoshi's laugh-riot, had two gold-digging wastrels with completely contrary names ('*pavitra aur bhakti ras se bharpoor*')—Amar and Prem. Prem had been Salman Khan's standard name in several huge hits, and by christening Aamir Amar, Santoshi invoked the romantic spirit of Rajesh Khanna for no apparent reason. But then, nothing in this classic was for any apparent reason!

While on the subject of Rajesh Khanna, a bus went from **Bombay to Goa** while the romantic superstar was at his peak. The driver's name was Rajesh and the conductor's name was Khanna (played by the film's producer–director Mehmood). It was said in those times that for a movie to become a hit, '*sirf Rajesh Khanna ka naam hi kaafi hai*'. It was quite ironic that on the bus run by Rajesh–Khanna, the next superstar of Bollywood took a ride.

David Dhawan directed **Rascals**, in which Sanjay Dutt played the role of Chetan Chauhan and Ajay Devgn was Bhagat Bhosle. Together, they were Chetan–Bhagat. The bestselling novelist was quite amused at this and tweeted, 'Saw the start of the new *Rascals* promo. I am speechless. Mr David Dhawan, I also have a pen. *Yaad rakhna* ;) The good thing is, takes two stars to handle my name. I could live with that ;)'

While **Bol Bachchan** had Scorpios rotating in the air, blindingly bright costumes and ear-splitting sound, it was a remake of the Hrishikesh Mukherjee classic **Gol Maal**, with Abhishek Bachchan playing the Amol Palekar role. In his first avatar, he was Abbas Ali and in a secular twist, he adopted the name Abhishek Bachchan for his second avatar. And as if that was not enough, Asrani's name in the movie was Shastri while his son (played by Krushna Abhishek) was called Ravi, making them Ravi–Shastri. That's what you could call 'setting the cat among the pigeons'.

19 Star Nicknames

Stars are usually known by flattering epithets (Big B) and jazzy initials (SRK). Sometimes, their names shorten (Sallu) or morph (KJo) into something that rolls off the tongue easily. But what do their friends call them? Their parents? Their relatives? What were they called before they became stars?

Pancham

Probably the most famous nickname in Bollywood, R.D. Burman's name had several stories behind it. The most credible version is the one in which he was named so by Ashok Kumar because he was unable to sing the fifth note (*pa*) right during the rehearsal of a song ('*Dol rahi hai naiya*' for the film **Shikari**) at home. That makes it the perfect nickname: a completely insignificant event bringing about a name that stayed throughout one's life and beyond.

Dadamoni

Literally meant 'a jewel among brothers'. That's what Abhash Kumar (aka Kishore Kumar) and Anup Kumar Ganguly called their elder brother, then a superstar of Hindi cinema—Ashok Kumar, the man who gave RD his nickname.

Munna

Amitabh Bachchan has been called the Big B, Amit and Lambooji—by various people. But his most affectionate nickname was the one given by his parents. The Star of the Millennium was their little boy—Munna.

Dabboo. Chintoo. Chimpoo. Lolo. Bebo.

The Kapoors have a penchant for silly nicknames. But then, what is a nickname if it is not silly? Randhir, Rishi, Rajiv, Karisma and Kareena respectively.

VD

Veeru Devgan's eldest son was named Vishal when he was born. When he was about to be launched by his father in a film called *Phool Aur Kaante*, his name was changed to Ajay. But for his old friends, he is still known by the initials of his birth name.

Baba

Sanjay Dutt is known for his heart of gold by friends across the industry—from superstars to spot boys. And as the son of a big star, he was first known to them as a little boy who came to the sets as Sanju baba. They still call him Baba.

Chichi

Govind Ahuja was derogatorily referred to as the Virar ka Chhokra when he started acting in movies. The south Bombay journalist lobby turned up their noses even more when they heard his nickname. But Govinda is still going strong.

Guddu. Duggu.

Bollywood's actor–director combo with a 100 per cent success ratio is the father–son duo with reflective nicknames—Rakesh and Hrithik Roshan respectively.

Bosky

Raakhee and Gulzar's only daughter—Meghna—has a pet name, Bosky. And Gulzar's bungalow in Bandra is called Boskyana.

Rinku

Sharmila Tagore. And if it is of any interest, her sister's nickname was Tinku.

Koko. Bonnie. Tito.

Silly, meaningless names. The only thing that explains them is the race to which the three belong. Who else but Bengalis would give such silly names to women as beautiful as Konkona Sen Sharma, Bipasha Basu and Sushmita Sen?

Piggy Chops

During the shooting of *Bluffmaster*, Abhishek Bachchan named her Piggy Chops and the name stuck within the unit. However, when it was time to give her credit for the cameo in *Taxi No. 9211*, producer Rohan Sippy listed the nickname and it entered national consciousness.

FILMI NICKNAMES

After going through the list of real-life nicknames of stars, here is a quick look at some of the nicknames stars had in films:

- *Munna*: In **Tezaab**, a conscientious police officer wanted to know the history of a criminal: '*Yeh Mahesh Deshmukh se Munna kaise ban gaya?* while in **Munna Bhai MBBS**, it was Dr Murli Prasad Sharma for parents who transformed into Munna Bhai for the Mumbai underworld.
- *Jackie*: Jaikishan was a flute player's son, who was taken under the wings of crime boss Pasha. And he became Jackie. When Jackie reformed, he went back to his original 'holy' name. This trick of anglicizing an Indian name to symbolize descent into villainy is common enough in Bollywood. The other example of freedom fighter's son Ramdas becoming Ronnie (Amitabh Bachchan) to his Portuguese masters in **Pukar**.
- *Tiger*: The uncontrollable maverick fighter—whose bosses are as scared of him as his enemies—has been portrayed by actors like Amitabh Bachchan in **Hum** (where his real name was Shekhar) and Salman Khan in **Ek Tha Tiger** (where his real name was Avinash Singh Rathore).
- *DJ*: The Delhi University drifter of **Rang De Basanti** who hung around the campus years after graduating was cool and had a suitably cool nickname. Except, his real name was a traditional Sikh name—Daljit.
- *Virus*: Khadoos professors are meant to be given cruel and funny nicknames. Viru Sahasrabuddhe of Imperial College of Engineering was given one such by attaching his surname's initial to his name. And the result was aptly irritating.

16

Excitement of Movies

Parde pe chamatkar hai, yeh chadhta sa bukhaar hai, sar pe junoon sawaar hai, khwabon ka karobaar hai

—*Title song from **Bombay Talkies***

Strange things happen around movies. Songs become movies. Great ideas don't become movies. People make movies within movies. People watch movies within movies. And when movies end, the controversies seem like another movie.

This section is about the strange goings-on before, during and after movies.

Imagining Things: 11 Greatest Movies to Not Have Been Made

Of course, an earlier list could have been one that is everyone's favourite—the Ten Favourite Movies of All. Bollywood. Hollywood. Regional. Whatever. But instead of going with that old favourite, we could do an interesting twist and come up with a list of Hindi films that were 'launched' but never made.

They had flashy *mahurats*. They had more stars than the Andromeda galaxy. They had storylines rivalling epics. They had everything going for them—except that they never got made. Dates and egos, deaths and eccentricities got in the way of these brilliant films, which may well have rewritten box-office history.

Ek

Just when we had finished gasping at *Devdas*'s budget (allegedly Rs 50 crore), Ram Gopal Varma announced a film on international terrorism called *Ek* with a budget of—hold your breath—Rs 100 crore (this was way back in 2003). Amitabh Bachchan, Nana Patekar, Ajay Devgn and an international cast were supposed to zoom across the major world capitals in a saga involving the Al Qaeda, CIA and RAW. When a journalist gasped at the budget, RGV pointed out that the budget was actually only $20 million and a top star like George Clooney or Julia Roberts got that kind of money for a single film. The logic was sound but no producer— neither Warner Bros nor Ramsay—came forward to pick up the tab. And after *Ram Gopal Varma Ki Aag*, they probably never will.

64 Squares

'Two players. One alive. One dead. A game unfinished' was the tantalizing line on the poster doing the rounds of Bollywood discussion forums. A game of chess with a dead man could have infinite possibilities and Vidhu Vinod Chopra felt that his first English-language film—

starring Amitabh Bachchan and Anupam Kher—should explore the emotions of two people across a chessboard. Amitabh and Anupam Kher have acted together in several films but none of these really pit them against each other, and this movie would have been the first time. Initially titled *Chess*, it was subsequently called *Move 5* and finally **64 Squares**. No details are available on the Vinod Chopra Films website but sources say it is back in development.

> *Bonus Production*: One of Vidhu Vinod Chopra's forthcoming productions was going to be the third instalment in the Munna Bhai series, **Munna Bhai Chale Amrika**—helmed by box-office midas Rajkumar Hirani. A trailer appeared, showing Munna and Circuit practising their English, and gags around George W. Bush seemed to be in place. However, an unsatisfactory first draft of the script and the lead actor's jail sentence have led to the film getting shelved. But we have to have a third Munna Bhai film, right? Right.

Galti Se/Jaan Boojh Ke

The film, which eventually released as *My Wife's Murder*, was intended with a twist quite unique to cinema in general, not just Indian cinema. Ram Gopal Varma intended to make two films, both of which were to start identically, about a man and his nagging wife. After the initial mood setting, the wife dies in both the films. But in the first one, the husband kills her accidentally, while in the second, it is a planned murder. The plots diverge from there and you never know where they end. He intended to release both the films (with identical casts) on the same day and invite the audience to sample one or both. But when the film released in Telugu (where the husband kills the wife *jaan boojh ke*) and had a controversial tag line ('Ever wished your wife was dead?'), it sparked off an avalanche of protests, and the Hindi version was a tame *galti se* version.

Bajirao Mastani

When Sanjay Leela Bhansali announced this film, there was a lot of banter on whether Salman would still have his faux-American accent while playing the Maratha chieftain. Nevertheless, a Maratha warrior's affair with a courtesan promised to be a great story. Sanjay Leela Bhansali directing a period film added to the allure. And if there was anything missing, then the casting ping-pong made up for it. After the success of *Hum Dil De Chuke Sanam*, it was Salman Khan and Aishwarya Rai. Then, Sallu beat up Ash and she walked off. Kareena agreed to sacrifice her multicrore fees to work with Bhansali. Salman stayed on. Bhansali got engaged in *Black* and to pacify Salman, he gave him a walk-on part in *Saawariya*. In the meantime, Kareena had walked off. When last heard, Salman had screamed 'I am not Bajirao' and sauntered off.

We now hear whispers of Ranveer Singh and Deepika Padukone getting ready to play the roles but we will believe them when we see the damn movie on screen.

Bonus Bajirao: This love story has been enticing film-makers for many years now. The trade magazines of the 1970s carried advertisements for a ***Bajirao Mastani***—with a stellar star cast of Rajesh Khanna and Hema Malini, directed by Manmohan Desai. 'Recreate a golden page from India's thrilling past,' the ads screamed. With all this hyperbole, I hope the film doesn't disappoint us!

Allwyn Kalicharan

At one point of time, Anurag Kashyap had an impressive body of critically acclaimed works, none of which had been released. When *Black Friday* eventually got a release, Anurag was hailed as the greatest thing to happen to Bollywood by no less than Danny Boyle. But even before that, he launched a sci-fi film with Anil Kapoor in the lead. The film was supposed to be about a cop in a dystopian Delhi of the future (apparently called Hastinapur) and those in the know swore that the city never looked as apocalyptic as it did in this film. The name itself was a twist on the famous refrigerator brand and a pun on the West Indian batsman— explained by a backstory. Anil Kapoor pulled out of the film and the producers felt no one would 'understand' the film, leading to a shelving of the project.

Time Machine

After the super success of *Mr India*, Shekhar Kapur consolidated his post-*Masoom* reputation as a director of intelligent, commercially successful films. Extending the mildly sci-fi theme of an invisible man, he launched *Time Machine*—starring Aamir Khan and Raveena Tandon. No film on time travel can ever be boring and this was slated to be a cracker. Except that Kapur was a brooding director and Aamir Khan was slowly upping his perfectionist gear as well. So, the scenes took a lot of time getting canned, made worse by the fact that Kapur also had international ambitions. In the end, Aamir started doing just one film a year (or less). Raveena got married and had a kid. Shekhar Kapur got an Oscar nomination and did not want to make masala films. And India still awaits a rocking film on time travel.

Apparently, Aamir has acquired the rights of the film from Shekhar Kapur and is on the lookout for a director to helm the project and for actors to replace the original cast.

Zameen

In the late 1980s (after *Saagar*), Ramesh Sippy assembled a star cast only he could have and started shooting *Zameen*. Based on a strong script by Manohar Shyam Joshi, the film had the two biggest heroines—Sridevi and Madhuri Dixit—appearing together for the first time apart from top stars like Vinod Khanna, Rajinikanth and Sanjay Dutt. The film was shelved after more than half the shooting had been completed.

While there were lots of speculations about script-related differences and ego clashes, Ramesh Sippy clarified that it was not the casting but the finances that blocked the film. The film's financier backed out and we lost the chance of seeing two divas on screen together.

Tara Rum Pum

Shekhar Kapur could well be the poster boy of unfinished classics. Some time after the ascent of A.R. Rahman in Hindi cinema, he realized that the Mozart of Madras was the ideal composer to help him create a fresh, new musical starring a fresh, new face. For the latter role, he zeroed in on Preity Zinta and it was rumoured that this would be her first lead role (after the supporting success of *Dil Se*). It all fizzled out in the end. (Yash Raj Films produced a film of the same name starring Saif Ali Khan and Rani Mukherji but with no connection to this film.)

Kalinga

Dilip Kumar returning to tinsel town to direct a multi-starrer was massive news. It was backed by Sudhakar Bokade who had produced films like *Saajan* and was a big name in the mid-1990s. Sure, there were apprehensions about Dilip Kumar's legendary perfectionism and eccentricity but Bokade had produced Nana Patekar's debut directorial venture *Prahaar* without a hitch. The shooting continued amidst uneasy rumours before the producer ran into financial difficulties with flops like *Sauda* and *Sapne Saajan Ke* and the film was quietly shelved. Occasionally, there have been declarations by Dilip Kumar that he would complete the film since it would otherwise be a blemish on his career, but no tangible progress has been seen. And IMDb.com forlornly lists Jackie Shroff as the only cast member.

Aakhri Mughal

This was supposed to be Abhishek Bachchan's launch vehicle. Directed by J.P. Dutta, it was the tale of Bahadur Shah Zafar's relationship with his son. Apparently, the rights were with Kamal Amrohi once upon a time and he had wanted to make the film with Amitabh Bachchan, after seeing him in *Zanjeer*. It did not happen then. It did not happen with the son. With all star-sons getting launched in all-singing-all-dancing-all-muscle-flexing roles, a debut like this would have been very different (to the point of being risky). But then, so was Abhishek's actual debut film—*Refugee*—with the same director. So, what was it? Was it the budget? Was it the beard AB Jr had to grow? We'll never know.

Dus

Mukul S. Anand had a really short career but he managed to establish his reputation as a maker of extravagant entertainers. He worked with some of the top stars of his time and at the time of his untimely death, he was working on a major terrorist saga titled *Dus*. Salman Khan, Sanjay Dutt, Raveena Tandon and Shilpa Shetty were the lead players. It was about a terrorist group led by Raveena Tandon (in her first negative role), who capture intelligence officer Sanjay Dutt and brainwashes him. His partner, Salman Khan, goes in to save him, assisted by Shilpa Shetty. Parts of the film were shot and even a promotional video was released but with the maker's demise, the film was never completed. Why was it called *Dus*, though? Sanjay and Salman were both part of an anti-terrorist cell called Force 10. (A terrorist plot was also central to *Dus*, directed by Anubhav Sinha, which released in 2005—starring Sanjay Dutt, Abhishek Bachchan, Zayed Khan and Shilpa Shetty.)

HONOURABLE MENTIONS

There were at least two movies that were launched with Amitabh Bachchan and Madhuri Dixit in the lead. And both of them had an amazing third lead. There was Tinnu Anand's *Shanakht* with AB, MD and Rajinikanth. And there was Inder Kumar's *Rishta* with Aamir Khan as the third star. But some jinx prevented this dynamite duo from having a release together (unless you count the '*Makhna*' song in *Bade Miyan Chote Miyan*). But with MD's comeback, we still live in hope.

Geet Gaata Chal: 24 Songs That Became Movies

A song from Chor Machaye Shor *became Bollywood's longest-running movie*

Qayamat Se Qayamat Tak, Daag—The Fire and *Dilwale Dulhania Le Jayenge* started three different trends.

QSQT was the first film to have a hugely popular abbreviation. *Daag* was the first film to have an appendage—The Subtitle. And *DDLJ* was the first film to start the trend of taking its title from a popular song. It would be better to clarify that these are probably not the very first movies to do so but definitely the inflection point because after these, each particular trend picked up like a rocket. A list of songs that went on to become titles of other films could be a never-ending one. Therefore, to keep the list manageable, a better idea would be to look at some of the famous examples. And some of the special ones.

The film that was ostensibly the 'tipping point' of the song-as-film trend, *Dilwale Dulhania Le Jayenge* (released in 1995) took its name from a song in *Chor Machaye Shor* (1970). It was one of the few films—if not the only one—which credited a person (Kirron Kher) for the 'title idea'.

One of the earliest examples of this—in 1960—was a film called **Mud Mud Ke Na Dekh**, obviously inspired by the famous dance number from **Shree 420** (1955). Incidentally, this (**MMKND**) was probably Prem Chopra's first movie.

The movie which has the maximum number of songs which went on to become film titles is Subhash Ghai's reincarnation drama **Karz**—with five of its songs made into films at last count! **Paisa Yeh Paisa, Main Solah Baras Ki, Dard-e-Dil** and **Ek Hasina Thi** are moderately successful films, based on songs from the blockbuster. Of course, Farah Khan's **Om Shanti Om** is the best known of the lot as it went on to become a monster hit giving credits and paying tributes to the original maker and star all the way.

Koi Mil Gaya (2003) took its name from a song in **Kuch Kuch Hota Hai** (1998). Both films have won the Filmfare Award for Best Film—as of now, this is the only such combination.

Hum Hain Rahi Pyar Ke (1993) was the first time a film title taken from a song (from **Nau Do Gyarah**) won the Filmfare Award for Best Film. It narrowly beat the trendsetter (**DDLJ**) by two years.

No winner of Filmfare Best Female Playback awards has been made into a film yet. On the other hand, four songs that won in the Best Male Playback Singer category have been turned into films—**Dil Toh Baccha Hai Ji** from **Ishqiya, Na Tum Jaano Na Hum** from **Kaho Naa Pyaar Hai, Papa Kahte Hain** from **QSQT** and **Roop Tera Mastana** from **Aradhana**.

The pair of **Na Tum Jaano Na Hum** and **Kaho Naa Pyaar Hai** indicates that there was only a two-year lag (thirty months, to be precise) between the original song and the movie that emerged from it. This is an amazingly short time difference. Of course, **Kaho Naa Pyaar Hai** was such a big hit that there was a scramble for everything connected to the film—hero, heroine, director, composer and even the song names.

However, the leader in the short-distance category is **Dil Toh Baccha Hai Ji** from **Ishqiya** in which the superhit Gulzar–Vishal musical output went from song (in January 2010) to film (in January 2011) in twelve months flat. Beat that!

Since we have a short-distance winner, maybe we could try to identify the long-distance winner as to which film and its original song had the maximum gap between them. Almost forty years after **Jis Desh Men Ganga Behti Hai** (1960) played the song 'Aa Ab Laut Chalen', Raj Kapoor's son Rishi made a film of the same name (1999).

Now this thirty-nine-year difference is not conclusive considering that at least two decades of difference can easily be taken as the norm. For example, *Jhoom Barabar Jhoom* (2007) was thirty-three years after *5 Rifles* (1974), *Kabhi Alvida Naa Kehna* (2006) was thirty years after *Chalte Chalte* (1976) and *Ta Ra Rum Pum* (2007) came twenty-eight years after *Baton Baton Mein* (1979). So, there might be a longer time-gap lurking somewhere out there . . .

One hit song from *Baton Baton Mein* has inspired two movies from its words—*Kabhi Khushi Kabhie Gham / Ta Ra Rum Pum*, which has been replicated by another hit song from *Karz*—*Ek Hasina Thi / Ekk Deewana Tha.*

To go one step deeper, we can now get a double-layer song-to-film transition. That is, a song being made into a film of which there is a song, which is made into another film.

Kamal Amrohi's *Pakeezah* (1971) had the famous '*Chalte chalte*', which was duly made into a film five years later and it catapulted Bappi Lahiri into gold-encrusted stardom. And *Kabhi Alvida Naa Kehna* (from a *Chalte Chalte* song) was made thirty years later.

Sudhir Mishra's first film, *Yeh Woh Manzil Toh Nahin*, featured what is probably Mirza Ghalib's most famous ghazal—'*Hazaaron khwaishein aisi*'—and that song became a film he directed in 2003. He subsequently wrote a film about the love story of a screenwriter and an actress set in 1950s Bollywood, naming it after the next line of the same ghazal—*Bahut nikle mere armaan.* When it was pointed out that people might mistake the film for a sequel to *Hazaaron Khwaishein Aisi*, he changed the name to that of yet another hit song—*Khoya Khoya Chand* (from *Kala Bazar*). A song from a 1960 film becoming a film in 2007. . . Forty-seven years is probably the longest time-gap considering the spans we were talking about three paragraphs earlier!

Meta: 10 Films within Films

There have been many films that have films being made as part of their stories. Some of them are the centrepiece. Some are relatively peripheral. And when you look at the biggest films that got 'made' in other films and the magnificent cast and crew they had, you wish some of them actually got made.

Om Shanti Om is probably the biggest tribute to the crazy world of Bollywood. Starting from the late '70s and going up to the present day, it simultaneously spoofed and saluted the whole gamut of filmi people—starting from masala directors to award-hungry stars. Needless to say, there was a procession of films that flitted in and out of the film. To start with, we had *Dreamy Girl*—Shantipriya's grandest hit, ripped off from the Hema Malini film of (almost) the same name. The film had, among other things, a typical filmi song ('Dhoom tana') that also featured Sunil Dutt.[1] There was another film called *Maa Bharti* being made in the film, starring Shantipriya, which had a fire scene and she had to be rescued by Om. This scene is reminiscent of the Sunil Dutt–Nargis's real-life love story on the sets of *Mother India*, where Nargis was rescued from a fire by Sunil Dutt. As you would have figured out, *Maa Bharti* is a literal translation of the real-life title! At a present-day Filmfare Awards function, we had the full roster of Best Actor nominees, all of them were made fun of quite mercilessly—Abhishek Bachchan in *Dhoom 5*, Akshay Kumar in *Return of Khiladi* and Om Kapoor in two identically filmed, identically written, identically scored films called *Phir Bhi Dil Hai NRI* and *Main Bhi Hoon Na*. And, of course, we had the film for which there was the shedding of so much blood, sweat and tears—literally. The film that was launched, then abandoned and then finally resurrected in a different avatar—**Om Shanti Om**.

---

[1] Footage from three typical Bollywood films—**Amrapali, Sachaa Jhutha** and **Jay Vejay**—from the 1960s and 1970s were taken, their negatives cleaned up and Deepika morphed on the scenes with the three heroes—Sunil Dutt, Rajesh Khanna and Jeetendra respectively.

Vidhu Vinod Chopra's second feature film, *Khamosh*, was a murder mystery unfolding during a film shoot in Pahalgam. Amol Palekar and Shabana Azmi were the lead stars in this typical masala film called *Aakhri Khoon*, which had a bathing scene, a rape, a suicide, promises of undying love between Niloufer and Vijaybabu, and bombastic dialogue. Some of the details were real (Shabana as the three-time National Award–winning actress) while some were not (Soni

On location for Aakhri Khoon

Razdan getting murdered). And some of them were deliciously self-referential. The director (played by Sadashiv Amrapurkar) kept repeating throughout the film, 'Arre, my next film *Shakuntala* will be a classic. This is just a thriller.' His screen name was Chandran. It could well have been Vidhu Vinod Chopra![2]

Hrishikesh Mukherjee's double-Amol, single-Utpal, mustachioed comedy—*Gol Maal*—had Deven Varma playing himself as the hero's friend. And when Amol Palekar landed up at the film studios to pick up a set of kurta–pajamas, there was a quick succession of filmi snippets. Amitabh Bachchan appeared as himself (shooting for *Jurmana*) and asked Deven Varma about the latter's films. Deven revealed that he was working for a 'mythological mystery suspense drama' called *Parvati Ka Pati Kaun?* In fact, the idea of twin brothers with and without a moustache came ostensibly from a film Deven was working in. Not to mention a series of filmi in-jokes about kurta sizes of various stars, long shooting times for films, and girl students seeking autographs (in uniforms straight out of *Guddi*)![3]

Behind-the-Scenes Alert: While on the subject of *Guddi*, we can doff a hat to the plethora of real films that were being made in that film. To bring Jaya Bhaduri face to face with the realism of the glamour factory, her uncle (Utpal Dutt) and hapless fiancé (Shamit Bhanja, in a role originally meant for Amitabh Bachchan) brought her to Bombay. As she met her idol Dharmendra, she saw the dust and grime of the studios where real-life

---

[2] Vidhu Vinod Chopra's next film was indeed a classic—*Parinda*.
[3] Both *Jurmana* and *Guddi* were also directed by Hrishikesh Mukherjee.

stars were shooting real-life films. Amitabh Bachchan (shooting for *Parwana*), Navin Nischol (shooting for *Nadaan*), Shatrughan Sinha and Vinod Khanna (shooting for *Mere Apne*), Dilip Kumar, Biswajeet and Mala Sinha (shooting for *Phir Kab Milogi*) were all seen making films within this film.

Luck By Chance, Zoya Akhtar's debut set in the film industry, had a long list of film stars in real and fictitious roles playing their parts in many films within the film.

The centrepiece of the film was a film called *Dil Ki Aag*, from which the lead Zafar Khan (Hrithik Roshan) dropped out and triggered off a chain of events that brought newcomer Vikram Jaisingh (Farhan Akhtar) into the limelight. The film was produced by industry veteran Romi Rolly (played with panache by Rishi Kapoor) whose flop-actor brother was making his directorial debut. The story of the film—a sister of the heroine murdered by the anti-hero—seemed very close to *Baazigar*, another film which made a newcomer a star and as the film's director proudly proclaimed, 'The original was a hit in the US!' On the other hand, Farhan's love interest and struggling actress Sona Mishra (Konkona Sen Sharma) was unable to break into the big league as the biggest film she had acted in was a B-grade potboiler—*Teer aur Talwar*, a poster of which hung from her wall.[4]

As the evocatively shot title sequence (featuring junior artistes and crew members) came to an end, we saw the director's name appear next to a film called *Kismet Talkies*. That was supposed to have been Zoya Akhtar's debut film's title!

In **Bollywood Calling**, Nagesh Kukunoor took a pointed look at the mainstream cinema of the country. Om Puri starred as the hapless producer—and then, reluctant director—of a typical multi-starrer masala mix called *Maut: The Death*. The title itself was a swipe at the craze for double-barrelled names in the industry. If the standard Bollywood formula of long-lost brothers growing up on opposite sides of the law was not enough, this film literally imported another complexity in the form of an American actor (since one of the brothers was born to a foreign mother!). Add to that a portly Navin Nischol playing a dacoit leader, the American actor having a terminal disease and the usual vagaries of tinsel town, and you don't worry about the film you are watching but about the film they are making in the film you are watching.

Antara Mali's tale in **Main Madhuri Dixit Banna Chahti Hoon** was the story of a million girls across the country who want to make it big in the film industry but don't know how.

---

[4] Some of the other posters visible in the film were decidedly tongue-in-cheek as they showed Sanjay Kapoor in Clint Eastwood–style films called *The Good, The Bad and The Worst* and *For a Few Rupees More!*

In a super-real atmosphere peopled by a film secretary (Govind Namdeo), wannabe heroes perpetually on the brink of stardom, and a sympathetic husband (played by scene-stealer Rajpal Yadav), Chutki's break came in the form of a title role in *Roshni*—in which she co-starred with Dev Anand, Anil Kapoor and Sachin Tendulkar(!), among others. Except that, the debut vehicle was a B-grade classic with duplicates of all the stars. And despite the derision of the city audience, the film ended on a note of hope—how Chutki's performance had been appreciated in this mess of a film, how the film had done very well in small centres and how more offers were coming in. The film also demonstrated the power of Madhuri Dixit as an icon of hope in the 1990s. After all, there isn't a film that says 'Main Amitabh Bachchan Banna Chahta Hoon'.

In Sudhir Mishra's **Khoya Khoya Chand**, the film industry of the 1950s came alive and we could identify hundreds of faces, traits, settings, words and music. The talented writer–director's (Shiney Ahuja) rise in the film industry and his tempestuous love affair with a heroine (Soha Ali Khan) evoked immediate comparisons with the lives of Guru Dutt and Waheeda Rehman. The slimy leading actor (Rajat Kapoor), the friendly assistant director (Vinay Pathak) and many other characters added to the authenticity. The film that was being made for an important part was *Ishq Aur Jung*, which opened with a majestic premiere at Regal Cinema. And the background of the industry ensured that there were many passing mentions of films and actors throughout.

Andaz Apna Apna kicked off its relentless laughathon with Amar (Aamir Khan) meeting Juhi Chawla, playing herself.[5] In the totally unreal sequence, Aamir appeared as a cyclist and gave a lift to the stranded actress. Within a blink, they were in love and Aamir was invited to her filmset as her 'special' guest. The film starred Govinda and seemed to be called *Pehra* (shown on the clapstick). It also seemed to have only one line of dialogue—'*Aa gale lag jaa*'—which was used by Govinda as a cue to hug Juhi, egged on by the director ('*Govinda, chipakke chipakke!*'). Again, the film packed in jokes about Shah Rukh's K-k-kiran, film stars' lack of punctuality and even one about Aamir's fussiness when it comes to choosing films.

Ram Gopal Varma set his first Hindi love story in Bollywood, where a chorus dancer—Mili Joshi—was suddenly catapulted into the starring role of a film due to two acts of providence. One, the country's biggest star—Raj Kamal (Jackie Shroff)—saw her dance like a dream on a beach. And two, the original heroine of the film married her chauffeur and retired. Walking the tightrope between reality and spoof, **Rangeela** was about the making of a film called

---

[5] During a stray discussion at the offices of Wah Wah Productions, there was a 'notice' of a forthcoming film, *Jungle Mein Oye Oye*, and Mehmood mentions a new film starring Prem (Salman Khan) called *Dracula Ki Mohabbat*. Deadly!

Rangeela—directed by Steven Kapoor (Gulshan Grover), whose competition was not Chopra or Mehra but Coppola and Spielberg. The stray dialogues seemed to indicate a love triangle, though no other actor was seen and only the hassled producer called PC (Avtar Gill) popped up to provide comic relief. There was also a tapori called Munna somewhere in the background who went about selling tickets to *Mr Bond* (also starring Raj Kamal) in 'black'.[6]

Sue McKinley's grandfather was a police officer in British India. His diary contained descriptions of Indian revolutionaries from the 1920s—Bhagat Singh, Chandrashekhar Azad, Ramprasad Bismil, Rajguru and Ashfaqullah Khan. The contents of that diary inspired Sue to quit her job at BBC London and come to India to make a documentary, *The Young Guns of India*.[7] To play the young revolutionaries, she roped in some frivolous Delhi University students, and her adventures while filming with them made for one hilarious story. While it was said to be a documentary, the supposed scenes from the film were dramatic recreations of the original events.

But the power of the scenes was so strong that as the shooting progressed, her actors could no longer remain detached and callous. They realized that the Indias of the present and of the 1920s were becoming alarmingly similar. As they saw the atrocities of the present day, their inner voices finally found the patriotic impulse that had inspired several past generations—*Rang De Basanti*.

HONOURABLE MENTION

While it is not a full-fledged film, we cannot exclude the segment from ***Bombay Talkies*** directed by Dibakar Banerjee. Based on a Satyajit Ray short story ('Potolbabu Filmstar'), it was the story of a passer-by who suddenly got recruited to play an 'extra' in a major film shoot starring Ranbir Kapoor. Nawazuddin Siddiqui played a stellar role as the drifter who decided to grab his two minutes of fame with both hands, confidence and conviction. The director of the 'film within the film' was never seen and only heard. It was Reema Kagti whose voice made an 'appearance' as the booming voice.

---

[6] *Blooper Alert*: In the poster of *Mr Bond*, the hero's name is written as Kishore ('In and As') though it is clearly referred to as Kamal's film. Incidentally, the producer's name was Jammu Patel—probably a play on Jhamu Sugandh, *Rangeela*'s producer.

[7] Incidentally, *The Young Guns of India* was the working title Rakeysh Omprakash Mehra and Kamlesh Pandey used when they were writing the first drafts of *Rang De Basanti*.

Inside Job: 11 Films Watched Inside Films

When Bollywood heroes and heroines are done with making films within films, they go to watch them. Sometimes the films they watch are picked up from real life and sometimes they are fictional.

In *Kala Bazar*, Dev Anand tried to make a quick buck by black-marketeering movie tickets. And the first movie that he scalped tickets for was the iconic blockbuster—*Mother India*. He got the idea when he passed a theatre playing *Do Ankhen Barah Haath* and heard blackmarketers continuously increase the price of tickets—starting with *sawaa ka do* and finally reaching *sawaa ka dus rupaiyah*. The entire plan of stealing to fund his capital requirements, recruiting helpers to smoothen the process of eventual scalping at the glittering premiere at Liberty Cinema were shown in detail. Even the reason for the easy sales was articulated by a waiting fan—'*Mehboob miyan ki phillum aur pehle din na dekhein?*' And as his sales happened, a procession of stars walked into the premiere. Pretty much all of Bollywood was there, except for Dev Anand.

In *Akayla*, Inspector Vijay Verma was at his wits' end. For a series of crimes, he had identified and arrested a dangerous criminal as the culprit, but every time, he managed to come up with an irrefutable alibi and walk free. To take his mind off the case, his girlfriend took him for a movie. It was *Seeta Aur Geeta*, coincidentally (or not) directed by the same director. Inspector Vijay was very excited by the daredevilry of the active twin though he grumbled that such things happened only in movies. Then a bulb lit up somewhere and he realized that his criminal was exactly like Ms Seeta and Ms Geeta: he had a twin. Talk about reel life imitating, well, reel life.

As the cons and counter-cons of *Bluffmaster* wound towards a conclusion, there was the small matter of exchanging Rs 3 crore of cash with some stolen jewellery. Abhishek Bachchan[1]

---

[1] Abhishek Bachchan is a great one for cinema hall rendezvous. In *Dhoom 2*, he met his mole—Sunehri—in a theatre showing the Pixar classic *Cars*. He didn't notice that his target—Mr A—was seated on the other side of his mole.

'killed' his partner Riteish Deshmukh and asked Nana Patekar to come to Maratha Mandir at 1 p.m. with the cash. As the suitcases changed hands in the dark, we realized it was *Shaan* that was playing. The trio of Amitabh–Shashi–Shatru were taking on Shaakaal in his den as the 'dead' Riteish Deshmukh landed up and 'killed' Abhishek—all the gunshots and groans getting muffled by the on-screen sounds. Two goofs can be pointed out in this scene:

1. Riteish Deshmukh asked for more cash and said that there was an hour left in the film, within which the money should be brought. This was clearly incorrect since the climax was on and it was a matter of a few minutes.
2. Maratha Mandir—for nearly the last 1,000 weeks—has been showing *Dilwale Dulhania Le Jayenge* at 11.30 a.m. They couldn't have reached the climax of *Shaan* at 1 p.m., when all this happened.

Late-night shows are a breeding ground for terrible things to happen. In *Ghar*, newly married couple Rekha and Vinod Mehra went for a late-night show of the Dharmendra-starrer *Loafer* (famous for the '*Aaj mausam bada beimaan hai*' song). When they were walking home after the show, a gang of goons attacked them—severely injuring the husband and abducting the wife. The wife's gang rape and the post-rape trauma formed the remainder of the movie.

> *Bonus Movie*: Even in **Shiva**, one of Nagarjuna's friends was attacked by goons when he was walking home after a movie show late at night.

Ram Gopal Varma created a morally ambiguous scene in **Satya** where his protagonist watched a movie with his girlfriend. When a police officer got to know of a dreaded gangster watching a movie, he wasted no time in swooping in and locking down the theatre. Satya was the underworld don who deserved to be arrested but the director manipulated the audience to feel strongly enough for him to wish his escape. As the trickle of people came out of the one unlocked door of the theatre, Satya engineered a devious ploy to get away, causing grievous harm to hundreds of people. Coincidentally or otherwise, the film that played during this escapade was J.P. Dutta's jingo-classic *Border*.

The film seems to have a jinx around it because it was also playing when a terrible fire raged through Delhi's Uphaar theatre (in 1997) and killed fifty-nine people.

Mohan Bhargav's return to his **Swades** was a full-fledged immersion into rural India including an open-air film show. The entire village turned up at the chowk as hand-operated projectors were cranked up and large white sheets were spread for a much-awaited spectacle. The film of the day was a Nasir Husain classic. *Pesh hai teen bhaiyon ke milne aur bichhadne ki saugaat, aaj ka cinema hai . . . Yaadon Ki Baaraat.* If we allow a bit of cheating, we can say that this is the second—and till date, last—time Aamir Khan and Shah Rukh Khan have appeared on screen together. SRK was the viewer when a kid Aamir (playing uncle Tariq's childhood version) was on the screen within the screen![2] The magic of Bollywood was aptly demonstrated as each scene was appreciated, cheered and whistled at by the audience. Eventually, a power cut played spoilsport and the truncated film show had to be replaced by a stargazing show conducted by the NASA scientist in the audience.

Faizal Khan (Nawazuddin Siddiqui) was the wasted son of dreaded gangster Sardar Khan (Manoj Bajpai). As he was growing up in a haze of charas and Bollywood-fuelled romanticism, the film which engulfed his consciousness was *Trishul.* Faizal was emotionally attached to the character of the illegitimate son—Amitabh Bachchan—watching it repeatedly and even crying at pivotal moments. He modelled himself after the Angry Young Man with the same hairstyle, similar sunglasses and mimicked Bachchan's gun-shooting style. In a moment of self-doubt, he did acknowledge that he may have become Shashi Kapoor instead but he rose beyond that to run the **Gangs of Wasseypur.**

Bonus Movies: Faizal's lady-love, Mohsina (Huma Qureshi) was a Bollywood buff too (aren't we all?) and had watched pretty much everything from **Dilwale Dulhania Le Jayenge** to **Rangeela**, though not **Karan Arjun.**

When four adolescent boys escape from their hostel at night to watch a film, their choice of director is not likely to be Shyam Benegal. It is more likely to be Kanti Shah—the Badshah of B in Bollywood. With cult classics like *Loha, Gunda* and *Phoolan Hasina Ramkali,* he is the darling of the hormonal masses. In **Udaan,** Rohan and his friends sneaked into *Angoor* (reverentially referred to as '*Kanti Shah Ke Angoor*' so that we don't confuse it with Gulzar's version). They were greeted by a bikini-clad woman prancing around on beach. She was introduced as Sapna, described as *jawani se bharpoor* and accompanied by supposedly sensuous moaning sounds. This visit to the cinema ended with the boys' discovery of their teacher in the same theatre (in a compromising position with a lady) and a subsequent

[2] The first (and 'real') time Aamir and SRK appeared on screen was for a guest appearance in the film *Pehla Nasha.* They were both part of Deepak Tijori's dream, who dreamt these stars would be cheering his ascendance on the Bollywood firmament.

expulsion from the school. True appreciation of cinematic brilliance is indeed rare in society.

In *Rockstar*, Nargis Fakhri escaped the confines of her home and St Stephen's College to watch a Hindi porn movie with Ranbir Kapoor. After creating an elaborate charade to get Nargis inside, they managed to catch a typical B-grade skin-fest called *Junglee Jawani* in a shady theatre called Amar Talkies. And for the rest of her life, Ranbir called Nargis by the same name. After *Rockstar* released, an actress called Ashika claimed that the scenes shown were actually from a movie called *Jungle Love*, of which she was the heroine. She threatened to sue the makers because she felt the homely image she had cultivated by acting in a family movie called *Jungle Love* was destroyed by Imtiaz Ali calling it *Junglee Jawani*.

In *Delhi Belly*, Vir Das got stood up by his girlfriend when they were about to watch a complete rockfest of a movie called *The Return of Disco Fighter*. This was obviously the much-awaited sequel of *Disco Fighter* ('He's a lover and a fighter' and 'Superhit of the Naughty '80s'), posters of which adorned his room. As he moped outside the theatre (PVR Rivoli), posters and cut-outs showed Aamir Khan in a hairy-chested, Lycra-encased, goggled avatar. He duly returned in the last scenes of the movie with a full-fledged item number and the dashing hero's signature line ('*Dil todoon haddi bhi, kung fu kheloon kabaddi bhi*').

Filmistaan was a wonderful film that was about the adventures of a film-crazy Indian assistant director (played brilliantly by Sharib Hashmi) who ended up getting kidnapped and hauled to Pakistan. At the Pakistani village where he was held hostage, pirated CDs ruled the roost and there was even an evening show of *Maine Pyar Kiya*. As Prem and Suman's love story unfolded, our hero conjured up a karaoke experience by mouthing each of the dialogues while being held prisoner by terrorists. Eventually, he was allowed to watch the climax and he saved the day in a way only a Bollywood buff can, thus earning the right to watch the next show—*Kuch Kuch Hota Hai*. And from his Pakistani fan club, he received the ultimate compliment: '*Tu toh chalta phirta Bombay Talkies hai!*'

HONOURABLE MENTION

Sometimes, it is not the movie but the poster. In *English Vinglish*, Sridevi went for a Hollywood film—*The Last Time I Saw Paris*—in the classical 1960s mould (starring Elizabeth Taylor) with her English class. The romantic pronouncements of the film paled when Sridevi walked out of the theatre and went past a row of posters in the lobby. The last poster was of a film starring Clark Gable and Ava Gardner. The name of the film was *Mogambo* and it was a lovely tribute to the erstwhile Miss Hawa Hawai.

OUTRAGE! 10 Movies That Offended People

Being multicultural has its pitfalls. Anything you say or do is likely to offend at least one of the country's many linguistic, regional or demographic groups. The outrage is almost always timed perfectly in the week before the release. With multiplexes booked and ad campaigns rolled out, the producers are a lot more malleable and willing to negotiate. I think we have reached a situation when there is almost a sense of anticlimax when a big movie releases without any chest-beating.[1]

When Mani Ratnam announced *Bombay,* the Shiv Sena objected to the title since the name of the metropolis was on its way to becoming Mumbai. This was justified by claiming that the film was set in a time when the city was indeed Bombay. Thus placated, Bal Thackeray demanded to preview the film as it had a character (played by Tinnu Anand) based on him. After the screening, Balasaheb demanded a change. But it was not because the character based on him was shown as inciting the riots. He objected to the character showing remorse towards the end. In a telling statement, Balasaheb explained that he was proud of what his party workers had done and he shouldn't be shown as being apologetic about it.

The irony of this situation wouldn't have been lost on Mani Ratnam though he chose to be pragmatic and made some minor changes to take out the 'remorse'.

Hindu pride was slighted by Deepa Mehta's *Fire* and there were several attacks on cinema halls showing the film. Bal Thackeray—and by extension, the Shiv Sena—was angry because the lesbian protagonists in the film were named after Hindu goddesses Sita and Radha and this apparently would hurt the sentiments of the millions of Hindus who worshipped them. He even claimed that there wouldn't have been any attacks if the characters were Muslim.

---

[1] The song '*Bhaag D.K. Bose*' from *Delhi Belly* was probably the biggest outrage-flop in recent times as not one Dilip Kumar or Deepak Kumar Bose sued the makers for outraging their modesty.

Despite winning several awards in international film festivals, *Fire* had a patchy release in India marred by violence, protests and counter-protests. It also marked Deepa Mehta as a 'controversial' film-maker among religious groups in India as her next film *Water* ran into trouble even before shooting could begin.[2]

The crowning glory of Govinda and Karisma Kapoor's innuendo-laden career came when Karisma burst out of every TV screen in the country crooning '*Sexy sexy sexy mujhe log bole*' (in Alisha Chinai's voice). This was from *Khuddar* (which came at the same time as other double-meaning behemoths like *Aankhen, Raja Babu, Dulaara*[3] et al). Whether Karisma's sexiness was undeniable or not, such frank admission in front of a general audience did not go down well with many moral guardian groups. After massive protests, outrage and discussions in Parliament, the word 'sexy' was changed to 'baby' before the release of the film (but after the 'sexy' version topped every chart it possibly could). While at it, one 'F.O.' in the song was also changed to 'N.O.'

Jo Bole So Nihaal—the familiar Sikh *jaikara*—became the title of a Sunny Deol movie. This deadly combination was seen as a record-smashing proposition in north India. As dialogue promos with Sunny *paaji* silencing American cops by screaming 'No if, no but . . . only Jatt' were all over the place, a protest erupted over the film's content and poster. The Shiromani Gurdwara Prabandhak Committee protested that scantily clad women next to the holy phrase on the film's posters offended the sensibilities of Sikhs. Other political and religious groups joined the fray claiming the use of a religious phrase for a commercial—and probably disreputable—venture to be patently wrong. The film's distributors in Punjab refused to release the film expecting trouble. To make matters worse, there were bomb blasts in a few theatres. If there was any will to exhibit or see this movie, the bomb blasts ended that and the movie made a quiet exit.

Bonus Outrage: There were also protests against the Akshay Kumar–starrer *Singh Is Kinng* for allegedly depicting Sikhs in bad light and even for showing Akshay as a Sikh with a trimmed beard. Disclaimers at the beginning and a scene in which Akshay expressed regret for trimming his beard managed to placate all concerned and the movie had a peaceful run.

---

[2] A detailed look at the travails of *Water* is available on page 279.

[3] For an analysis of Govinda's landmark attempt at playback singing in *Dulaara*, do check out page 397.

Before the release of *My Name Is Khan*, Shah Rukh Khan—as owner of Kolkata Knight Riders—supported the inclusion of Pakistani players in IPL and promptly earned the wrath of Bal 'Who Else' Thackeray. Demanding an apology and retraction, thousands of Shiv Sainiks laid siege on theatres. Simultaneously, armchair activism kicked in as celebrities tweeted their support for SRK and Karan Johar, pledging to see the movie in theatres. Millions of people 'protested' by watching the film and used the hashtag *#MyNameIs* to register their support. Eventually, Bal Thackeray withdrew his opposition to the release—albeit through a vitriolic editorial in *Saamna*—and the movie went on to become a huge box-office grosser.

Bonus Outrage: Just ahead of *Fanaa*, Aamir Khan showed his solidarity with Medha Patkar's Narmada Bachao Andolan. Protests erupted in Gujarat that threatened to block the release of *Fanaa* unless Aamir retracted his statement. There was tacit support from the administration as security agencies refused to guarantee the safety of cinegoers and the film did not release in the state—though there was no official ban on it.

The normally peaceful Catholics of India rose in protest when Shiney Ahuja played a priest in *Sins*. Instead of the benevolent paternal figures we were used to, Shiney turned out to be a lust-crazed psychopath who killed, raped, swore and turned into a bloody mess. The Jammu and Kashmir government banned it. The Minorities Commission asked for an 'explanation' from the Censor Board for passing it. Christian organizations protested in front of theatres. But to be fair, the protests were not violent and took the Catholic way of writing letters to the relevant authorities and observing sit-in dharnas. Thank God for some non-violent people!

Nobody knew the existence of an organization called Salon and Beauty Parlours Association till SRK—no stranger to controversy—announced the launch of *Billu Barber*. But then, the entire country got to know that they had serious objections to the word 'barber' and wanted the film to be renamed *Billu Hairdresser*. People everywhere fell off their chairs laughing but when they got up and looked at the posters carefully, the 'Barber' had indeed been dropped from the posters (in some cases, taped over) and the film was released simply as *Billu*.[4]

'There are some references to the city of Mumbai as "Bombay" in the film. If this hurts the sentiments of any member of the audience, it is completely unintentional and we unreservedly

---

[4] It was rumoured that following protests from Knight Riders all over the country, SRK would call his IPL team Kolkata but this turned out to be false.

apologize for the same. The city of Mumbai is an integral part of the film and respecting the sentiments of its residents and the society at large is our primary motive.'

Wake Up Sid opened with this ponderous disclaimer and there are no prizes for guessing which member(s) of the audience had hurt sentiments. This time, it was Junior Mr Thackeray—Raj of Maharashtra Navnirman Sena—who objected to the Bombay references and promptly disrupted screenings in Bombay—sorry, Mumbai—and Poona—sorry, Pune. Eager to inherit his uncle's rabble-rousing mantle, Raj forced producer Karan Johar to apologize (for his 'creative mistake') and insert the disclaimer during the first week.

Prakash Jha's *Aarakshan* was cleared by the Censor Board but it ran into an avalanche of protests even before its release. Without seeing the film, several political parties decided some dialogues and scenes were derogatory towards the backward classes. In anticipation of unrest, three states—Uttar Pradesh, Andhra Pradesh and Punjab—banned the release of the movie. While the makers offered to make changes and even appealed to the Supreme Court, only AP and Punjab lifted the ban and the movie did not open in UP—thus denting box-office collections in the crucial first week. Eventually, the Supreme Court lifted the ban even in Uttar Pradesh and everyone would have been quite surprised to see *Aarakshan* only had a backdrop of reservation and the plot was mainly about an idealistic teacher trying to reform the education system.

Dibakar Banerjee's *Shanghai* faced a hiccup just ahead of its release when one Tajinder Pal Singh Bagga,[5] president of Bhagat Singh Kranti Sena, filed a PIL to delete the song '*Bharat Mata ki jai*' from the film and ban the sale of audio CDs of the soundtrack. In his twenty-four-page petition, he noted that 'Bharat Mata has been presented in most humiliating, outraging and most insulting manner'. Naming the Ministry of Information and Broadcasting as Respondent No. 1 and the Central Board of Film Certification as Respondent No. 2, the petitioner prayed for the above action so as to 'restrain certain malicious people from bringing pride and honour of India into disrepute and disrespect'. The Delhi High Court rejected the petition and the film was released with the song, to much critical acclaim.

---

[5] Mr Bagga has a stellar career in outrage. He had assaulted senior lawyer Prashant Bhushan (part of Anna Hazare's team) in his office. He had also thrown a shoe at Hurriyat leader Syed Ali Shah Geelani, ironically shouting '*Bharat Mata ki jai*' while doing so.

17

Yes? No? Maybe?

Tum jo ho, woh tum nahin ho. Woh woh hai. Woh jo hai, woh woh nahin hai.
Woh tum ho. Tum jo ho, woh tum nahin ho. Woh jo hai, woh woh nahin hai.
Main jo hoon, main main hoon ya main bhi woh nahin hoon, jo main hoon?
                              —*Salman Khan in* **Andaz Apna Apna**

Often things in Bollywood are not what they seem. Directors don't only direct. Actors don't only act. Heroes sometimes become heroines. Gender is not what it seems. Some people exist only in two dimensions. Some exist only in our imagination. Even stars who are famous for one thing end up doing a lot of the other.

This section looks at people who are not what they seem.

Acting Talent: 10 Directors Who Have Acted

Ever since Hitchcock set a precedent of fleetingly appearing in his films, *hazaar* directors have followed suit. Putting oneself in a cameo in one's own directorial venture is the easiest act of vanity (and/or cost-saving) one can indulge in. The other obvious way a director has appeared in a film is by playing himself.[1] However, there have also been instances when an acclaimed director has been seen as an acting talent and given roles by others—making it interesting to decipher whether the decision was economic, creative, an act of flattery or just random!

Subhash Ghai has been the most faithful follower of the Hitchcockian credo. In each of his directorial attempts since **Hero**, he has popped up either mouthing inane lyrics or as a very visible part of the scenery. This must probably be a vicarious pleasure for him since the director was an acting graduate from FTII and started his career as an actor. He acted in six films including a film called **Gumrah**, where he was one of the lead players (along with Reena Roy and Danny Denzongpa). His biggest film remains **Aradhana**, where he played Prakash—Junior Rajesh Khanna's air force buddy who got to introduce the hero's second coming with a great line: 'Pehle Prakash aata hai, phir Suraj nikalta hai.' His rather uneventful acting career soon gave way to a very eventful directing career as he got his big break to direct **Kalicharan**— starring the boyfriend of his **Gumrah** co-star. He has never looked back since then.

Vijay Anand was the writer–director who could do no wrong. During the '60s, he directed, in succession, **Tere Ghar Ke Samne**, **Guide**, **Teesri Manzil** and **Jewel Thief** followed shortly by **Johny Mera Naam**—a very rare record. Apart from a few cameos in his own films, Vijay

---

[1] This is again fertile ground for appearances. **Luck By Chance**, for example, has cameos by Rajkumar Hirani and Karan Johar playing themselves. Karan Johar has also played himself in **Home Delivery**, where Viveik Oberoi's character was writing a script for him.

Anand acted as the lead in *Kora Kagaz* and *Main Tulsi Tere Aangan Ki*.[2] The first was a story about a crumbling marriage. The second was about his forced marriage despite having a son with a prostitute. His performances—especially in *Kora Kagaz*—were very good though he was overshadowed by his leading ladies in both films. Jaya Bhaduri and Nutan won Filmfare Awards for Best Actress for these two films.

Mahesh Manjrekar hit box-office gold with his Hindi directorial debut *Vaastav* and earned his acting chops with *Kaante* soon after. As the quirky Balli, he carved a niche among the bigger stars in the movie and both his careers have run simultaneously ever since. He has done meaty roles in several Salman Khan blockbusters—*Dabangg, Wanted* and *Bodyguard*. He has had two unusual 'husband' roles in Sanjay Gupta productions—*Musafir* and *Dus Kahaniyaan*— both of which had an element of cuckolding. With his stylized and exaggerated acting style, he might just be remembered more for his acting roles than for directing.

Farhan Akhtar started off as a director and his production company also made its mark for its offbeat but reasonably successful ventures. *Rock On!* was a buddy film with a difference. In this film about four band-members attempting a dysfunctional revival, the director (Abhishek Kapoor) wanted the lead actors to sing their own songs and approached Farhan to play the lead. After this, there was no looking back. He played lead roles in three major films after that—*Luck By Chance, Karthik Calling Karthik* and *Zindagi Na Milegi Dobara*—and they got him lots of favourable press. He then went on to play the title role in *Bhaag Milkha Bhaag* directed by Rakeysh Omprakash Mehra, which required a lot of physical and mental preparation and won him awards in truckloads. The critical and commercial success of the film was testimony to his growing stature as an actor and commercial clout as a star and his first film (as an actor) that he did not produce. Most recently, Farhan has played the lead in *Shaadi Ke Side Effects* and is looking even more dashing.[3]

Anurag Kashyap—after spending several angry years on the fringes of Bollywood—entered it gingerly as he got success and recognition. As his equity improved, he got noticed for his acting skills as well. He had a substantial role in Zoya Akhtar's *Luck By Chance*, where he played—with understated comic effect—a writer with 'arty' pretensions and 'commercial' compulsions. He was supposed to be the copier from a Hollywood DVD but his background

---

[2] Anybody wants to make a sequel—*Main Bharta Tere Baingan Ka*?

[3] Interestingly, Farhan also starred in *The Fakir of Venice*, an offbeat venture in which he played a conman who brings a fake fakir for an art installation in Venice. It did not get a major release in India but his performance was much appreciated in the festival circuit.

came through in a brilliant scene where he described a completely avant-garde, surreal climax for the masala film and was brought down to earth by the producer who called him 'Ay film institute...' Among his other roles, a difficult and extraordinary performance was in Onir's *I Am*, as a father who sexually abused his son. It was a chilling role and he drew on his childhood experiences to play it.

Bonus Brother: Abhinav Kashyap, director of **Dabangg** and Anurag's younger brother, has also done a small role in a big film. In Mani Ratnam's **Yuva**, he was the student activist who was beaten up by Lallan (Abhishek Bachchan) in a moving car and eventually reached the Assembly as one of the four young leaders.

Tigmanshu Dhulia as Ramadhir Singh, the don of Wasseypur

Tigmanshu Dhulia directed **Shagird** which had Anurag Kashyap playing a small role as a UP don, Bunty bhaiyya. The compliment was returned when Tigmanshu was recruited to act in **Gangs of Wasseypur**. His preparation as an actor probably started when he joined the National School of Drama. He played what Anurag Kashyap called the 'longest role in the film', a mafia don who aged fifty years during the course of the film and garnered gushing praise from all and sundry. As main villain Ramadhir Singh, he was the man whose blood three generations of Khans were lusting for.

That Rajkumar Santoshi acted in a short film called **Halo** is almost not known. Directed by acclaimed cinematographer Santosh Sivan, this was an experimental film about a little girl's attempt to find her missing dog called Halo. Rajkumar Santoshi played the little girl's affectionate father, a cute bald character who did his daughter's bidding and wanted to keep her happy. While the film never got a theatrical release, it did win the National Award for the Best Children's Film (in 1995).

Ashutosh Gowariker started his showbiz career as an actor. He acted in *Kachchi Dhoop*, a TV serial directed by Amol Palekar in which he co-starred with another future star, Bhagyashree.

Around the same time, he also did a small role in **Naam**—which made a star out of Sanjay Dutt—as a taxi-driver. In the late '80s to the early '90s, he acted in several small roles, of which two still stand out: he played second fiddle to Shah Rukh Khan in **Chamatkar** and **Kabhi Haan Kabhi Naa**. In the former, he was the crooked captain of the rival cricket team while in the latter, he was the bandana-wearing, no-nonsense leader of Windows, the band in which SRK played. In 1993, he got his break as a director (**Pehla Nasha**) and moved away from acting. Interestingly, his directorial debut had cameos by both Aamir Khan and Shah Rukh Khan, with whom he went on to make two huge films.

Sudhir Mishra was part of the initial batches of FTII, the first crusaders for meaningful cinema who collaborated with batchmates and colleagues to produce films they believed in. In this struggle, Sudhir Mishra ended up acting in—probably filling in—several small character roles in the mid-'80s. One of his larger and well-acted roles was in Vidhu Vinod Chopra's **Khamosh**, about a series of murders during a film shooting. As the laconic cinematographer with a menacing look, it seemed he wasn't up to any good. But then in a murder mystery, nobody seems to be up to any good! He did a bit part in **Jaane Bhi Do Yaaro** as well. Towards the later part of his career, he appeared in a largish role in Madhur Bhandarkar's **Traffic Signal**. He played a ganja-smoking mafia don, who was not shy of beating up bank officers who called on his number to offer home loans.

The feisty and firebrand Farah Khan made her acting debut under her own direction in **Om Shanti Om**, as a hot-headed extra who got into fisticuffs with SRK in the opening scene. She plunged headlong into acting with **Shirin Farhad Ki Toh Nikal Padi**, cast against Boman Irani. In Bela Bhansali Sehgal's directorial debut, she played a middle-aged Parsi woman with her usual chutzpah. The quirks and idiosyncrasies of the Parsi community got a new twist with her over-the-top acting style as she grappled with the idea of dating a forty-five-year-old lingerie salesman who insisted she didn't need a padded bra!

> *Bonus Farah*: Strictly speaking, Farah Khan's first screen appearance happened in the 1980s when she appeared as a backup dancer in a few films.
>
> She first choreographed a song for M.S. Sathyu's **Kahan Kahan Se Guzar Gaya** and got the assignment because the director lived in her building. Since the budget was very low, she became a backup dancer as well for the exotic song 'Kali mai, diya salai'.
>
> Talking of the exotic, Farah and Sajid Khan appeared in a song in Ramsay Brothers' **3D Saamri** with tons of mud on their face, coming out of a crypt! The dance was a copy of Michael Jackson's 'Thriller' and Bappi Lahiri sang the song.

Her other known appearance was in *Jalwa* where she danced behind Archana Puran Singh in the hit song '*Feeling hot hot hot*'.

Homework: Check out the songs on YouTube and identify Farah in them!

HONOURABLE MENTIONS

Before Rajkumar Hirani's first three directorial ventures broke box-office records in succession, he took baby steps from making trailers to doing other small jobs to becoming an editor. One of his earliest—if not his only—acting assignment was a television commercial for Fevicol. As two groups of burly men tried to pull apart a Fevicol-fixed joint, Rajkumar Hirani—sporting pitch-dark bushy hair and a moustache—happily egged them on and in his usual good-natured way explained the benefits of the adhesive ('*Yeh Fevicol ka mazboot jodh hai, tootega nahin*'). This obviously doesn't count as a movie appearance but you would agree it is too good to ignore.

Raju Hirani's producer deserves a mention for a minuscule—though not insignificant—part in *Jaane Bhi Do Yaaro*. Vinod Chopra (soon to append a Vidhu before his name) appeared in the iconic Mahabharata scene as—hold your breath—Duhshasan! He threw bombastic lines about outraging Draupadi's modesty and jumped about the stage in glee before he was unceremoniously replaced by a bespectacled Duhshasan (Ravi Baswani joining the fray)![4] And of course, in a nod towards his FTII friends, Kundan Shah named the two male leads Vinod Chopra and Sudhir Mishra.

---

[4] He followed up this stellar role with a deadly appearance in his own film—*Parinda*. For the opening scene in Anna's den, Vidhu Vinod Chopra played the corpse.

Music Makers: 10 Singing Stars

Kishore Kumar was the only star in Bollywood to totally blur the line between acting and singing, moving between screen and microphone with consummate ease. Apart from him, singing stars have been a bit of a novelty and usually a cause for breathless PR blitzes ('I did my own stunts') and great trivial value, if not always great musical value.

Ashok Kumar sang not out of commercial considerations but a technical one. He started acting when playback singing didn't exist and actors had to flex their vocal cords. So, there he was—perched on the branch beside Devika Rani—happily singing '*Main ban ka panchhi ban ke sang sang doloon re*' in **Achhut Kanya**. Even in his biggest hit movie, **Kismet**, he sang a very popular number ('*Dheere dheere aa re baadal*') in his own voice. One may now laugh at the nasal sing-song voice (largely due to the early recording systems), but Ashok Kumar was clearly a good singer because he continued to sing for himself even after playback singing became common. His biggest hit song was probably '*Rail gaadi*' from **Aashirwad**, the first rap song in Hindi. His tune and diction were quite brilliant in the fast-moving song, zipping between the million railway stations of India.

Amitabh Bachchan in a singing avatar in Silsila

There are some things that Amitabh Bachchan did with so much sincerity that they became popular. And then there are some things that he had to do because he was phenomenally popular, but he did them sincerely anyway. Playback singing probably falls in the second category; he started his singing career with *Mr Natwarlal* ('*Mere paas aao mere doston*'), which was at the peak of his stardom. The song—framed like a conversation with a group of kids—went on to become a huge hit and paved the way for more. Since then, the Big B has sung for many movies and music videos. He has sung a song with a parallel version by someone as accomplished as Lata Mangeshkar ('*Neela aasmaan so gaya*' in *Silsila*). He has sung Rabindra Sangeet for a film he didn't act in ('*Ekla chalo re*' in *Kahaani*). He has sung a song that has become an integral part of an Indian festival ('*Rang barse*' in *Silsila*). In short, he has been magnificent.

When an already successful heroine plays the title role of a Yash Chopra movie, the success becomes a foregone conclusion and people search for myths instead. *Chandni* was such a film and Sridevi was such an actress. Her legend increased manifold as she did pretty much everything in the film—from comedy to tragedy, from subtle emotion to hyperbolic melodrama, from dance to singing. She sang the title song of the film—'*Chandni o meri Chandni*'—with her customary exuberance and pre-empted all criticism of her singing talent with a mix of bubbly exclamations and measured singing. Lots of '*shona shona shona*' and '*bade woh ho*' were thrown about during the song to make it a reasonable success in a hugely successful album.

For better or for worse, the 1990s belonged to Govinda. Supported by David Dhawan, he took over Bollywood with his trademark mixture of bright (aka garish) costumes, exaggerated (aka uncouth) comedy and energetic (aka vulgar) choreography. You can also add playback singing to the list. Quite appropriately, Govinda's biggest hit in his own voice was a song that almost got buried in an avalanche of controversy. In *Dulaara*, he sang the landmark '*Meri pant bhi sexy*' and sent the moral police into whatever the opposite of orgasm is.[1] Govinda suggestively rubbed each part of his body as he declared each item of his clothing—including his handkerchief—to be wildly sexy. His tapori-style diction and slightly rasping voice proved to be perfect for this song (composed by Nikhil–Vinay) as he reduced even Alka Yagnik to a supporting singer in the song.

Tuneless Alert: Govinda has sung in several other films like *Aankhen*, *Haseena Maan Jaayegi*, etc. but none of these songs was as popular.

---

[1] It was reported that the Censor Board had suggested that the offending word be changed to 'fancy' but the movie released in its pristine glory and flopped soon afterwards.

The perfectionist Mr Khan flexed his vocal chords in *Ghulam*, by which time he had completely shifted to his 'method' style and worked on only one film at a time. As Mumbai tapori Sidhu putting line on an upmarket chick, he was supposed to be seriously out of his depth. Instead, he made her an offer she couldn't refuse and asked her out to Mumbai's most popular 'outing' destination—'*Aati kya Khandala?*' Under Jatin–Lalit's baton, Aamir offered Rani Mukherji chikki at Lonavla, photos at the ghats and even a trip to the 'otterfoll'. When the song became a huge hit, it started debates about the decline of poetry in Hindi film lyrics but then, what do you expect a tapori to say to his girlfriend—'*Tum aa gaye ho, noor aa gaya hai?*'[2]

When the Badshah of Bollywood sang his first song for *Josh*—sibling banter turned into a ditty—he brought into it a panache that took things to a level higher than what less fortunate people would have been able to. Aishwarya Rai on screen and Hema Sardesai off screen played foil to SRK's semi-rap style description of his romantic escapades—'*Apun bola tu meri laila*'—which would have been the perfect song for music director Anu Malik to sing, if not SRK! Peppering it with tons of *ae, re, la* and random faux–Goa lingo, SRK managed to support the visual slapstick with an aural one as well. SRK has occasionally done a few stray lines of dialogues within songs (in *Mohabbatein* and *Baadshah*, for example) but surely that doesn't qualify as singing. Evil people say even *Josh* doesn't qualify as singing, but . . .

Javed Akhtar's son wears many hats—scriptwriter, director, producer, actor . . . and singer. Strangely, despite his good looks, his first three avatars came a lot before the last two, though the latter ones are now threatening to overtake the first two. When Abhishek Kapoor wanted a lead actor who could sing for his rock-band-redux tale, his choice was—quite obviously, in hindsight—Farhan Akhtar. With his chiselled good looks and endearing lisp, Farhan just dug into the role of the corporate captain by day and rock vocalist by night. After *Rock On!* Farhan's subsequent films were not 'musical' enough or had only background vocals. Only in *Zindagi Na Milegi Dobara* was a song required in his own voice and Farhan duly obliged us with the superhit '*Senorita*'.

Hrithik Roshan, Bollywood's Greek god, made his singing debut in home production *Kites*, which sank with such speed that his singing sequence got lost in the flotsam. He followed it up with another number in *Guzaarish*, which made an even faster exit from the theatres and our minds. Indulgent uncle Rajesh Roshan, who composed for *Kites*, had only good things to say about his nephew. Hrithik was third-time-lucky in *Zindagi Na Milegi Dobara* where he surprised everybody with his rendition of '*Senorita*'. Since three major stars sang for the

---

[2] Yes, he can say that too. '*Tum aa gaye ho, Noor aa gaya hai . . . chalo, teenon milke Khandala chalte hain!*'

song—making it something of a rarity in Bollywood—the 'making of' video went viral and it transpired that Hrithik was asked to sing on the fly, without planning or reservation. Well, he *is* perfect then.

Since '*Senorita*' has been such a key part of this discussion, it would be churlish not to mention the third member of the singing party—Abhay Deol—about whom composer Shankar said, 'It adds to the character of the song because his voice sticks out.' Not like a sore thumb, if we may add.

Ever since technology rendered playback singing by the lead pair optional, it has become quite a rarity to have both the lead players of a movie sing. **London Paris New York** was such a rare movie in which both lead players Ali Zafar (also the music composer) and Aditi Rao Hydari sang. Ali Zafar, of course, is a composer–singer first and actor later but Aditi Rao Hydari became the unconventional voice in '*Woh dekhne mein*' and '*Thehri si zindagi*'. In the latter version, she brought out a 'demure' counterpoint to Ali Zafar's practised style while the first one was a solo female version—a little subdued but fresh nevertheless.

And the final name in the list has to be the one who is never wrong—Dong *jo kabhi wrong nahin hota*. In **Tahalka**, Amrish Puri was the slit-eyed, pigtailed, head-tattooed super-villain of Dongri La. His opening scene—also his singing debut—was an elaborate song-and-dance sequence in which he sang the number which has passed into seriously cult territory ever since—'*Shom shom shom shom shamo shasha*'. This is probably the only song with only one line (as above) repeated endlessly during its three-minute span. During the song, he played a shehnai-like instrument, a banjo, a sitar (like a guitar)[3] and his pigtail like an iktara—all this while dancing energetically with women in golden bustiers. Phew!

Bonus Kid on the Block: Ayushmann Khurrana made a super-successful acting and singing debut in **Vicky Donor**, winning a Filmfare award for Best Male Playback for his efforts. The slow, romantic '*Paani da rang*' was a tune he composed in college (along with friend Rochak Kohli) nearly a decade before it was finally seen on screen.

---

[3] A detailed study of the string instruments in Bollywood is available on page 230.

Under Cover: 11 Songs in Disguise

As the climax approaches (or a crisis is precipitated), there is a need to storm the villain's den. The Z-category security of the den can only be breached by outlandish costumes, nubile nymphets and foot-stomping music to divert attention. A very potent set-piece of the '80s and the '90s, songs in disguises brought a touch of the exotic and unpredictable to the mundane act of polishing off the villain.

Jewel Thief
Song: '*Honthon pe aisi baat*'
Objective: Stealing the crown jewels of the prince of Sikkim on 26 January, the day of his coronation.
Disguise: The world-famous jewel thief (despite having his pictures plastered across all newspapers in the country) simply put on a Sikkimese dress and hat. He was supported by a full-fledged dance troupe led by a lady (Vyjayanthimala) who was in love with him. But the disguise—or the lack of it—was redundant since it was a trap and the police had the place surrounded.

Kranti
Song: '*Chana jor garam*'
Objective: Storming a British fortress to rescue freedom fighters—Dilip Kumar and Manoj Kumar—who were already on the noose.
Disguise: Shatrughan Sinha and Hema Malini became two musically inclined chanasellers, who infiltrated the fort to drug the guards with their narcotic-laden chana. While Shatru put on a dhoti–kurta and a chanawala cap, Hema went in with no disguise. But then, with a shimmying midriff like hers, who's bothered about her face?

401

Desh Premee

Song: '*Gore nahin hum kaale sahi*'

Objective: Don (Prem Chopra—not a mafia don, that was his name) entered the country as the member of an African band called Santana. Amitabh Bachchan (son of the older AB) had been presumed dead and he needed a cover to return and expose his enemies. He became part of the band.

Disguise: In a supreme irony, Hema Malini—the fairest of them all—became a dark African with a proper Afro wig (though her skin retained an orangish hue) too. She was accompanied by Amitabh Bachchan and Prem Chopra (also in black make-up and wig) as the three of them did a rocking performance at a nightclub and nobody could figure out their real identity.

Shaan

Song: '*Yamma yamma*'

Objective: To consign Shaakaal's (Kulbhushan Kharbanda) evil island to the bottom of the ocean but after rescuing Raakhee from his clutches.

Disguise: None! Amitabh Bachchan, Shashi Kapoor, Parveen Babi and Bindiya Goswami put on a scintillating dance show so that Shatrughan Sinha could sneak in and execute Shaakaal's—well—execution. Shaakaal had been looking for them and yet there was no attempt to look different—except the heroines got into gypsy costumes. Needless to say, the baldy baddie identified them in a jiffy. He was only waiting for the song to get over.

Andhaa Kaanoon

Song: '*Ek taraf hum tum, ek taraf saare*'

Objective: For Rajinikanth to sing a cool song in his Hindi debut. What else? Okay, baba—it was all for killing Anthony D'Costa (Pran), a heinous villain responsible for murdering Rajini's father and raping his sister.

Disguise: The lead dancer and Rajini's lady-love (Reena Roy) was a dancer at Three Aces disco to start with. So, her shiny red costume wasn't really a disguise. Rajini wore a shiny black leather costume with a jazzy golden chest-piece though you could hardly see beyond his curly wig, French beard and cool goggles. Yes, you parched souls, yes. Rajini and goggles together in one sequence mean mayhem, without even counting his bloodshot eyes behind them.

Mr India

Song: '*Hawa Hawaii*'

Objective: Crime reporter Seema Soni (Sridevi) chanced upon a cross-connection on her boss's erratic phone. Local crime boss Daaga was inviting international don Mr Walcott to a devious tête-à-tête, to be accompanied by a dance performance by an international star.

Disguise: Sridevi sauntered into the party as dancing diva Miss Hawa Hawaii, wearing a fruity hat and an over-the-top demeanour. Since nobody had—very conveniently—seen how the original Miss Hawa Hawaii looked, her curvaceous body (most notably thunderous thighs[1]) was licence enough to make people believe her to be the 'item girl'. If there was any lingering doubt, her iconic performance removed it.

Mohra

Song: '*Tu cheez badi hai mast mast*'
Objective: Inspector Amar (assisted by his girlfriend Roma—Raveena Tandon) wanted to catch a drug smuggler (Tej Sapru) closing a deal at Queenside Club. Unknown to them, a vigilante (Sunil Shetty) was also planning to kill the smuggler.
Disguise: The ever-popular, super-flexible dancers! Akshay Kumar wore sunglasses (inside a nightclub in the evening), a bandana and a quasi-Arabian outfit while Raveena Tandon was in shimmering white clothing that did immense justice to her midriff. Paresh Rawal literally brought in colour by putting on black make-up (see inspiration above, **Desh Premee**) which came off at an opportune moment, rendering the entire exercise redundant.

Baazi

Song: '*Dole dole dil dole*'
Objective: Police officer Amar Damji (Aamir Khan) was on the run, after being falsely accused of murder and terrorism. To reach the people who framed him, he let out a bait about a club dancer called Julie Braganza who had proof of Amar Damji's innocence.
Disguise: When the villains landed up at Wicked Club (subtle!) to meet Julie Braganza, it was a fully made-up, fully waxed, fully endowed Aamir Khan who met them.[2] Strictly speaking, the song wasn't at the villain's den but he stormed the den right after the song.

Karan Arjun

Thanks to an elaborate reincarnation-cum-revenge-cum-love story plot, **Karan Arjun** was probably the only movie that had *two* songs in disguise.

Song 1: '*Gupchup gupchup*' which was about getting into the same charpai with the behnoi.
Objective: Make off with the arms cache that the villains (Amrish Puri, Ranjeet et al) were smuggling.

---

[1] The song's lyrics paid a tribute (intentional or otherwise) to the thunder and lightning of her thighs as Kavita Krishnamurthy crooned '*Bijli giraane main hoon aayee.*'

[2] For a detailed exposition on 'drag' appearances, turn to page 404.

Disguise: City tapori Mamta Kulkarni as Rajasthani dancer in ghagra–choli along with full supporting troupe and throaty Ila Arun-esque vocals. While the villains were enacting their wet dreams, SRK and Salman made off with the guns.

Song 2: '*Jai Maa Kali*', a disco hymn to the goddess.
Objective: Smuggle Kajol out of the clutches of her tyrannical father (Ranjeet), while they were doing a pre-nup prayer[3] at a cavernous Kali temple.
Disguise: Bare-chested and dhotis (for the heroes) with a bandana and army-style face markings. When Kajol's family stood up to complete their puja, she took one step back and merged with the dancers behind her (who were also in disguise, thoughtfully in exactly the same costume Kajol was dressed in).

Bade Miyan Chote Miyan
Song: '*Assi chutki nabbe taal, ragadke beeda mooh mein daal*'
Objective: Amitabh Bachchan and Govinda would sing, dance and feed the villains drugged *khaini* so that the police could attack and arrest them.
Disguise: None. Since logic has never been David Dhawan's forte, he got the two heroes to land up in their regular costumes. Their ploy of drugging the villains with khaini failed spectacularly as the villains saw through them and made them sing and dance till the late-arriving police saved the day. You could say they were male versions of Basanti!

Manmohan Desai Double Bill
The element of surprise in rescuing loved ones from the clutches of Amrish Puri (or Jeevan) plays an invaluable role and nobody does it better than Manmohan Desai.

In **Amar Akbar Anthony**, he put three different kinds of beards on his three male stars for the climax. Amar was a one-man band party. Akbar was a sherwani-clad elderly tailor. Anthony was a Catholic priest in a cassock. And the song truthfully claimed they were miracle-workers—'*Anhoni ko honi kar de . . .*'

In **Naseeb**, the suspension of disbelief was even more spectacular. There was a matador. There was a cossack. There was Charlie Chaplin. The three heroines seemed to have walked straight out of the Arabian Nights, a flamenco show and *My Fair Lady*. '*Rang jamaane aaye hain*', they declared, and delivered as per expectation. In a rotating restaurant atop a Bombay skyscraper, they did *udaao sabke hosh*.

---

[3] Yes, prayer. Not agreement. This is the centuries-old Indian culture. Jai Hind! Jai Maharashtra!

BLESSINGS IN DISGUISE

- Sridevi in *Mr India*: Charlie Chaplin. Ms Hawa Hawaii, the exotic dancer. Soldier in Mogambo's den. While the second one probably came naturally to Sridevi, she nevertheless pulled off a stunning act as Charlie in a gambling den.
- Kamal Haasan in *Chachi 420*: While he donned only one role, Kamal Haasan showed us the heights to which disguises can be taken. Clothes, body type, gait, facial features were all altered in an effort to change the film's young hero into a middle-aged aunty.
- Hrithik Roshan in *Dhoom 2*: Queen of England. An old janitor. A bandana-clad hipster. One of Snow White's seven dwarfs. Even a marble statue. Playing the ace thief, our hunky hero totally rocked the different looks that allowed him to clean out museums across the world.
- Vidya Balan in *Bobby Jasoos*: Beggar. Roadside astrologer. Office peon. Peer. Obese aunty. As a lady detective, our acting powerhouse used twelve different looks to chase her suspects all around Hyderabad.

Life's a Drag: 10 Drag Appearances

When the pioneering Phalke made his films, he didn't have a choice. Women were not allowed to perform in this newfangled thingamajig called bioscope and Dadasaheb's heroines were mostly—well—heroes. But since then, Bollywood has had strange notions of what constitutes entertainment and muscular he-men have appeared in ghagra–cholis and what not, revealing hairy midriffs and faux-cleavage. Ewww.

Most of the things Kishore Kumar did in **Half Ticket** had no logic. But all the things Kishore Kumar did in the movie were loads of fun. Including playing a gypsy girl where he sang a duet with *himself*. Kishore Kumar brought his brand of hysterical humour to this song, where he 'romanced' Pran (playing diamond smuggler Raja Babu), the same guy who was hunting for him to get back the diamonds he had hidden in Kishore's pocket. Kishore Kumar and Pran enacted the song ('*Aake seedhi lagi jaise dil pe*') and Kishore Kumar sang for both voices as only he could.[1]

As the name **Bluff Master** indicates, Shammi Kapoor—in the title role—played a whole lot of things that he wasn't. Including a female qawwali singer! Shammi—as Munni bai—heaved his bosom, arched his eyebrows and made coy gestures to match Saira Banu in the *nakhra* department. The audience in the packed auditorium seemed to lap up both the performances. The song ('*Oye chali chali kaise yeh hawa yeh chali*') was composed by Kalyanji–Anandji and the whole crazy caper was directed by Manmohan Desai (who was just sharpening his skills before he presented Dharmendra wearing skirts and Zeenat Aman wearing pants in **Dharam Veer**, though that wasn't a drag outing.)

Film-makers believe that the 'charms' of a drag song increase manifold if the hero is really manly

---

[1] For another example of Kishore-in-drag in **Half Ticket**, do check out the chapter on People in Pictures (Page 418).

in reality. There cannot be any other reason behind Dara Singh playing a woman in *Lootera*. He rubbed his silky smooth legs to create waves of lust among the assembled audience. Since the performance was happening aboard a ship, one can only assume that the sailors—having spent months sailing—had rather lenient standards for evaluating female pulchritude. His objective was to woo the sailors on the villains' ship along with a bevy of beauties (all of whom were burly men in drag) with the most out-of-place lyrics ('*Patli kamar nazuk umar*'). Eventually, the she-male army strangled the villainous sailors with their wigs as soon as the song finished.

Trivia Alert: Both the above songs were sung by Shamshad Begum, who seems to be a drag-song queen.

In *Rafoo Chakkar*, Rishi Kapoor and Paintal—two down-on-the-luck musicians—witnessed a murder and dressed up as girls to get attached to a girl's college excursion group. The plot was reminiscent of the Hollywood comedy *Some Like It Hot* and the two stars just lived it up—wooing the heroines as males and advising them on romantic affairs as females. Dev and Devi made alternate appearances throughout the film, embracing heroines and dodging villains. And also singing the hit song of the film—'*Chhuk chhuk chhak chhak, Bombay se Baroda tak*'.

Bonus Movie: In *Khiladi*, Akshay Kumar and Deepak Tijori became girls to hitch a ride on the girls' college bus and to become room-mates to Ayesha Jhulka and Sabeeha respectively. To complicate things, sports teacher Tinnu Anand—known to have a glad eye—promptly fell in love with Deepak Tijori.

An evil dictator presiding over an evil empire takes an Indian major's daughter hostage, challenging him to win her back within a year. To pull off this feat, the major puts together a team of crack commandos. To demonstrate the 'crackness' of the commandos, regular action films generally put up scenes of great daredevilry. *Tahalka* was not a regular action flick. To introduce the commando team—Javed Jaffrey, Aditya Pancholi and (horror of horrors) Naseeruddin Shah—the director put them in drag as they tried to hit on some girls. Naseeruddin Shah's legendary body of work stands insignificant in front of this hair-raising scene where he appeared in a swimsuit and a wig. Suffice it to say, the song is one of the many iconic set-pieces that separate a 'man-film' (pun not intended) like *Tahalka* from the boys.

In *Baazi*, Aamir Khan was a Special Branch officer but while on the trail of arms smugglers, he was framed for the murder and rape of the police commissioner's daughter (oh, no!) and sentenced to prison. When he escaped from prison to prove his innocence (oh, yes!), he was then falsely accused of the commissioner's murder (oh, no!). In a strange strategy (that makes perfect sense in Bollywood and none in the real world), he sent a letter from 'Julie Braganza' baiting that 'she' had the real story about the rape. In a nightclub with an Eiffel Tower replica, Aamir became Julie and wiggled his hips, flaunted smooth legs, waved permed hair and sang a song. And it didn't end with the song. The 'sexy' Julie was then presented for Deputy CM Chaubey's pleasure, who took great pains to strip the beauty—only to reveal the long nozzle. Of a gun. (Uffoh, I know what you were thinking, perverts!)

What Aamir can do, SRK can do too—probably better. In one role in *Duplicate*, he was dreaded gangster Mannu out to take revenge—in the most innovatively gruesome ways possible—on his rivals. To this end, he entered the apartment of Dhingra (played by Sharat Saxena) and performed a sexy striptease to the accompaniment of wine and whips before putting a bullet through his mouth. Shah Rukh's make-up was perfect as was the 'cleavage' though he put on an artificial skin on his legs to avoid the obviously painful exercise of waxing.

> *Bonus Movie*: In *Trimurti*, SRK was again a *gaon ki gori* (complete with pallu and nose ring) who sneaked into his girlfriend's house as a domestic help carrying a glass of milk and was soon coochie-cooing with her.

Kamal Haasan became *Chachi 420*—the father desperate enough to become a woman in order to spend time with his daughter. Kamal's CV already included playing a dwarf and a leper by then and he gleefully added Lakshmi Godbole, a Maharashtrian governess to it. As the Chachi, the legendary actor steered clear of the usual amateurishness of drag make-up and imported make-up artistes from Hollywood to become the woman his father-in-law (Amrish Puri) fell in love with. From the jowl on her face to the voluminous breasts to the traditionally worn saree, Kamal Haasan was a fully endowed woman in the movie. He was nominated for Best Actor in the Filmfare Awards. He would have probably won if he had been nominated as Best Actress.

> *Bonus Movies*: Talking of aunties, Govinda draped a garish pink saree in *Aunty No. 1* to become Kader Khan's object of affection. Govinda was a woman (a Singaporean nurse, to be specific) again in the climax of *Coolie No. 1*, where he fought the entire gang of villains in a grey sequined skirt.

Murdering in the guise of a woman is one thing. Stealing the British Queen's crown as a woman is quite another. In **Dhoom 2**, Hrithik Roshan was master thief Mr A. The film opened with him skydiving to land atop a train passing through the deserts of Namibia. We don't know why the British Royal family was passing through Namibia along with the crown but Mr A did manage to get into the high-security enclosure where the crown was kept, dressed as the Queen herself. The security guard ushered her in and Mr A was out in a jiffy with the crown in his backpack. Mr A pulled off a series of heists in the movie putting on mind-boggling get-ups, but for the sheer surprise value, the British Queen was probably the best of the lot.

And finally, the last entry on the list has to be the biggest star of Bollywood—Amitabh Bachchan—in the song that created excitement and controversy in equal measure. In Prakash Mehra's **Lawaaris**, the Big B played a series of 'wives' to the tune of a popular folk song—'*Mere angane mein tumhara kya kaam hai*'. As the song went from *moti, chhoti, lambi, kaali, gori*, Amitabh appeared in different types of grotesque costumes from saree to ghagra–choli to salwar–kameez. The song went on to become a massive hit though when it first played on screen, Jaya Bachchan was repulsed enough to walk out of the theatre. But the song also had such tremendous durability that for years on end, it was the song that drew maximum applause in Amitabh's international shows. And of course, when Amitabh Bachchan sang '*Jiski biwi chhoti*', he ran backstage to bring his own *chhoti naati biwi* to play her part in the sequence. She was never repulsed after that first time.[2]

Reverse Drag: Rani Mukherji as Veer Pratap Singh in Dil Bole Hadippa

---

[2] During the live shows, a new stanza was occasionally added to the song—'*Jiski biwi bhaengi, uska bhi bada naam hai*'. And the stanza ended with lyrics inspired by another popular film song: '*Kissi pe nigahen, kissi pe nishana / Kalyanji ko dekhe, Anandji deewana!*'

LGBT: 14 Instances of Alternative Sexuality

Bollywood has not received as much flak for anything as it has received for 'gay jokes'. And unlike other weaknesses—where they have tried to make amends—this one has gone on unabated, with stereotyping happening by the truckload. In the avalanche of crass humour, there have been occasional attempts at a serious/realistic portrayal but the propensity is still to sneak in a character with floppy hands and be done with it.

Lesbian

Deepa Mehta's *Fire* was probably the first film to openly depict a lesbian relationship, which unfolded between two sisters-in-law of a traditional Indian family. One of their husbands (Javed Jaffrey) was a philanderer while the other (Kulbhushan Kharbanda) was overtly religious, both eschewing marital sex. Shabana Azmi and Nandita Das were wonderfully real as the repressed women who sought each other's company for sexual intimacy. Needless to say, the film came under fire because lesbianism was said to be 'against Indian culture' and the cinematic value got forgotten in the chaos.

For every sensitive depiction of a lesbian relationship, there are ten titillatory ones. Fortunately (if you support Gay Pride) or unfortunately (if you are in an engineering college), this ratio has not happened in India. Most film-makers have steered clear of lesbian titillation, except for a select few. Karan Razdan made *Girlfriend* about a 'love triangle' in which one girl (Isha Koppikar) got ballistic when the other (Amrita Arora) got into a heterosexual relationship (with Ashish Chaudhary, who didn't know whether he was coming[1] or going). The guy was left peeping as the two girls put on some serious action. The movie ended with a slash-fest when Isha Koppikar attacked her lover and her lover's lover with sharp objects and a sharper tongue. Oh, I didn't mean tongue in that sense, you pervert!

---

[1] Pun intended.

410

Gay

To kick off the list of gay characters in Bollywood, we can start with one of the earliest—Pinku (Anupam Kher) in *Mast Kalandar*. Sporting a flaming pink mohawk, he had all the usual mannerisms that were to become the stereotype for gay roles in the future. While this was a full-fledged character, a bit part in *Sholay*—as a convict in Asrani's jail—is most likely to be Bollywood's first gay character.

The crime and punishment of being gay in India: Rahul Bose in Onir's I Am

Onir's *I Am* (as well as *My Brother Nikhil*) was one of the few realistic films on homosexuality. Rahul Bose played Omar in one of the four short films that made up the complete feature and it was an eerily real depiction of the harassment gay people routinely undergo in our country—at the hands of the police and society.

Reema Kagti's *Honeymoon Travels Pvt Ltd* brought together six disparate couples on a group honeymoon. Vikram Chatwal and Sandhya Mridul faced a strange dilemma when he turned out to be a closet homosexual and had agreed to marry a desi girl because he thought she would be docile enough not to make the news public. Sandhya Mridul, of course, was far from docile but she agreed to play along with him because the marriage accorded her freedom and affluence, which was an acceptable compromise for her.

> *Bonus Movies*: Madhur Bhandarkar started off with a realistic depiction of closet homosexuality in *Page 3* but when he made *Fashion*, he managed to exaggerate the realism with popular stereotypes and most of the gay characters became jokes.

In *Dostana*, Abhishek Bachchan and John Abraham pretended to be gay partners to get into a shared apartment with Priyanka Chopra. Immediately, all the floppy-handed mannerisms started as did the insinuation that homosexuality was somewhat perverse ('*Maa da laadla bigad gaya*'). After a movie full of jokes poked at homosexuals, the pièce de résistance was a climactic kiss between the two hunks—much to the amusement of people inside the movie and repulsion among those outside.[2]

> *Bonus Movie*: The most well-known Bollywood gay joke is, of course, Kantaben. Played by Sulbha Arya, she was Saif Ali Khan's domestic help in **Kal Ho Naa Ho** and was all scandalized at the hint of Saif's homosexual relationship with SRK.

The final movie with a gay theme is **Dunno Y Na Jaane Kyon**, known for its serious intent and absolutely hilarious execution. While the movie was shown at some gay film festivals, it received thunderous slaps from Indian critics and audiences as it became one of those so-bad-it's-good movies. A married businessman's affair with a male prostitute (while his wife slept with his brother and his mother slept with random men) turned out to be amateurish in all aspects, doing more harm than good to Indian gay cinema.

Bisexual

Naming **Razia Sultan** in this list is a controversial choice but it had to be done. The song '*Khwab ban kar koi aayega*' was picturized with a swan-headed boat in an indoor pool where Parveen Babi caressed Hema Malini's body with a huge pink feather. She interrupted the song to kiss Hema (hiding behind the aforementioned feather) as the oarswomen nudged and winked. While the lesbian undertones were clear, Hema was shown to be fantasizing about Dharmendra riding towards her on a horse as she drifted between male dreams when asleep and enjoying female attention when awake.

When the promos of **Dedh Ishqiya** began circulating, Huma Qureshi and Arshad Warsi's 'hot scenes' were the talk of the gossip columns. But when the film hit the theatres, the romance seemed to have shifted a little bit and it was Madhuri Dixit who walked into the sunset with Huma. With their intellectual and physical charms, the two actresses were just leading the two actors along in an elaborate con. In a pivotal scene, the two heroines giggled with and tickled each other as Babban and his Khalujaan looked on bemused.

---

[2] The hunks of **Dostana** merely pretended to be gay. In another Karan Johar production—**Student of the Year**—Rishi Kapoor played a gay college principal. This is probably the first instance where a mainstream Bollywood hero (though past his prime) has played a gay character. Karan Johar also directed a segment in **Bombay Talkies** where the lead character (Randeep Hooda) played a married man coming out of the closet and (sort of) accepting his sexuality.

Transvestite

Eunuchs are a common feature in boisterous song-and-dance sequences. '*Tayyab Ali pyar ka dushman*' from **Amar Akbar Anthony** started a trend that continued well into the '90s. Eunuchs with important roles are relatively fewer.

The most 'famous' eunuch of Bollywood was Maharani of **Sadak**. Sadashiv Amrapurkar gave a memorable performance as the brothel madam who would do anything to keep her girls in control. She led her army of goons, including the foreign 'side hero' (played by Gavin Packard), to heap untold misery on anyone who opposed her trafficking empire. Be it her shaving in a saree (*saree mein dadhi banana!*) or her sing-song threats or her heavy bangles with which she maimed Sanjay Dutt, she was eminently scary. The character was impactful enough for Filmfare to start a new category altogether—Best Villain—to give her (sorry, him) an award.

Mahesh Bhatt returned to the eunuch theme with a 'sensitive' story—**Tamanna**. In the movie, Pooja Bhatt was Tamanna who was rescued from a garbage dump by a eunuch (played by Paresh Rawal). Based on a true story, the movie looked at how the eunuch raised the girl and ensured a good education for her before Tamanna started hating her for being a eunuch. All of that was resolved with loads of sentiment before a subplot of Tamanna's real father emerged.

> *Clairvoyance Alert*: Mahesh Bhatt proved that he was way ahead of his time as the biological father of Tamanna was a politician, who refused to accept her for fear of a scandal. This movie predated the N.D. Tiwari case by nearly fifteen years.

Amol Palekar made **Daayra**, a story about the sexual exploitation of women in rural India. Sonali Kulkarni played a rape victim who was rescued and rehabilitated by a transvestite (played by Nirmal Pandey). The film made a strong statement about masculinity and gender in the context of sexual assault. The transvestite was capable of identifying with the victim's pain but was not able to protect her. The film did very well in the festival circuit and in something like a world record, Nirmal Pandey and Sonali Kulkarni were jointly awarded the Best Actress award at the Valenciennes Film Festival (1998).

Transformers: 10 Characters Who Changed Beyond Recognition

Very few film industries in the world run on adrenaline like Bollywood does. And one of the staple sources of hormone is the 'emergence' of the hero(ine). Wronged by humanity at large and Amrish Puri in particular, the hero decides to take up arms. A montage of shots shows him pumping iron/practising dance steps/running as if the devil was after him. Intercut by shots of the heroine feeding him juice/mother feeding him gajar ka halwa/coach feeding him *hausla*. Hallelujah—the He-man is born and the climax is precipitated.

A good-natured but socially inept person (aka geek) fell in love with an angel. For good measure, the person was old (I.S. Johar in **Shagird**), fat (Govinda in **Partner**) or a non-Marathi *manoos* in Mumbai (Amol Palekar in **Chhoti Si Baat**). He sought the help of a dude (also known as 'date doctor') who appreciated the deepness of the geek's love and coached him to dating heaven (read: action on first date). The coaches were radically different—from macho man (Salman Khan) to effeminate hero (Joy Mukherjee) to the indescribable Colonel Julius Nagendranath Wilfred Singh (Ashok Kumar). But the leading ladies were floored and romantic rivals were vanquished—except in **Shagird**, where the coach himself was the rival.

The world's most famous transformation story happened when a Cockney flower girl became a London socialite. *My Fair Lady* has been adapted a billion times, in a million languages. Basu Chatterjee directed **Manpasand**, the Hindi version where Dev Anand tried to make a lady out of Tina Munim—a loud-mouthed seller of neem *datuns* on Mumbai local trains. The '*Rain in Spain*' transformed into '*Charu Chandra ka chanchal chitwan*' as the desi Dr Higgins ran the whole gamut of training for Kamli—from gait to giggle, from etiquette to petticoat (sorry, dress sense). Needless to say, many complications arose when the woman thought the whole exercise was for true love while the man was just trying to win a bet with his friend. And do note how Tina Munim has transformed beyond the film as well . . .

A criminal wanted in eleven countries was killed. But the police officer in pursuit decided to keep that information a secret and infiltrated his gang with a lookalike. Thus was born the tale of *Don*. The lookalike was a street singer from eastern UP—with a liking for paan and gaan. The criminal, on the other hand, was a suave and ruthless rake who went from one-night stands to gunfights without batting an eyelid. The change took all of three minutes of screen time and involved watching some random footage that the police had shot of the international smuggler. This lack of homework was explained by giving the 'Don' a bout of amnesia when he went back to the gang. That way, the gangsters themselves trained their nemesis.

In *Yaarana*, a villager with a golden voice was discovered and experts unanimously agreed on his potential to become India's biggest singing star with Polydor, then India's snazziest music label. But in the glitzy world of showbiz, a country bumpkin needed twinkle-toes and starry vibes to complement the golden voice. To this end, Kishen the Villager was enrolled in language classes, etiquette classes and dance classes. Of course, mayhem ensued immediately afterwards. He gave the language teacher a tongue twister ('*kachcha paapad, pakka paapad*'), the etiquette guy a limb-twister and the fellow dancers a kick (literally) in the behind. Eventually, it took a beautiful instructor (Neetu Singh) and loads of senti speeches to kick-start the change. What a transformation it was then! Nowadays, we see it every year on Indian Idol.

After Ramlal Sharma won the super-prestigious interschool cycle race ages ago, nobody from Model School of Dehradun was good enough to win it back. Till Mr Sharma's two sons came along. When the elder one, Ratan, got into fisticuffs with the rich brats of Rajput College and was thrown off a cliff, it was the cue for the director's cousin, producer's nephew and Ratan's hitherto-good-for-nothing younger brother—Sanjaylal Sharma—to enter the race. And enter he did. With a training regime involving push-ups, weights and power-cycling, he was up and running in a jiffy. Ably assisted by his girlfriend, Anjali, Sanju trained hard, raced harder and in the sharpest cycle race this side of Tour de France, he pipped Rajput to win and, as they say, *Jo Jeeta Wohi Sikandar*.

In *Khoon Bhari Maang*, a gold-digger married a millionaire heiress—who was rather, ahem, plain-looking. He promptly pushed her off a boat into the jaws of a crocodile and returned happily to marry his moll. Except that Rekha had survived the sharks of Bollywood—and a crocodile was not going be the end of her. With a hideously chewed-up face, Rekha sold her diamonds and flew abroad to a plastic surgeon. She returned to India with a new face, newer make-up and such an attitude that her husband resumed wooing her in seven minutes!

Apparently, the good plastic surgeon managed to infuse some mutated genes during the operation because Rekha took over the climax of the film with leather jacket, stilettos and whips. Don't get naughty ideas. She used those to dump her hubby into the jaws of the aforementioned crocodile.

After a whole lot of solo transformations, it was the turn of an entire village. Thanks to the hotheaded Bhuvan, Champaner had no choice but to learn cricket and play a team of Englishmen in *Lagaan*. Not an easy task for people who had grown up on gilli-danda. Fortunately, a British coach was at hand and desperation made you do the strangest of things. Very soon, the elderly Ishwar Vaid was keeping wickets. The chicken farmer, Bhura, was snapping up balls instead of cocks(!). The ironsmith, Arjan, was wielding a bat in the same way he handled a sledgehammer. A handicapped, the scavenger Kachra was turning the ball square. And the village madman, Guran, was behaving like, well, Sreesanth. In probably the longest—but highly engaging—transformation shown in Hindi cinema, the ragtag team of eleven cricketers came together like a symphony, played like a dream and ended on such a high that, 150 years later, we are still to fall out of love with the game.

Most transformations in Bollywood happen so fast that they seem like magic. But they aren't. Except in *Koi Mil Gaya*. After his pregnant mother was caught in a freak road accident, Rohit had an abnormal birth and was a child with special needs. Having a slowly developing brain, he was the butt of all jokes—not least because of his sing-song voice. Basically, he was Hrithik Roshan As Never Seen Before. Enter an alien who could convert solar power into supernatural power. Add to that the guilt trip of being partially responsible for Rohit's abnormality and you had the translucent blue alien transforming the scrawny Rohit into a muscle-bound Mr Universe lookalike (aka Hrithik Roshan As We Know Him). Soon, he was slam-dunking basketballs, tearing shirts with his bulging biceps and singing songs with Preity Zinta.

Sequel Alert: He even went on to invent a time machine and father a superhero. Here's one transformation too big for one film to contain.

Om Shanti Om was about a grand plan to recreate the '70s in the present day, and that needed the audacity of India's biggest superstar—Om Kapoor aka OK! Looking for a girl who looked like yesteryear's star—Shantipriya—OK stumbled upon Sandy, a teenager from Bangalore with a predilection for blue hot pants and pink bubble gum. While the looks fitted to a T, the dialogue delivery did not. Nor did she fit into the elaborate costumes from the Golden Age of Bollywood. With the help of another yesteryear actress, Sandy went on to become Shanti with repeated costume changes, the blessings of many well-wishers and parroting that one line about the value of a pinch of vermilion that had the potential of making a heroine's career in Bollywood—'*Ek chutki sindoor ki keemat tum kya jaano, Ramesh Babu? Ishwar ka ashirwaad hota hai ek chutki sindoor. Suhagan ke sar ka taaj hota hai ek chutki sindoor.*'

In a transformation, one is a changee. The other is a changer—or coach—who brings it all about. Except, in **Karthik Calling Karthik**, the two were the same. A hard-working, highly intelligent doormat called Karthik changed into a smooth-talking, sharp-dressing rake called Karthik over one extended shopping session. All thanks to the counselling session provided by that confident dude on the phone with all the answers—who was also Karthik. Karthik called Karthik every night and gave handy hints on wooing long-legged lasses away from their boyfriends, convincing the boss to give hefty raises and bullying nasty neighbours into submission. The hero Karthik followed the coaching of the on-phone Karthik blindly—and the world was at his feet. He ignored only one teeny-weeny warning—don't tell anybody about this coaching. And you know what happens when people don't listen to coaches, don't you?

ACTORS WHO CHANGED IN REALITY

At various stages of their careers, actors have put themselves through regimes that have completely altered their looks (and our perception of them).

- *Arjun Kapoor, Sonam Kapoor*: As two hugely overweight kids, the Kapoor cousins went through rigorous diets and gym routines to look what they do now. Salman Khan was instrumental behind training Arjun and grooming him to become a star.
- *Shah Rukh Khan*: For **Om Shanti Om**, SRK developed 'six packs' which became India's most discussed body part for several weeks running up the film's release. It also started an unspoken war between the three Khans with Aamir following suit with a similar look (in Ghajini) and Salman sneering about having been-there-done-that.
- *Sanjay Dutt*: Bollywood's original bodybuilder was Sanjay Dutt who returned from drug rehab and sculpted a kickass physique for himself. He is said to have been the inspiration for several younger stars including Salman Khan.
- *Vidya Balan*: In stark contrast to the weight loss regimes heroines go through, Vidya Balan put on an astounding twelve kilos for her role in **The Dirty Picture**. Gorging on bananas, burgers and pasta, Vidya's—ahem—full figure brought the raunch that was required for the role.

Framed: 10 People Seen in Pictures

Often, the cast of a movie gathers in front of a photograph to pay homage to a departed soul. Sometimes, crime-fighters circulate pictures of criminals to identify them. And ever so rarely, a crime gets photographed and the game is afoot. It is often gratifying to take a closer look at the people in the pictures. Instead of the standard-issue 'father oil painting' that is part of every haveli film set, directors sometimes slip in a filmi 'Easter egg' that makes the search worth its while.

In *Half Ticket*, the super-quirky Kishore Kumar played himself, a kiddie version of himself and his own mother in the same manic comedy. When Kishore Kumar's father—disgusted with his monkeying around—threw him out of the house, he went to his mother's picture and complained bitterly against his father before bidding goodbye and leaving home. His mother in the picture—wearing a saree, a big bindi and a gentle smile—was none other than the comic genius himself.

Bonus Mother Photo: Dev Anand did several mind-blowing things in *Awwal Number* but if one has to choose a particularly iconic piece (and that's a difficult task, mind you), it has to be the choice of his mother in the film. As Dev Anand and Aditya Pancholi reminisced about their departed mother in one scene, her photo appeared in a meadow where they were hanging out and it was Cindy Crawford. Yes, Cindy Crawford—with a blue ribbon as garland. Wow. Just, wow!

Shakti Samanta's superhit *Kati Patang* traced the story of a young girl who fled from her own wedding and ended up impersonating a widow. The widow's in-laws welcomed her into their home and we got to see a few snatches of her late husband's photographs. As it turned out, they were of Sujit Kumar, the durable character actor who gained fame by driving the jeep while Rajesh Khanna sang '*Mere sapnon ki rani*'.[1] This was an interesting detail because usually such photographs have an unknown person scowling at us. Probably Shakti Samanta was very good friends with Sujit Kumar and used him to have a known face as the 'husband'.

Hrishikesh Mukherjee's *Gol Maal* ended in a car chase where Utpal Dutt was arrested for reckless driving. He was soon seated in the police station, dressed in a baniyan and pyjamas. In walked a clean-shaven senior police officer who immediately suspected him of having international criminal linkages—because of his impeccable English. (Example: '*You are not a police officer. You are a foolish officer.*') At this point, the police officer opened his drawer to find a picture of 'famous bandit, dacoit, murderer, smuggler, 420, Mr Pascal D'Costa'. The likeness was striking because the clean-shaven criminal (wearing a cap, cravat and cigarette) was Utpal Dutt himself.

Jaane Bhi Do Yaaro had two photographers in the lead and we had a Lifetime full of pictures. The photo that defined the course of the movie was one taken accidentally. The duo took a photograph of a performing monkey for a contest they wanted to enter. When they took a print in their studio, there was some action captured in a mirror the monkey was holding. Further enlargement revealed a murder. The photograph showed builder Tarneja (Pankaj Kapur) shooting someone as well as the outstretched arms of the falling victim (later revealed to be Satish Shah as Commissioner D'Mello) while his assistant (Satish Kaushik) looked on.

In Sai Paranjpye's *Katha*, we had a clerk (Naseeruddin Shah) diligently balancing the books while a conman (Farooque Shaikh) was suavely balancing his stories with people who matter. He fibbed his way into a high-flying job in the same company as a clerk and was soon invited to the boss's house parties. No sooner had he got there than he started romancing both the boss's wife and daughter. The daughter's role was played by Winnie Paranjpye and she showed him a picture of her late mother (the boss's first wife). The conman immediately complimented the daughter on her similarities with her mother and started flirting with her. He was not lying about the similarities. The lady in the (garlanded) picture was indeed Sai Paranjpye, Winnie's mother in real life.

In *Dilwale Dulhania Le Jayenge*, Raj Malhotra was the first person in the history of his college to have flunked. He was unsure how his father would take it but Dharamvir Malhotra

---

[1] Incidentally, the opening scenes of *Kati Patang* showed a wedding scene (from which Asha Parekh would flee) where the band was playing '*Mere sapnon ki rani*'.

('matric fail') was not your usual Bollywood dad. A self-made millionaire, he firmly believed a college degree was not going to make his son a billionaire and was rather proud that his son had continued the family tradition of failing. Popping a bottle of champagne, he took his son through a line-up of pictures of their ancestors—'*Mere pardada Diwan Brijnath, kabhi school nahin gaye. Mere dada Diwan Dwarkanath, chauthi fail. Mere pitaji aur tere dada, Diwan Pushkarnath, aathvi fail.*' And in the oil paintings, the ancestors looked exactly like Dharamvir Malhotra. They were all paintings of Anupam Kher in different retro looks.

Karan Johar is a much-confessed Yash Raj fan and much of his style is an extension of the YRF brand of film-making. In *Kabhi Khushi Kabhie Gham*, there was a situation very similar to the previous one. Like *DDLJ*, Amitabh Bachchan as Yashvardhan Raichand 'introduced' his father to his son (SRK) and repeated the Raichand family values (which, for the record, were significantly different from the Addams Family Values). The bearded gentleman in the picture, with a regal air and piercing gaze, was also Amitabh Bachchan.

Farah Khan's movies are compendia of in-jokes. You catch some of them in the first viewing and keep adding some on subsequent viewings. And you have to keep a sharp eye on the end credits. In *Om Shanti Om*, our hero (v1.0) had a very unheroic name—Om Prakash Makhija. With a name like that he had no hopes of making it to the big league, he complained to his mother, and said he wanted to change it. The mother—an accomplished junior artiste who missed stardom by a whisker[2]—was prone to overacting and screamed '*Nahiiin!*' Soon, she was standing in front of her late husband's picture and lamenting this blasphemy. On closer inspection (of the end credits, not the picture), one realized the moustachioed man in the picture was Nakul Kamte, the film's sound designer.

> *Bonus Father Photo*: Directors seem to get these ideas when Farah Khan is around. In *Shirin Farhad Ki Toh Nikal Padi*, we got fleeting glimpses of Boman Irani's father—an officer in uniform—in his b/w photo. The father was also Boman Irani.
>
> *Bonus Mother Photo*: Farah Khan also paid a tribute to her mother Menka Irani in *Om Shanti Om* by using one of her B&W pictures in a scene. (Menka, BTW, is the elder sister of Honey and Daisy Irani.)

---

[2] For the mother's filmi credentials, see the chapter 'Yo Yo: 10 Famous Casting Flip-flops' on page 276.

In *Kahaani*, Vidya Bagchi had just one photograph of her missing husband. With only that, she landed up in unknown Calcutta and started looking for him. The picture was a self-photo taken on the day of their wedding as the couple posed for the camera with a blindingly happy smile. Nobody had ever seen, known or heard of Mr Bagchi. His face resembled that of one Milan Damji, an employee of the National Data Centre, and the HR executive, Ms Agnes DeMello, remembered that after seeing the photo. But before she could convey her thoughts to Vidya, an insurance agent called Bob Biswas visited her. And the mystery of the man in the photograph remained unsolved. The actor who was Arnab Bagchi in the photograph is Indraneil Sengupta, a leading Bengali actor.

The most remarkable twist to the cliché of the dead-father-in-a-photograph could have only been given by an actor of the stature of Naseeruddin Shah in *Jaane Tu Ya Jaane Na*. As Amar Singh Rathore, he was Jai's (Imran Khan) dearly departed dad framed in a picture. From his perch on the wall, he was constantly bickering with his wife (played by Naseer's wife in real life, Ratna Pathak Shah) on the non-violent upbringing she was providing to a *Ranjhaur ke Rathore*. Fathers in Bollywood are comical or serious or angry or happy or dead. In this movie, he was all of them simultaneously . . . what a picture!

CHASING PICTURES

You see a person in a picture and not in real life. And then you find him.

- *Baazigar*: Ajay Sharma wooed Seema and then threw her off a roof, just before he was supposed to marry her. Then he started wooing Priya (Seema's sister) as Vicky Malhotra and soon got engaged to her as well. On the day of the engagement, Seema's friend from college—Anjali—bumped into Priya and found Vicky to be very familiar. She went back to her old photo albums to find 'Vicky' romancing Seema. She was about to reveal this to Priya when Vicky intercepted the call and landed up at her hotel room. And he wasn't going to let the offending photograph go out in the open.
- *Sarfarosh*: ACP Rathore was on a mission to stop the influx of illegal arms into the country. And when all clues dried up and witnesses got killed, he found the picture of a bar-girl that led him to the dance bar district of Mumbai. An estranged officer of the force—Inspector Salim—joined in the search and tapped his source in Sangam Bar. His source gave him a lead to—not the girl but—what they were looking for . . . the next link in the illegal arms chain. The bar-girl remained in the picture and went out of the movie.

Woh Kaun Tha? 8 Characters That Didn't Exist

Bollywood is littered with characters with larger-than-life screen presence, great dialogues, fantastic styling and super chemistry with co-stars. Basically, they have everything to make them memorable. And sometimes, they *are* nothing. They don't exist. Several memorable characters of Bollywood are figments of other characters' imagination.

SPOILER ALERT

The presence or absence of some of these characters is shrouded in mystery and they have an element of suspense in their revelation. Readers are hereby warned that this chapter may unveil part of the suspense.

Amar was the *Jewel Thief*—wanted all over India. Amar had six toes on his right foot. He got engaged in Gangtok to a beautiful woman called Shalu. He gave her a diamond-studded ring. He had mistresses all over. His friends called him Prince. He had an uncanny similarity to one Vinay and many people mistook Vinay for him. Vinay was the happy-go-lucky son of the police commissioner, who had an eye for gems. Shalu and her brother insisted that he was Amar. Only when he showed a five-toed right foot were they convinced otherwise. But Vinay's similarity to a wanted criminal meant that the police were soon looking for him while he had to look for Amar. He went on a chase from Mumbai to Pune to Calcutta to Gangtok to find him. But how do you find a person who doesn't exist? Or . . . does he?

The team of *Jewel Thief* came up with another crime caper, again with a guy who was nobody. Despite the unambiguous title—*Johny Mera Naam*—nobody was sure who Johny really was. The movie was about the two sons of a police officer who grew up on different sides of the law. Mohan (Pran) became a criminal while Sohan (Dev Anand) became a CID officer. In walked a petty thief called Johny who befriended a gangster in jail and was inducted to deliver some precious stones. He did so with the trademark style of Dev Anand and the ingenuity of Vijay Anand, soon becoming a gang member and befriending the beautiful Hema Malini. There were suspicions of crossing and double-crossing as people suspected the non-existence of Johny and they wanted to get the guy calling himself Johny talking.

In *Anand*, Rajesh Khanna was always trying to make friends by catching the friendly vibes transmitted by passing strangers on his 'antenna'. And he befriended strangers by giving them a friendly whack and calling them Murarilal. Murarilal and Anand supposedly went back a long way. Murarilal had taken Anand to Qutab Minar and '*beer pilake out kar diya tha*'. Most of Anand's victims could only mumble their confusion. Till Johnny Walker came along. He caught this icebreaker smoothly by becoming Murarilal and identifying Anand to be 'Jaichand'. He even poked fun at his inability to hold a drink ('*do hi peg mein Dilli chhod gaye?*') and described their friendship as chaddi-buddies ('*hum bachpan mein ek hi saath padha karte they*'). Murarilal and Jaichand were getting along nicely till Dr Bhaskar Banerjee came along and broke the spell. '*Iska naam Jaichand nahin, Anand hai.*' The prompt reply was, '*Main bhi Murarilal nahin, Isabhai hoon. Isabhai Suratwala.*'

Gol Maal had the best-known non-existent character in Bollywood—Lakshmanprasad Dashrathprasad Sharma, the clean-shaven 'younger brother' of Ramprasad Dashrathprasad Sharma. The brother was invented on the spur of the moment to save a job and his character traits were in brilliant contrast to the 'elder' brother. Firstly, he was the brash city slicker with a nickname (Lucky). He had varied interests from the India–Pakistan hockey Test match to Western music concerts by Asha Puthli. His talents (music) were diametrically opposite to his brother's (accountancy). But when you think about it, you realize Amol Palekar was a bloody good Bollywood hero because all these diverse traits, interests and talents actually resided in one person!

You stop by at a fair on your way back from office. You get into a ferris wheel with a very beautiful woman. When you are at the top, the ferris wheel gets stuck and you have to spend the entire night with the woman, high above the city (though you don't become a member of the mile high club). Question: What do you tell your wife when you get home? In *Aaj Ki Taaza Khabar*, Sunil (Kiran Kumar) was the man in a jam who placated his livid wife with the story of a fictitious friend called Champak Bhumia. Soon, the suspicious wife had written to Champak Bhumia, asking to meet him. Sunil convinced his friend Amit (played brilliantly by Asrani) to play Champak Bhumia. The fake Champak discharged his duties admirably till . . . till one more Champak Bhumia (Paintal) landed up.

Bonus Movie: In ***Anthony Kaun Hai***, Arshad Warsi played Champ who assumed the identity of Anthony Gonsalves, a shady blackmailer. The name Champ was the shortened version of Champak, probably a nod towards the original Champak Bhumia.

Double Bonus Movie: In ***Golmaal Returns***, Ajay Devgn unwittingly spent a (platonic) night with Celina Jaitley on her yacht. He too invented a friend called Anthony Gonsalves—a bloody popular name for shady characters—to placate his suspicious wife.

In ***Do Aur Do Paanch***, two conmen landed up in a boarding school to kidnap a millionaire's son. One of them assumed the cover of one Ram Singh, who was supposed to be the son of the principal's best friend. His problem was that the principal's daughter was the real Ram's childhood friend and was likely to ask questions he didn't know answers to. To solve this tricky problem, he invented a fictitious childhood friend called Suresh. In one brilliant scene, Amitabh totally flummoxed Parveen Babi with his invocation of this mysterious childhood friend. Suresh was a fat boy. Suresh was with Deepak in the USA. They used to take away Suresh's candies. Jimmy went with Suresh too. Suresh asked Ram not to write letters to others. Suresh's fiancée had her clothes stolen and she had to keep wearing the same clothes for sixteen days. So on and so forth.

'*Mukhtar Singh ka naam toh suna hoga tumne?*' Kallu used to tell stories of Mukhtar Singh—the dreaded goon who scared both the police and the public. When he passed through a busy market, the roads emptied. He was big—and bad—enough to collect taxes on behalf of the government. He asked Kallu to pay road tax because his long legs damaged roads more. Kallu, the daredevil that he was, flattened him in a jiffy. Then, he proceeded to dispatch Mukhtar Singh's deadly Alsatian with ease. But one street mongrel barked at Kallu to scare him to death and revealed the bag of salt you were supposed to take with his story. You see, Mukhtar Singh didn't exist. Kallu invented him to cook up stories and glorify himself. These stories went on till Kallu ran into Shahni Seth and transformed into ***Kaalia***.

He came from London to Calcutta for an IT project. He used to call his wife quite regularly for the first two weeks but then the calls stopped. The wife—nearly eight months pregnant—came to the city and started hunting for him with one photograph and some scraps of information. His family stayed near Thakurpukur. He studied in Kalagachhia Kailash Kamini High School. He stayed in room number 15 of Mona Lisa Guest House during his stay. While she was looking for him, many people wanted to stop her. And that included the deputy chief of the Intelligence Bureau as well as an insurance agent called Bob Biswas.

His wife called herself Vidya (pronounced Bidda in Calcutta) Venkatesan. His name was Arnab Bagchi but the strange thing was that he did not exist—not in any records, not in any memories, not in any nook or cranny of Calcutta. And that was the *Kahaani*. One minute . . . if he did not exist, where did the wife come from?

STARS WHO DIDN'T EXIST (IN CREDITS)

Bollywood is full of instances where people did things out of goodwill and they didn't receive any credit. These titbits are part of Bollywood folklore and never officially acknowledged.

- *R.D. Burman*: While S.D. Burman was officially the composer of *Aradhana*, he fell ill while working on the soundtrack. It is widely believed that his son and then assistant R.D. Burman took over and the songs 'Mere sapnon ki rani' and 'Kora kaagaz tha yeh man mera' were composed by Burman Jr. Seeing the younger composer's talent, Shakti Samanta officially took him on as composer for his next production—*Kati Patang*.
- *Rekha*: Rekha has often been the go-to person for dubbing of a variety of high-profile roles. In *Waaris*, heroine Smita Patil passed away just after the shooting was completed and her voice was dubbed by Rekha. Even Sridevi's voice in *Aakhree Raasta* was dubbed by Rekha because the South Indian actress had just started in Hindi films and her Hindi wasn't fluent enough.
- *Salim–Javed*: In *Baghban*, the two legendary writers unofficially came together because Amitabh Bachchan wanted his final speech to be written by Javed Akhtar. The writer obliged. Before Amitabh's speech, Salman Khan had to say a few lines too and he requested father Salim Khan to write for him. This writer also obliged and those two speeches remain Salim–Javed's last—though unofficial—partnership.

QS Cutie: 19 Early Films of Aamir Khan

Aamir Khan's first lead role, in **Qayamat Se Qayamat Tak**, quickly caught the imagination of teenage girls in the country. He was married by then but that information was kept under wraps to keep his lover-boy image alive.[1] One of his biggest contributions to Bollywood has been the fact that he brought the work ethic of doing one film at a time and immersing himself into it completely. However, before this 'method' period (which started in the mid-'90s), Aamir Khan had a 'mad' period when he did a series of delightfully crazy films that straddled the entire gamut of box-office performances (superhit to unmitigated disaster) and critical attention (deafening applause to pelting eggs).

Holi

This was Aamir's first film, made before **QSQT**. Directed by Ketan Mehta, it was the output of an FTII student workshop about a college hostel where things went from bad to worse as small issues around examinations and student brawls went out of hand. Aamir was one of the leaders of a gang of students and the film's cast included a plethora of stars (like Naseeruddin Shah, Om Puri, Deepti Naval) and future stars who went on to become Aamir's regular collaborators—Ashutosh Gowariker, Amole Gupte, Raj Zutshi. And as mentioned earlier, he was credited by his original name—Aamir Hussain—in the film.

Raakh

Aamir Khan's second release was a critical success and a box-office disaster. Aditya Bhattacharya (son of director Basu Bhattacharya) directed this gritty, dark film about a young man hunting down his girlfriend's rapists. Aamir played the young man, assisted by a cynical cop, played by

---

[1] His wife, Reena Dutt, appeared briefly in the '*Papa kehte hain*' song, as a giggling teenager at the college party. And the girl sitting next to her in the same song was Nuzhat, Imran Khan's mother and Aamir Khan's cousin.

Pankaj Kapur. Teenage girls, who went to see the chocolate-box hero of *QSQT*, were shocked to see him in this avatar and they quickly went out and warned their friends.

Love Love Love

The usual rich-girl–poor-boy formula paired the hot couple of Juhi and Aamir, but the film sank without a trace. Neither the music nor the treatment of the hackneyed plot could interest audiences. The standard act of the hero being upstaged at parties by the brash villain seemed to be a little too jaded by now. They even repeated Dalip Tahil in Aamir's dad's role from *QSQT* but it remained a Dud Dud Dud.

Jawani Zindabaad

Noble themes seldom make entertaining movies. But at least they are applauded for their stand. This one—on anti-dowry—got shafted both ways. It was too frivolous for an issue-based film and too serious to be an out-and-out entertainer. Farha starred opposite Aamir, Javed Jaffrey starred alongside and all of them contributed to the abominable wastage of celluloid.

Deewana Mujh Sa Nahin

Aamir Khan's first pairing with Madhuri Dixit and his first film wearing spectacles bombed spectacularly. He played a fashion photographer to Madhuri's supermodel character, following her devotedly in the total conviction that she would eventually realize that it was a match made in heaven while she remained blissfully unaware of his existence. A tremendously bad film later, all got settled in true filmi style.

Awwal Number

This is not an Aamir Khan film, actually. Any film which has Dev Anand cannot be anybody else's. One of the greatest films of the so-bad-that-it's-good genre, this cricket film had Aamir as Sunny, who made it to the Indian cricket team and took India to a last-ball victory in the last one-day match of a series we had already lost. In between, he romanced Ekta (a plump Dev Anand discovery). There was a gossip item that in a scene for which Aamir and Ekta had to roll on the ground, he passed out under Ekta's weight.

Tum Mere Ho

A snake film! Aamir was the son of a snake charmer and wore strange headgear made of cowries, waistcoats without anything under them and Juhi Chawla all over himself. *Ichhadhari nagin*, *kabila*, *inteqam*, *qurbani* and similar words of the genre were bandied about as Juhi died of snakebite and was revived, killing the audience in the process. Eventually the film did not survive either.

Dil

Just when his professional obituary was being written, Aamir appeared in this college romance opposite Madhuri Dixit. Their earlier flop did nothing to raise the expectations and neither did the non-entity director–producer. It must have been the lucky tree in Ooty around which the title song was shot that turned this film into a monster hit. The music was a super success, the loud comedy was appreciated in college campuses all over India and the Aamir–Madhuri pairing was feted as the Next Big Thing. They have never appeared in a film again together. Yet.

Dil Hai Ke Manta Nahin

Aamir Khan's fabled perfectionism started to show as Pooja Bhatt expressed concern in an interview that she thought he would go from cinema to cinema, seeing if the seats were okay and the ACs were working right! As Raghu Jaitley—the motormouthed reporter, Aamir did a competent job and the film was a runaway success. Nadeem–Shravan's music was hugely popular and the film was re-released with one song added later.

Afsana Pyar Ka

Aamir and the heroine studied in the same college. He irritated her and she challenged him to fight the college boxing champion. Aamir's honourable and valiant behaviour in the boxing ring caused a change of heart. Wait! This is the story of *Dil*. Well yes, but *APK* had the same story as well! This Aamir–Neelam starrer had at least one very good rain song ('*Tip tip tip tip baarish shuru ho gayee*') and a convoluted subplot about his estranged parents as well. But everybody had this feeling that they had seen the film already.

Isi Ka Naam Zindagi

A Bengali comedy *Banchharam-er Bagan* (Banchharam's Garden) was—for reasons beyond the limits of human comprehension—remade in Hindi. The zamindar's role was reprised by Shakti Kapoor, and Pran played the garden's owner. Aamir was his grandson, a role that was almost insignificant in the original Bengali version but expanded miraculously—and needlessly—in Hindi.

Daulat Ki Jung

Sometimes, Hindi film titles tell you the entire story of the film. This was one such title that made the entire star cast, music and direction of the film irrelevant. As per laws of the land, children of business rivals are not allowed to marry unless they endure eighteen reels of terrible pain. What was really unfortunate was that we had to endure the same agony.

Parampara

Yash Chopra's directional venture was a tri-generational saga starring Sunil Dutt, Vinod Khanna and Aamir Khan (as also Saif, as part of the third generation). '*Yeh shaadi nahin ho sakti*', '*Bhagwaan ko sakshi maan kar tumhe apna loonga*', '*Main tumhe jaidaad se bedakhal kar doonga*' and a million other familiar bombasts exploded as Aamir–Saif appeared towards the second half, while Vinod Khanna romanced Ramya and Ashwini Bhave for the most part of the film.

Jo Jeeta Wohi Sikandar

Riverdale came alive and Aamir Khan played the quintessential Archie to a brilliant soundtrack by Jatin–Lalit. Aamir—in his late twenties—played a schoolboy in white uniform but did not look too out of place. Director Mansoor Khan did an excellent job of getting the angst of the lower middle-class Model School against the rich, spoilt brats of Rajput School. Aamir's performance was overlooked by Filmfare which gave Anil Kapoor (for *Beta*, of all things) the prize. And that was the last time we saw Aamir at award functions.

Hum Hain Rahi Pyar Ke

Aamir Khan was credited for ghost-directing the film, which was officially directed by Mahesh Bhatt (then helming about half a dozen films simultaneously, some of which supposedly directed entirely over the phone). Since the film was produced by Aamir's father and Aamir was slowly developing an intellectual aura, it was unanimously decided that he be credited for the direction. Whoever directed the film did a competent job of making a nice comedy about Aamir's adventures with his nephews and niece, a murderous Sindhi creditor and a south Indian lover.

Andaz Apna Apna

In one of the most manic comedies ever, Aamir and Salman were paired for the first—and last—time as two wastrels out to marry heiress Raveena, where they also met her secretary Karishma. Raveena was played by Raveena Tandon and Karishma was played by Karisma Kapoor (or were they?). Mogambo ka bhatija, Vasco da Gama ki gun and a villain called Teja (who was a twin of Raveena's father) were all in the fray. Confused? Don't be. Leave your brains aside and die laughing.

Aatank Hi Aatank

The Godfather has spawned many copies, none of them probably as bad as this one. Aamir played Michael Corleone, who had to take a break from singing songs with Juhi Chawla to join the family business. Rajinikanth was thoroughly underutilized as Sonny and Pooja Bedi dropped in as the second lead. Aamir went around with an AK-47 from hotel to hotel, killing his enemies in elevators.

Baazi

Ashutosh Gowariker and Aamir Khan came together for the first time in this cops-and-terrorists tale, with a climax lifted straight out of *Die Hard*. Aamir Khan played Special Branch cop Amar Damji and took on several get-ups including that of Julie Braganza, she of silken thighs and cleavage! Heroine Mamta Kulkarni had an inconsequential role but rumours of an affair between the two of them surfaced during the making.

Akele Hum Akele Tum

A remake of *Kramer vs. Kramer*, Aamir Khan played a self-obsessed music composer ignoring his talented wife, Manisha Koirala. The couple fought for custody of their son and the ending was altered to suit Bolly sensibilities. The film had fantastic music (by Annu Malik) and even better digs at the contemporary music scene. Satish Shah played Gulbadan Kumar, owner of a music company, and there was a composer-duo (one short and paunchy and the other dapper and French-bearded) called Amar–Kaushik. Basically, the producers—Venus—took a major dig at their biggest competitors.

The other Aamir Khan release of 1995 was **Rangeela**, in which he delivered a fantastic performance, but his transformation to a moody perfectionist was complete. Ram Gopal Verma was so cheesed off with him that he said that the waiter in the famous hotel scene (*'AC chalu hai, sir'*) acted better than Aamir. Aamir himself had vowed never to work with actors like Salman Khan who did not share his perfectionist work ethic. By doing so, Aamir became a great actor and changed the way the film industry works but it is certainly less fun.

Nowadays, he restricts himself only to the most unusual projects, does some-great-some-record-shattering films, is a whiz at marketing his films and has become the voice of our conscience with *Satyameva Jayate*. He also speaks sonorously on the choice of his films and the importance of his craft. Maybe an intrepid film journalist should pin him down and ask him to explain the creative rationale behind '*Khambe jaisi khadi hai / Ladki hai ya chhadi hai*'.

AAMIR'S HAIR APPARENT

After Aamir chose to concentrate on one film at a time, he always immersed himself in the role—even changing physically to portray the character perfectly. And each character has that one tic or reason that makes it stick in our memories.

- *Lagaan – Once Upon a Time in India*: In order to portray the wide-eyed innocence of the nineteenth-century villager he was playing, Aamir used eyelash-curler to make his eyes look bigger and in line with Bhuvan's character. It was very subtly done and brought out the character's idealism perfectly.

- *Dil Chahta Hai*: This was the first film where Aamir's look started a trend, with his cool hair and goatee being imitated by all and sundry. The look was created by Avan Contractor, whose Bollywood debut created a stir and spawned many imitations.

- *The Rising: Ballad of Mangal Pandey*: Due to the long time the film took to make, this was Aamir's longest 'look' as he retained it for nearly two years. He even appeared in an ad campaign for Titan watches sporting his luxuriant moustache and flowing mane.

- *Taare Zameen Par*: The character Aamir played was adored by the children and that was not only for the freedom he gave his students but also for the cool gelled 'mohawk' hair style he sported. Again, a look created by Avan Contractor.

- *Ghajini*: This was Aamir got himself eight packs in answer to SRK's six for *Om Shanti Om*. The body was a result of a punishing gym routine and the haircut—a buzz cut with channels by Avan Contractor, again—an output of what the team envisaged how skull sutures look like after complicated brain surgeries.

- *3 Idiots*: After the 'built body' of Ghajini, Aamir lost a ton of weight to become a twenty-year-old engineering student. His wardrobe was all about light T-shirts and cargo pants, while his hair was practically short.

Nishabd: 10 Silent Scenes of Amitabh Bachchan

One of the mandatories of any list of Hindi film trivia is the story how Amitabh Bachchan was rejected in an audition for All India Radio. And also that one of his earlier mentors (Sunil Dutt) did not find the legendary voice attractive enough to give him a speaking part in **Reshma Aur Shera**. While his fabled baritone has always been a huge draw, there are some iconic scenes in which he did not use his magical voice. And said much more than what lesser mortals did with flared nostrils, bared biceps and haired chests.

Anand

As Anand Sehgal stood at the twilight of his life and sang the melancholic '*Kahin doorjab din dhal jaaye*', his host—Dr Bhaskar Banerjee—silently walked up the stairs, came up behind him and waited for the song to end. Despite the restraint and the measured body language, enough charisma seeped through for a nation to take note of the arrival of the next superstar. Not a very easy task, considering that it all happened when Rajesh Khanna was singing a massive hit.

Deewaar

Vijay Verma rose to the top of the Bombay underworld. And his mentor—Daavarsaab—handed over his chair to the heir. As an envious colleague watched in awe, Vijay Verma slowly circled the coveted chair, sat down with an air of finality and then plonked his feet on the table. The *lambi race ka ghoda* had finally come good.

Don

What do you notice when Helen is in a thigh-high slit skirt, dancing away? A lot, if the person she is trying to seduce is a smuggler wanted in eleven countries. The gangster did nothing beyond getting dressed in a green shirt and a green-and-white check blazer. The subdued lust, the arrogance, the imperious behaviour all shone through as he sauntered around. SRK did the same scene twenty-eight years later. Did he succeed? Well, as they said, '*Don ko pakadna mushkil hi nahin . . .*'

Kaala Patthar

Probably the angriest role of the Angry Young Man, this film had quite a few silent passages which spoke more than the entire filmography of Nana Patekar. One was a scene in which AB was confronted with a knife—and he walked up to the goon and gripped the knife at the blade. As the blood trickled through, the pain and the anger on his face was something only he can pull off. The second one was a sequence of one-upmanship instigated by the garrulous Shatrughan Sinha—who snatched away the light from his beedi. AB calmly went up to him, picked the beedi out of Shatrughan's mouth, lit his own, stubbed the other out and walked away.

Yaarana

Emily Post came to Ganga-kinare. Kisanwa was being groomed into superstar Kishan by Ram Sethi (a regular feature of many Amitabh Bachchan films). As Kishan failed spectacularly with the fork and knife in a comic mime sequence, he dared his teacher to do a physical equivalent of a tongue-twister. Slap your knees with both hands. Get your right hand to touch your left ear and left hand to touch your nose. Slap again. Get your left hand to touch your right ear and right hand to touch your nose. Repeat (till your nose turns red with ill-timed slaps). He did it so effortlessly—and just as effortlessly, we rolled in helpless laughter.

Satte Pe Satta

A dreaded criminal came out of jail and slowly shuffled towards a waiting car. He had salt-and-pepper hair, eerily light eyes, a gaunt face and the stoop of a burdened man. Also, he was supposed to be identical to a lively, happy man—seen in just the previous scene. Actors of today would probably starve themselves to achieve that lean and hungry look while the man did it in alternate shifts of shooting with a little help from undereye make-up, contact lenses and a whole lot of acting talent. And the menace that he exuded when he crouched out of the jail door was not something that comes out of rehearsals. It was pure magic.

Main Azaad Hoon

Azaad tried to bring about a compromise between sugar-mill workers and sugarcane farmers. Admittedly, a difficult task, it came about after a long meeting. And when the farmers asked him to address the gathering, he was too overcome with emotion to speak. He fought back tears, choked a little, smiled a little and raised his right fist in a well-known gesture of *inquilaab*! The crowd roared in approval.

Sholay

The widow of the Thakur household went around the balcony at sunset, lighting the lamps. A mercenary sat outside his cottage across the courtyard and played a haunting tune on his mouth organ. On-screen love has never been so understated, yet so eloquent. The legends abound . . . it was RD who played the mouth organ. The lighting of dusk was so delicate that it took a fortnight to shoot the scene. And the players on screen were as much in love in real life.

Ek Ajnabee

A retired armyman tried to exorcise the demons of his past. He drank heavily to shut out the brutal scenes in his memory. The eternal Hindi film cliché of a troubled man drowning his sorrows was given a soundless dimension as the man drank, cried, contemplated suicide, crumpled up in agony and exhausted himself at the end of it all. One of the longest silent scenes in recent times, any lesser actor would have ended up making it a yawn. He kept you on a gut-wrenching edge.

Shakti

A dreaded smuggler—Vijay—was released from jail for a short while to attend his mother's funeral. His fury at his adversaries' act slowly morphed into grief as he walked into the room and saw the dead body. He eventually knelt down in front of his estranged father and started weeping. The father and son held each other tightly and they kept weeping. Two of Hindi cinema's best actors didn't speak a word but said volumes.

Sarkar

HONOURABLE MENTIONS

This film was an ensemble of his moods—angry, amused, frustrated, relaxed, tired, energetic, devastated, victorious, benevolent—almost like the nine rasas, of which Ram Gopal Varma seems to have prepared a slideshow. No one scene stood out. Not one scene was forgettable either. And it all added up to a textbook on acting.

Amul's tribute to the baap of them all

INSPIRED BY: AMITABH BACHCHAN

While Rajinikanth seems to be the pinnacle of cinematic stardom, his journey towards divinity started with a series of films in the late 70s and early 80s, which were almost frame-by-frame copies of Amitabh Bachchan hits.

- *Billa*: **Don** (As SRK starred in a *Don* remake, Ajith starred as David Billa in the Tamil remake.)
- *Thee*: **Deewaar** (Lock, stock and badge copy including minor characters like Rahim Chacha.)
- *Mr Bharath*: **Trishul** (He even went to the villain's den in an ambulance.)
- *Maaveeran*: **Mard** (Dara Singh acted as the hero's father in the Tamil version as well.)
- *Velaikkaran*: **Namak Halaal** (Rajini-saar even did a Tamil reprise of the Vijay Merchant–Vijay Hazare monologue.)
- *Padikathavan*: **Khud-daar** (Taxi with human emotions, slimy younger brother . . . all there, scene for scene.)

QUIZ: DO YOU KNOW VIJAY?

Match the fifteen Vijays to the films in which they appeared in.

A	Aakhree Raasta	1	Vijay Verma
B	Aankhen	2	Vijay Verma
C	Agneepath	3	Vijay Verma
D	Akayla	4	Vijay Khanna
E	Bbuddah Hoga Terra Baap	5	Vijay Kumar
F	Deewaar	6	Vijay Kumar
G	Dostana	7	Vijay Kumar
H	Ek Rishta: The Bond of Love	8	Vijay Pal Singh
I	Ganga (Bhojpuri)	9	Vijay Shandelia
J	Kaala Patthar	10	Vijay Srivastava
K	Shaan	11	Vijay Dinanath Chavan
L	Shahenshah	12	Vijay Kapoor
M	Shakti	13	Vijay Singh Rajput
N	Trishul	14	Viju
O	Zanjeer	15	Thakur Vijay Singh

436

18

On Endings

Khel tumne shuru kiya hai. Vaada karta hoon khatam main karoonga.
—*Madan Puri in **Deewaar***

This section is about how things end.

Picture Abhi Baaki Hai: 16 Unusual 'The End's

And having writ moves on . . . and there is no END.
—Closing line from Yash Chopra's ***Waqt***

Indian cinegoers are programmed to jump up like a jack-in-the-box whenever a movie approaches some sort of resolution. Even before the entire cast gets in position for the mandatory family portrait, you have busy souls treading over toes and bumping into seats in their crazed desire to reach the parking lot before anyone else can get there. No Indian ever sees the 'The End' card, or at least, they try their best not to. If they do succeed, they miss out on some cool endings—which seem to be getting snazzier by the day and sometimes a little quirky even. Before the end card comes on, there is a lot to say—even if the story is over.

Message
Movies always ended with a 'The End' card—superimposed on hugging siblings, embracing lovers and crying parents. But film-makers try to give a complete closure . . . just in case you thought this was the interval and some explosive plot detail would be revealed later.

In the thriller ***Benaam***, the viewers were requested: 'Please don't reveal THE END' just as Om Prakash (in ***Chupke Chupke***) requested audiences—in his trademark style—not to reveal the plot.[1]

Shakti Samanta was a pioneer of this brand of last-minute commentary. After Rajesh Khanna (the son) lovingly hugged Sharmila Tagore (the mother) and touched her feet, we were allowed to leave with an end card which said—'***Aradhana** is complete*'. And when an elderly

---

[1] This request was started by Alfred Hitchcock himself when he requested *Psycho* audiences—'Please don't give away the ending. It's the only one we have.'

438

Rajesh Khanna half-smilingly–half-tearfully waved to Sharmila Tagore (and presumably his shining teeth were symbols of his undying love) we were informed—'*This is Amar Prem*'—as the frame froze.

Sometimes, the message is subtle—especially if the director wants to get a wee bit naughty. In *Seeta Aur Geeta*, the two Hema Malinis dispatched the villains with a mix of whips and tears and married the two leading men (Dharmendra and Sanjeev Kumar). There was a bit of tomfoolery with each of the two men almost getting into the bed of the wrong Hema. Once the confusion was settled, 'The End' came on screen within an inverted red triangle—the familiar symbol for family planning. Presumably, the director wanted to discourage their having twins to scotch the possibilities of sequels.

Symmetry

It would be interesting to mention two of Ramesh Sippy's films—*Sholay* and *Shakti*—for an interesting symmetry of their opening and closing scenes. In *Sholay*, the film opened with a train chugging into a station; a police officer got off and proceeded on a journey through the ravines to meet Thakur Baldev Singh. The film closed with a train—carrying the lead pair—chugging out of the same station as the Thakur saw it go off. Even in *Shakti*, the film opened with a 'toy train' entering a hill station and a grandson got off, welcomed by his grandfather. And in the closing scene, the same grandson went off by a similar train, seen off by his grandpa. Intentional? Coincidental?

Bloopers

A very popular concept for end credits all over the world is to show the shooting bloopers from the unused footage. Jackie Chan films are the most famous proponents of this since you sometimes don't realize the intricacy of the stunt till you see the set-up and the failed attempts. The super-popular (though slightly inexplicably so) *Golmaal* series directed by Rohit Shetty follows this format quite religiously. With their spinning cars, stunts atop ferris wheels and timed bum-kicks, it is imperative to know whether they got it right the first time or whether they landed on their bums.

Story Completion

Sometimes, the film ends on a high and there is a need—either for closure or for comic relief—to describe what the main characters went on to do.

In *Rock On!* the futures of the main characters were described through subtitles as a hauntingly beautiful song (about dreams coming true) played on. The band members of Magik and their spouses had started following their dreams and they rocked on.

Rab Ne Bana Di Jodi had a humorous photo album of Suri-ji and Taani-ji's Japanese honeymoon (won in a Sumo-wrestling championship, no less) with their gradually increasing intimacy. Starting with the kimono-clad couple in Japanese tea-rooms, the album ended with them in a bedroom scene just before the U-rated censor certificate could be challenged.

These two films had sure-shot happy endings and no 'spoiler alerts' were required. Ramesh Sharma's critically acclaimed *New Delhi Times* had probably the most damning story continuation but that cannot be revealed without spoiling the suspense.

Cast

Farah Khan has developed and—with three films—patented a completely innovative way of acknowledging the unsung members of her cast. In all her films, the cast and crew appear on screen with great fanfare, usually jiving to the tune of a hit song. In *Main Hoon Na*, the crew was at a fair dancing to the tune of '*Yeh fizaaein*'. In *Om Shanti Om*, they walked the red carpet for a glitzy premier—but with a twist. The spot boys arrived in a Merc while the director herself got off an auto (when the carpet itself was being rolled back). In *Tees Maar Khan*, one part of the crew was shown in the 'village' where the film was shot and the others were at the Oscar awards ceremony (where, presumably, the film won handsomely).

Song

The one draw that keeps the audience—or at least, some part of it—glued to the seats is a hit song while the credits roll.

Dibakar Banerjee has perfected this art of creating a huge musical draw with a rocking number to go with the end credits. In *Khosla Ka Ghosla*, it was '*Chak de phattey*' with the entire cast in a construction ensemble, trying to seal Anupam Kher in a wall á la Anarkali. In *Love Sex Aur Dhokha*, the title song—to the accompaniment of cast members in jazzy music video costumes—brought up the end.

This concept of having a music video during the credits is essentially a Hollywood concept, where the poor dears cannot have songs within the movie and place the biggest hit from the soundtrack in the end. This is becoming increasingly popular but one of the earliest Indian films to replicate this was Kaizad Gustad's *Bombay Boys*, which ended with a rap song by Javed Jaffrey, who enlightened us on the bhais of Mumbai with a music video he featured in as well. And the way he announced the song was reason enough for a lot of people to stop leaving: *Kyunki . . . abhi khatam nahin hua, ch*****!*

A music video by Loki Local to bring proceedings to an end

YASH CHOPRA (1932–2012)

When 'The End' of ***Jab Tak Hai Jaan*** came on, it was The End in more ways than one. The end credits of the film had a wonderful montage of Yash Chopra during its making, his passion and confidence oozing from every frame. The title of the film prophetically described his desire to work till the very end of his life and the montage was a befitting tribute to that. And the very last frame had him saying 'Action' before it dissolved into black: 'and he lives on . . . forever.'

End Mein Twist? 10 Last-scene Cameos

Kahaani mein twist is something Bollywood just cannot do without. And no twist can be better than the one that comes in the end. And no end twist worth its salt can be without a jaw-dropping appearance of a major star delivering the punchline. Bollywood directors and producers have always cashed in their brownie points to create this plot device, where a star lands up unannounced and blows our minds.

STATUTORY DECLARATION: Since this chapter is dealing with the last scenes of movies, spoilers are inevitable. Readers are expected to refer to the offer document before concluding the sale. Oh sorry—wrong warning.

Starring Sanjeev Kumar and Vidya Sinha, **Pati Patni Aur Woh** was an extramarital comedy—though scrubbed clean of any sexuality. In fact, there was no hint of sex with the other woman (Ranjeeta) as the 'unfaithful' husband was content taking her out to dinners and drives—giving the excuse of his wife's fictional illness. His standard prop was a set of medicine bottles, ostensibly for his wife's treatment. When the affair was discovered, there was embarrassment and contrition as the other woman tearfully exited. Just when we had heard enough lectures about man's ingrained waywardness, in walked the replacement secretary—Parveen Babi as Miss Neeta—in a stunning yellow dress. As she demurely walked in, Sanjeev Kumar just about managed to close his gaping mouth and solemnly pulled out some medicine bottles from the drawer.

In the 1980s, Amitabh Bachchan was *the* draw. You just had to have him in your film—one way or the other! Gul Anand, producer of frothy comedies like **Khatta Meetha** and **Chashme Buddoor**, shared a good rapport with the Big B and got him to do surprising cameos in both these films. The more dramatic one came in the climax of his least successful film—**Hero Hiralal**. At the end of the movie, Hero Hiralal (Naseeruddin Shah) had been christened

Mohabbat ka Maseeha and was about to kill himself in a widely publicized spectacle of death. Without dwelling on the logic of the film (or the lack thereof), let me jump to the point where the heroine Roopa (Sanjana Kapoor, in the Most Miscast Role in Bollywood History) had to reach the venue where her lover was being killed. And who better to save the day than our friendly neighbourhood superstar? Amitabh Bachchan arrived in a Mercedes (with the '*Main hoon Don*' music in the background) and took it upon himself to ensure a 'happy ending'. He got into the driver's seat himself and drove the heroine to her destination. And disappeared—though not before tying a handkerchief around his neck in the Hiralal style!

Kabhi Haan Kabhi Naa followed the swings in the fortunes of regular guy Sunil (SRK in a super-cute role) going about his life in Goa. As his poor academic record and significantly better musical talents see-sawed, so did his luck with sweetheart Anna (Suchitra Krishnamoorthi) and eventually it all ended with his gracious heartbreak. After being best man at Anna's wedding, Sunil sat despondent on a pavement when a new girl in town came up to him and asked for directions. As the camera first showed her legs and eventually her face, the audience was delighted to find Juhi Chawla. Within a minute, Sunil had picked up all her luggage, offered to walk her to her destination and explained the good luck behind spotting shooting stars. Just when we were getting a little sad about Sunil's 'no', in walked a 'yes' and allowed us to leave with a smile.

Deewana Mastana was a ping-pong match between Anil Kapoor and Govinda to win Juhi Chawla's hand. In the end, the lady asked both the gentlemen to arrive at the office of the 'Registarer of Marriage Court' (sic). When they both landed up in the full attire of a groom, they were sweetly introduced to one Mr Prem—played by Salman Khan. Salman was the secret lover of Juhi in the film and emerged in the very last scene to elope in his standard lover-boy-Prem image. Within a second, our two heroes were standing witness to the wedding in front of marriage registrar Kader Khan (the second cameo!) and watching the couple ride into the sunset. Hey—it was not over yet! Almost immediately, Raveena Tandon appeared in the horizon and our dynamic duo chased after her and the wooing routine started all over again.

Aamir Khan's loudest film—beating *Ishq* very narrowly, though—was **Mela**. A mid-'70s film (surprisingly made in the 1990s) kicked off when Aamir came across Twinkle Khanna in a semi-conscious state. The *dukhbhari dastaan* of her brother being killed by Daku Gujjar Singh was enough to melt Aamir's heart but not his partner Faisal's. But when a heroine falls in love with one hero and calls the other her brother, dacoits get blown away in the flood of emotions. And after an ear-shattering climax, we had the trio driving away in their truck when . . . when Aishwarya Rai literally fell from the heavens. Three shots of love-struck gazes later, we had

Faisal and Ash perched on the top of the truck as he fed her oranges and heard her *dukhbhari dastaan* while the title song brought about the end.

Within the first half of **Taxi No. 9211**, John Abraham had lost his entire fortune, his girlfriend and all his hopes—thanks to the eponymous cab and its ill-tempered driver. A combative second half later, he had managed to win back most of it except his girl. As he left his newfound mentor's home late in the night and the ladies in the audience had a niggling feeling of happiness at his single status, the dude banged his car into another.

And breaking all the hearts in the audience, we had Priyanka Chopra stepping out of the other car. After a brief altercation about the damages, the duo was batting eyelids and swaying foolishly as '*Chahiye thoda pyar, thoda pyar chahiye*' blared in the background. Priyanka Chopra was soon sharing her mobile number (left tantalizingly incomplete at 98200 5214) and setting the stage for more.

A love story between a chef and a radio jockey in Australia could have been a Hollywood rom-com but Yash Raj is nothing if it isn't cool! They put Saif Ali Khan and Preity Zinta in **Salaam Namaste** to first be enemies, then friends, then lovers, then live-in partners and finally parents. As the film veered towards the plot of the Hugh Grant–starrer *Nine Months*, the fluffy romance went out of the window and all the emotions of a pregnancy stepped in. Soon—in true Bolly-style, we had Preity going into labour and being rushed to the hospital. To complicate matters further, Tania Zaetta (Arshad Warsi's wife in the film) went into labour at the same time. And to reprise a role done by Robin Williams in *Nine Months*, in walked Dr Vijay Kumar, MD, DGO. Abhishek Bachchan put on bottle-bottom glasses and a bumbling style as he landed up to deliver the two babies in an operation theatre suffused with an air of mayhem![1]

> *Bonus Movie*: Abhishek Bachchan was seen right at the end of **Ek Ajnabee**, taking over from the ageing Amitabh Bachchan as the bodyguard of the little girl. Except that the little girl had also grown up to become Lara Dutta in a double-barrelled last-scene cameo.

Strictly speaking, this was not the very last scene of the film but then, Amitabh Bachchan—when inducted for a guest appearance—is usually someone with a lever in the climax. In the Shah

---

[1] This was not the only cameo in **Salaam Namaste**. Arshad Warsi's real-life wife (Maria Goretti) and son (Zeke) appeared in a bookshop which Saif visited. Preity Zinta's then real-life boyfriend, Ness Wadia, played a man reading a newspaper in a bus by which Preity travelled.

Rukh Khan–starrer *Paheli*, he was a cowherd who offered his services to solve the problem of identifying the real SRK. When the real SRK had left his village in search of a livelihood, a ghost had taken his place and won over everyone in the family. When the original SRK returned, nobody knew which was which. The unnamed cowherd brought in some of his folksy common sense and—in a test of wits between the two SRKs—managed to separate the real from the unreal.

Iqbal was about a deaf-and-mute boy's (Shreyas Talpade) quest to break into the India team as a fast bowler. Assisted by coach (Naseeruddin Shah) who had his own demons to fight and a spunky sister (Shweta Prasad), he burst on to the national cricket scene and in a very satisfying climax, took his state team (Andhra Pradesh) to victory in the Ranji Trophy and also secured a berth in the national team. On cue, India's most famous fast bowler turned up to congratulate this newbie. Kapil Dev has appeared in Hindi films every now and then but this was probably his most apt appearance, dispensing advice to a budding pacer. And also because Iqbal had nicknamed one of his buffaloes Kapil!

Though not his best work by far, Vishal Bhardwaj's *7 Khoon Maaf* had a fair degree of unpredictability. A Ruskin Bond short story ('Susanna's Seven Husbands') was expanded by the author to get a feature-length screenplay out of it. Priyanka Chopra's murderous spree with her six husbands was depicted in gory detail and in the closing scenes of the film, she was spotted with an old man in a bar. The old man was none other than Ruskin Bond himself and it seemed that he was scheduled to be the seventh victim. As it turned out, the author of the story—who holds all the strings, anyways—was not going to be an easy victim to dispatch and Susanna's seventh husband turned out to be one hell of guy!

QUIZ: NAAM TOH SUNA HOGA . . .

Actors have often played characters with the same name. Match the characters with the same name.

1	Ajit in *Yaadon Ki Baaraat*	A	Annu Kapoor in *Hum*
2	Ajit in *Zanjeer*	B	Goga Kapoor in *Coolie*
3	Amitabh Bachchan in *Jaadugar*	C	Kulbhushan Kharbanda in *Shaan*
4	Amitabh Bachchan in *Kaalia*	D	Mahesh Thakur in *Hum Saath Saath Hain*
5	Manoj Bajpayee in *Gangs of Wasseypur*	E	Paresh Rawal in *Sardar*
6	Nana Patekar in *Parinda*	F	Rajesh Khanna in *Roti*
7	Paresh Rawal in *Daud*	G	Ranveer Singh in *Band Baaja Baaraat*
8	Satyen Kappu in *Deewaar*	H	Rehman in *Chacha Bhatija*
9	Shah Rukh Khan in *Karan Arjun*	I	Suchitra Krishnamoorthi in *Kabhi Haan Kabhi Naa*
10	Shatrughan Sinha in *Kaala Patthar*	J	Vijayeta Pandit in *Love Story*
11	Sonam Kapoor in *Delhi 6*	K	Saurabh Shukla in *Satya*

ANSWERS

1 C Both the Salim–Javed villains were called Shaakaal. 2 H Again Salim–Javed characters, both called Teja. 3 B Goga was Goga Kapoor's default option and Big B's only foray. 4 K Before he became Kaalia, AB was Kallu Mama's namesake. 5 E Both were Sardars (Khan and Vallabh bhai Patel respectively). 6 I Mafia don and Goan teenager had a name in common—Anna. 7 J Ek villain aur ek heroine—both Pinky. 8 D The fallen union leader and the son-in-law of India's largest joint family were both Anand Babu. 9 A Arjun Singh, simple. 10 F Both were fugitives who tried to live—Mangal Singh. 11 G Curiously enough, they were both Bittu Sharma.

446

19

Unendings

Given Up for Dead for People Who Came Back
for More

*Meri maa kehti thi kahaani ke anth mein sab theek ho jaata hai. Aur agar theek
na ho, toh samajh kahaani khatam nahin hui.*

— *Fardeen Khan in* **Om Jai Jagdish**[1]

This section is about people who hadn't had enough.

---

[1] The more famous version of this quote is, of course, from **Om Shanti Om**, where Shah Rukh Khan announced
'*Picture abhi baaki hai . . .*'

Given Up for Dead: 10 People Who Came Back for More

For some dreams, one lifetime is not enough.
—Publicity line for ***Om Shanti Om***

Be it revenge or be it love, sometimes you have to come back from the dead to find your life's meaning. Botched-up murder attempts, wrong records, misunderstandings or plain good luck have given stars leases of life in Hindi movies and they have made the most of it by kicking ass—literally and figuratively.

The Wife, Her Boyfriend and/or Evil Accomplice

While it was not the first, it was still the original. And the title explained where the dead returned from—***Do Gaz Zameen Ke Neeche***. A rich 'scientist' was tricked into marriage by a seductress and then killed off by her accomplices—a *mama* and a paramour. They killed him on a sunny afternoon[1] and cremated him before throwing his remains into a river.[2] After the burial, the movie was overrun by a zombie who seemed to be the scientist coming back from the dead. Soon, it became a crazed blood-fest of the villain's attempts to kill the zombie and all of that coming to nought. In Ramsay horror flicks, the ghost is the evil spirit, neutralized by scantily clad heroines with crucifixes nestled in their cleavage or by muscular heroes with hefty trishuls. Here, the villains were fighting a zombie. Oh—and it wouldn't spoil the suspense if I say the 'scientist' was conducting experiments to raise the dead.

---

[1] Sigh. The Ramsay Brothers don't even know what sun is. They killed him on a rainy night.
[2] Bwahaha. Read the title again, pardner.

In *Sabse Bada Khiladi*, Mamta Kulkarni was in love with city slicker Mohnish Behl. Her millionaire father died, stipulating in his will that she would have to marry a country bumpkin (Akshay Kumar) to get her inheritance. Divorce not being an option, they decided to kill him. The poison was administered via a venomous apple, passed into Akshay's mouth during a passionate kiss by Mamta. Nothing happened to her while Akshay dropped dead almost instantaneously. They hid him in a freezer, from which he jumped out and had to be stuffed back in again. And just when they had finally disposed of the dead body (which involved bribing a cop—Gulshan Grover), a cop Akshay Kumar turned up. As cop Akshay started chasing the villains, bumpkin Akshay popped out from every nook and corner where Mohnish and Mamata went. Do you know what happens when villains see constant visions of their murder victim? Yes, they confess to their crimes.

In *Do Anjaane*, a critically wounded man was found on the railway tracks; he also had amnesia. A rich family adopted him. Several years passed before he had another accident and remembered his past life. He was Amit Roy, whose wife Rekha wanted to act in movies as a shady 'friend' (Prem Chopra) egged her on. During a train journey, the shady friend pushed Amit off the train and convinced Rekha that he had accidentally fallen off. Before you could say Bhanurekha Ganeshan, Rekha had entered the film industry, acted in a hit movie and become a major star of the Bengali film industry. Amit now returned as a Punjabi producer who wanted to make a movie based on his story—with Rekha in the lead. The story turned out to be about a man, his ambitious wife and their shady friend. Amitabh used this plot to make his wife repent, his shady friend regret and also reunite with his ten-year-old son. Not bad for a dead man.

Evil Husbands and their Magnificent Machinations

By the way, husbands are evil too. Husband (Kabir Bedi) threw ugly, rich wife (Rekha) into the jaws of a crocodile. Crocodile chewed off half her face. Husband claimed the inheritance. But the lack of a dead body meant he had to wait for seven years for the fortune. Lack of a dead body also meant rich wife was not dead and on her way to a plastic surgeon (Tom Alter). She got an altered (heh heh) face and a killer attitude before she came back to Bombay for vengeance. This was the story of *Khoon Bhari Maang*. Before she extracted revenge, she offered glimpses of herself to the husband and her children. The husband was so horny to see this new sex bomb that he fell for her hook, line and sinker. The children were more perceptive and when they saw her, they seemed to remember their 'dead' mother. Of course, the climax was a suitably bloody and gory battle between Rekha and Kabir Bedi—with the crocodile also weighing in, this time on Rekha's side.

Bonus Trivia: When Rekha returned to Bombay after her plastic surgery, she got into a cab and gave her home address as '10th Road, Juhu Vile Parle Scheme'. The most famous house on that road is called Prateeksha.

When *Sleeping with the Enemy* became a monster hit in the USA, the world fell in love with Julia Roberts all over again and Indian film-makers fell in love with the plot. As many as three films (with major stars) released almost simultaneously around 1995–96. In *Agnisakshi*, *Yaraana* and *Daraar*, Manisha Koirala, Madhuri Dixit and Juhi Chawla faked their own deaths to escape from the clutches of an abusive husband (Nana Patekar, Raj Babbar and Arbaaz Khan respectively) and found love in the arms of a sweet guy (Jackie Shroff, Rishi Kapoor and Rishi Kapoor again respectively). The deaths were close to the original (off a yacht in *Daraar*), very different from the original (a car accident in *Yaraana*) and a mix of the two (car falling into a river in *Agnisakshi*). The directors—Partho Ghosh, David Dhawan and Abbas–Mustan—managed to string in several hit songs, idiosyncrasies of the stars (think Nana Patekar's deadpan style, Arbaaz Khan's wooden delivery) and a lot of *bhartiya naari* sentiments to conjure up movies that were very similar to the original and yet nothing like it.

Mistaken Identity

Pyaasa was the classic tragedy about an unsung poet, Vijay. His poetry was rejected by publishers. His brothers threw him out of their house. Only a prostitute and a *tel maalishwala* understood him. Out on one of his aimless roams across the city, he gave away his coat to a beggar who then came under a train. Since the face was badly mutilated, everybody recognized the coat and assumed Vijay to be dead. And bingo—his brilliant poetry found recognition. His publisher claimed credit. His brothers claimed royalties. Everybody claimed a piece of the poet's pie, while Vijay was himself consigned to a mental asylum—unaware of his fame. When he managed to escape, he lost his sense of balance and became cannon fodder for his adversaries. You can get a sense of his existentialist angst when he arrived at his own 'memorial' service and then lamented, '*Yeh duniya agar mil bhi jaaye toh kya hai . . .*' *Abbe, duniya nahin chahiye toh wapas kyun aaya?*

Dharmendra was released from Nasik Central Jail, where he had been imprisoned for embezzling his bank. He got into a train but a pickpocket stole his prison papers and money. While escaping, the thief came under the train and died. He was identified by Dharmendra's papers in his pocket and thus started the saga of *Jeevan Mrityu*. His second coming was dedicated to taking revenge on the people who framed him. After his 'official' death, his honesty and intelligence helped him become a millionaire's second-in-command. And with the millions at his command, he came back—as a Sikh, Bikram Singh. He took apart the businesses and lives of the three villains, reunited with his girlfriend (Raakhee) and even played Cupid to his assistant.

Twist in the Love Story

The multi-country love triangle—*Sangam*—was about Raj Kapoor's obsessive love for Vyjayanthimala and her soft corner for Rajendra Kumar, which was subtly reciprocated. But since Raj professed his love for Vyjayanthimala to Rajendra first, the latter decided to exit honourably. Complications arose when Raj—an air force pilot—was assigned to the front and his plane was shot down. Presuming him to be dead, Rajendra Kumar and Vyjayanthimala rekindled their romance and were about to marry when Raj returned. The movie took the predestined Bollywood formula of the heroine reverting to the original lover in the case of a triangle and the only good thing that emerged out of Raj Kapoor's interim death was the hit song—'*Yeh mera prem patra padh kar*'.

One generation later, Raj Kapoor's son Rishi was the man who upturned the Bollywood Love Triangle Formula in *Deewana*. Rishi was 'killed' by evil uncle Amrish Puri while his mother and wife (Divya Bharti) managed to escape. The young widow couldn't recover from the trauma and was destined to a lifetime of grief shrouded in white. In walked a flamboyant upstart and reminded her (and us) that you needed love in your life: '*Koi na koi chahiye pyar karne wala*'. A young boy called Shah Rukh Khan swept Divya Bharti off her feet and just when they had got married, Rishi returned. According to the formula, Divya Bharti should have reverted to him. But whether it was an acceptance of the newly liberalized country or a freshly minted superstar, that did not happen. Rishi Kapoor didn't get the girl. But to know how, you have to watch the movie.

End Piece

Yeh Vaada Raha had one of the most stupefying returns from the dead. Rishi Kapoor and Poonam Dhillon were in love when they met with a terrible accident and Poonam's face was badly disfigured. Rishi's mother—who wasn't in favour of the match—told him that Poonam had died in the accident. While Rishi moped for Poonam, she got plastic surgery done on her face and turned into—hold your breath—Tina Munim. When Poonam–Tina landed up at Rishi's doorstep to announce herself, she found him to be engaged to another girl and it was her turn to mope. Soon, Tina (who was actually Poonam) had been co-opted to sing with Rishi to raise money for an orphanage in Poonam's (who was now Tina) memory.

Whatay climax it was when Rishi finally managed to figure out how the new girl had the same voice as his dead girlfriend. (To ensure continuity of voice, Jaya Bhaduri dubbed for both the heroines.)

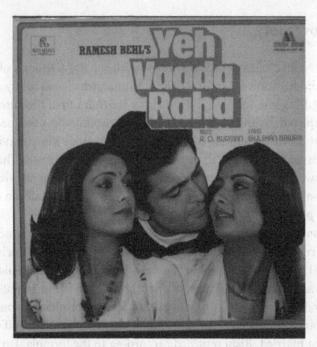

What if I told you there are two people in this poster?

Bonus Warning: In the mid-'90s, the title track of ***Yeh Vaada Raha*** also came back from the dead and got made into a music video featuring three bimbettes in pink hot pants seductively offering to speak sexy somethings to lonely (read horny) souls on the phone. A Mumbai number (022-6400895) flashed tantalizingly on the screen, which was a welcome change from the ISD numbers that usually offered these services. People who called that number would have been distressed to find that they had been connected to Bandra police station.

'Bahut Shukriya, Badi Meherbani . . .'

Readers of my blog Calcutta Chromosome, and buyers of my previous book have been inspiring, to say the least. Their comments and suggestions were invaluable in writing this one.

Bollybook stands on the shoulders of those Good Samaritans who upload videos and update information on YouTube and IMDb.

For this book, and even generally, I have taken assistance from Bollywood fans across the globe.

Abhishek Mukherjee (@ovshake42) wrestled the hundred unwieldy chapters into manageable sections and untiringly pointed out the ones I missed.

Aneela Z Babar (@AneelaBabar), Beth Watkins (@bethlovesbolly) and Pavan Jha (@p1j) do not know how much they helped.

When not furthering the cause of good cinema, Neeraj Ghaywan (@ghaywan) and Shiladitya Bora (@ShiladityaBora) furthered the cause of this book.

Facebook groups like *I Love Trashy Hindi Movies* and *Indian Film Quiz* have often been sounding boards for ideas.

Udayan Chakrabarti was the first reader of the first draft of the book. I remain grateful for his honest and thoughtful rudeness.

Nilendu Misra reminded me of hundreds of forgotten movies and obscure anecdotes that eventually made their way into the book. I hope he agrees to co-author a book with me some day.

Udayan Mitra was that dream editor who saw this book to be much bigger and better than I ever imagined. And then shared his insights and erudition over many glasses of cold coffee.

While mothers were taking their children to see *Born Free*, Rita Chaudhuri took me to see *Yaarana*. Instead of Rabindra Sangeet, she introduced me to R.D. Burman. I can never thank her enough for that.

Dyujoy and Drishti Chaudhuri gave me passive inspiration as my secret desire is for them to grow up and love Hindi cinema. And maybe even trivia around Hindi cinema.

Some things, I said right at the beginning. The rest, I have said here.

Images Courtesy and Copyright

AB Corp Limited
Paa

Abhinav Bhatt (minimalmovieposters.in)
Minimalist poster of *Deewaar*

Anticlock Films Pvt. Ltd (anticlockfilms.com)
I Am (Omar)

Anurag Kashyap Films Pvt. Ltd (akfpl.com) and Viacom 18 Motion Pictures (viacom18.com)
Gangs of Wasseypur

Anurag Kashyap Films Pvt. Ltd
Udaan (Photographer: Ishika Mohan)

Dibakar Banerjee Productions
Love Sex Aur Dhokha

Faiza Ahmed Khan (director)
Supermen of Malegaon (Photographer: Ameet Mallapur)

Gujarat Cooperative Milk Marketing Federation (amul.com)
Advertisements of Amul Butter

HT Media Ltd (hindustantimes.com)
Photograph of press conference of *Water*

Kunal Kundu (behance.net/kunalkundu)
Illustration of Kishore Kumar

MAD Entertainment Limited
Cheeni Kum

Madras Talkies (madrastalkies.com)
Dil Se and *Guru*

National Film Development Corporation Limited (nfdcindia.com)
Jaane Bhi Do Yaaro

Pritish Nandy Communications (pritishnandycom.com)
Fatso, Jhankaar Beats, and *Shabd*

PVR Pictures Ltd (pvrpictures.com)
Taare Zameen Par

Red Chillies Entertainment Pvt. Ltd (redchillies.com)
Main Hoon Na, Phir Bhi Dil Hai Hindustani, and Company logo of Red Chillies

Rose Audio Visuals Pvt. Ltd (roseaudiovisuals.com)
Kasme Vaade, London Paris New York, and *Yeh Vaada Raha*

Vinod Chopra Films Pvt. Ltd (vinodchopra.com)
Lage Raho Munna Bhai and *3 Idiots*

Vinod Chopra Productions Pvt. Ltd (vinodchopra.com)
Ferrari Ki Sawaari, Khamosh, Munna Bhai MBBS, and *Parineeta*

Yash Raj Films Pvt. Ltd (yashrajfilms.com)
Chak De India, Dhoom 2, Dil Bole Hadippa, Dilwale Dulhania Le Jayenge, Ek Tha Tiger Ishaqzaade, Jhoom Barabar Jhoom, Kaala Patthar, Ladies vs Ricky Bahl, Rocket Singh: Salesman of the Year, Silsila, and *Veer Zaara*

Index